ADOBE® DREAMWEAVER® CS3
REVEALED

Adobe | Approved Certification Courseware

ADOBE® DREAMWEAVER® CS3
REVEALED

Sherry Bishop

COURSE TECHNOLOGY
CENGAGE Learning™

Adobe® Dreamweaver® CS3—Revealed

Sherry Bishop

Vice President, Technology and Trades ABU: David Garza

Director of Learning Solutions: Sandy Clark

Managing Editor: Larry Main

Senior Acquisitions Editor: James Gish

Product Managers: Jane Hosie-Bounar, Nicole Bruno

Editorial Assistant: Sarah Timm

Marketing Director: Deborah Yarnell

Marketing Manager: Kevin Rivenburg

Marketing Specialist: Victoria Ortiz

Content Product Managers: Heather Furrow, Tintu Thomas

Developmental Editor: Barbara Waxer

Technical Editors: Ann Fisher, John Shanley

Art Director: Bruce Bond

Cover Design: Lisa Kuhn, Curio Press, LLC

Cover Photo: © Art Wolfe/Getty Images

Text Designer: Ann Small

Proofreader: Christine Clark

Indexer: Kevin Broccoli

For product information and technology assistance, contact us at
Cengage Learning Customer & Sales Support, 1-800-354-9706

For permission to use material from this text or product, submit all requests online at **cengage.com/permissions**. Further permissions questions can be emailed to **permissionrequest@cengage.com**

Some of the product names and company names used in this book have been used for identification purposes only and may be trademarks or registered trademarks of their respective manufacturers and sellers.

Adobe® InDesign®, Adobe® Photoshop®, Adobe® Illustrator®, Adobe® Flash®, Adobe® Dreamweaver®, and Adobe® Creative Suite® are trademarks or registered trademarks of Adobe Systems, Inc. in the United States and/or other countries. Third party products, services, company names, logos, design, titles, words, or phrases within these materials may be trademarks of their respective owners.

The Adobe Approved Certification Courseware logo is a proprietary trademark of Adobe. All rights reserved.

ISBN-13: 978-1-4283-1964-6

ISBN-10: 1-4283-1964-6

Course Technology
25 Thomson Place,
Boston, Massachusetts, 02210.

Cengage Learning is a leading provider of customized learning solutions with office locations around the globe, including Singapore, the United Kingdom, Australia, Mexico, Brazil and Japan. Locate your local office at: **international.cengage.com/region**

Cengage Learning products are represented in Canada by Nelson Education, Ltd.

For your lifelong learning solutions, visit **course.cengage.com**
Visit our corporate website at **cengage.com**

Course Technology , a part of Cengage Learning, and *Adobe Dreamweaver CS3—Revealed* are independent from ProCert Labs, LLC and Adobe Systems Incorporated, and are not affiliated with ProCert Labs and Adobe in any manner. This publication may assist students to prepare for an Adobe Certified Expert exam, however, neither ProCert Labs nor Adobe warrant that use of this material will ensure success in connection with any exam.

Printed in the United States of America
2 3 4 5 6 7 8 9 11 10 09 08

Revealed Series Vision

The Revealed Series is your guide to today's hottest multimedia applications. These comprehensive books teach the skills behind the application, showing you how to apply smart design principles to multimedia products such as dynamic graphics, animation, Web sites, software authoring tools, and digital video.

A team of design professionals including multimedia instructors, students, authors, and editors worked together to create this series. We recognized the unique learning environment of the multimedia classroom and created a series that:

- Gives you comprehensive step-by-step instructions
- Offers in-depth explanation of the "Why" behind a skill
- Includes creative projects for additional practice
- Explains concepts clearly using full-color visuals

It was our goal to create a book that speaks directly to the multimedia and design community—one of the most rapidly growing computer fields today. We think we've done just that, with a sophisticated and instructive book design.

—The Revealed Series

Author's Vision

This book introduces you to a fascinating program that will inspire you to create rich and exciting Web sites.

Many talented and creative individuals created this text for you.

The Project Manager, Jane Hosie-Bounar, guided and directed the team from start to finish. She is a talented and tireless individual—the ultimate professional and visionary.

Barbara Waxer, the Development Editor, brought so much talent to the table—a gift for design, a strong command of our wonderful English language, and a deep understanding of copyright issues. She is great fun to work with, no matter how tedious the task you are tackling!

The designs from Anita Quintana helped give birth to a new Web site for this book, Carolyne's Creations. She definitely helped to raise the banner standards! Thank you, Anita.

The copyright content was generously provided by my editor, Barbara Waxer. Additional information on locating media on the Internet and determining its legal use is available in her Revealed Series book *Internet Surf and Turf Revealed: The Essential Guide to Copyright, Fair Use, and Finding Media*.

Ann Fisher and John Shanley, the Technical Editors, carefully tested each step to make sure that the end product was error-free. They gave exceptional feedback as they reviewed each chapter. This part of the publishing process is what truly sets Cengage Learning and Course Technology apart from other publishers.

Tintu Thomas, Heather Furrow, and Elena Montillo, our Content

Product Managers, kept the schedule on track. We thank them for keeping up with the many details and deadlines.

Special thanks go to Jim Gish, Senior Acquisitions Editor. This was my first opportunity to work with Jim, and it was certainly a pleasant one. He and Sandy Clark, the Director of Learning Solutions, have embraced the Revealed books with enthusiasm and grace.

The Beach Club (www.beachclubal.com) in Gulf Shores, Alabama, generously allowed us to use several photographs of their beautiful property for The Striped Umbrella Web site. Florence Pruitt, the club director, was extremely helpful and gracious.

I hope you enjoy reading and working through the book. Dreamweaver is such an outstanding Web development tool. It plays easily with both the professional Web developer and the beginning student. We are all indebted to the inspired team at Adobe.

Typically, your family is the last to be properly thanked. My husband, Don, continues to support and encourage me every day, as he has for the last thirty-seven years. Our travels with our children and grandchildren provide happy memories for me and content for the Web sites. This book leans fairly strongly in the direction of my precious grandchildren Jacob, Emma, Thomas, and Caroline. You will see their faces peeking out from some of the pages.

—Sherry Bishop

Introduction to Adobe Dreamweaver CS3

Welcome to *Adobe Dreamweaver CS3—Revealed*. This book offers creative projects, concise instructions, and complete coverage of basic to intermediate Dreamweaver skills, helping you to create polished, professional-looking Web sites. Use this book both in the classroom and as your own reference guide.

This text is organized into 12 chapters. In these chapters, you will explore the many options Dreamweaver provides for creating dynamic Dreamweaver Web sites.

What You'll Do

A What You'll Do figure begins every lesson. This figure gives you an at-a-glance look at what you'll do in the chapter, either by showing you a page or pages from the current project or a tool you'll be using.

Comprehensive Conceptual Lessons

Before jumping into instructions, in-depth conceptual information tells you "why" skills are applied. This book provides the "how" and "why" through the use of professional examples. Also included in the text are tips and sidebars to help you work more efficiently and creatively, or to teach you a bit about the history or design philosophy behind the skill you are using.

Step-by-Step Instructions

This book combines in-depth conceptual information with concise steps to help you learn Dreamweaver CS3. Each set of steps guides you through a lesson where you will create, modify, or enhance a Dreamweaver CS3 Web site. Step references to large colorful images and quick step summaries round out the lessons. The Data Files for the steps are provided on the CD at the back of this book.

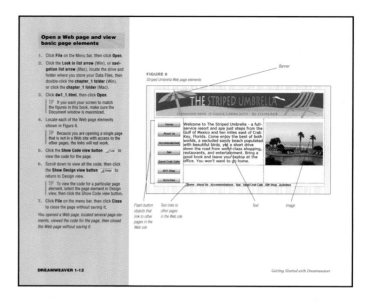

Projects

This book contains a variety of end-of-chapter materials for additional practice and reinforcement. The Skills Review contains hands-on practice exercises that mirror the progressive nature of the lesson material. The chapter concludes with four projects; two Project Builders, one Design Project, and one Portfolio Project. The Project Builders and the Design Project require you to apply the skills you've learned in the chapter. Portfolio Projects encourage students to use their creativity to create a Web site of their own design.

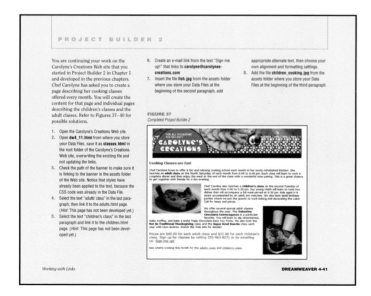

CHAPTER 1   GETTING STARTED WITH DREAMWEAVER

CHAPTER 3 WORKING WITH TEXT AND IMAGES

CHAPTER 4 WORKING WITH LINKS

CHAPTER 5 USING HTML TABLES TO LAY OUT A PAGE

CHAPTER 6   MANAGING A WEB SERVER AND FILES

CHAPTER 7 **USING STYLES AND STYLE SHEETS FOR DESIGN**

CHAPTER 8 **COLLECTING DATA WITH FORMS**

CHAPTER 10 ADDING MEDIA OBJECTS

CONTENTS

CONTENTS

CHAPTER 12 WORKING WITH LIBRARY ITEMS AND SNIPPETS

Intended Audience

This text is designed for the beginner or intermediate user who wants to learn how to use Dreamweaver CS3. The book is designed to provide basic and in-depth material that not only educates, but also encourages you to explore the nuances of this exciting program.

Approach

The text allows you to work at your own pace through step-by-step tutorials. A concept is presented and the process is explained, followed by the actual steps. To learn the most from the use of the text, you should adopt the following habits:

- Proceed slowly: Accuracy and comprehension are more important than speed.
- Understand what is happening with each step before you continue to the next step.
- After finishing a skill, ask yourself if you could do it on your own, without referring to the steps. If the answer is no, review the steps.

Icons, Buttons, and Pointers

Symbols for icons, buttons, and pointers are shown in the step each time they are used. Icons may look different in the files panel depending on the file association settings on your computer.

Fonts

The Data Files contain a variety of commonly used fonts, but there is no guarantee that these fonts will be available on your computer. In a few cases, fonts other than those common to a PC or a Macintosh are used. If any of the fonts in use is not available on your computer, you can make a substitution, realizing that the results may vary from those in the book.

Windows and Macintosh

Adobe Dreamweaver CS3 works virtually the same on Windows and Macintosh operating systems. In those cases where there is a significant difference, the abbreviations (Win) and (Mac) are used.

System Requirements

For a Windows operating system:
Intel® Pentium® 4, Intel Centrino®, Intel Xeon®, or Intel Core™ Duo (or compatible) processor

Microsoft® Windows® XP with Service Pack 2 or Windows Vista™ Home Premium, Business, Ultimate, or Enterprise (certified for 32-bit editions)

512MB of RAM

1GB of available hard-disk space (additional free space required during installation)

1,024×768 monitor resolution with 16-bit video card

DVD-ROM drive

Internet or phone connection required for product activation

Broadband Internet connection required for Adobe Stock Photos* and other services.

For a Macintosh operating system:
PowerPC® G4 or G5 or multicore Intel® processor

Mac OS X v.10.4.8

512MB of RAM

1.4GB of available hard-disk space (additional free space required during installation)

1,024×768 monitor resolution with 16-bit video card

DVD-ROM drive

Internet or phone connection required for product activation

Broadband Internet connection required for Adobe Stock Photos* and other services.

Building a Web Site

You will create and develop a Web site called The Striped Umbrella in the lesson material in this book. Because each chapter builds off of the previous chapter, it is recommended that you work through the chapters in consecutive order.

Data Files

To complete the lessons in this book, you need the Data Files on the CD in the back of this book. Your instructor will tell you where to store the files as you work, such as the hard drive, a network server, or a USB storage device. The instructions in the lessons will refer to "where you store your Data Files" when referring to the Data Files for the book.

When you copy the Data Files to your computer, you may see lock icons that indicate that the files are read- only when you view them in the Dreamweaver Files panel. To unlock the files, right-click on the locked file name in the Files panel, and then click Turn off Read Only.

Images vs Graphics

Many times these terms seem to be used interchangeably. For the purposes of this text, the term images is used when referring to pictures on a Web page. The term graphics is used as a more encompassing term that refers to non-text items on a Web page such as photographs, logos, navigation bars, Flash animations, graphs, background images, and drawings. You may define these terms in a slightly different way, depending on your professional background or business environment.

Preference Settings

The learning process will be much easier if you can see the file extensions for the files you will use in the lessons. To do this in Windows, open Windows Explorer, click Organize, Folder and Search Options, click the View tab, then uncheck the box Hide Extensions for Known File Types. To do this for a Mac, go to the Finder, click the Finder menu, and then click Preferences. Click the Advanced tab, then select the Show all file extensions check box.

To view the Flash content that you will be creating, you must set a preference in your browser to allow active content to run. Otherwise, you will not be able to view objects such as Flash buttons.

To set this preference in Internet Explorer, click Tools, Internet Options, Advanced, then check the box Allow active content to run in files on My Computer. Your browser settings may be slightly different, but look for similar wording. When using Windows Internet Explorer 7, you can also click the information bar when prompted to allow blocked content.

Creating a Portfolio

The Portfolio Project and Project Builders allow students to use their creativity to come up with original Dreamweaver designs. You might suggest that students create a portfolio in which they can store their original work.

Web Sites Used in Figures

Each time a Web site is used for illustration purposes in a lesson, where necessary a statement acknowledging that we obtained permission to use the Web site is included, along with the URL of the site. Sites whose content is in the public domain, such as federal government Web sites, are acknowledged as a courtesy.

GETTING STARTED WITH
DREAMWEAVER

1. Explore the Dreamweaver workspace

2. View a Web page and use Help

3. Plan and define a Web site

4. Add a folder and pages and set the home page

5. Create and view a site map

GETTING STARTED WITH
DREAMWEAVER

Introduction

Adobe Dreamweaver CS3 is a Web development tool that lets you create dynamic, interactive Web pages containing text, images, hyperlinks, animation, sounds, video, and other elements. You can use Dreamweaver to create individual Web pages or complex Web sites consisting of many Web pages. A **Web site** is a group of related Web pages that are linked together and share a common interface and design. You can use Dreamweaver to create design elements such as text, tables, and interactive buttons, or you can import elements from other software programs. You can save Dreamweaver files in many different file formats, including XHTML, HTML, JavaScript, CSS, or XML, to name a few. **XHTML** is the acronym for eXtensible HyperText Markup Language, the current standard language used to create Web pages. You can still use **HTML** (HyperText Markup Language) in Dreamweaver; however, it is no longer considered the standard language. In Dreamweaver, you can easily convert existing HTML code to XHTML-compliant code. You use a browser to view your Web pages on the Internet. A **browser** is a program, such as Microsoft Internet Explorer

or Mozilla Firefox, that lets you display HTML-developed Web pages.

Using Dreamweaver Tools

Creating an excellent Web site is a complex task. Fortunately, Dreamweaver has an impressive number of tools that can help. Using Dreamweaver's design tools, you can create dynamic and interactive Web pages without writing a word of code. However, if you prefer to write code, Dreamweaver makes it easy to type and edit the code directly and see the visual results of the code instantly. Dreamweaver also contains organizational tools that help you work with a team of people to create a Web site. You can also use Dreamweaver's management tools to help you manage a Web site. For instance, you can use the **Files panel** to create folders to organize and store the various files for your Web site, add pages to your Web site, and set the **home page**, the first page that viewers see when they visit the site. You can also use the **site map**, a graphical representation of how the pages within a Web site relate to each other, to view and edit the navigation structure of your Web site. The **navigation structure** is the way viewers navigate from page to page in your Web site.

Tools You'll Use

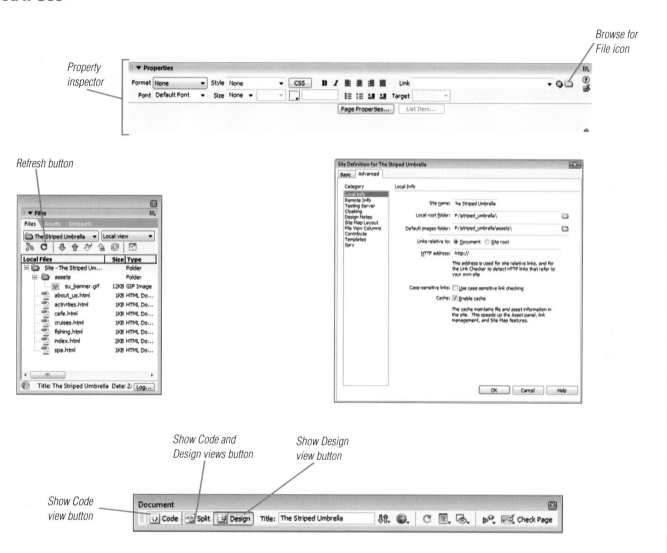

Browse for File icon

Property inspector

Refresh button

Show Code and Design views button

Show Design view button

Show Code view button

EXPLORE THE
DREAMWEAVER WORKSPACE

What You'll Do

In this lesson, you will start Dreamweaver, examine the components that make up the Dreamweaver workspace, and change views.

Examining the Dreamweaver Workspace

The **Dreamweaver workspace** is designed to provide you with easy access to all the tools you need to create Web pages. Refer to Figure 1 as you locate the components described below.

The **Document window** is the large white area in the Dreamweaver program window where you create and edit Web pages. The **menu bar**, located above the Document window, includes menu names, each of which contains Dreamweaver commands. To choose a menu command, click the menu name to open the menu, then click the menu command. Directly below the menu bar is the Insert bar. The **Insert bar** includes seven groups of buttons displayed as tabs: Common, Layout, Forms, Data, Spry, Text, and Favorites. Clicking a tab on the Insert bar displays the buttons and menus associated with that group. For example, if you click the Layout tab, you will find buttons for using div tags, used for creating blocks of content on pages, the Table button, used for inserting a table, and the

Frames button, used for selecting one of thirteen different frame layouts.

QUICKTIP

To display the categories using a drop-down menu as in previous versions of Dreamweaver, click the current Insert bar list arrow, and then click Show as Menu. To change back to the tab display, click the Insert bar list arrow, and then click Show as Tabs.

The **Document toolbar** contains buttons and drop-down menus you can use to change the current work mode, preview Web pages, debug Web pages, choose visual aids, and view file-management options. The **Standard toolbar** contains buttons you can use to execute frequently used commands also available on the File and Edit menus. The **Style Rendering toolbar** contains buttons that can be used to render different media types, but is available only if your document uses media-dependent style sheets. An example of a media-dependent style sheet would be one used to create and format pages for a cell phone. The **Coding toolbar** contains buttons that are used when working directly in the code. These, along with the Standard toolbar, are not part of the default workspace setup and might not be displayed when you open Dreamweaver.

The **Property inspector**, located at the bottom of the Dreamweaver window, lets you view and change the properties of a selected object. The Property inspector is context sensitive, which means it changes according to what is selected in the Document window. The **status bar** is located below the Document window. The left side of the status bar displays the **tag selector**, which shows the HTML tags used at the insertion point location. The right side displays the window size and estimated download time for the current page, as well as the Select tool, used for page editing, the Hand tool, used for panning, and the Zoom tool, used for magnifying.

A **panel** is a window that displays information on a particular topic or contains related commands. **Panel groups** are sets of related panels that are grouped together. To view the contents of a panel in a panel group, click the panel tab. Panel groups can be collapsed and docked on the right side of the screen, or undocked by dragging the gripper on the left side of the panel group title bar. To collapse or expand a panel group, click the expander arrow on the left side of the panel group title bar, as shown in Figure 2, or just click the name of the panel group. When you first start Dreamweaver, the CSS, Application, Tag Inspector, and Files panel groups appear by default. Panels can be opened using the Window menu commands or the corresponding shortcut keys.

Working with Dreamweaver Views

A **view** is a particular way of displaying page content. Dreamweaver has three working views. **Design view** shows the page as it would appear in a browser and is primarily used for designing and creating a Web page. **Code view** shows the underlying HTML code for the page; use this view to read or edit the underlying code. **Code and Design view** is a combination of Code view and Design view. Code and Design view is the best view for **debugging** or correcting errors because you can immediately see how code modifications change the appearance of the page. The view buttons are located on the Document toolbar.

FIGURE 1
Dreamweaver CS3 workspace

FIGURE 2
Panels in Files panel group

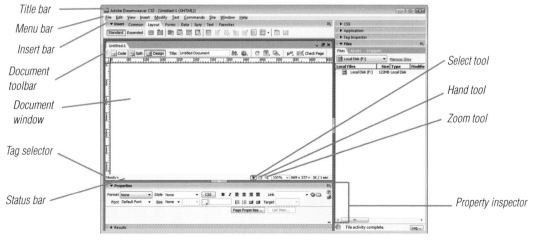

Start Dreamweaver (Windows)

1. Click the **Start button**  on the taskbar.

2. Point to **All Programs**, click **Adobe Web Premium CS3**, then click **Adobe Dreamweaver CS3**, as shown in Figure 3.

   TIP The name of your Adobe suite may differ from the figure.

3. If the Default Editor dialog box opens, click **OK**.

You started Dreamweaver CS3 for Windows.

FIGURE 3
Starting Dreamweaver CS3 (Windows)

Click Adobe Dreamweaver CS3

Choosing a workspace layout (Windows)

If you are starting Dreamweaver in Windows for the first time after installing it, you might see the Workspace Setup dialog box, which asks you to choose between the Designer, Coder, or Dual Screen layouts. All three layouts are built with an integrated workspace using the Multiple Document Interface (MDI). The **Multiple Document Interface** means that all document windows and panels are positioned within one large application window. In the Designer workspace layout, the panels are docked on the right side of the screen and the Design view is the default view. In the Coder workspace layout, the panels are docked on the left side of the screen and the Code view is the default view. However, the panels may be docked on either side of the screen in both Coder and Designer layouts. To change the workspace layout, click Window on the menu bar, point to Workspace Layout, and then click the desired layout.

FIGURE 4
Starting Dreamweaver CS3 (Macintosh)

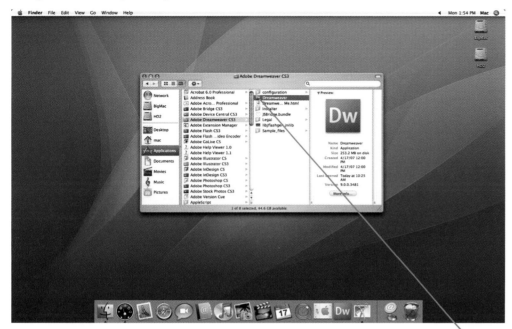

Dreamweaver CS3
application

1. Click **Finder** in the Dock, then click **Applications**.

2. Click the **Adobe Dreamweaver CS3 folder**, then double-click the **Dreamweaver CS3 application,** as shown in Figure 4.

   TIP   Once Dreamweaver is running, you can add it to the Dock permanently by [control]-clicking the Dreamweaver icon, then clicking Keep In Dock.

You started Dreamweaver CS3 for Macintosh.

Using two monitors for optimum workspace layout

A third option you have for workspace layout is Dual Screen layout. **Dual Screen layout** is the layout you would choose when you are using dual monitors while working with Dreamweaver. The Document window and Property inspector are displayed on the first monitor and the panels are displayed on the second monitor. It is quite seamless to work between the two monitors and provides optimum workspace by allowing you to have multiple panels open without compromising your Document window space.

Change views and view panels

1. Click **HTML** in the Create New category on the Dreamweaver Welcome Screen.

   The Dreamweaver Welcome Screen provides shortcuts for opening files or for creating new files or Web sites.

   TIP If you do not want the Dreamweaver Welcome Screen to appear each time you start Dreamweaver, click the Don't show again check box on the Welcome Screen or remove the check mark next to Show Welcome Screen in the General category of the Preferences dialog box.

2. Click the **Show Code view button** [Code] on the Document toolbar.

   The default code for a new document appears in the Document window, as shown in Figure 5.

   TIP The Coding toolbar is available only in Code view.

3. Click the **Show Code and Design views button** [Split] on the Document toolbar.

4. Click the **Show Design view button** [Design] on the Document toolbar.

   (continued)

Show Code view button

Show Code and Design views button

Show Design view button

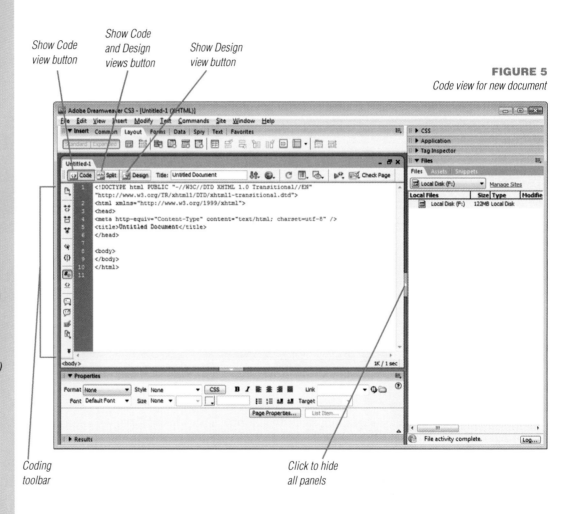

FIGURE 5
Code view for new document

Coding toolbar

Click to hide all panels

Getting Started with Dreamweaver

FIGURE 6
Displaying a panel group

Expander arrow

Drag to undock or "float" panel group

Application panel group with four panels

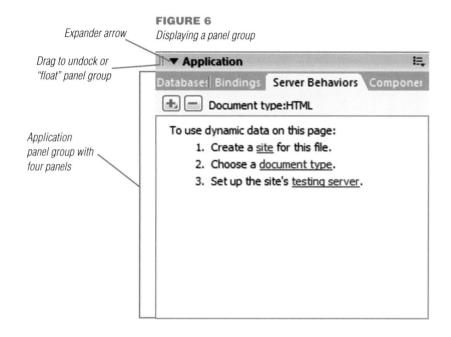

5. Click **Application** on the panel group title bar, then compare your screen to Figure 6.

    TIP   If the Application panel group is not displayed, click Window on the menu bar, then click Server Behaviors. The Server Behaviors panel is in the Application panel group.

6. Click each panel name tab to display the contents of each panel.

7. Click **Application** on the panel group title bar to collapse the Application panel group.

8. View the contents of the CSS and Files panel groups, then collapse the CSS panel group.

9. Close the open document.

You viewed a new Web page using three views, opened panel groups, viewed their contents, then closed panel groups.

Hiding and Displaying Toolbars
To hide or display the Insert, Style Rendering, Document, or Standard toolbars, click View on the menu bar, point to Toolbars, then click Insert, Style Rendering, Document, or Standard. The Coding toolbar is available only in Code view and appears vertically in the Document window. By default, the Insert and Document toolbars appear in the workspace.

VIEW A WEB PAGE
AND USE HELP

What You'll Do

 In this lesson, you will open a Web page, view several page elements, and access the Help system.

Opening a Web Page

After starting Dreamweaver, you can create a new Web site, create a new Web page, or open an existing Web site or Web page. The first Web page that appears when viewers go to a Web site is called the **home page**. The home page sets the look and feel of the Web site and directs viewers to the rest of the pages in the Web site.

Viewing Basic Web Page Elements

There are many elements that make up Web pages. Web pages can be very simple and designed primarily with text, or they can be media-rich with text, images sound, and movies, creating an enhanced interactive Web experience. Figure 7 is an example of a Web page with several different page elements that work together to create a simple and attractive page.

Most information on a Web page is presented in the form of **text**. You can type text directly onto a Web page in Dreamweaver or import text created in other programs. You can then use the Property inspector to format text so that it is attractive and easy to read. Text should be short and to the point to prevent viewers from losing interest and leaving your site.

Hyperlinks, also known as **links**, are image or text elements on a Web page that users click to display another location on the page, another Web page on the same Web site, or a Web page on a different Web site.

Images add visual interest to a Web page. The saying that "less is more" is certainly true with images, though. Too many images cause the page to load slowly and discourage viewers from waiting for the page to download. Many pages have **banners**, which are images displayed across the top of the screen that can incorporate a company's logo, contact information, and links to the other pages in the site.

Navigation bars are bars that contain multiple links that are usually organized in rows or columns. Sometimes navigation bars are used with an image map. An **image map** is an image that has been divided into sections, each of which contains a link.

Getting Started with Dreamweaver

Flash button objects are Flash objects that can be created in Dreamweaver and can serve as links to other files or Web pages. You can insert them onto a Web page without requiring the Adobe Flash program to be installed. They add visual interest to a Web page.

Getting Help

Dreamweaver has an excellent Help feature that is both comprehensive and easy to use.

When questions or problems arise, you can use the commands on the Help menu to find the answers you need. Clicking the Using Dreamweaver command opens the Adobe Help Viewer that contains two links you can use to search for answers in different ways. The Contents link lists Dreamweaver Help topics by category. The Index link lets you view topics in alphabetical order. The Search text box at the top of the window lets you enter a keyword to search for a specific topic.

You can use the Browse box to view other Adobe products' Help topics. On a Macintosh, you can view topics by Index or Table of Contents, and use Search text box. Context-specific help can be accessed by clicking the Help button on the Property inspector.

FIGURE 7
Common Web page elements

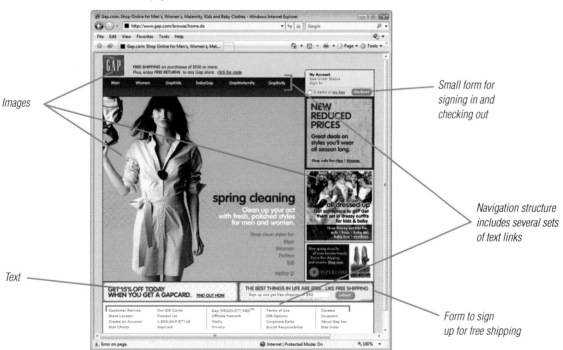

Images

Text

Small form for signing in and checking out

Navigation structure includes several sets of text links

Form to sign up for free shipping

Gap Web site used with permission from Gap Inc. – www.gap.com

Open a Web page and view basic page elements

1. Click **File** on the Menu bar, then click **Open**.

2. Click the **Look in list arrow** (Win), or **navigation list arrow** (Mac), locate the drive and folder where you store your Data Files, then double-click the **chapter_1 folder** (Win), or click the **chapter_1 folder** (Mac).

3. Click **dw1_1.html**, then click **Open**.

   TIP If you want your screen to match the figures in this book, make sure the Document window is maximized.

4. Locate each of the Web page elements shown in Figure 8.

   TIP Because you are opening a single page that is not in a Web site with access to the other pages, the links will not work.

5. Click the **Show Code view button** ⟨⟩ Code to view the code for the page.

6. Scroll down to view all the code, then click the **Show Design view button** Design to return to Design view.

   TIP To view the code for a particular page element, select the page element in Design view, then click the Show Code view button.

7. Click **File** on the menu bar, then click **Close** to close the page without saving it.

You opened a Web page, located several page elements, viewed the code for the page, then closed the Web page without saving it.

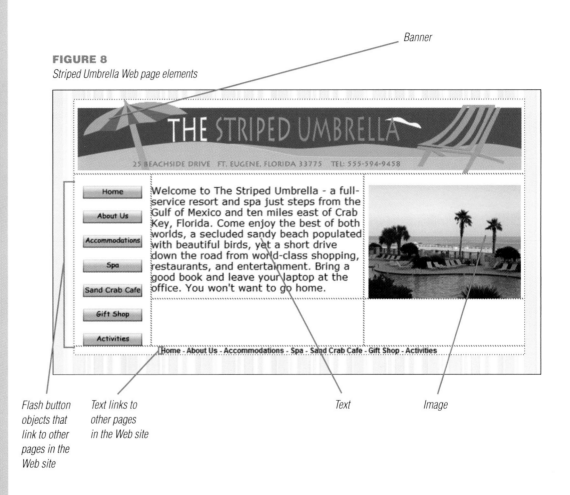

FIGURE 8
Striped Umbrella Web page elements

Banner

Flash button objects that link to other pages in the Web site

Text links to other pages in the Web site

Text

Image

FIGURE 9

Dreamweaver Help window

1. Click **Help** on the menu bar, then click **Dreamweaver Help.**

   The Adobe Help Viewer window opens with Dreamweaver CS3 as the active program to browse for help.

   TIP   You can also open the Help feature by pressing [F1] (Win).

2. Click to place the insertion point in the Search text box.

3. Type **saving** in the Search text box (Win).

4. Press **[Enter]** (Win) or **[return]** (Mac), then scroll down to view the topics.

   TIP   You may have to select "Dreamweaver CS3" from the list of available programs in the list.

5. If necessary, select **saving** in the Search text box, type **"save files"** (be sure to type the quotation marks), then press **[Enter]** (Win) or **[return]** (Mac).

   Because you placed the keywords in quotation marks, Dreamweaver listed fewer topics found.

6. Click the second topic in the topic list.

   Information on accessing sites, a server, and local drives appears in the right frame, as shown in Figure 9.

7. Scroll down and scan the text.

8. Close the Dreamweaver Help window.

You used Dreamweaver Help to read information about connecting to a server to edit files.

PLAN AND DEFINE A
WEB SITE

What You'll Do

 In this lesson, you will review a Web site plan for The Striped Umbrella, a beach resort and spa. You will also create a root folder for The Striped Umbrella Web site, and then define the Web site.

Understanding the Total Process

Creating a Web site is a complex process. It can often involve a large team of people working in various roles to ensure that the Web site contains accurate information, looks good, and works smoothly.

Figure 10 illustrates the phases in a Web site development project.

Planning a Web Site

Planning is probably the most important part of any successful project. Planning is an *essential* part of creating a Web site, and is a

FIGURE 10
Phases of a Web site development project

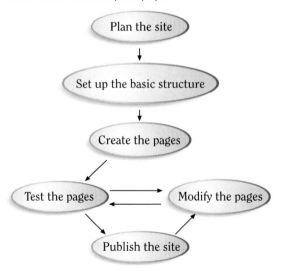

continuous process that overlaps the subsequent phases. To start planning your Web site, you need to create a checklist of questions and answers about the site. For example, what are your goals for the Web site? Who is the audience you want to target? Teenagers? Children? Sports Enthusiasts? Senior citizens? How can you design the site to appeal to the target audience? The more questions you can answer about the site, the more prepared you will be when you begin the developmental phase. Because of the

public demand for "instant" information, your plan should include not just how to get the site up and running, but how to keep it current. Table 1 lists some of the basic questions you need to answer during the planning phase for almost any type of Web site. From your checklist, you should create a statement of purpose and scope, a timeline for all due dates, a budget, a task list with work assignments, and a list of resources needed. You should also include a list of deliverables, such as a preliminary story-

board, page drafts, and art-work for approval. The due dates for each deliverable should be included in the timeline.

Setting Up the Basic Structure

Once you complete the planning phase, you need to set up the structure of the site by creating a storyboard. A **storyboard** is a small sketch that represents every page in a Web site. Like a flowchart, a storyboard shows the relationship of each page in the Web site to all the other pages. Storyboards are very

TABLE 1: Web Site Planning Checklist

question	examples
1. Who is the target audience?	Seniors, teens, children
2. How can I tailor the Web site to reach that audience?	Specify an appropriate reading level, decide the optimal amount of multimedia content, use formal or casual language
3. What are the goals for the site?	Sell a product, provide information
4. How will I gather the information?	Recruit other employees, write it myself, use content from in-house documents
5. What are my sources for rich media content?	Internal production department, outside production company, my own photographs
6. What is my budget?	Very limited, well financed
7. What is the timeline?	Two weeks, one month, six months
8. Who is on my project team?	Just me, a complete staff of designers
9. How often should the site be updated?	Every 10 minutes, once a month
10. Who will update the site?	Me, other team members

helpful when planning a Web site, because they allow you to visualize how each page in the site is linked to others. You can sketch a storyboard using a pencil and paper or using a graphics program on a computer. The storyboard shown in Figure 11 shows all the pages that will be contained in The Striped Umbrella Web site that you will create in this book. Notice that the home page appears at the top of the storyboard, and that it has four pages linked to it. The home page is called the **parent page**, because it is at a higher level in the Web hierarchy and has pages linked to it. The pages linked below it are called **child pages**. The Activities page, which is a child page to the home page, is also a parent page to the Cruises and Fishing pages. You can refer to this storyboard as you create the actual links in Dreamweaver. More detailed storyboards will also include all document names, images, text files, and link information.

QUICKTIP

You can create a storyboard on a computer using a software program such as Microsoft Word, PowerPoint, or Paint; Corel Paintshop Pro; or Adobe Illustrator. You might find it easier to make changes to a computer-generated storyboard than to one created on paper.

In addition to creating a storyboard for your site, you should also create a folder hierarchy for all of the files that will be used in the Web site. Start by creating a folder for the Web site with a descriptive name, such as the name of the company.

This folder, known as the **root folder** or **local root folder**, will store all the Web pages or HTML files for the site. Then create a subfolder called **assets** in which you store all of the files that are not Web pages, such as images and sound files. You should avoid using spaces, special characters, or uppercase characters in your folder names to ensure that all your files can be read and linked successfully on all Web servers, whether they are Windows- or UNIX-based.

After you create the root folder, you need to define your Web site. When you **define** a Web site, the root folder and any folders and files it contains appear in the **Files panel**, the panel you use to manage your Web site's files and folders. Using the Files panel to manage your files ensures that the site links work correctly when the Web site is published. You also use the Files panel to add or delete pages.

Creating the Web Pages and Collecting the Page Content

This is the fun part! After you create your storyboard, you need to gather the files that will be used to create the pages, including text, images, buttons, video, and animation. Some of these files will come

FIGURE 11
The Striped Umbrella Web site storyboard

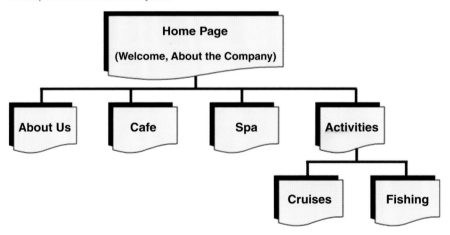

from other software programs, and some will be created in Dreamweaver. For example, you can create text in a word-processing program and insert it into Dreamweaver, or you can create and format text in Dreamweaver. Images, tables, colors, and horizontal rules all contribute to making a page attractive and interesting. In choosing your elements, however, you should always carefully consider the file size of each page. A page with too many graphical elements might take a long time to load, which could cause visitors to leave your Web site. Before you actually add content to each page, however, it is a good idea to use the Files panel to add all the pages to the site according to the structure you specified in your storyboard. Once all the blank pages are in place, you can add the content you collected. This will allow you to create and test the navigation links you will need for the site. The blank pages will act as placeholders. Some designers prefer to add pages as they are created and build the links as they go. It is a personal preference.

Testing the Pages

Once all your pages are completed, you need to test the site to make sure all the links work and that everything looks good. It is important to test your Web pages using different browser software. The two most common browsers are Microsoft Internet Explorer and Mozilla Firefox. You should also test your Web site using different versions of each browser. Older versions of Internet Explorer do not support the latest Web technology. You should also test your Web site using a variety of screen sizes. Some viewers may have small monitors, while others may have large, high-resolution monitors. You should also consider connection download time. Although more people use cable modems or DSL (digital subscriber line) some still use slower dial-up modems. Testing is a continuous process, for which you should allocate plenty of time.

Modifying the Pages

After you create a Web site, you'll probably find that you need to keep making changes to it, especially when information on the site needs to be updated. Each time you make a change, such as adding a new button or image to a page, you should test the site again. Modifying and testing pages in a Web site is an ongoing process.

Publishing the Site

Publishing a Web site means that you transfer all the files for the site to a **Web server**, a computer that is connected to the Internet with an IP (Internet Protocol) address, so that it is available for viewing on the Internet. A Web site must be published or users of the Internet cannot view it. There are several options for publishing a Web site. For instance, many Internet Service Providers (ISPs) provide space on their servers for customers to publish Web sites, and some commercial Web sites provide limited free space for their viewers. Although publishing happens at the end of the process, it's a good idea to set up Web server access in the planning phase. Use the Files panel to transfer your files using the FTP (File Transfer Protocol) capability. **FTP** is the process of uploading and downloading files to and from a remote site.

Dreamweaver also gives you the ability to transfer files using the FTP process without creating a Web site first. You simply enter login information to an FTP site to establish a connection by clicking New in the Manage Sites dialog box, and then clicking the FTP option.

Create a root folder (Windows)

1. Click the **Start button** 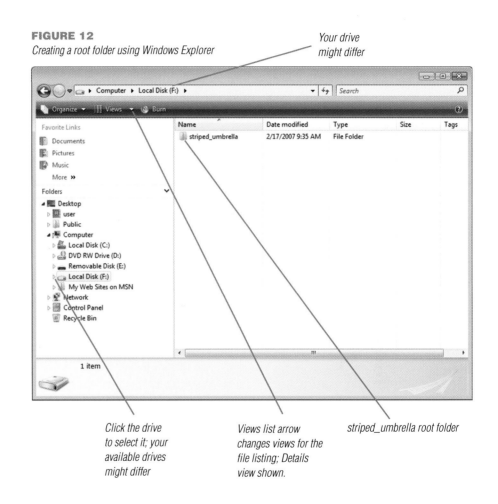 on the taskbar, point to **All Programs**, click **Accessories**, then click **Windows Explorer**.

   TIP   You can also right-click the Start button, then click **Explore.**

2. Navigate to the drive and folder where you will create a folder to store your files for The Striped Umbrella Web site.

3. Click **Organize** on the toolbar, then click **New Folder.**

4. Type **striped_umbrella,** to rename the folder, then press **[Enter]**.

   The folder is renamed striped_umbrella, as shown in Figure 12.

   TIP   Your desktop will look different from Figure 12 if you are not using Windows Vista.

5. Close Windows Explorer.

   TIP   You can also use the Files panel to create a new folder by clicking the Site list arrow, selecting the drive and folder where you want to create the new folder, right-clicking, selecting New Folder, then typing the new folder name.

You created a new folder to serve as the root folder for The Striped Umbrella Web site.

FIGURE 12
Creating a root folder using Windows Explorer

Your drive might differ

Click the drive to select it; your available drives might differ

Views list arrow changes views for the file listing; Details view shown.

striped_umbrella root folder

FIGURE 13

Creating a root folder using a Macintosh

1. Double-click the **hard drive icon** on the desktop, then use Finder to navigate to the drive and folder where you will create a folder to store your files for The Striped Umbrella Web site.

2. Click **File** on the menu bar, then click **New Folder**.

3. Type **striped_umbrella** to rename the folder, as shown in Figure 13.

You created a new folder to serve as the root folder for The Striped Umbrella Web site.

Define a Web site

1. Return to Dreamweaver, then click **Dreamweaver Site** in the Create New category on the Welcome Screen.

2. Click the **Advanced tab** (if necessary), then type **The Striped Umbrella** in the Site name text box.

   The Basic tab can be used instead of the Advanced tab if you prefer to use a wizard.

   | TIP   It is acceptable to use uppercase letters in the site name because it is not the name of a folder or a file.

3. Click the **Browse for File icon** 📁 next to the Local root folder text box, click the **Select list arrow** (Win) or the **navigation list arrow** (Mac) in the **Choose local root folder for site The Striped Umbrella dialog box,** click the **drive and folder** where your Web site files will be stored, then click the **striped_umbrella folder**.

4. Click **Open** (Win) or **Choose** (Mac), then click **Select** (Win).

5. Verify that the Enable cache check box is checked, as shown in Figure 14.

6. Verify that the Links relative to option button is set to Document.

   This setting is very important to make sure your links work correctly.

You created a Web site and defined it with the name The Striped Umbrella. You then verified that the correct options were selected in the Site Definition dialog box.

FIGURE 14
Site Definition for The Striped Umbrella dialog box

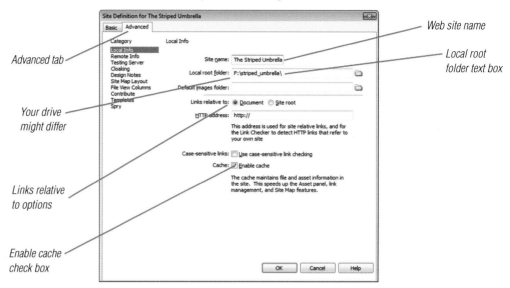

Advanced tab

Your drive might differ

Links relative to options

Enable cache check box

Web site name

Local root folder text box

Understanding IP addresses and domain names

To be accessible over the Internet, a Web site must be published to a Web server with a permanent IP address. An **IP address** is an assigned series of numbers, separated by periods, that designates an address on the Internet. To access a Web page, you can enter either an IP address or a domain name in the address text box of your browser window. A **domain name** is a Web address that is expressed in letters instead of numbers and usually reflects the name of the business represented by the Web site. For example, the domain name of the Adobe Web site is *www.adobe.com,* but the IP address is 192.150.20.61. Because domain names use descriptive text instead of numbers, they are much easier to remember. Compare an IP address to your Social Security number and a domain name to your name. Both your Social Security number and your name are used to refer to you as a person, but your name is much easier for your friends and family to use than your Social Security number. You can type the IP address or the domain name in the address text box of the browser window to access a Web site. The domain name is also referred to as a URL, or Uniform Resource Locator.

FIGURE 15

Setting the Remote Access for The Striped Umbrella Web site

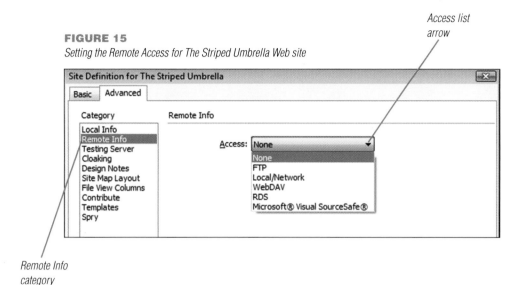

Remote Info
category

1. Click **Remote Info** in the Category list, click the **Access list arrow**, then choose the method you will use to publish your Web site, as shown in Figure 15.

   TIP If you do not have the information to publish your Web site, choose None. You can specify this information later.

2. Enter any necessary information in the Site Definition dialog box based on the setting you chose in Step 1, then click **OK**.

   TIP Your instructor will give you the necessary information to publish your Web site.

You set up the remote access information to prepare you for publishing your Web site.

Understanding the process of publishing a Web site

Before publishing a Web site so that viewers of the Web can access it, you should first create a local root folder, called the **local site**, to house all the files for your Web site. This folder usually resides on your hard drive. Next, you need to gain access to a remote server. A **remote server** is a Web server that hosts Web sites and is not directly connected to the computer housing the local site. Many Internet Service Providers, or ISPs, provide space for publishing Web pages on their servers. Once you have access to a remote server, you can then use the Remote Info category in the Site Definition dialog box to enter information such as the FTP host, host directory, login, and password. After entering this information, you can then use the Put File(s) button in the Files panel to transfer the files to the designated remote server. Once the site is published to a remote server, it is called a **remote site**.

ADD A FOLDER AND PAGES
AND SET THE HOME PAGE

What You'll Do

In this lesson, you will set the home page. You will also create a new folder and new pages for the Web site, using the Files panel.

Adding a Folder to a Web Site

After defining a Web site, you need to create folders to organize the files that will make up the Web site. Creating a folder called **assets** is a good beginning. You can use the assets folder to store all non-HTML files, such as images or sound files. After you create the assets folder, it is a good idea to set it as the default location to store the Web site images. This saves a step when you import new images into the Web site.

DESIGNTIP   **Creating an effective navigation structure**

When you create a Web site, it's important to consider how your viewers will navigate from page to page within the site. A navigation bar is a critical tool for moving around a Web site, so it's important that all text, buttons, and icons used in a navigation bar have a consistent look across all pages. If a complex navigation bar is used, such as one that incorporates JavaScript or Flash, it's a good idea to include plain text links in another location on the page for accessibility. Otherwise, viewers might become confused or lost within the site. A navigation structure can include more links than those included in a navigation bar, however. For instance, it can contain other sets of links that relate to the content of a specific page and which are placed at the bottom or sides of a page in a different format. No matter what navigation structure you use, make sure that every page includes a link back to the home page. Don't make viewers rely on the Back button on the browser toolbar to find their way back to the home page. It's possible that the viewer's current page might have opened as a result of a search and clicking the Back button will take the viewer out of the Web site.

Setting the Home Page

The home page of a Web site is the first page that viewers see when they visit your Web site. Most Web sites contain many other pages that all connect back to the home page. Dreamweaver uses the home page that you have designated as a starting point for creating a **site map**, a graphical representation of the Web pages in a Web site. When you **set** the home page, you tell Dreamweaver which page you have designated to be your home page. The home page filename usually has the name index.html (.htm), or default.html (.htm).

Adding Pages to a Web Site

Web sites might be as simple as one page or might contain hundreds of pages. When you create a Web site, you can add all the pages and specify where they should be placed in the Web site folder structure in the root folder. Once you add and name all the pages in the Web site, you can then add the content, such as text and graphics, to each page. It is better to add as many blank pages as you think you will need in the beginning, rather than adding them one at a time with all the content in place. This will enable you to set up the navigation structure of the Web site at the beginning of the development process and view how each page is linked to others. When you are satisfied with the overall structure, you can then add the content to each page. This is strictly a personal preference, however. You can also choose to add and link

pages as they are created, and that will work just fine, too.

You have a choice of several default document types you can generate when you create new HTML pages. The default document type is designated in the Preferences dialog box. XHTML 1.0 Transitional is the default document type when you install Dreamweaver and will be used throughout this book. It's important to understand the terminology—the pages are still called HTML pages and the file extension is still HTML, but the document type will be XHTML 1.0 Transitional.

Using the Files panel for file management

You should definitely use the Files panel to add, delete, move, or rename files and folders in a Web site. It is very important that you perform these file-maintenance tasks in the Files panel rather than in Windows Explorer (Win) or in the Finder (Mac). Working outside of Dreamweaver, such as in Windows Explorer, can cause linking errors. You cannot take advantage of Dreamweaver's simple yet powerful site-management features unless you use the Files panel for all file-management activities. You may choose to use Windows Explorer (Win) or the Finder (Mac) only to create the root folder or to move or copy the root folder of a Web site to another location. If you move or copy the root folder to a new location, you will have to define the Web site again in the Files panel, as you did in Lesson 3 of this chapter. Defining a Web site is not difficult and will become routine for you after you practice a bit. If you are using Dreamweaver on multiple computers, such as in labs or at home, you will have to define your sites the first time you change to a different computer.

Add a folder to a Web site (Windows)

1. Right-click **The Striped Umbrella site** in the Files panel, then click **New Folder**.

2. Type **assets** in the folder text box, then press **[Enter]**.

   | TIP To rename a folder, double-click the folder name, then type the new name.

3. Compare your screen to Figure 16.

You used the Files panel to create a new folder in the striped_umbrella folder and named it 'assets'.

Add a folder to a Web site (Macintosh)

1. Press and hold **[control]**, click the **striped_umbrella folder**, then click **New Folder**.

2. Type **assets** in the new folder name text box, then press **[return]**.

   | TIP To rename a folder, click the folder name text box, then press **[return]**.

3. Compare your screen to Figure 17.

You used the Files panel to create a new folder under the striped_umbrella folder and named it 'assets'.

FIGURE 16

The Striped Umbrella site in Files panel with assets folder created (Windows)

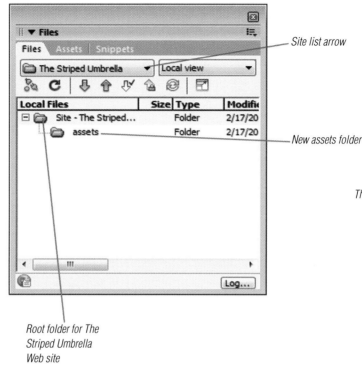

Site list arrow

New assets folder

Root folder for The Striped Umbrella Web site

FIGURE 17

The Striped Umbrella site in Files panel with assets folder created (Macintosh)

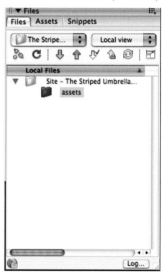

FIGURE 18

*Site Definition for The Striped Umbrella dialog box with assets folder
set as the default images folder*

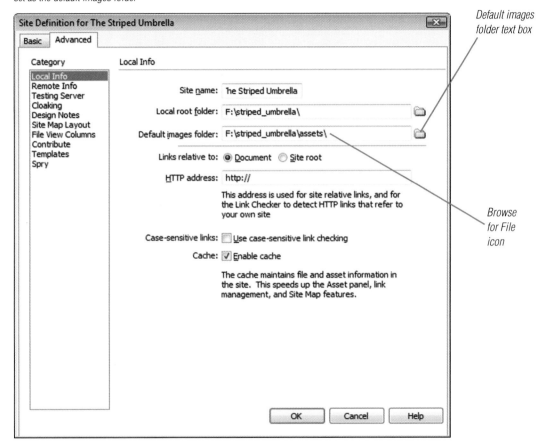

Default images
folder text box

Browse
for File
icon

Set the default images folder

1. Click the **Site list arrow** next to The Striped Umbrella in the Site text box on the Files panel, click **Manage Sites**, then click **Edit**.

2. Click the **Browse for File icon** 📁 next to the Default images folder text box.

3. If necessary, navigate to your striped_umbrella folder, double-click the **assets folder** (Win) or click the **assets folder** (Mac), then click **Select** (Win) or **Choose** (Mac).

   Compare your screen to Figure 18.

4. Click **OK**, then click **Done**.

You set the assets folder as the default images folder so that imported images will be automatically saved in it.

Set the home page

1. Open **dw1_2.html** from where you store your Data Files.

   The file has several elements in it, including a banner image.

2. Click **File** on the menu bar, click **Save As**, click the **Save in list arrow** (Win) or the **Where list arrow** (Mac), navigate to the striped_umbrella folder, select **dw1_2.html** in the File name text box (Win) or select **dw1_2** in the Save As text box (Mac), then type **index**.

3. Click **Save**.

   The file extension .html is automatically added to the filename. As shown in Figure 19, the title bar displays the drive where the root folder is stored, the root folder name, the filename of the page (index.html), and the document type (XHTML) in parentheses. (Win) The information within the brackets is called the **path**, or location of the open file in relation to other folders in the Web site.

4. When asked to update links, click **No**.

   The banner image is no longer visible and the page contains a broken link to the image. This is because although you saved the .html file under a new name in the Web site's root folder, you have not yet copied the image file into the Web site's assets folder. The link to the banner image is still linked to the Data Files folder. You will fix this in the next set of steps.

5. Right-click (Win) or [control]-click (Mac) **index.html** in the Files panel, then click **Set as Home Page**.

You opened a file, saved it with the filename index, then set it as the home page.

FIGURE 19
index.html copied to the striped_umbrella root folder — Path for file

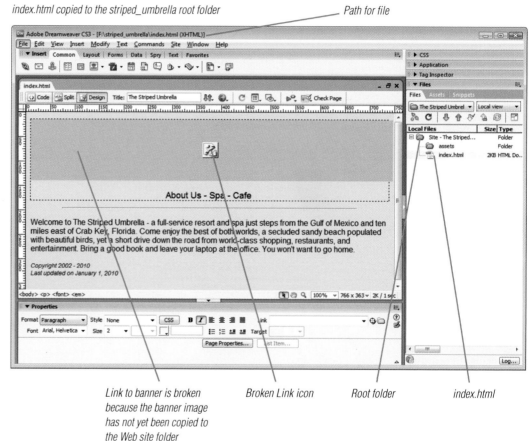

Link to banner is broken because the banner image has not yet been copied to the Web site folder

Broken Link icon   Root folder   index.html

FIGURE 20
Property inspector showing properties of The Striped Umbrella banner

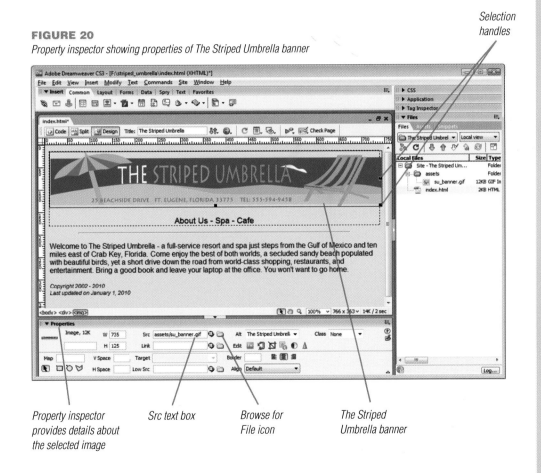

Selection handles

Property inspector provides details about the selected image

Src text box

Browse for File icon

The Striped Umbrella banner

1. Click **The Striped Umbrella banner broken link placeholder** to select it.

   Selection handles appear around the broken link. To correct the broken link, you must copy the image file from the Data Files folder into the assets folder of your Web site.

2. Click the **Browse for File icon** 📁 next to the Src text box in the Property inspector, click the **Look in list arrow** (Win) or **navigation list arrow** (Mac), navigate to the assets folder in your Data Files folder for this chapter, click **su_banner.gif**, click **OK** (Win) or **Choose** (Mac), then click in a blank part of the page.

   TIP If you do not see the su-banner.gif file listed in the Files panel, click the Refresh button ⟳ on the Files panel toolbar.

   The file for the Striped Umbrella banner, su_banner.gif, is automatically copied to the assets folder of The Striped Umbrella Web site, the folder that you designated as the default images folder. The Src text box shows the path of the banner to the assets folder in the Web site, and the banner image is visible on the page.

3. Compare your screen to Figure 20.

   TIP Until you copy a graphic from an outside folder to your Web site, the graphic is not part of the Web site, and the image will appear as a broken link.

You saved The Striped Umbrella banner in the assets folder.

Add pages to a Web site (Windows)

1. Click the **plus sign** to the left of the assets folder (if necessary) to open the folder and view its contents, su_banner.gif.

   TIP If you do not see a file listed in the assets folder, click the Refresh button ⟳ on the Files panel toolbar.

2. Right-click the **striped_umbrella root folder**, click **New File**, type **about_us.html** to replace untitled.html, then press **[Enter]**.

   Each new file is a page in the Web site.

   TIP If you create a new file in the Files panel, you must type the filename extension (.html) manually. If you create a new file using the File menu or the Welcome Screen the file-name extension will be added automatically.

3. Repeat Step 2 to add five more blank pages to The Striped Umbrella Web site, then name the new files **spa.html**, **cafe.html**, **activities.html**, **cruises.html**, and **fishing.html**.

   TIP Make sure to add the new files to the root folder, not the assets folder. If you accidentally add them to the assets folder, just drag them to the root folder.

4. Click the **Refresh button** ⟳ on the Files panel to list the files alphabetically, then compare your screen to Figure 21.

You added the following six pages to The Striped Umbrella Web site: about_us, activities, cafe, cruises, fishing, and spa.

FIGURE 21
New pages added to The Striped Umbrella Web site (Windows)

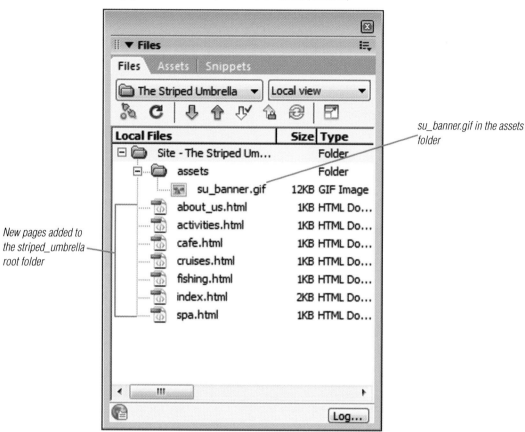

su_banner.gif in the assets folder

New pages added to the striped_umbrella root folder

FIGURE 22

New pages added to The Striped Umbrella Web site (Macintosh)

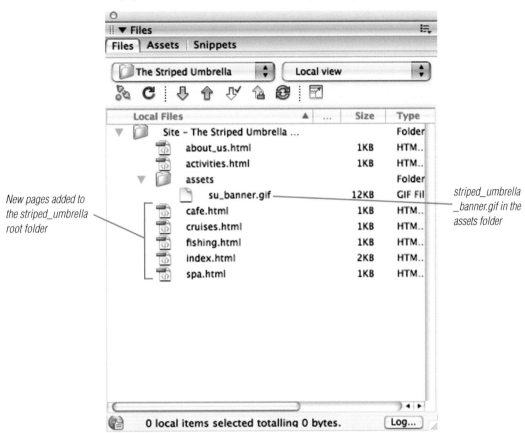

New pages added to the striped_umbrella root folder

striped_umbrella _banner.gif in the assets folder

1. Click the **triangle** to the left of the assets folder to open the folder and view its contents.

   TIP If you do not see a file listed in the assets folder, click the Refresh button C on the Files panel.

2. [control]-click the **striped_umbrella root folder**, click **New File**, type **about_us.html** to replace untitled.html, then press **[return]**.

   TIP If you create a new file in the Files panel, you must type the filename extension (.html) manually.

3. Repeat Step 3 to add five more blank pages to The Striped Umbrella Web site, then name the new files **spa.html, cafe.html, activities.html, cruises.html,** and **fishing.html.**

4. Click the **Refresh button** C to list the files alphabetically, then compare your screen to Figure 22.

You added six pages to The Striped Umbrella Web site: about_us, activities, cafe, cruises, fishing, spa.

CREATE AND VIEW
A SITE MAP

What You'll Do

 In this lesson, you will create and view a site map for The Striped Umbrella Web site.

Creating a Site Map

As you add new Web pages to a Web site, it is easy to lose track of how they all link together. You can use the site map feature to help you keep track of the relationships between pages in a Web site. A **site map** is a graphical representation of the pages in the Web site and shows the folder structure for the Web site. You can find out details about each page by viewing the visual clues in the site map. For example, the site map uses icons to indicate pages with broken links, e-mail links, and links to external Web sites. It also indicates which pages are currently **checked out**, or being used by other team members.

Viewing a Site Map

You can view a site map using the Map view in the Files panel. You can expand the Files panel to display both the site map and the Web site file list. You can specify that the site map show a filename or a page title for each page. You can also edit page titles in the site map. Figure 23 shows the site map and file list for The Striped Umbrella Web site. Only the home page and pages that are linked to the home page will display in the site map. As more child pages are added, the site map will display them using a **tree structure**, or a diagram that visually represents the way the pages are linked to each other.

DESIGNTIP **Verifying page titles**

When you view a Web page in a browser, its page title is displayed in the browser window title bar. The page title should reflect the page content and set the tone for the page. It is especially important to use words in your page title that are likely to match keywords viewers might enter when using a search engine. Search engines compare the text in page titles to the keywords typed into the search engine. When a title bar displays "Untitled Document," the designer has neglected to give the page a title. This is like giving up free "billboard space" and looks very unprofessional.

Using Site Maps to Help Visitors Find Your Pages

It is very helpful to include an image of the site map, or a site listing, in a Web site to help viewers understand the navigation structure of the site. Using Dreamweaver, you have the options of saving a site map for printing purposes or for displaying a site map on a page in a Web site. Windows users can save site maps as either a BMP (bitmapped) file or as a PNG (Portable Network Graphics) file. Macintosh users can save site maps as PICT or JPEG files. The PNG and JPEG formats are best for inserting the site map on a Web page. Another option to help search engines find your Web pages is to create an **XML site map**, or a listing of the Web site links that can be made available to search engines such as Google, MSN, or Yahoo.

Submitting a site map to search engines is intended to help visitors find your pages, but does not replace the standard methods that search engines use to locate pages based on information entered in search text boxes. For more information on XML site maps, visit *http://www.sitemaps.org/*. This is a Web site sponsored jointly by Google, Yahoo, and Microsoft.

FIGURE 23
The Striped Umbrella site map

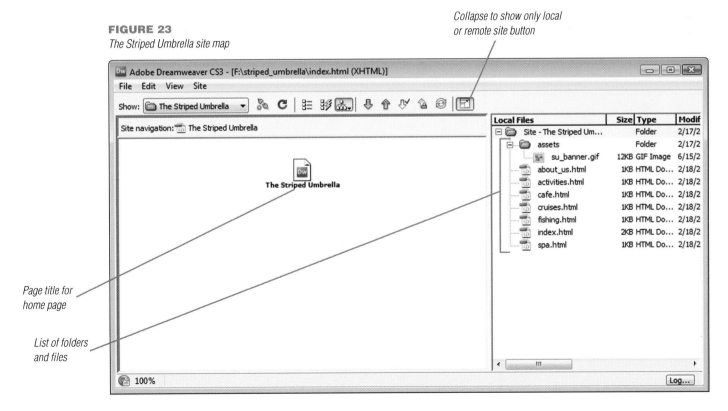

Collapse to show only local or remote site button

Page title for home page

List of folders and files

Select site map options

1. Click the **Site list arrow** next to The Striped Umbrella in the Files panel, click **Manage Sites**, click **The Striped Umbrella** (if necessary), then click **Edit** to open the Site Definition dialog box.

2. Click **Site Map Layout** in the Category list.

3. Verify that index.html is specified as the home page in the Home page text box, as shown in Figure 24.

   TIP If the index.html file is not specified as your home page, click the Browse for File icon next to the Home page text box, then locate and double-click index.html.

4. Click the **Page titles option button**.

5. Click **OK**, then click **Done**.

You designated index.html as the home page for The Striped Umbrella Web site to create the site map. You also specified that page titles are displayed in the site map instead of filenames.

FIGURE 24
Options for the site map layout

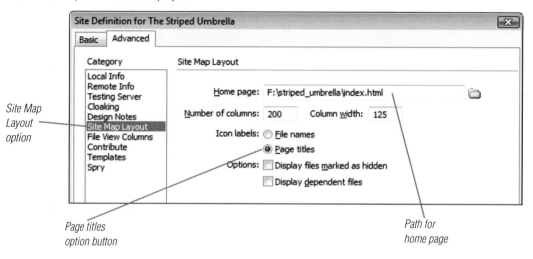

Site Map Layout option

Page titles option button

Path for home page

POWER USER SHORTCUTS

to do this:	use this shortcut:
Open a file	[Ctrl][O] (Win) or ⌘ [O] (Mac)
Close a file	[Ctrl][W] (Win) or ⌘ [W] (Mac)
Create a new file	[Ctrl][N] (Win) or ⌘ [N] (Mac)
Save a file	[Ctrl][S] (Win) or ⌘ [S] (Mac)
Dreamweaver Help	F1
Show panels	F4
Show page titles in Site Map	[Ctrl][Shift][T] (Win) or [Shift] ⌘ [T] (Mac)

FIGURE 25
Expanding the site map

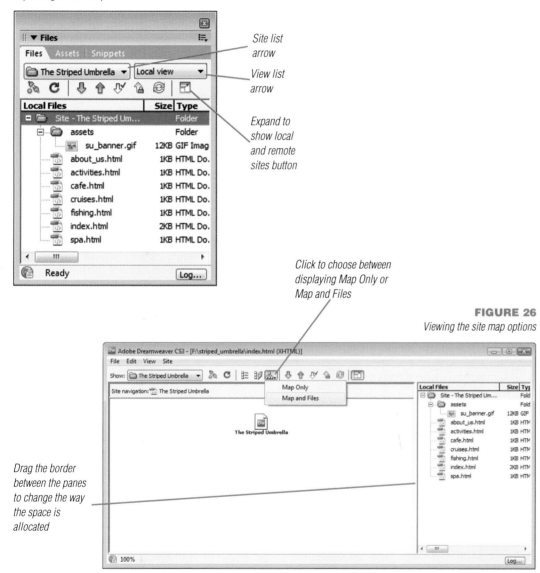

Site list
arrow

View list
arrow

Expand to
show local
and remote
sites button

Click to choose between
displaying Map Only or
Map and Files

FIGURE 26
Viewing the site map options

Drag the border
between the panes
to change the way
the space is
allocated

View a site map

1. Click the **Expand to show local and remote sites button** on the Files panel toolbar, as shown in Figure 25, to display the expanded site map.

   The site map shows the home page and pages that are linked to it. Because there are no pages linked to the home page, the site map shows only the home page.

   TIP You can drag the border between the two panes on the screen to resize them.

2. Click the **Site map button**, then click **Map and Files** if you don't see the index page icon on the site map, as shown in Figure 26.

3. Click **View** on the menu bar, point to **Site Map Options**, then click **Show Page Titles** to deselect it (Win) or click **View,** point to **Site Map Options**, then click **Show Page Titles** (Mac).

   The filename, index.html, is now displayed instead of the page title, The Striped Umbrella.

4. Click the **Collapse to show only local or remote site button** on the toolbar to collapse the site map.

   The file list appears again in the Files panel.

5. Click **File** on the menu bar, then click **Exit** (Win) or click **Dreamweaver** on the menu bar, and then click **Quit Dreamweaver** (Mac).

   TIP If you are prompted to save changes, click No.

You expanded the site map and viewed the index page with the page title and then the filename. You then collapsed the site map.

Explore the Dreamweaver workspace.

1. Start Dreamweaver.
2. Create a new document.
3. Change the view to Code view.
4. Change the view to Code and Design views.
5. Change the view to Design view.
6. Expand the Application panel group.
7. View each panel in the Application panel group.
8. Collapse the Application panel group.
9. Close the page without saving it.

View a Web page and use Help.

1. Open the file dw1_3.html from where you store your Data Files.
2. Locate the following page elements: a table, a banner, an image, and some formatted text.
3. Change the view to Code view.
4. Change the view to Design view.
5. Use the Dreamweaver Help command to search for information on panel groups.
6. Display and read one of the topics you find.
7. Close the Dreamweaver Help Viewer window.
8. Close the page without saving it.

Plan and define a Web site.

1. Select the drive and folder where you will store your Web site files using Windows Explorer or the Macintosh Finder.
2. Create a new root folder called **blooms**.
3. Close Windows Explorer or the Finder (Mac), then activate the Dreamweaver application.
4. Create a new site called **blooms & bulbs**.
5. Specify the blooms folder as the Local root folder.
6. Verify that the Enable cache check box is selected.
7. Use the Remote Info category in the Site Definition for the blooms & bulbs dialog box to set up Web server access. (*Hint*: Specify None if you do not have the necessary information to set up Web server access.)
8. Click **OK**, then click Done to close the Site Definition for the blooms & bulbs dialog box.

Add a folder and pages and set the home page.

1. Create a new folder in the blooms root folder called **assets**.
2. Edit the site to set the assets folder as the default location for the Web site images.

3. Open the file dw1_4.html from where you store your Data Files, save this file in the blooms root folder as **index.html**, then click No to updating the links.
4. Set index.html as the home page.
5. Select the broken image link for the blooms & bulbs banner on the page.
6. Use the Property inspector to browse for blooms_banner.jpg, then select it to automatically save it in the assets folder of the blooms & bulbs Web site.
7. Create seven new pages in the Files panel, and name them: **plants.html**, **classes.html**, **newsletter.html**, **annuals.html**, **perennials.html**, **water_plants.html**, and **tips.html**.
8. Refresh the view to list the new files alphabetically.

Create and view a site map.

1. Use the Site Definition dialog box to verify that the index.html file is shown as the home page.
2. View the expanded site map for the Web site.
3. Show the page titles, as shown in Figure 27.
4. Show the file names.
5. Collapse the site map, then close index.html.

FIGURE 27
Completed Skills Review

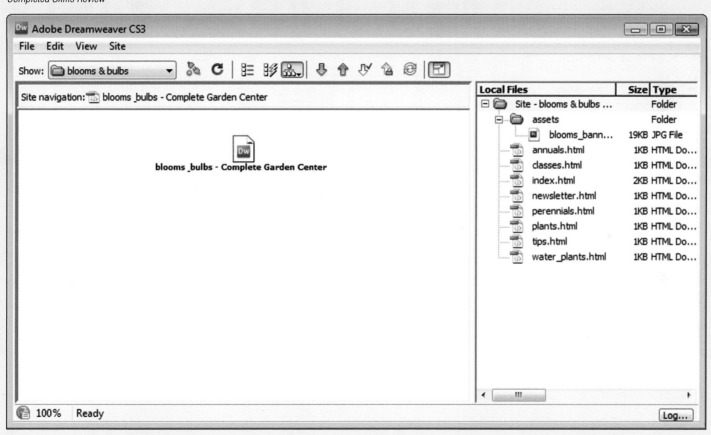

You have been hired to create a Web site for a travel outfitter called TripSmart. TripSmart specializes in travel products and services. In addition to selling travel products, such as luggage and accessories, they sponsor trips and offer travel advice. Their clients range from college students to families to vacationing professionals. The owner, Thomas Howard, has requested a dynamic Web site that conveys the excitement of traveling.

1. Using the information in the preceding paragraph, create a storyboard for this Web site, using either a pencil and paper or a software program such as Microsoft Word. Include the home page with links to four child pages named **catalog.html**, **newsletter.html**, **services.html**, and **destinations.html**. Include two child pages under the destinations page named **amazon.html** and **kenya.html.**

2. Create a new root folder named **tripsmart** in the drive and folder where you store your Web site files.

3. Start Dreamweaver, then create a Web site with the name **TripSmart**. Set the tripsmart folder as the local root folder for the Web site.

4. Create an assets folder and set it as the default location for images.

5. Open the file dw1_5.html from where you store your Data Files, then save it in the tripsmart root folder as **index.html**.

6. Correct the path for the banner by selecting the banner on the page, browsing to the original source in the Data Files folder, then selecting the file to copy it automatically to your TripSmart assets folder.

7. Set index.html as the home page.

FIGURE 28
Completed Project Builder 1

8. Create six additional pages for the site, and name them as follows: **catalog.html**, **newsletter.html**, **services.html**, **destinations.html**, **amazon.html**, and **kenya.html**. Use your storyboard and Figure 28 as a guide.

9. Refresh the Files panel.

10. View the site map for the Web site. (*Hint*: View the site map with the site map option set to show filenames rather than page titles.)

11. Collapse the site map, then close any open pages.

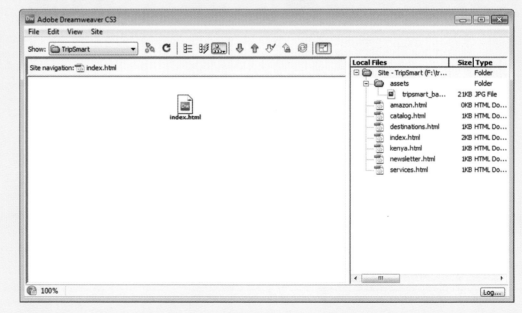

Your company has been selected to design a Web site for a catering business called Carolyne's Creations. In addition to catering, Carolyne's services include cooking classes and daily specials available as take-out meals. She also has a retail shop that stocks gourmet treats and kitchen items.

1. Create a storyboard for this Web site that includes a home page and child pages named **shop.html, classes.html, catering.html,** and **recipes.html.** Create two more child pages under the classes.html page called **children.html** and **adults.html**.

2. Create a new root folder for the Web site in the drive and folder where you save your Web site files, then name it **cc**.

3. Create a Web site with the name Carolyne's Creations, using the cc folder for the root folder.

4. Create an assets folder for the Web site and set the assets folder as the default location for images.

5. Open dw1_6.html from the where you store your Data Files then save it as **index.html** in the cc folder.

6. Save the cc_banner.jpg file in the assets folder.

7. Set index.html as the home page.

8. Using Figure 29 and your storyboard as guides, create the additional pages shown for the Web site.

9. View the site map with page titles displayed, as shown in Figure 29, then show the file-names before you collapse the site map.

10. Close the index file.

FIGURE 29
Completed Project Builder 2

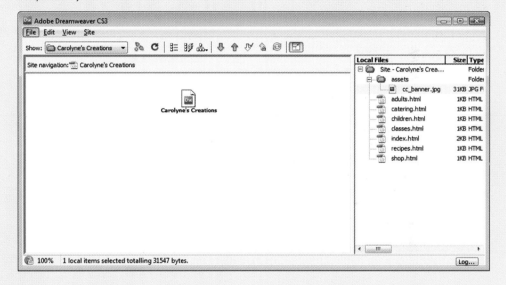

Figure 30 shows the Audi Web site, a past selection for the Adobe Site of the Day. To visit the current Audi Web site, connect to the Internet, then go to *www.audi.com*. The current page might differ from the figure because dynamic Web sites are updated frequently to reflect current information. The main navigation structure is accessed through the links along the right side of the page. The page title is Audi Worldwide > Home.

Go to the Adobe Web site at *www.adobe.com,* click the Showcase link (at the bottom right corner of the page), then click the current Site of the Day. Explore the site and answer the following questions:

1. Do you see page titles for each page you visit?
2. Do the page titles accurately reflect the page content?
3. View the pages using more than one screen resolution, if possible. For which resolution does the site appear to be designed?

4. Is the navigation structure clear?
5. How is the navigation structure organized?

6. Why do you think this site was chosen as a Site of the Day?

FIGURE 30
Design Project

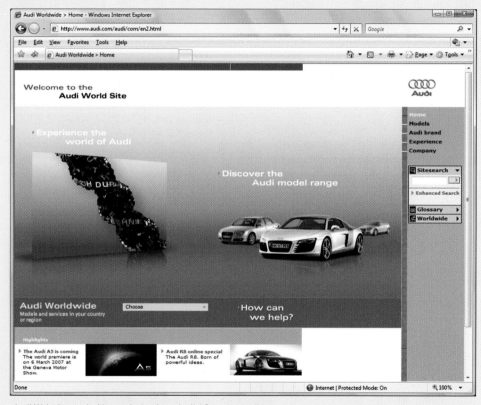

Audi Web site used with permission from Audi AG – www.audi.com

PORTFOLIO PROJECT

The Portfolio Project will be an ongoing project throughout the book, in which you will plan and create an original Web site without any Data Files supplied. The focus of the Web site can be on any topic, organization, sports team, club, or company that you would like. You will build on this Web site from chapter to chapter, so you must do each Portfolio Project assignment in each chapter to complete your Web site. When you finish this book, you should have a completed Web site that would be an excellent addition to a professional portfolio.

1. Decide what type of Web site you would like to create. It can be a personal Web site about you, a business Web site that promotes a fictitious or real company, or an informational Web site that provides information about a topic, cause, or organization.

2. Write a list of questions and answers about the Web site you have decided to create.

3. Create a storyboard for your Web site to include at least four pages. The storyboard should include the home page with at least three child pages under it.

4. Create a root folder and an assets folder to house the Web site assets, then set it as the default location for images.

5. Create a blank page named **index.html** as a placeholder for the home page, then set it as the home page.

6. Begin collecting content, such as pictures or text to use in your Web site. You can use a digital camera to take photos, scan pictures, or create your own graphics using a program such as Adobe Fireworks or Adobe Illustrator. Gather the content in a central location that will be accessible to you as you develop your site.

chapter

2

DEVELOPING A
WEB PAGE

1. Create head content and set page properties

2. Create, import, and format text

3. Add links to Web pages

4. Use the History panel and edit code

5. Modify and test Web pages

Introduction

The process of developing a Web page requires several steps. If the page is a home page, you need to spend some time crafting the head content. The head content contains information used by search engines to help viewers find your Web site. You also need to choose the colors for the page background and text. You then need to add the page content, format it attractively, and add links to other pages in the Web site or to other Web sites. Finally, to ensure that all links work correctly and are current, you need to test them regularly.

Understanding Page Layout

Before you add content to a page, consider the following guidelines for laying out pages:

Use White Space Effectively. A living room crammed with too much furniture makes it difficult to appreciate the individual pieces. The same is true of a Web page. Too many text blocks, links, animations, and images can be distracting. Consider leaving some white space on each page. White space, which is not necessarily white, is the area on a Web page that contains no text or graphics.

Limit Multimedia Elements. Too many multimedia elements, such as images,

video clips, or sounds, may result in a page that takes too much time to load. Viewers may leave your Web site before the entire page finishes loading. Use multimedia elements only if you have a good reason.

Keep It Simple. Often the simplest Web sites are the most appealing and are also the easiest to create and maintain. A simple, well-designed Web site that works well is far superior to a complex one that contains errors.

Use an Intuitive Navigation Structure. Make sure the navigation structure is easy to use. Viewers should always know where they are in the site and be able to easily find their way back to the home page. If viewers get lost, they may leave the site rather than struggle to find their way around.

Apply a Consistent Theme. To help give pages in your Web site a consistent appearance, consider designing your pages using elements that relate to a common theme. Consistency in the use of color and fonts, the placement of the navigation links, and the overall page design gives a Web site a unified look and promotes greater ease-of-use and accessibility. Template-based pages and style sheets make this task much easier.

Tools You'll Use

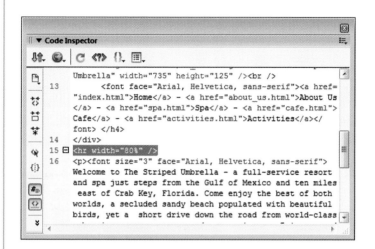

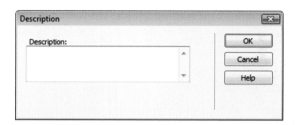

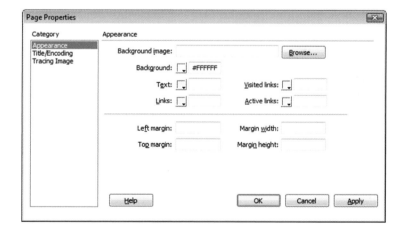

CREATE HEAD CONTENT AND
SET PAGE PROPERTIES

What You'll Do

 In this lesson, you will learn how to enter titles, keywords, and descriptions in the head content section of a Web page. You will also change the background color for a Web page.

Creating the Head Content

A Web page is composed of two distinct sections: the head content and the body. The **head content** includes the page title that is displayed in the title bar of the browser and some important page elements, called meta tags, that are not visible in the browser. Page titles are not to be confused with filenames, the name used to store each file on the server. **Meta tags** are HTML codes that include information about the page, such as keywords and descriptions. Meta tags are read by screen readers (for viewers who have visual impairments) and are also used to provide the server information such as the PICS rating for the page. PICS is the acronym for **Platform for Internet Content Selection**. This is a rating system for Web pages that is similar to rating systems used for movies. **Keywords** are words

---

DESIGNTIP **Using Web-safe colors**

Prior to 1994, colors appeared differently on different types of computers. In 1994, Netscape developed the first **Web-safe color palette**, a set of colors that appears consistently in all browsers and on Macintosh, Windows, and UNIX platforms. The evolution of video cards has made this less relevant today, although understanding Web-safe colors may still prove important given the limitations of other online devices, such as cell phones and PDAs. If you want your Web pages to be viewed across a wide variety of computer platforms, choose Web-safe colors for all your page elements. Dreamweaver has two Web-safe color palettes, Color Cubes and Continuous Tone, each of which contains 216 Web-safe colors. Color Cubes is the default color palette. To choose a different color palette, click Modify on the menu bar, click Page Properties, click the Appearance category, click the Background, Text, or Links color box to open the color picker, click the color picker list arrow, and then click the color palette you want.

that relate to the content of the Web site. A **description** is a short paragraph that describes the content and features of the Web site. For instance, the words "beach" and "resort" would be appropriate keywords for The Striped Umbrella Web site. Search engines find Web pages by matching the title, description, and keywords in the head content of Web pages with keywords that viewers enter in search engine text boxes. Therefore, it is important to include concise, useful information in the head content. The **body** is the part of the page that appears in a browser window. It contains all the page content that is visible to viewers, such as text, images, and links.

Setting Web Page Properties

When you create a Web page, one of the first design decisions that you should make is choosing the **background color**, or the color that fills the entire Web page. The background color should complement the colors used for text, links, and images that are placed on the page. Many times, images are used for backgrounds for either the entire page or a part of the page, such as a table background. A strong contrast between the text color and the background color makes it easier for viewers to read the text on your Web page. You can choose a light background color with a dark text color, or a dark background color with a light text color. A white background with dark text, though not terribly exciting, provides good contrast and is the easiest to read for most viewers. Another design decision you need to make is whether to change the **default font** and **default link colors**, which are the colors used by the browser to display text, links, and visited links. The default color for **unvisited links**, or links that the viewer has not clicked yet, is blue. In Dreamweaver, unvisited links are simply called **links**. The default color for **visited links**, or links that have been previously clicked, is purple. You change the background color, text, and link colors using the color picker in the Page Properties dialog box. You can choose colors from one of the five Dreamweaver color palettes, as shown in Figure 1.

QUICKTIP

Many design decisions are implemented through the use of Cascading Style Sheets, or CSS. We will initially use the Page Properties dialog box to set page properties such as the background color. Later we will learn to do this using Cascading Style Sheets.

FIGURE 1
Color picker showing color palettes

Click list arrow to choose a color palette

Web-safe palettes

DESIGNTIP Making pages accessible to viewers of all abilities

Not all of your viewers will have perfect vision and hearing or full use of both hands. There are several techniques you can use to ensure that your Web site is accessible to individuals with disabilities. These techniques include using alternate text with images, avoiding certain colors on Web pages, and supplying text as an alternate source for information that is presented in an audio file. Adobe provides much information about Web site compliance with Section 508 accessibility guidelines. For more information, visit the Adobe Web site at *www.adobe.com/accessibility/*. Here you will find suggestions for creating accessible Web sites, an explanation of Section 508, and information on how people with disabilities use assistive devices to navigate the Internet.

Edit a page title

1. Start Dreamweaver, click the **Site list arrow** on the Files panel, then click **The Striped Umbrella** (if necessary).

2. Double-click **index.html** in the Files panel to open The Striped Umbrella home page, click **View** on the menu bar, then click **Head Content**.

   The Title icon ⊞ and Meta icon 🔲 are now visible in the head content section, as shown in Figure 2.

3. Click the **Title icon** ⊞ in the head content section.

   The page title The Striped Umbrella appears in the Title text box in the Property inspector.

4. Click the end of The Striped Umbrella text in the Title text box in the Property inspector, press **[Spacebar]**, type **beach resort and spa, Ft. Eugene, Florida**, then press **[Enter]** (Win) or **[return]** (Mac).

   Compare your screen with Figure 3. The new title is better, because it incorporates the words "beach resort" and "spa" and the location of the resort—words that potential customers might use as keywords when using a search engine.

   TIP You can also change the page title using the Title text box on the Document toolbar.

   You opened The Striped Umbrella Web site, opened the home page in Design view, viewed the head content section, and changed the page title.

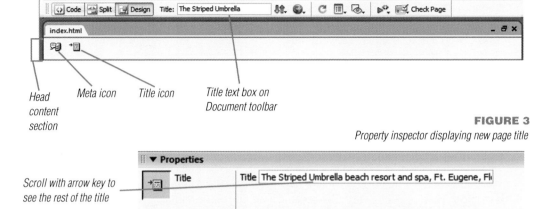

FIGURE 2
Viewing the head content

Head content section   Meta icon   Title icon   Title text box on Document toolbar

FIGURE 3
Property inspector displaying new page title

Scroll with arrow key to see the rest of the title

▼ Properties
Title   Title | The Striped Umbrella beach resort and spa, Ft. Eugene, Fl

---

DESIGNTIP   **Using appropriate content for your target audience**

When you begin developing the content for your Web site, you need to decide what content to include and how to arrange each element on each page. You must design the content with the audience in mind. What is the age group of your audience? What reading level is appropriate? Should you use a formal or informal tone? Should the pages be simple, containing mostly text, or rich with images and multimedia files? Your content should fit your target audience. Look at the font sizes used, the number and size of images and animations used, the reading level, and the amount of technical expertise needed to navigate your site, and then evaluate them to see if they fit your audience. If they do not, you will be defeating your purpose. Usually, the first page that your audience will see when they visit your Web site is the home page. The home page should be designed so that viewers will understand your site's purpose and feel comfortable finding their way around the pages in your site. To ensure that viewers do not get lost in your Web site, make sure you design all the pages with a consistent look and feel. You can use templates and Cascading Style Sheets to maintain a common look for each page. **Templates** are Web pages that contain the basic layout for each page in the site, including the location of a company logo or a menu of buttons. **Cascading Style Sheets** are sets of formatting attributes that are used to format Web pages to provide a consistent presentation for content across the site.

FIGURE 4
Insert bar displaying the HTML category

Common tab

Your icon may differ
depending on what
was last selected

Keywords
command

Head list arrow

FIGURE 5
Keywords dialog box

Keywords

Enter keywords

1. Click the **Common tab** on the Insert bar (if necessary).

2. Click the **Head list arrow**, as shown in Figure 4, then click **Keywords**.

   TIP Some buttons on the Insert bar include a list arrow indicating that there is a menu of choices beneath the current button. The button that you select last will appear on the Insert bar until you select another.

3. Type **beach resort, spa, Ft. Eugene, Florida, Gulf of Mexico, fishing, dolphin cruises** in the Keywords text box, as shown in Figure 5, then click OK

   The Keywords icon appears in the head content section and the keywords appear in the Keywords text box in the Property inspector.

You added keywords relating to the beach to the head content of The Striped Umbrella home page.

DESIGNTIP   **Entering keywords and descriptions**

Search engines use keywords, descriptions, and titles to find pages after a user enters search terms. Therefore, it is very important to anticipate the search terms your potential customers would use and include these words in the keywords, description, and title. Many search engines display page titles and descriptions in their search results. Some search engines limit the number of keywords that they will index, so make sure you list the most important keywords first. Keep your keywords and descriptions short and concise to ensure that all search engines will include your site. To choose effective keywords, many designers incorporate the use of focus groups to have a more representative sample of words that potential customers or clients might use. A **focus group** is a marketing tool that asks a group of people for feedback about a product, such as its impact in a television ad or the effectiveness of a Web site design.

Enter a description

1. Click the **Head list arrow** on the Insert bar, then click **Description**.

2. In the Description text box, type **The Striped Umbrella is a full-service resort and spa just steps from the Gulf of Mexico in Ft. Eugene, Florida**.

   Your screen should resemble Figure 6.

3. Click **OK**.

   The Description icon appears in the Head Content section and the keywords appear in the Description text box in the Property inspector.

4. Click the **Show Code view button** [‹›] Code on the Document toolbar.

   Notice that the title, keywords, and description appear in the HTML code in the document window, as shown in Figure 7.

   TIP   You can also enter and edit the meta tags directly in the code in Code view.

5. Click the **Show Design view button** 🖳 Design to return to Design view.

6. Click **View** on the menu bar, then click **Head Content** to close the head content section.

You added a description of The Striped Umbrella resort to the head content of the home page. You then viewed the home page in Code view and examined the HTML code for the head content.

FIGURE 6
Description dialog box

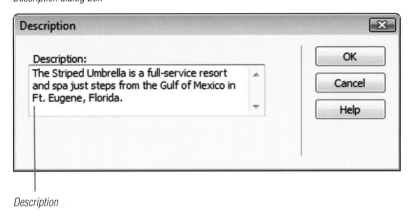

Description

FIGURE 7
Head Content displayed in Code view

Opening HTML tag

Head tags

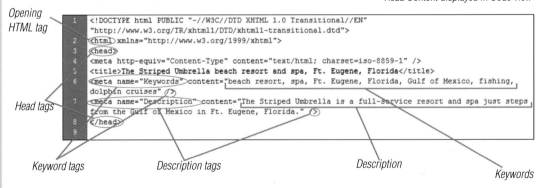

Keyword tags   Description tags   Description   Keywords

FIGURE 8

Page Properties dialog box

Default Color button

Background color box

Hexadecimal number for white

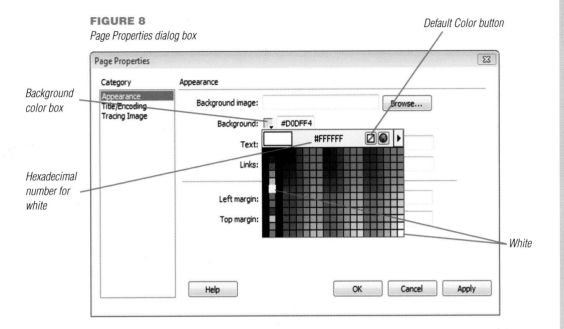

White

1. Click **Modify** on the menu bar, then click **Page Properties** to open the Page Properties dialog box.

2. Click the **Background color box** [▼] to open the color picker, as shown in Figure 8.

3. Click the last color in the bottom row (white).

4. Click **Apply**, then click **OK**.

   Clicking Apply lets you see the changes you made to the Web page without closing the Page Properties dialog box.

   TIP If you don't like the color you chose, click the Default Color button [☑] in the color picker to switch back to the default color.

   The background color of the Web page is now white. The black text against the white background provides a nice contrast and makes the text easy to read.

   You used the Page Properties dialog box to change the background color to white.

Understanding hexadecimal values

Each color is assigned a **hexadecimal value**, a value that represents the amount of red, green, and blue present in the color. For example, white, which is made of equal parts of red, green, and blue, has a hexadecimal value of FFFFFF. Each pair of characters in the hexadecimal value represents the red, green, and blue values. The hexadecimal number system is based on 16, rather than 10 in the decimal number system. Because the hexadecimal number system includes only numbers up to 9, values after 9 use the letters of the alphabet. "A" represents the number 10 in the hexadecimal number system. "F" represents the number 15.

CREATE, IMPORT, AND
FORMAT TEXT

What You'll Do

In this lesson, you will apply HTML heading styles and HTML text styles to text on The Striped Umbrella home page. You will also import a file and set text properties for the text on the new page.

Creating and Importing Text

Most information in Web pages is presented in the form of text. You can type text directly in Dreamweaver, import, or copy and paste it from another software program. When using a Windows computer to import text from a Microsoft Word file, you use the Import Word Document command. Not only will the formatting be preserved, but Dreamweaver will generate clean HTML code. When you import text, it is important to keep in mind that visitors to your site must have the same fonts installed on their computers as the fonts applied to the imported text. Otherwise, the text may appear incorrectly. Some software programs may be able to convert text into graphics so that the text retains the same appearance no matter which fonts are installed. However, text converted into graphics is no longer editable. If text does not have a font specified, the default font

Using keyboard shortcuts

When working with text, the standard Windows keyboard shortcuts for Cut, Copy, and Paste are very useful. These are [Ctrl][X] (Win) or [⌘][X] (Mac) for Cut, [Ctrl][C] (Win) or [⌘][C] (Mac) for Copy, and [Ctrl][V] (Win) or [⌘][V] (Mac) for Paste. You can view all Dreamweaver keyboard shortcuts using the Keyboard Shortcuts dialog box, which lets you view existing shortcuts for menu commands, tools, or miscellaneous functions, such as copying HTML or inserting an image. You can also create your own shortcuts or assign shortcuts that you are familiar with from using them in other software programs. To view or modify keyboard shortcuts, click the Keyboard Shortcuts command on the Edit menu (Win) or Dreamweaver menu (Mac), then select the shortcut key set you want. The Keyboard Shortcuts feature is also available in Adobe Fireworks and Flash. Each chapter includes a list of keyboard shortcuts relevant to that chapter.

will apply. This means that the default font on the user's computer will be used to display the text. Keep in mind that some fonts may not display the same on both a Windows and a Macintosh computer. It is wise to stick to the standard fonts that work well with both systems.

Formatting Text Using the Property Inspector

Because text is more difficult and tiring to read on a computer screen than on a printed page, you should make the text in your Web site attractive and easy to read. You can format text in Dreamweaver by changing its font, size, and color, just as you would in other software programs. To apply formatting to text, you first select the text you want to enhance, and then use the Property inspector to apply formatting attributes, such as font type, size, color, alignment, and indents.

Changing Fonts

You can format your text with different fonts by choosing a font combination from the Font list in the Property inspector. A **font combination** is a set of three fonts that specify which fonts a browser should use to display the text of your Web page. Font combinations are used so that if one font is not available, the browser will use the next one specified in the font combination. For

example, if text is formatted with the font combination Arial, Helvetica, sans serif, the browser will first look on the viewer's system for Arial. If Arial is not available, then it will look for Helvetica. If Helvetica is not available, then it will look for a sans-serif font to apply to the text. Using fonts within the default settings is wise, because fonts set outside the default settings may not be available on all viewers' computers.

Changing Font Sizes

There are two ways to change the size of text using the Property inspector. You can select a font size between 1 and 7 (where 1 is the smallest and 7 is the largest), or you can change the font size relative to the default base font. The **default base font** is size 3. For example, choosing +1 in the Size list increases the font size from 3 to 4. Font sizes on Windows and Macintosh computers may differ slightly, so it's important to view your page on both platforms, if possible.

Formatting Paragraphs

You can format blocks of text as paragraphs or as different sizes of headings. To format a paragraph as a heading, click anywhere in the paragraph, and then select the heading size you want from the Format list in the Property inspector. The Format list contains six different heading formats. Heading 1 is the largest size, and

Heading 6 is the smallest size. Browsers display text formatted as headings in bold, setting them off from paragraphs of text. You can also align paragraphs with the alignment buttons on the Property inspector and indent paragraphs using the Text Indent and Text Outdent buttons on the Property inspector.

QUICKTIP

Mixing too many different fonts and formatting attributes on a Web page can result in pages that are visually confusing or difficult to read.

Using HTML Tags Compared to Using CSS

The standard practice today is to use Cascading Style Sheets (CSS) to handle most of the formatting and placement of Web page elements. In fact, the default preference in Dreamweaver is to use CSS rather than HTML tags. However, this is a lot to learn when you are just beginning, so we are going to disable this preference temporarily until we study CSS in depth in the next chapter. At that point, we will again set the default preference to using CSS instead of HTML tags by clicking Edit (Win) or Dreamweaver (Mac) on the menu bar, clicking Preferences, and then checking the Use CSS instead of HTML tags check box.

Enter text

1. Position the insertion point directly after "want to go home." at the end of the paragraph, press **[Enter]** (Win) or **[return]** (Mac), then type **The Striped Umbrella**.

   Pressing [Enter] (Win) or [return] (Mac) creates a new paragraph. The HTML code for a paragraph break is <p>. The tag is closed with </p>.

   TIP   If the new text does not assume the formatting attributes as the paragraph above it, click the Show Code and Design views button 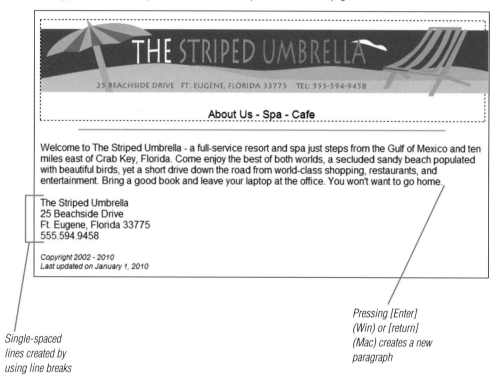 , position the cursor between the period after "home" and the font tag, then go back to the page in Design view and insert a new paragraph.

2. Press and hold **[Shift]**, press **[Enter]** (Win) or **[return]** (Mac), then type **25 Beachside Drive**.

   Pressing and holding [Shift] while you press [Enter] (Win) or [return] (Mac) creates a line break. A line break places a new line of text on the next line down without creating a new paragraph. Line breaks are useful when you want to add a new line of text directly below the current line of text and keep the same formatting. The HTML code for a line break is <br />.

3. Add the following text below the 25 Beachside Drive text, using line breaks after each line:

   Ft. Eugene, Florida 33775

   555.594.9458

4. Compare your screen with Figure 9.

   You entered text for the address and telephone number on the home page.

FIGURE 9

Entering the address and telephone number on The Striped Umbrella home page

THE STRIPED UMBRELLA

25 BEACHSIDE DRIVE   FT. EUGENE, FLORIDA 33775   TEL: 555-594-9458

About Us - Spa - Cafe

Welcome to The Striped Umbrella - a full-service resort and spa just steps from the Gulf of Mexico and ten miles east of Crab Key, Florida. Come enjoy the best of both worlds, a secluded sandy beach populated with beautiful birds, yet a short drive down the road from world-class shopping, restaurants, and entertainment. Bring a good book and leave your laptop at the office. You won't want to go home.

The Striped Umbrella
25 Beachside Drive
Ft. Eugene, Florida 33775
555.594.9458

Copyright 2002 - 2010
Last updated on January 1, 2010

Single-spaced lines created by using line breaks

Pressing [Enter] (Win) or [return] (Mac) creates a new paragraph

FIGURE 10

Formatting the address on The Striped Umbrella home page

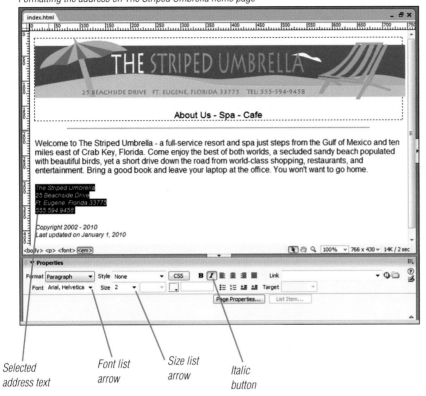

Selected address text

Font list arrow

Size list arrow

Italic button

1. Select the entire address and telephone number, as shown in Figure 10, then click the **Italic button** *I* in the Property inspector to italicize the text.

    When you have applied the italic style to selected text, the HTML code is <em>.

    TIP   To create bold text, the HTML tag is <strong></strong>; to underline text, the HTML code is <u></u>.

2. With the text still selected, click the **Size list arrow**, click **2**, then compare your screen to Figure 10.

3. Save your work, then close the document.

You formatted the address and phone number for The Striped Umbrella by changing the font style to Italic and changing the size to 2.

Preventing data loss

When you are ready to stop working with a file in Dreamweaver, it is a good idea to save your changes, close the page or pages on which you are working, and exit Dreamweaver. Doing this will prevent the loss of data if power is interrupted. In some cases, loss of power can corrupt an open file and render it unusable.

Save an image file in the assets folder

1. Open dw2_1.html from where you store your Data Files, save it as **spa.html** in the striped_umbrella folder, overwriting the existing file, then click **No** in the Update Links dialog box.

2. Select **The Striped Umbrella** banner.

   Updating links ties the image or hyperlink to the Data Files folder. Because you already copied su_banner.gif to the Web site, the banner image is visible. Notice that the Src text box shows the link is to the Web site assets folder, not to the Data Files folder.

3. Click the **Spa image broken link placeholder** to select it, click the **Browse for File icon** 📁 in the Property inspector, navigate to the chapter_2 assets folder, click **the_spa.jpg**, click beside the icon to deselect it, then click **OK** (Win) or **Choose** (Mac).

   Because this image was not in the Web site, it appears as a broken link. Using the Browse for File icon 📁 selects the source of the original image file. Dreamweaver automatically copies the file to the assets folder of the Web site and it is visible on the page. You may have to deselect the new image to see it replace the broken link.

4. Click the **Refresh button** 🔁 on the Files panel toolbar, then click the **plus sign** (Win) or **expander arrow** (Mac) next to the assets folder in the Files panel, (if necessary).

   A copy of the_spa.jpg file appears in the assets folder, as shown in Figure 11.

You opened a new file, saved it as the new spa page, and fixed a broken link by copying the image to the assets folder.

FIGURE 11
Image file added to The Striped Umbrella assets folder

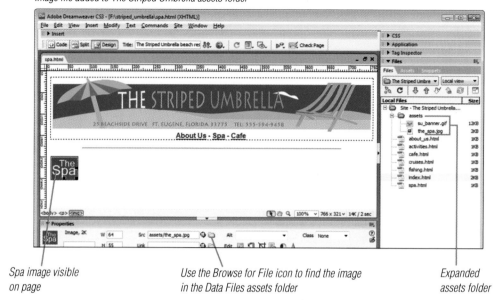

Spa image visible on page

Use the Browse for File icon to find the image in the Data Files assets folder

Expanded assets folder

Choosing filenames for Web pages

When you choose a name for a Web page, you should use a descriptive name that reflects the contents of the page. For example, if the page is about your company's products, you could name it products.html. You should also follow some general rules for naming Web pages, such as naming the home page **index.html**. Most file servers look for the file named index.html to use as the initial page for a Web site. Do not use spaces, special characters, or punctuation in Web page filenames or in the names of any images that will be inserted in your Web site. Spaces in filenames can cause errors when a browser attempts to read a file, and may cause your images to load incorrectly. You should also never use a number for the first character of a filename. To ensure that everything will load properly on all platforms, including UNIX, assume that filenames are case-sensitive and use lowercase characters. Files are saved with the .htm or .html file extension. Although either file extension is appropriate, the default file extension is .html. Use underscores in place of spaces. Forbidden characters include * & ^ % $ # @ ! / and \.

FIGURE 12
Clean Up Word HTML dialog box

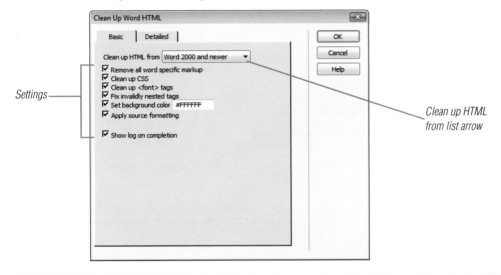

Settings

Clean up HTML
from list arrow

Importing and Linking Microsoft Office documents (Windows)

Adobe makes it easy to transfer data between Microsoft Office documents and Dreamweaver Web pages. When importing a Word or Excel document, click File on the menu bar, point to Import, then click either Word Document or Excel Document. Select the file want to import, then click the Formatting list arrow to choose between importing Text only (unformatted text); Text with structure (paragraphs, lists, and tables); Text, structure, basic formatting (bold, italic and Text), structure, full formatting (bold, italic, styles) before you click Open. The option you choose depends on the importance of the original structure and formatting. Always use the Clean Up Word HTML command after importing a Word file. You can also create a link to a Word or Excel document on your Web page. To do so, drag the Word or Excel document from its current location to the location on the Web page where you would like the link to appear. (If the document is located outside the Web site, you can browse for it using the Site list arrow on the Files panel.) Next, select the Create a link option button in the Insert Document dialog box, then save the file in your root folder so it will be uploaded when you publish your site. If it is not uploaded, the link will be broken.

Import text

1. Click **Edit** (Win) or **Dreamweaver** (Mac) on the menu bar, click **Preferences**, then click **General** on the left (if necessary).

2. Verify that the Use CSS instead of HTML tags check box is not checked, then click **OK**.

   TIP   It is very important to remove the check mark in the Use CSS instead of HTML tags check box at this time. After we explore CSS, we will restore this default preference. This is not a recommended practice. It is being suggested only to facilitate the learning process for a beginning Web designer.

3. Click to the right of the spa graphic on the spa.html page, then press **[Enter]** (Win) or **[return]** (Mac).

4. Click **File** on the menu bar, point to **Import**, click **Word Document**, double-click the **chapter_2 folder** from where you store your Data Files, then double-click **spa.doc** (Win), or double-click **spa.doc** from where you store your Data Files, select all, copy, close spa.doc, then paste the copied text on the spa page in Dreamweaver (Mac).

5. Click **Commands** on the menu bar, then click **Clean Up Word HTML**.

   TIP   If a dialog box appears stating that Dreamweaver was unable to determine the version of Word used to generate this document, click OK, click the Clean up HTML from list arrow, then choose a version of Word.

6. Make sure each check box in the Clean Up Word HTML dialog box is checked, as shown in Figure 12, click **OK**, then click **OK** again to close the Clean Up Word HTML Results window.

You imported a Word document, then used the Clean Up Word HTML command.

Set text properties

1. Expand the Insert bar (if necessary), click the Common tab, then place the insertion point anywhere within the words "Spa Services."

2. Click the **Format list arrow** in the Property inspector, click **Heading 4,** click the **Show Code and Design views button** ⟨Split⟩ on the Document toolbar, then compare your screen to Figure 13.

   The Heading 4 format is applied to the paragraph. Even a single word is considered a paragraph if there is a hard return or paragraph break after it. The HTML code for a Heading 4 tag is <h4>. The tag is then closed with </h4>. The level of the heading tag follows the h, so the code for a Heading 1 tag is <h1>.

3. Click the **Align Center button** ≡ in the Property inspector to center the heading.

   When the paragraph is centered, the HTML code 'align="center"' is added to the <h4> tag.

4. Select the words **Spa Services**, click the **Font list arrow**, then click **Arial**, **Helvetica**, **sans-serif**.

   Because setting a font is a character command, you must select all the characters you want to format before applying a font.

   TIP You can modify the font combinations in the Font list by clicking Text on the menu bar, pointing to Font, then clicking Edit Font List.

   (continued)

FIGURE 13
Code for Headings 4 tags

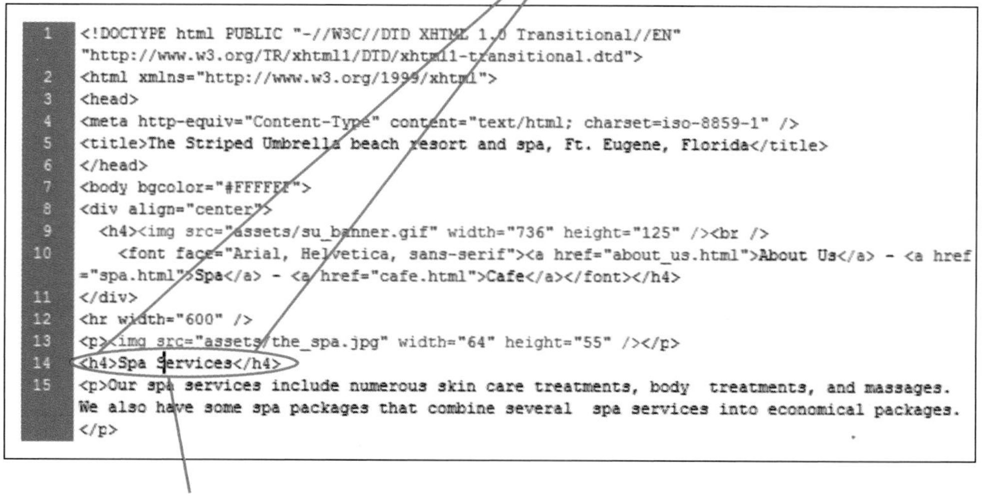

Code for <h4> tags

```
1   <!DOCTYPE html PUBLIC "-//W3C//DTD XHTML 1.0 Transitional//EN"
    "http://www.w3.org/TR/xhtml1/DTD/xhtml1-transitional.dtd">
2   <html xmlns="http://www.w3.org/1999/xhtml">
3   <head>
4   <meta http-equiv="Content-Type" content="text/html; charset=iso-8859-1" />
5   <title>The Striped Umbrella beach resort and spa, Ft. Eugene, Florida</title>
6   </head>
7   <body bgcolor="#FFFFFF">
8   <div align="center">
9     <h4><img src="assets/su_banner.gif" width="736" height="125" /><br />
10      <font face="Arial, Helvetica, sans-serif"><a href="about_us.html">About Us</a> - <a href
    ="spa.html">Spa</a> - <a href="cafe.html">Cafe</a></font></h4>
11  </div>
12  <hr width="600" />
13  <p><img src="assets/the_spa.jpg" width="64" height="55" /></p>
14  <h4>Spa Services</h4>
15  <p>Our spa services include numerous skin care treatments, body  treatments, and massages.
    We also have some spa packages that combine several  spa services into economical packages.
    </p>
```

Insertion point within the Spa Services text

FIGURE 14
Formatted Spa Services text

About Us - Spa - Cafe

Spa Services

Our spa services include numerous skin care treatments, body treatments, and massages. We also have some spa packages that combine several spa services into economical packages.

Skin Care Treatments

DESIGNTIP **Choosing fonts**

There are two classifications of fonts: sans-serif and serif. **Sans-serif fonts** are block-style characters that are often used for headings and subheadings. The headings in this book use a sans-serif font. Examples of sans-serif fonts include Arial, Verdana, and Helvetica. **Serif fonts** are more ornate and contain small extra strokes at the beginning and end of the characters. Some people consider serif fonts easier to read in printed material, because the extra strokes lead your eye from one character to the next. This paragraph you are reading uses a serif font. Examples of serif fonts include Times New Roman, Times, and Georgia. Many designers feel that a sans-serif font is preferable when the content of a Web site is primarily intended to be read on the screen, but that a serif font is preferable if the content will be printed. When you choose fonts, you need to keep in mind the amount of text each page will contain and whether most viewers will read the text on-screen or print it. A good rule of thumb is to limit each Web site to no more than three font variations. Using more than three may make your Web site look unprofessional and suggest the "ransom note effect." The phrase **ransom note effect** implies that fonts have been randomly used in a document without regard to style, similar to a ransom note made up of words cut from various sources and pasted onto a page.

---

5. With the heading still selected, click the **Text Color button** ☐ in the Property inspector to open the color picker, then click the first **dark blue color** in the third row (#000066).

   The HTML code added when the font color is designated is <font color="#000066">. The font color tag is closed with </font>.

   TIP   You can also type #000066 in the color text box in the Property inspector to select the color in Step 5.

6. Click to the left of the "O" in Our spa services, press and hold [Shift], scroll to the end of the text, click to place the insertion point after the end of the last sentence on the page, then release [Shift].

7. Click the **Font list arrow** in the Property inspector, click **Arial, Helvetica, sans-serif**, click the **Size list arrow** in the Property inspector, then click **3**.

   TIP   To change the size of selected text, use either the Format list arrow or the Size list arrow, but not both.

8. Click anywhere on the page to deselect the text, save your work, then compare your screen to Figure 14.

9. Close the spa page.

You formatted the Spa Services text using the Heading 4 style and the Arial, Helvetica, sans-serif font combination. Next, you centered the heading on the page and changed the text color to a dark blue. You then selected the rest of the text on the page and changed it to the Arial, Helvetica, sans-serif font combination with a text size of 3.

ADD LINKS TO
WEB PAGES

What You'll Do

 In this lesson, you will open the home page and add links to the navigation bar that link to the About Us, Spa, Cafe, and Activities pages. You will then insert an e-mail link at the bottom of the page and create page titles for the untitled pages in the site map.

Adding Links to Web Pages

Links provide the real power for Web pages. Links make it possible for viewers to navigate all the pages in a Web site and to connect to other pages anywhere on the Web. Viewers are more likely to return to Web sites that have a user-friendly navigation structure. Viewers also enjoy Web sites that have interesting links to other Web pages or other Web sites.

To add links to a Web page, first select the text or image that you want to serve as a link, and then specify a path to the page to which you want to link in the Link text box in the Property inspector. After you add all your links, you can open the site map to see a diagram of how the linked pages relate to each other.

When you create links on a Web page, it is important to avoid **broken links**, or links that cannot find their intended destinations. You can accidentally cause a broken link by typing the incorrect address for the link in the Link text box. Broken links are often caused by companies merging, going out of business, or simply moving their Web site addresses.

In addition to adding links to your pages, you should provide a **point of contact**, or a place on a Web page that provides viewers with a means of contacting the company. A common point of contact is a **mailto: link**, which is an e-mail address that viewers with questions or problems can use to contact someone at the company's headquarters.

Using Navigation Bars

A **navigation bar** is an area on a Web page that contains links to the main pages of a Web site. Navigation bars are usually located at the top or side of the main pages of a Web site and can be created with text, images, or a combination of the two. To make navigating a Web site as easy as possible, you should place navigation bars in the same position on each Web page. Navigation bars are the backbone of a Web site's navigation structure, which includes all navigation aids for moving around a Web site. You can, however, include additional links to the main pages of the Web site elsewhere on the page. The Web page in Figure 15 shows an example of a navigation bar that contains both text and image links that use JavaScript. Notice that when the mouse is placed on an item in the navigation bar, the image expands to include more information.

Navigation bars can also be simple and contain only text-based links to the pages in the site. You can create a simple navigation bar by typing the names of your Web site's pages at the top of your Web page, formatting the text, and then adding links to each page name. It is always a good idea to provide plain text links for accessibility, regardless of the type of navigation structure you choose to use.

FIGURE 15
The Coca-Cola Web site

Coca-Cola Web site used with permission from The Coca-Cola Company - www.coca-cola.com

Create a navigation bar

1. Open **index.html** (the home page).

2. Position the insertion point to the left of "A" in About Us, then drag to select **About Us - Spa - Cafe**.

3. Type **Home - About Us - Spa - Cafe - Activities**, as shown in Figure 16.

   These five text labels will serve as a navigation bar. You will add the links later.

You created a new navigation bar using text, replacing the original navigation bar.

Format a navigation bar

1. Select **Home - About Us - Spa - Cafe - Activities** (if necessary), click the **Size list arrow** in the Property inspector, then click **None**.

   None is equal to size 3, the default text size. The None setting eliminates any prior size formatting that was applied to the text.

   TIP If your Property inspector is not visible, click Window on the menu bar, then click Properties to open it.

2. Click the **Format list arrow** in the Property inspector, then click **Heading 4**.

3. Click the **Font list arrow** in the Property inspector, click **Arial, Helvetica, sans-serif** (if necessary), compare your screen to Figure 17, then deselect the text.

   TIP An asterisk after the filename in the title bar indicates that you have altered the page since you last saved it. After you save your work, the asterisk does not appear.

You formatted the new navigation bar, using a heading and a font combination.

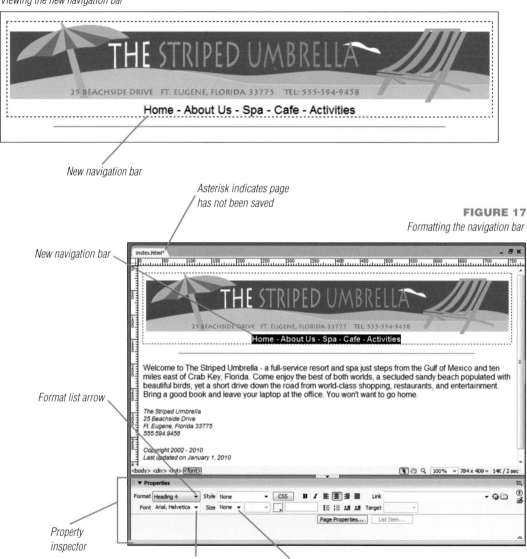

FIGURE 16
Viewing the new navigation bar

New navigation bar

Asterisk indicates page has not been saved

FIGURE 17
Formatting the navigation bar

New navigation bar

Format list arrow

Property inspector

Font list arrow

Size list arrow

FIGURE 18

Selecting the Home link

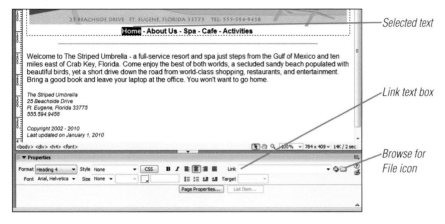

Selected text

Link text box

Browse for File icon

FIGURE 19

Select File dialog box

Striped Umbrella local root folder

index.html page

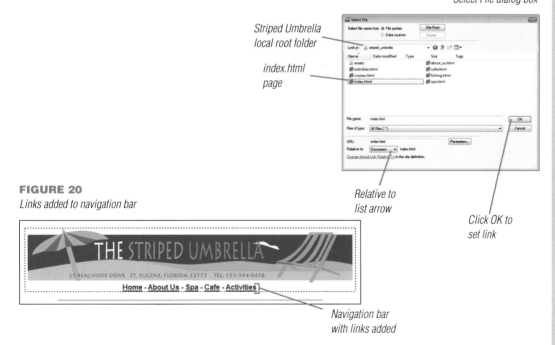

Relative to list arrow

Click OK to set link

FIGURE 20

Links added to navigation bar

Navigation bar with links added

Add links to Web pages

1. Double-click **Home** to select it, as shown in Figure 18.

2. Click the **Browse for File icon** 📁 next to the Link text box in the Property inspector, then navigate to the striped_umbrella root folder (if necessary).

3. Verify that the link is set Relative to Document in the Relative to: list.

4. Click **index.html** as shown in Figure 19, click **OK** (Win) or **Choose** (Mac), then click anywhere on the page to deselect Home.

   Home now appears in blue with an underline, indicating it is a link. However, clicking Home will not open a new page because the link is to the home page. It might seem odd to create a link to the same page on which the link appears, but this will be helpful when you copy the navigation bar to other pages in the site. Always provide viewers a link to the home page.

5. Repeat Steps 1–4 to create links for About Us, Spa, Cafe, and Activities to their corresponding pages in the striped_umbrella root folder.

6. When you finish adding the links to the other four pages, deselect all, then compare your screen to Figure 20.

You created a link for each of the five navigation bar elements to their respective Web pages in The Striped Umbrella Web site.

Create an e-mail link

1. Place the insertion point after the last digit in the telephone number, then insert a line break.

2. Click the **Common tab** on the Insert bar (if necessary), then click the **Email Link button** to insert an e-mail link.

3. Type **Club Manager** in the Text text box, type **manager@stripedumbrella.com** in the E-Mail text box, as shown in Figure 21, then click **OK** to close the Email Link dialog box.

   If you do not retain the formatting from the previous line (Size 2, Italic), use the History panel to undo Steps 1–3. Switch to Code view and place the insertion point immediately to the right of the telephone number, then repeat the steps again in Design view.

4. Save your work.

   Notice that the text "mailto:manager@striped_umbrella.com," appears in the Link text box in the Property inspector. When a viewer clicks this link, a blank e-mail message window opens in the viewer's default e-mail software, where the viewer can type a message. See Figure 22.

   TIP   You must enter the correct e-mail address in the E-Mail text box for the link to work. However, you can enter any descriptive name, such as customer service or Bob Smith in the Text text box. You can also enter the e-mail address as the text if you want to show the actual e-mail address on the Web page.

You inserted an e-mail link to serve as a point of contact for The Striped Umbrella.

FIGURE 21
Email Link dialog box

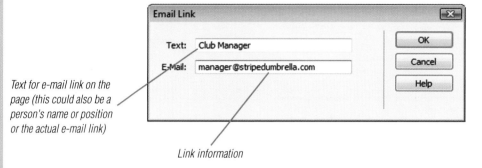

Text for e-mail link on the page (this could also be a person's name or position or the actual e-mail link)

Link information

FIGURE 22
mailto: link on the Property inspector

mailto: link

FIGURE 23

The Striped Umbrella site map

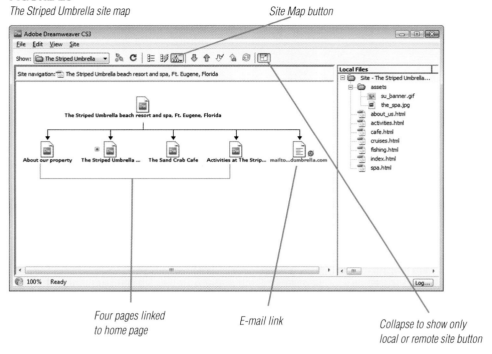

Site Map button

Four pages linked to home page

E-mail link

Collapse to show only local or remote site button

1. Click the **Expand to show local and remote sites button** 🗗 on the Files panel to expand the site map.

   The site map shows the home page, the four pages that are linked to it, and the e-mail link on the home page.

   TIP If you don't see the site map on the left window, click the Site Map button list arrow, 🗺, then click Map and Files.

2. Click **View** on the Files panel menu bar, point to **Site Map Options**, then click **Show Page Titles** (Win), or click the **Options menu**, point to **View**, point to **Site Map Options**, then click **Show Page Titles** (Mac) (if necessary).

3. Select the first Untitled Document page in the site map, select the words **Untitled Document**, type **About our property**, then press **[Enter]** (Win) or **[return]** (Mac).

   When you select a page title in the site map, the corresponding file is selected in the Local Files panel. Be careful before entering a new page title in the Site map. If the option is set to filenames rather than page titles, you will accidentally change the filename.

4. Repeat Step 3 for the other two Untitled Document pages, naming them **The Sand Crab Cafe** and **Activities at The Striped** Umbrella, respectively, as shown in Figure 23.

5. Click the **Collapse to show only local or remote site button** 🗗 on the toolbar to collapse the site map.

You viewed the site map and added page titles to the untitled pages.

USE THE HISTORY
PANEL AND EDIT CODE

What You'll Do

In this lesson, you will use the History panel to undo formatting changes you make to a horizontal rule. You will then use the Code Inspector to view the HTML code for the horizontal rule. You will also insert a date object and then view its code in the Code Inspector.

Using the History Panel

Throughout the process of creating a Web page, it's likely that you will make mistakes along the way. Fortunately, you have a tool named the History panel to undo your mistakes. The **History panel** records each editing and formatting task performed and displays them in a list in the order in which they were completed. Each task listed in the History panel is called a **step**. You can drag the **slider** on the left side of the History panel to undo or redo steps, as shown in Figure 24. You can also click in the bar to the left of a step to undo all steps below it. You click the step to select it. By default, the History panel records 50 steps. You can change the number of steps the History panel records in the General category of the Preferences dialog box. However, keep in mind that setting this number too high might require additional memory and could affect Dreamweaver's performance.

Understanding other History panel features

Dragging the slider up and down in the History panel is a quick way to undo or redo steps. However, the History panel offers much more. It has the capability to "memorize" certain tasks and consolidate them into one command. This is a useful feature for steps that are executed repetitively on Web pages. Some Dreamweaver features, such as drag and drop, cannot be recorded in the History panel and are noted by a red "x" placed next to them. The History panel does not show steps performed in the Files panel.

Viewing HTML Code in the Code Inspector

If you enjoy writing code, you occasionally might want to make changes to Web pages by entering the code rather than using the panels and tools in Design view. You can view the code in Dreamweaver using Code view, Code and Design views, or the Code Inspector. The **Code Inspector**, shown in Figure 25, is a separate window that displays the current page in Code view. The advantage of using the Code Inspector is that you can see a full-screen view of your page in Design view while viewing the underlying code in a floating window that you can resize and position wherever you want.

You can add advanced features, such as JavaScript functions, to Web pages by copying and pasting code from one page to another in the Code Inspector. A **JavaScript** function is a block of code that adds dynamic content such as rollovers or interactive forms to a Web page. A **rollover** is a special effect that changes the appearance of an object when the mouse moves over it.

QUICK TIP

If you are new to HTML, you can use the Reference panel to find answers to your HTML questions. The Reference panel is part of the Code panel group and contains many resources besides HTML help, such as JavaScript help.

FIGURE 24
The History panel

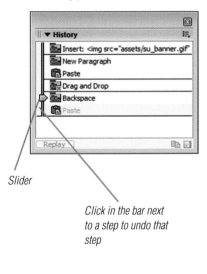

Slider

Click in the bar next to a step to undo that step

FIGURE 25
Code Inspector

Code displayed in the Code Inspector

View Options menu

Page displayed in Design view behind the Code Inspector

Use the History panel

1. Click **Window** on the menu bar, then click **History**, **if necessary**.

   The History panel opens and displays steps you have recently performed.

2. Click the **History panel options menu**, click **Clear History**, as shown in Figure 26, then click **Yes** to close the warning box (if necessary).

3. Select the **horizontal rule** on the home page.

   A **horizontal rule** is a line used to separate page elements or to organize information on a page.

4. Select the number in the W text box in the Property inspector, type **90**, click the **list arrow** next to the W text box, click **%**, then compare your Property inspector to Figure 27.

5. Using the Property inspector, change the width of the horizontal rule to 80%, click the **Align list arrow**, then click **Left**.

6. Drag the **slider** on the History panel up to Set Width: 90%, as shown in Figure 28.

   The bottom two steps in the History panel appear gray, indicating that these steps have been undone.

7. Click the **History panel options menu,** then click **Close panel group** to close the History panel.

You formatted the horizontal rule, made changes to it, then used the History panel to undo some of the changes.

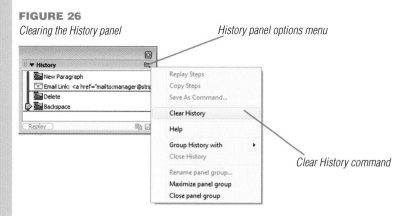

FIGURE 26
Clearing the History panel

History panel options menu

Clear History command

FIGURE 27
Property inspector settings for horizontal rule

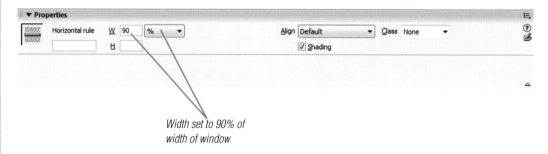

Width set to 90% of width of window

FIGURE 28
Undoing steps using the History panel

Set Width: 90%

Slider

Steps that have been undone

FIGURE 29

Viewing the View Options menu in the Code Inspector

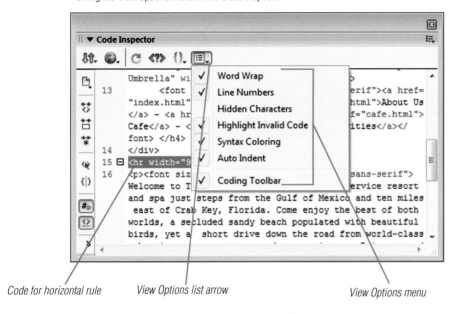

Code for horizontal rule   View Options list arrow   View Options menu

---

POWER USER SHORTCUTS

to do this:	use this shortcut:
Select All	[Ctrl][A] (Win) or ⌘ [A] (Mac)
Copy	[Ctrl][C] (Win) or ⌘ [C] (Mac)
Cut	[Ctrl][X] (Win) or ⌘ [X] (Mac)
Paste	[Ctrl][V] (Win) or ⌘ [V] (Mac)
Line Break	[Shift][Enter] (Win) or [Shift][return] (Mac)
Show or hide the Code Inspector	[F10] (Win) or [option][F10] (Mac)
Preview in browser	[F12] (Win) or [option][F12] (Mac)

Use the Code Inspector

1. Click the **horizontal rule** to select it (if necessary), click **Window** on the menu bar, then click **Code Inspector**.

   The Code Inspector highlights the code for the horizontal rule.

   | TIP   You can also press [F10](Win) or [option][F10] (Mac) to display the Code Inspector.

2. Click the **View Options list arrow** on the Code Inspector toolbar to display the View Options menu, then click **Word Wrap** (if necessary), to activate Word Wrap.

   The Word Wrap feature forces text to stay within the confines of the Code Inspector window, allowing you to read without scrolling sideways.

3. Click the **View Options list arrow**, then verify that the Word Wrap, Line Numbers, Highlight Invalid Code, Syntax Coloring, Auto Indent, and the Coding Toolbar menu items are checked, as shown in Figure 29.

4. Select **90%** in the horizontal rule width code, then type **80%**.

5. Click **Refresh** in the Property inspector.

   After typing in the Code Inspector, you must refresh your changes to see them.

You changed the width of the horizontal rule by changing the code in the Code Inspector.

Use the Reference panel

1. Click the **Reference button** 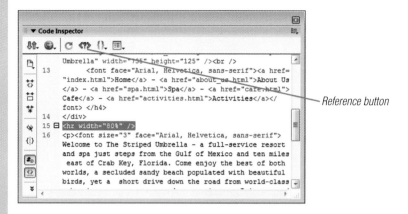 on the Code Inspector toolbar, as shown in Figure 30, to open the Results panel group with the Reference panel visible.

   TIP Verify that the horizontal rule is still selected, or you will not see the horizontal rule description in the Reference panel.

2. Read the information about horizontal rules in the Reference panel, as shown in Figure 31, right-click the **Results panel group title bar,** then click **Close panel group** (Win) or click the **Results panel option list** in the Results panel title bar, then click **Close panel group** (Mac) to close the Results panel group.

3. Close the Code Inspector.

You read information about horizontal rule settings in the Reference panel.

FIGURE 30
Reference button on the Code Inspector toolbar

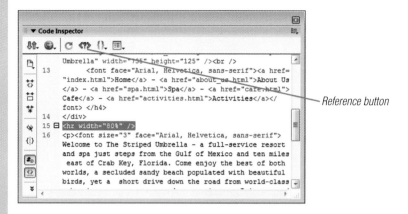

Reference button

FIGURE 31
Viewing the Reference panel

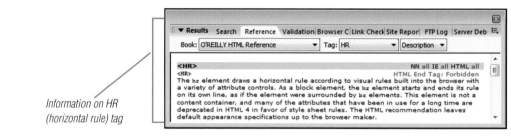

Information on HR (horizontal rule) tag

Inserting comments

A handy Dreamweaver feature is the ability to insert comments into HTML code. Comments can provide helpful information describing portions of the code, such as a JavaScript function. You can create comments in any Dreamweaver view, but you must turn on Invisible Elements to see them in Design view. Use the Edit, Preferences, Invisible Elements, Comments option to enable viewing of comments; then use the View, Visual Aids, Invisible Elements menu option to display them on the page. To create a comment, click the Common tab on the Insert bar, click the Comment button, type a comment in the Comment dialog box, and then click OK. Comments are not visible in browser windows.

FIGURE 32
Insert Date dialog box

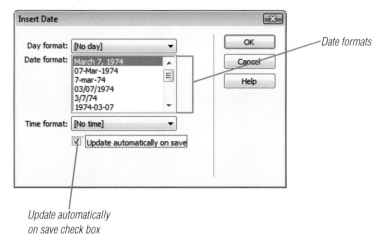

Date formats

Update automatically
on save check box

FIGURE 33
Viewing the date object in Code view

```
18    25 Beachside Drive<br />
19    Ft. Eugene, Florida 33775<br />
20    555.594.9458<br />
21    <a href="mailto:manager@stripedumbrella.com">Club Manager</a></em></font></p>
22  <p><font size="2" face="Arial, Helvetica, sans-serif"><em>Copyright 2002 - 2010 <br />
23    Last updated on
24         <!-- #BeginDate format:Am1 -->February 22, 2007<!-- #EndDate -->
25  </em></font></p>
26  </body>
27  </html>
28
```

Code for date object

Insert a date object

1. Scroll down the page (if necessary), to select **January 1, 2010**, then press **[Delete]** (Win) or **[delete]** (Mac).

2. Click the **Date button** 🗓 on the Insert bar, then click **March 7, 1974** in the Date format text box.

3. Click the **Update automatically on save checkbox**, as shown in Figure 32, click **OK**, then deselect the text.

4. Click the **Show Code and Design views button** ⬒ Split .

    Notice that the code has changed to reflect the date object, which is set to today's date, as shown in Figure 33. (Your date will be different.) The new code is highlighted with a light yellow background, indicating that it is a date object, automatically coded by Dreamweaver, rather than a date that has been manually typed on the page by the designer.

5. Return to Design view.

You inserted a date object that will be updated automatically when you open and save the home page.

MODIFY AND TEST
WEB PAGES

What You'll Do

In this lesson, you will preview the home page in the browser to check for typographical errors, grammatical errors, broken links, and overall appearance. After previewing, you will make slight formatting adjustments to the page to improve its appearance.

Testing and Modifying Web Pages

Testing Web pages is a continuous process. You never really finish a Web site, because there are always additions and corrections to make. As you add and modify pages, you must test each page as part of the development process. The best way to test a Web page is to preview it in a browser window to make sure that all text and image elements appear the way you expect them to. You should also test your links to make sure they work properly. You also need to proofread your text to make sure it contains all the necessary information for the page with no typographical or grammatical errors. Designers typically view a page in a browser, return to Design view to make necessary changes, and then view the page in a browser again. This process may be repeated many times before the page is ready for publishing. In fact, it is sometimes difficult to stop making improvements to a page and move on to another project. You need to strike a balance among quality, creativity, and productivity.

DESIGNTIP **Using "Under Construction" pages**

Many people are tempted to insert an unfinished page as a placeholder for a page that will be finished later. Rather than have real content, these pages usually contain text or an image that indicates the page is not finished, or "under construction." You should not publish a Web page that has a link to an unfinished page. It is frustrating to click a link for a page you want to open only to find an "under construction" note or image displayed. You want to make the best possible impression on your viewing audience. If you cannot complete a page before publishing it, at least provide enough information on it to make it "worth the trip."

Testing a Web Page Using Different Browsers and Screen Sizes

Because users access the Internet using a wide variety of computer systems, it is important to design your pages so that all browsers and screen sizes can display them well. You should test your pages using different browsers and a wide variety of screen sizes to ensure the best view of your page by the most people possible. Although the most common screen size that designers use today is 1024 × 768, many viewers restore down individual program windows to a size comparable to 800 × 600 to be able to have more windows open simultaneously on their screen. In other words, people use their "screen real estate" according to their personal work style. To view your page using different screen sizes, click the Window Size pop-up menu in the status bar (Win) or at the bottom of the document window (Mac), then choose the setting you want to use. Table 1 lists the Dreamweaver default window screen sizes. Remember also to check your pages using Windows and Macintosh platforms. Some page elements such as fonts, colors, table borders, layers, and horizontal rules may not appear consistently in both.

Testing a Web Page As Rendered in a Mobile Device

There is another preview feature with Dreamweaver that allows you to see what a page would look like if it were viewed on a mobile hand-held device, such as a Blackberry. To use this feature, click the Preview/Debug in Browser button on the Document toolbar, then click Preview in Device Central.

TABLE 1: Dreamweaver Default Window Screen Sizes

window size (inside dimensions of the browser window without borders)	monitor size
592W	
536 × 196	640 × 480, default
600 × 300	640 × 480, maximized
760 × 420	800 × 600, maximized
795 × 470	832 × 624, maximized
955 × 600	1024 × 768, maximized
544 × 378	Web TV

Modify a Web page

1. Click the **Restore Down button** on the index.html title bar to decrease the size of the home page window (Win) or skip to Step 2 (Mac).

   TIP You cannot use the Window Size options if your Document window is maximized (Win).

2. Click the **Window Size list arrow** on the status bar, as shown in Figure 34, then click **600 × 300 (640 × 480, Maximized)**, (if necessary).

   A viewer using this setting will be forced to use the horizontal scroll bar to view the entire page.

3. Click the **Window Size list arrow**, then click **760 × 420 (800 × 600, Maximized)**.

4. Replace the period after the last sentence, "You won't want to go home." with an exclamation point.

5. Shorten the horizontal rule to 75%.

6. Click the **Maximize button** on the index.html title bar to maximize the home page window.

7. Save your work.

You viewed the home page using two different window sizes and you made simple formatting changes to the page.

FIGURE 34
Window screen sizes

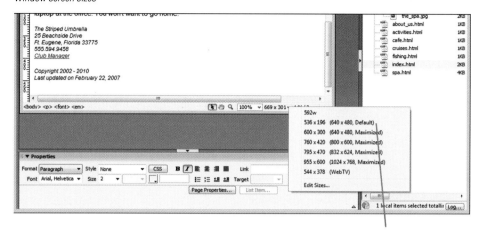

Size choices for viewing the page

Using smart design principles in Web page layout

As you view your pages in the browser, take a critical look at the symmetry of the page. Is it balanced? Are there too many images compared to text, or vice versa? Does everything "heavy" seem to be on the top or bottom of the page, or do the page elements seem to balance with the weight evenly distributed between the top, bottom, and sides? Use design principles to create a site-wide consistency for your pages. Horizontal symmetry means that the elements are balanced across the page. Vertical symmetry means that they are balanced down the page. Diagonal symmetry balances page elements along the invisible diagonal line of the page. Radial symmetry runs from the center of the page outward, like the petals of a flower. These principles all deal with balance; however, too much balance is not good, either. Sometimes it adds interest to place page elements a little off center or to have an asymmetric layout. Color, white space, text, and images should all complement each other and provide a natural flow across and down the page. The rule of thirds—dividing a page into nine squares like a tic-tac-toe grid—states that interest is increased when your focus is on one of the intersections in the grid. The most important information should be at the top of the page where it is visible without scrolling, or "above the fold," as they say in the newspaper business.

FIGURE 35

Viewing The Striped Umbrella home page in the Firefox browser

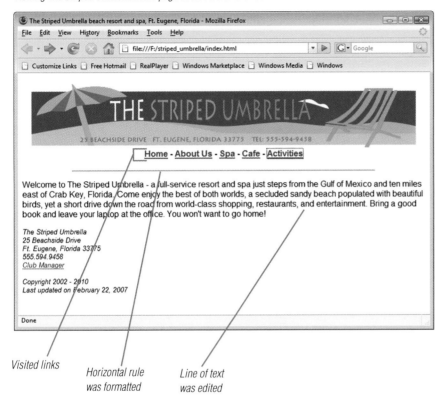

Visited links

Horizontal rule was formatted

Line of text was edited

1. Click the **Preview/Debug in browser button** 🌐, on the Document toolbar, then choose your browser from the menu that opens.

   The Striped Umbrella home page opens in your default browser.

   > TIP If previewing the page in Internet Explorer 7, click the Information bar when prompted to allow blocked content.

2. Click each link on the navigation bar, then after each click, use the Back button on the browser toolbar to return to the home page.

   Pages with no content at this point will appear as blank pages. Compare your screen to Figure 35.

3. Close your browser window, then close all open pages.

You viewed The Striped Umbrella home page in your browser and tested each link on the navigation bar.

DESIGNTIP **Choosing a window size**

Today, the majority of viewers are using a screen resolution of 1024×768 or higher. Because of this, more content can be displayed at one time on a computer monitor. Some people may use their whole screen to view pages on the Internet. Others may choose to allocate a smaller area of their screen to the browser window. In other words, people tend to use their "screen real estate" in different ways. The ideal Web page will not be so small that it tries to spread out over a larger screen size or so large that the viewer has to use horizontal scroll bars to read the page content. Achieving the best balance is one of the design decisions that must be made during the planning process.

Create head content and set Web page properties.

1. Open the blooms & bulbs Web site.
2. Open the index page and view the head content.
3. Change the page title to **blooms & bulbs - Your Complete Garden Center**.
4. Insert the following keywords: **garden**, **plants**, **nursery**, **flowers**, **landscape**, **blooms & bulbs**.
5. Insert the following description: **blooms & bulbs is a premier supplier of garden plants for both professional and home gardeners.**
6. Switch to Code view to view the HTML code for the head content, then switch back to Design view.
7. Open the Page Properties dialog box to view the current page properties.
8. Change the background color to a color of your choice.
9. Change the background color to white again, then save your work.

Create, import, and format text.

1. Select the current navigation bar and replace it with **Home**, **Featured Plants**, **Garden Tips**, and **Classes**. Use the [Spacebar] and a hyphen to separate the items.
2. Using the Property inspector, apply the Heading 4 format to the navigation bar.

3. Create a new paragraph after the paragraph of text and type the following text, inserting a line break after each line.
   blooms & bulbs
   Highway 43 South
   Alvin, Texas 77511
   555.248.0806
4. Italicize the address and phone number lines and change the font to Arial, Helvetica, sans-serif and the size to 2.
5. Change the copyright and last updated statements to size 2.
6. Save your work, then close the home page.
7. Open dw2_2.html and save it as **tips.html** in the blooms & bulbs Web site, overwriting the existing file, but not updating links.
8. Click the broken image link below the blooms & bulbs banner, browse to the chapter_2 Data Files folder, select the garden_tips.jpg in the assets folder, then click OK to save a copy of it in the blooms & bulbs Web site.
9. Place the insertion point under the Garden Tips graphic.
10. Import gardening_tips.doc from where you store your Data Files, using the Import Word Document command, then use the Clean Up Word HTML command. (*Hint*: The Use CSS instead of HTML tags option should be turned off before executing the following steps.)
11. Format all of the text on the page using the following attributes: Font: Arial, Helvetica, sans-serif, Alignment: Align Left, and Style: None.

12. Select the Seasonal Gardening Checklist heading, then use the Property inspector to center the text.
13. Use the Property inspector to format the selected text with a Heading 3 format.
14. Apply the color #003366 (the dark blue color in the third row) to the text.
15. Select the rest of the text on the page except for the Seasonal Gardening Checklist heading, then set the size to 3.
16. Select the Basic Gardening Tips heading, then format this text in bold, with the color #003366.
17. Save your work and close the tips page.

Add links to Web pages.

1. Open the index page, then use the Property inspector to link Home on the navigation bar to the index.html page in the blooms & bulbs Web site.
2. Link Featured Plants on the navigation bar to the plants.html page.
3. Link Garden Tips on the navigation bar to the tips.html page.
4. Link Classes on the navigation bar to the classes.html page.
5. Using the Insert bar, create an e-mail link under the telephone number.
6. Type **Customer Service** in the Text text box and **mailbox@blooms.com** in the E-Mail text box.
7. Open the plants.html page, add a page title called **Our Featured Plants**, then save the page.
8. Open the classes.html page and add the page title **Classes Offered**, then save your work.

Use the History panel and edit code.

1. Open the History panel, then clear its contents.
2. Delete the current date in the Last updated on statement on the home page and replace it with a date that will update automatically when the file is saved.
3. Change the font for the last updated on statement using the font of your choice.
4. Use the History panel to go back to the original font and style settings for the last updated on statement.
5. Close the History panel.

6. Examine the code for the last updated on statement.
7. Save your work.

Modify and test Web pages.

1. Using the Window Size pop-up menu, view the home page at 600 × 300 (640 × 480, Maximized) and 760 × 420 (800 × 600, Maximized), then maximize the Document window.
2. View the page in your browser. (*Hint:* If previewing the page in Internet Explorer 7, click the Information bar when prompted to allow blocked content.)

3. Verify that all links work correctly, then close the browser.
4. On the home page, change the text "Stop by and see us soon!" to **We ship overnight**.
5. Save your work, then view the pages in your browser, comparing your screens to Figure 36 and Figure 37.
6. Close your browser.
7. Adjust the spacing (if necessary), save your work, then preview the home page in the browser again.
8. Close the browser, then save and close all open pages.

FIGURE 36
Completed Skills Review, home page

Home - Featured Plants - Garden Tips - Classes

Welcome to blooms & bulbs. We carry a variety of plants and shrubs along with a large inventory of gardening supplies. Our four greenhouses are full of healthy young plants just waiting to be planted in your yard. Our staff includes a certified landscape architect, three landscape designers, and six master gardeners. We offer detailed landscape plans tailored to your location as well as planting and regular maintenance services. We ship overnight.

blooms & bulbs
Highway 43 South
Alvin, Texas 77511
555.248.0806
Customer Service

Copyright 2001 - 2010
Last updated on March 10, 2007

FIGURE 37
Completed Skills Review, tips page

We have some planting tips we would like to share with you as you prepare your gardens this season. Remember, there is always something to be done for your gardens, no matter what the season. Our experienced staff is here to help you plan your gardens, select your plants, prepare your soil, assist you in the planting, and maintain your beds. Check out our calendar for a list of our scheduled classes. All classes are free of charge and on a first-come, first-served basis!

Seasonal Gardening Checklist:

Fall – The time to plant trees and spring blooming bulbs.
Winter – The time to prune fruit trees and finish planting your bulbs.
Spring – The time to prepare your beds, plant annuals, and apply fertilizer to established plants.
Summer – The time to supplement rainfall so that plants get one inch of water per week.

Developing a Web Page

You have been hired to create a Web site for a TripSmart, a travel outfitter. You have created the basic framework for the Web site and are now ready to format and edit the home page to improve the content and appearance.

1. Open the TripSmart Web site, then open the home page.
2. Enter the following keywords: **travel**, **traveling**, **trips**, and **vacations**.
3. Enter the following description: **TripSmart is a comprehensive travel store. We can help you plan trips**, **make travel arrangements**, **and supply you with travel gear**.
4. Change the page title to **TripSmart - Serving All Your Travel Needs**.

5. Select the existing navigation bar and replace it with the following text links: **Home**, **Catalog**, **Services**, **Destinations**, and **Newsletter**. Type hyphens between each text link.
6. Replace the date in the last updated statement with a date that will update automatically on save.
7. Type the following address two lines below the paragraph about the company, using line breaks after each line:
   TripSmart
   1106 Beechwood
   Fayetteville, AR 72704
   555.848.0807

8. Insert an e-mail link in the line below the telephone number, using **Customer Service** for the Text text box and **mailbox@tripsmart.com** for the E-mail text box in the Email Link dialog box.
9. Italicize TripSmart, the address, phone number, and e-mail link and format it to size 2, Arial, Helvetica, sans-serif.
10. Link the navigation bar entries to index.html, catalog.html, services.html, destinations.html, and newsletter.html.
11. View the HTML code for the page.
12. View the page using two different window sizes, then test the links in your browser window.
13. View the site map.

14. Create the following page titles:
catalog.html = **TripSmart Catalog**
services.html = **TripSmart Services**
destinations.html = **TripSmart Featured
Destinations**
newsletter.html = **TripSmart Newsletter**

15. Verify that all the page titles are entered
correctly, then collapse the site map.

16. Preview the home page in your browser,
then test all the links. (*Hint:* If previewing
the page in Internet Explorer 7, click the
Information bar when prompted to allow
blocked content.).

17. Compare your page to Figure 38, close the
browser, then save and close all open pages.

FIGURE 38
Completed Project Builder 1

Home - Catalog - Services - Destinations - Newsletter

Welcome to TripSmart - the smart choice for the savvy traveler. We're here to help you with all your travel needs.
Choose customized trips to any location or our Five-Star Tours, recently rated number one in the country by
Traveler magazine. With over 30 years of experience, we can bring you the best the world has to offer.

TripSmart
1106 Beechwood
Fayetteville, AR 72704
555.848.0807
Customer Service

Copyright 2002 - 2010
Last updated on March 10, 2007

Developing a Web Page

Your company has been selected to design a Web site for a catering business named Carolyne's Creations. You are now ready to add content to the home page and apply formatting options to improve the page appearance, using Figure 39 as a guide.

1. Open the Carolyne's Creations Web site, then open the home page.
2. Place the insertion point in front of the sentence beginning "Give us a call" and type **Feel like a guest at your own party**.

3. Center the navigation bar.
4. Change the navigation bar to the Heading 4 format.
5. Add the following address below the paragraph using line breaks after each line:
   Carolyne's Creations
   496 Maple Street
   Seven Falls, Virginia 52404
   555.963.8271
6. Enter another line break after the telephone number and type **E-mail**, then add an e-mail link using Carolyne Kate for the text and carolyne@carolynescreations.com for the e-mail address.

7. Apply the Verdana, Arial, Helvetica, sans-serif font to the contact information, then apply any other formatting of your choice.
8. Create links from each navigation bar element to its corresponding Web page.
9. Replace the date that follows the text "Last updated on" with a date object, then save your work.

10. View the completed page in your default browser, then test each link. (*Hint*: If previewing the page in Internet Explorer 7, click the Information bar when prompted to allow blocked content.)

11. Close your browser.

12. View the site map, then title any untitled pages with appropriate titles.

13. Save your work, then close all pages.

FIGURE 39
Completed Project Builder 2

Angela Lou is a freelance photographer. She is searching the Internet looking for a particular type of paper to use in printing her digital images. She knows that Web sites use keywords and descriptions in order to receive "hits" with search engines. She is curious about how they work. Follow the steps below and write your answers to the questions.

1. Connect to the Internet, then go to *www.snapfish.com* to see the Snapfish Web site's home page, as shown in Figure 40.
2. View the page source by clicking View on the menu bar, then clicking Source (Internet Explorer) or Page Source (Netscape Navigator or Mozilla Firefox).
3. Can you locate a description and keywords? If so, what are they?
4. How many keywords do you find?
5. Is the description appropriate for the Web site? Why or why not?
6. Look at the numbers of keywords and words in the description. Is there an appropriate number? Or are there too many or not enough?

7. Use a search engine such as Google at *www.google.com*, then type the words **photo quality paper** in the Search text box.

8. Click the first link in the list of results and view the source code for that page. Do you see keywords and a description? Do any of them match the words you used in the search?

FIGURE 40
Design Project

Snapfish Web site used with permission from Snapfish - www.snapfish.com

In this assignment, you will continue to work on the Web site you defined in Chapter 1. In Chapter 1, you created a storyboard for your Web site with at least four pages. You also created a local root folder for your Web site and an assets folder to store the Web site asset files. You set the assets folder as the default storage location for your images. You began to collect information and resources for your Web site and started working on the home page.

1. Think about the head content for the home page. Add the title, keywords, and a description.

2. Create the main page content for the home page and format it attractively.

3. Add the address and other contact information to the home page, including an e-mail address.

4. Consult your storyboard and design the navigation bar.

5. Link the navigation bar items to the appropriate pages.

6. Add a last updated on statement to the home page with a date that will automatically update when the page is saved.

7. Edit and format the page content until you are satisfied with the results.

8. Verify that each page has a page title by viewing the site map.

9. Verify that all links, including the e-mail link, work correctly.

10. When you are satisfied with the home page, review the checklist questions shown in Figure 41, then make any necessary changes.

11. Save your work.

FIGURE 41
Portfolio Project checklist

Web Site Checklist

1. Do all pages have a page title?
2. Does the home page have a description and keywords?
3. Does the home page contain contact information, including an e-mail address?
4. Do all completed pages in the Web site have consistent navigation links?
5. Does the home page have a "last updated on" statement that will automatically update when the page is saved?
6. Do all pages have attractively formatted text?
7. Do all paths for links and images work correctly?
8. Does the home page view well using at least two different screen resolutions?

3

WORKING WITH TEXT
AND IMAGES

1. Create unordered and ordered lists

2. Create, apply, and edit Cascading Style Sheets

3. Add styles and attach Cascading Style Sheets

4. Insert and align images

5. Enhance an image and use alternate text

6. Insert a background image and perform site maintenance

3 WORKING WITH TEXT
AND IMAGES

Introduction

Most Web pages contain a combination of text and images. Dreamweaver provides many tools for working with text and images that you can use to make your Web pages attractive and easy to read. Dreamweaver also has tools that help you format text quickly and ensure a consistent appearance of text elements across all your Web pages.

Formatting Text as Lists

If a Web page contains a large amount of text, it can be difficult for viewers to digest it all. You can break up the monotony of large blocks of text by breaking them up into smaller paragraphs or organizing them as lists. You can create three types of lists in Dreamweaver: unordered lists, ordered lists, and definition lists.

Using Cascading Style Sheets

You can save time and ensure that all your page elements have a consistent appearance by using **Cascading Style Sheets (CSS)**. CSS are sets of formatting instructions, usually stored in a separate file, that control the appearance of content on a Web page or throughout a Web site. You can use CSS to define consistent formatting attributes for page elements such as text and tables throughout your Web site. You can then apply the formatting attributes you define to any element in a single document or to all of the pages in a Web site.

Using Images to Enhance Web Pages

Images make Web pages visually stimulating and more exciting than pages that contain only text. However, you should use images sparingly. If you think of text as the meat and potatoes of a Web site, the images would be the seasoning. You should add images to a page just as you would add seasoning to food. A little seasoning enhances the flavor and brings out the quality of the dish. Too much seasoning overwhelms the dish and masks the flavor of the main ingredients. Too little seasoning results in a bland dish. There are many ways to work with images so that they complement the content of pages in a Web site. There are specific file formats used to save images for Web sites to ensure maximum quality with minimum file size. You should store images in a separate folder in an organized fashion.

Tools You'll Use

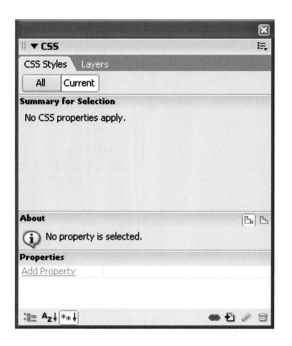

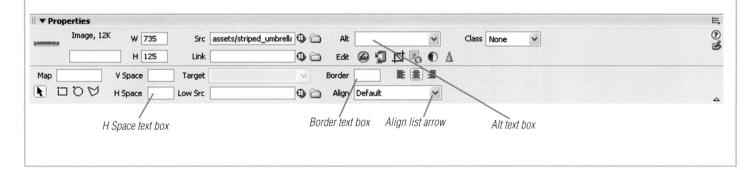

H Space text box   Border text box   Align list arrow   Alt text box

CREATE UNORDERED AND
ORDERED LISTS

What You'll Do

Spa Packages

- Spa Sampler
  Mix and match any three of our services.
- Girl's Day Out
  One hour massage, a facial, a manicure, and a pedicure.

Call the Spa desk for prices and reservations. Our desk is open from 7:00 a.m. until 5:00 p.m.

Questions you may have

1. How do I schedule Spa services?
   Please make appointments by calling The Club desk at least 24 hours in advance. Please arrive 15
   minutes before your appointment to allow enough time to shower or use the sauna.
2. Will I be charged if I cancel my appointment?
   Please cancel 24 hours before your service to avoid a cancellation charge. No-shows and cancellations
   without adequate notice will be charged for the full service.
3. Are there any health safeguards I should know about?
   Please advise us of medical conditions or allergies you have. Heat treatments like hydrotherapy and
   body wraps should be avoided if you are pregnant, have high blood pressure, or any type of heart
   condition or diabetes.
4. What about tipping?
   Gratuities are at your sole discretion, but are certainly appreciated.

In this lesson, you will create an unordered list of spa services on the spa page. You will also import text with questions and format them as an ordered list.

Creating Unordered Lists

Unordered lists are lists of items that do not need to be placed in a specific order. A grocery list that lists items in a random order is a good example of an unordered list. Items in unordered lists are usually preceded by a **bullet**, or a small raised dot or similar icon. Unordered lists that contain bullets are sometimes called **bulleted lists**. Although you can use paragraph indentations to create an unordered list, bullets can often make lists easier to read. To create an unordered list, first select the text you want to format as an unordered list, then use the Unordered List button in the Property inspector to insert bullets at the beginning of each paragraph of the selected text.

Formatting Unordered Lists

In Dreamweaver, the default bullet style is a round dot. To change the bullet style to a square, expand the Property inspector to its full size, as shown in Figure 1, click List Item in the Property inspector to open the List Properties dialog box, and then set the style for bulleted lists to Square. Be aware, however, that not all browsers display square bullets correctly, in which case the bullets will appear differently.

Creating Ordered Lists

Ordered lists, which are sometimes called **numbered lists**, are lists of items that are presented in a specific order and that are preceded by numbers or letters in sequence. An ordered list is appropriate for a list in which each item must be executed according to its specified order. A list that provides numbered directions for driving from Point A to Point B or a list that provides instructions for assembling a bicycle are both examples of ordered lists.

Formatting Ordered Lists

You can format an ordered list to show different styles of numbers or letters by using the List Properties dialog box, as shown in Figure 2. You can apply numbers, Roman numerals, lowercase letters, or uppercase letters to an ordered list.

Creating Definition Lists

Definition lists are similar to unordered lists but do not have bullets. They are often used with terms and definitions, such as in a dictionary or glossary. To create a definition list, select the text to use for the list, click Text on the menu bar, point to List, and then click Definition List.

FIGURE 1
Expanded Property inspector

Property inspector expanded to its full size

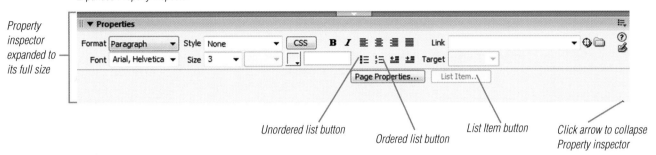

Unordered list button

Ordered list button

List Item button

Click arrow to collapse Property inspector

List type list arrow

FIGURE 2
Choosing a numbered list style in the List Properties dialog box

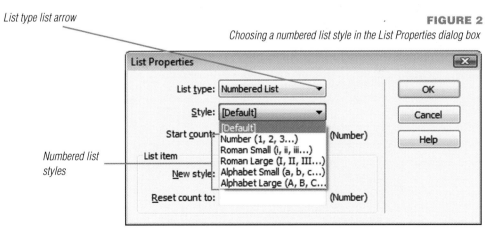

Numbered list styles

Create an unordered list

1. Open the spa page in The Striped Umbrella Web site.

2. Select the three items under the Skin Care Treatments heading.

3. Click the **Unordered List button** 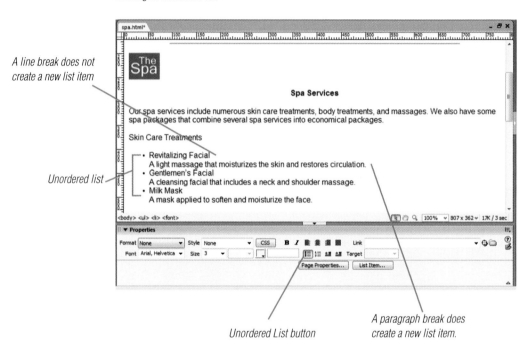 in the Property inspector to format the selected text as an unordered list, click anywhere to deselect the text, then compare your screen to Figure 3.

   Each spa service item and its description is separated by a line break. That is why each description is indented under its corresponding item, rather than formatted as a new list item. You must enter a paragraph break to create a new list item.

4. Repeat Step 3 to create unordered lists of the items under the Body Treatments, Massages, and Spa Packages headings, being careful not to include the contact information in the last sentence on the page as part of your last list.

   TIP Pressing [Enter] (Win) or [return] (Mac) once at the end of an unordered list creates another bulleted item. To end an unordered list, press [Enter] (Win) or [return] (Mac) twice.

You opened the spa page in Design view and formatted four spa services lists as unordered lists.

FIGURE 3

Creating an unordered list

A line break does not create a new list item

Unordered list

Unordered List button

A paragraph break does create a new list item.

Spa Services

Our spa services include numerous skin care treatments, body treatments, and massages. We also have some spa packages that combine several spa services into economical packages.

Skin Care Treatments

- Revitalizing Facial
  A light massage that moisturizes the skin and restores circulation.
- Gentlemen's Facial
  A cleansing facial that includes a neck and shoulder massage.
- Milk Mask
  A mask applied to soften and moisturize the face.

FIGURE 4
List Properties dialog box

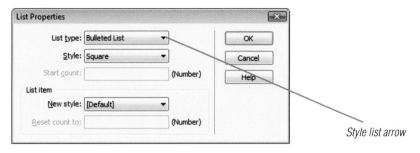

Style list arrow

FIGURE 5
HTML tags in Code view for unordered list

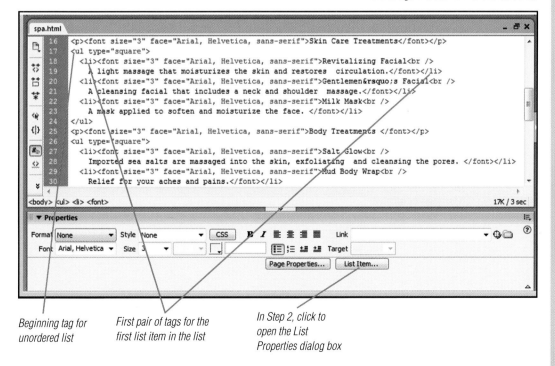

Beginning tag for unordered list

First pair of tags for the first list item in the list

In Step 2, click to open the List Properties dialog box

Format an unordered list

1. Click any of the items in the first unordered list to place the insertion point in the list.

2. Expand the Property inspector (if necessary), click **List Item** in the Property inspector to open the List Properties dialog box, click the **Style list arrow**, click **Square**, as shown in Figure 4, then click **OK**.

   The bullets in the unordered list now have a square shape.

3. Repeat Step 2 to format the next three unordered lists.

4. Position the insertion point to the left of the first item in the first unordered list, then click the **Show Code view button** <> Code toolbar to view the code for the unordered list, as shown in Figure 5.

   Notice that there is a pair of HTML codes, or tags, surrounding each type of element on the page. The first tag in each pair begins the code for a particular element, and the last tag ends the code for the element. For instance, the tags <ul></ul> surround the unordered list. The tags <li> and </li> surround each item in the list.

5. Click the **Show Design view button** Design on the toolbar.

You used the List Properties dialog box to apply the Square bullet style to the unordered lists. You then viewed the HTML code for the unordered lists in Code view.

Create an ordered list

1. Place the insertion point at the end of the page, after the word "5:00 p.m."

2. Use the Import Word Document command to import questions.doc from where you store your Data Files (Win) or open questions.doc from where you store your Data Files, select all, copy, then paste the copied text on the page (Mac).

   The inserted text appears on the same line as the existing text.

   > TIP Remember to remove the check mark in the Use CSS instead of HTML tags check box in the General section of the Preferences dialog box before importing Word text.

3. Place the insertion point to the left of the text "Questions you may have," click **Insert** on the menu bar, point to **HTML**, then click **Horizontal Rule**.

   A horizontal rule appears and helps to separate the unordered list from the text you just imported.

4. Select the text beginning with "How do I schedule" and ending with the last sentence on the page.

5. Click the **Ordered List button** in the Property inspector to format the selected text as an ordered list.

6. Deselect the text, then compare your screen to Figure 6.

You imported text on the spa page. You also added a horizontal rule to help organize the page. Finally, you formatted selected text as an ordered list.

FIGURE 6
Creating an ordered list

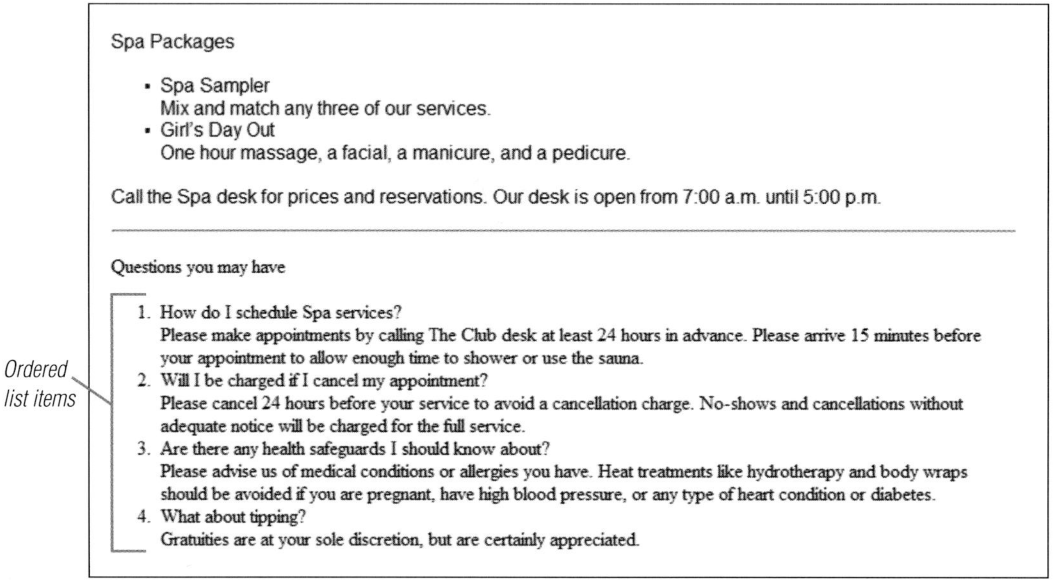

Spa Packages

- Spa Sampler
  Mix and match any three of our services.
- Girl's Day Out
  One hour massage, a facial, a manicure, and a pedicure.

Call the Spa desk for prices and reservations. Our desk is open from 7:00 a.m. until 5:00 p.m.

Questions you may have

1. How do I schedule Spa services?
   Please make appointments by calling The Club desk at least 24 hours in advance. Please arrive 15 minutes before your appointment to allow enough time to shower or use the sauna.
2. Will I be charged if I cancel my appointment?
   Please cancel 24 hours before your service to avoid a cancellation charge. No-shows and cancellations without adequate notice will be charged for the full service.
3. Are there any health safeguards I should know about?
   Please advise us of medical conditions or allergies you have. Heat treatments like hydrotherapy and body wraps should be avoided if you are pregnant, have high blood pressure, or any type of heart condition or diabetes.
4. What about tipping?
   Gratuities are at your sole discretion, but are certainly appreciated.

Ordered list items

FIGURE 7
Spa page with ordered list

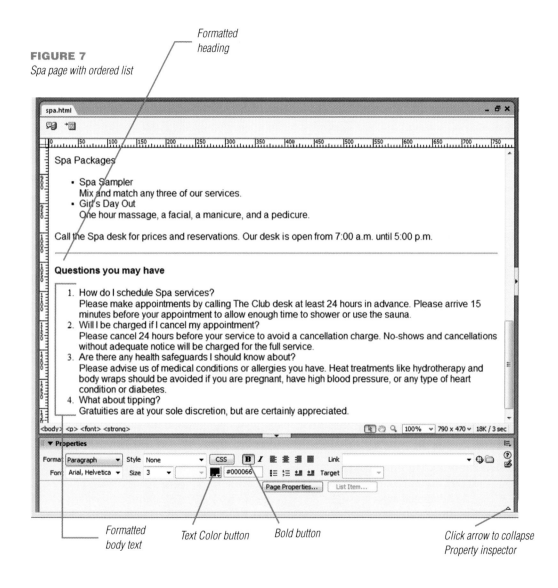

Formatted heading

Formatted body text

Text Color button

Bold button

Click arrow to collapse Property inspector

1. Select all the text below the horizontal rule, then change the font to Arial, Helvetica, sans-serif, size 3.

2. Select the heading "Questions you may have," then click the **Bold button** **B** in the Property inspector.

3. Click the **Text Color button** in the Property inspector to open the color picker, click the first **dark blue color** in the third row, color #000066, deselect the text, then compare your screen to Figure 7.

   TIP If you want to see more of your Web page in the Document window, you can collapse the Property inspector.

5. Save your work.

You applied a new font and font size to the ordered list. You also formatted the "Questions you may have" heading.

CREATE, APPLY, AND EDIT
CASCADING STYLE SHEETS

What You'll Do

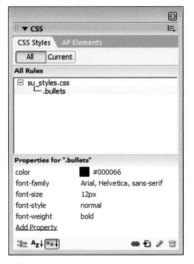

 In this lesson, you will create a Cascading Style Sheet file for The Striped Umbrella Web site. You will also create styles named bullets and heading and apply them to the spa page.

Understanding Cascading Style Sheets

CSS are made up of sets of formatting attributes called rules, which define the formatting attributes for individual styles, and are classified by where the code is stored. Sometimes the terms "style" and "rule" seem to be used interchangeably to refer to a rule in a style sheet. The code can be saved in a separate file (**external style sheets**), as part of the head content of an individual Web page (**internal or embedded styles**) or as part of the body of the HTML code (**inline styles**). External CSS style sheets are saved as files with the .css extension and are stored in the directory structure of a Web site, as shown in Figure 8. They are the preferred method for creating and using styles.

CSS are also classified by their function. A **Class style** can be used to format any page element. An **HTML style** is used to redefine an HTML tag. An **Advanced style** is used to format combinations of page elements. In this chapter, we will use class styles stored in external style sheet files.

Using the CSS Styles Panel

You use the buttons on the CSS Styles panel to create, edit, and apply styles. To add a style, use the New CSS Rule dialog box to name the style and specify whether to add it to a new or existing style sheet. You then use the CSS Rule definition dialog box to set the formatting attributes for the style. Once you add a new style to a style sheet, it appears in a list in the CSS Styles panel. To apply a style, you select the text to which you want to apply the style, and then choose a style from the Style list in the Property inspector. You can apply CSS styles to elements on a single Web page or to all of the pages in a Web site. When you make a change to a style, all page elements formatted with that style are automatically updated. Once you create a CSS style sheet, you can attach it to the remaining pages in your Web site.

The CSS Styles panel is used for managing your styles. The Properties pane displays properties for a selected style at the bottom of the panel. You can easily change a property's value by clicking an option from a drop-down list.

Comparing the Advantages of Using Style Sheets

You can use CSS styles to save an enormous amount of time. Being able to define a rule and then apply it to page elements on all the pages of your Web site means that you can make hundreds of formatting changes in a few minutes. In addition, style sheets create a more uniform look from page to page and they generate cleaner code. Using style sheets separates the development of content from the way the content is presented. Pages formatted with CSS styles are much more compliant with current accessibility standards than those with manual formatting.

QUICKTIP

For more information about Cascading Style Sheets, visit *www.w3.org* or view a tutorial at *www.adobe.com/go/vid0152*.

Understanding CSS Style Sheet Code

You can see the code for a CSS style by opening a style sheet file. A CSS style consists of two parts: the selector and the declaration. The **selector** is the name of the tag to which the style declarations have been assigned. The **declaration** consists of the property and the value. For example, Figure 9 shows the code for the su_styles.css style sheet. In this example,

the first property listed for the .bullets style is font-family. The value for this property is Arial, Helvetica, sans-serif. When you create a new CSS, you will see it as an open document in the Document window. Save this file as you make changes to it.

FIGURE 8

Cascading Style Sheet file created in striped_umbrella root folder

New Cascading
Style Sheet file

FIGURE 9

su_styles.css style sheet file

```
1   .bullets {
2       font-family: Arial, Helvetica, sans-serif;
3       font-size: 14px;
4       font-style: normal;
5       font-weight: bold;
6       color: #000066;
7   }
8
```

Create a Cascading Style Sheet and a style

1. Click **Edit** (Win) or **Dreamweaver** (Mac) on the menu bar, click **Preferences**, click the **General category**, if necessary, click the **Use CSS instead of HTML tags check box**, then click **OK** to turn this default option back on.

   From this point forward, we will use CSS rather than HTML tags to format text. The Property inspector font sizes will be shown in pixels rather than HTML text sizes, as shown in Figure 10. You can also set font sizes using values such as "small" or "medium."

2. Expand the CSS panel group, then click the **CSS Styles panel tab** (if necessary).

3. Click the **Switch to All (Document) Mode button** **All**, click the **New CSS Rule button** in the CSS Styles panel to open the New CSS Rule dialog box, verify that the Class option button is selected, then type **bullets** in the Name text box.

   > TIP Class names are preceded by a period. If you don't enter a period when you type the name, Dreamweaver will add the period for you.

4. Click the **Define in list arrow**, click **(New Style Sheet File)** (if necessary), compare your screen with Figure 11, then click **OK**.

5. Type **su_styles** in the File name text box (Win) or the Save As text box (Mac), then click **Save** to open the CSS Rule Definition for .bullets in su_styles.css dialog box.

   The .bullets rule will be stored within the su_styles.css file.

   (continued)

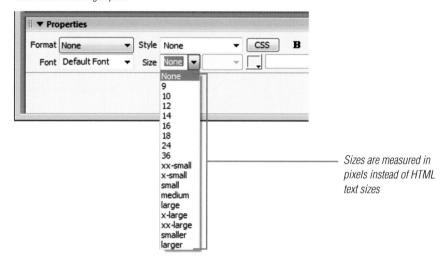

Sizes are measured in pixels instead of HTML text sizes

FIGURE 11
New CSS Rule dialog box

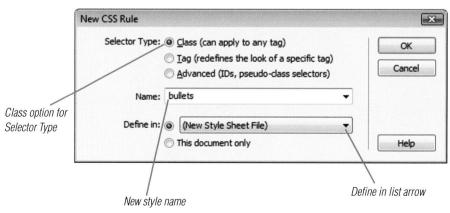

Class option for Selector Type

New style name

Define in list arrow

FIGURE 12

CSS Rule Definition for .bullets in su_styles.css dialog box

Type category selected

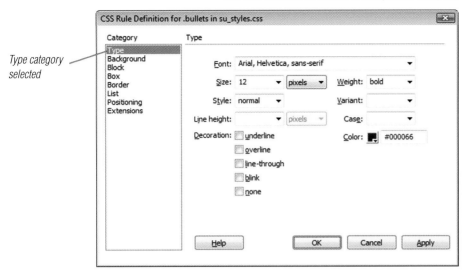

FIGURE 13

CSS Styles panel with bullets style added

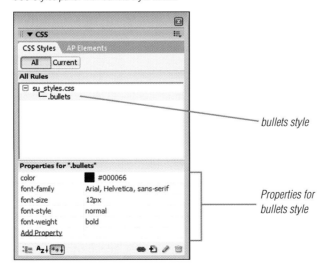

bullets style

Properties for bullets style

6. Verify that Type is selected in the Category list, set the Font to **Arial, Helvetica, sans-serif,** set the Size to **12 pixels**, set the Weight to **bold**, set the Style to **normal**, set the Color to **#000066**, compare your screen to Figure 12, then click **OK**.

7. Click the **plus sign** (Win) or the **expander arrow** (Mac) next to su_styles.css in the CSS Styles panel and expand the panel (if necessary) to list the .bullets style, then select the **bullets style**.

   The CSS style named .bullets and the style properties appear in the CSS Styles panel, as shown in Figure 13.

You created a Cascading Style Sheet file named su_styles.css and a style called .bullets.

Apply a Cascading Style Sheet

1. Click **View** on the menu bar, point to **Toolbars**, then click **Style Rendering**.

2. Verify that the **Toggle Displaying of CSS Styles button** 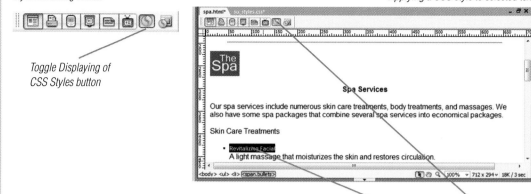 on the Style Rendering toolbar is active, as shown in Figure 14.

   TIP You can determine if the Toggle Displaying of CSS Styles button is active if it has an outline around the button. As long as this button is active, you do not have to display the toolbar on the screen.

   You can use the Toggle Displaying of CSS Styles button to see how styles affect your page.

3. Select the text "Revitalizing Facial," as shown in Figure 15, then use the Property inspector to set the Font to **Default Font**, the Size to **None**, and the Style to **bullets**.

   TIP Before you apply a style to selected text, you need to remove all formatting attributes such as font and color from that text, or the style will not be applied correctly.

4. Repeat Step 1 to apply the bullets style to each of the spa services bulleted items in the unordered lists, then compare your screen to Figure 16.

   The font size is too small, which you will fix in the next lesson.

You applied the bullets style to each item in the Spa Services category lists.

FIGURE 14
Style Rendering toolbar

Toggle Displaying of CSS Styles button

FIGURE 15
Applying a CSS style to selected text

Style applied

Toggle Displaying of CSS Styles button

FIGURE 16
Unordered list with bullets style applied

bullets style applied to each of the Spa Services items

Using the Style Rendering toolbar

The Style Rendering toolbar allows you to render your page as different media types, such as print, TV, or handheld. To display it when a page is open, click View on the menu bar, point to Toolbars, and then click Style Rendering. The buttons on the Style Rendering toolbar allow you to see how your page will look as you select different media types. The next to the last button on the toolbar is the Toggle Displaying of CSS Styles button, which you can use to view how a page looks with styles applied. It works independently of the other buttons. The last button is the Design-time Style Sheets button, which you can use to show or hide particular combinations of styles while you are working in the Document window.

FIGURE 17

Editing a style

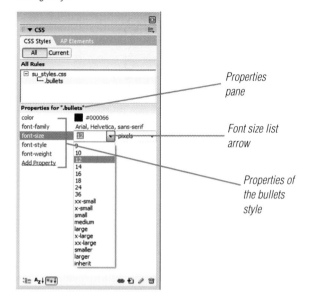

Properties
pane

Font size list
arrow

Properties of
the bullets
style

FIGURE 18

Viewing the changes made to the bullets style

Text that has
the bullets style
applied to it is
now larger

Skin Care Treatments

- **Revitalizing Facial**
  A light massage that moisturizes the skin and restores circulation.
- **Gentlemen's Facial**
  A cleansing facial that includes a neck and shoulder massage.
- **Milk Mask**
  A mask applied to soften and moisturize the face.

Body Treatments

- **Salt Glow**
  Imported sea salts are massaged into the skin, exfoliating and cleansing the pores.
- **Mud Body Wrap**
  Relief for your aches and pains.
- **Seaweed Body Wrap**
  Seaweed is a natural detoxifying agent that also helps improve circulation.

Massages

Edit a Cascading Style Sheet

1. Click **.bullets** in the CSS Styles panel.

   The style's properties and values are displayed in the Properties pane, the bottom part of the CSS Styles panel, as shown in Figure 17. You can also click the **Edit Style button** 🖉 in the CSS Styles panel to open the CSS Rule Definition for .bullets dialog box.

   TIP .bullets in the CSS Styles panel if you do not see .bullets. Click the plus sign (Win) or expander arrow (Mac) to the left of su_styles.css in the CSS Styles panel if you do not see .bullets. Click the plus sign (Win) or expander arrow (Mac) to the left of <style> if you do not see su_styles.css.

2. Click **12px** in the CSS Styles panel, click the **font-size list arrow**, click **14**, then compare your screen to Figure 18.

   The text is larger, reflecting the changes you made to the bullets style.

   TIP If you position the insertion point in text that has a CSS style applied to it, that style is displayed in the Style text box on the Property inspector.

You edited the bullets style to change the font size to 14 pixels. You then viewed the results of the edited style in the unordered list.

ADD STYLES AND ATTACH
CASCADING STYLE SHEETS

What You'll Do

 In this lesson, you will add a style to a Cascading Style Sheet. You will then attach the style sheet file to the index page and apply one of the styles to text on the page.

Understanding External and Embedded Style Sheets

When you are first learning about CSS, the terminology can be very confusing. In the last lesson, you learned that external style sheets are a separate file in a Web site saved with the .css file extension. You also learned that CSS can be part of an html file, rather than a separate file. These are called internal, or embedded, style sheets. External CSS files are created by the Web designer. Embedded style sheets are created automatically by Dreamweaver when the Preference is set to Use CSS instead of HTML tags. When this preference is set, any formatting choices you make using the Property inspector will automatically create a style. The code for these styles will reside in the head content for that page. These styles will be automatically named style1, style2, and so on. You can rename the styles as they are created to make them more recognizable for you to use, for example, body_text, subheading, or address. Embedded style sheets apply only to a single page, although you can copy them into the code in other pages. Remember that style sheets can be used to format much more than text objects. They can be used to set the page background, link properties, tables, or determine the appearance of almost any object on the page. Figure 19 shows the code for some embedded styles. The code resides in the head content of the Web page.

When you have several pages in a Web site, you will probably want to use the same CSS style sheet for each page to ensure that all your elements have a consistent appearance. To attach a style sheet to another document, click the Attach Style Sheet button on the CSS Styles panel to open the Attach External Style Sheet dialog box, make sure the Add as Link option is selected, browse to locate the file you want to attach, and then click OK. The styles contained in the attached style sheet will appear in the CSS Styles panel, and you can use them to apply styles to text on the page. External style sheets can be attached, or linked, to any page. This is an extremely powerful tool. If you decide to make a change in a style, it will automatically be made to every object that it formats.

FIGURE 19

Code for embedded styles shown in Code view

```
1   <!DOCTYPE html PUBLIC "-//W3C//DTD XHTML 1.0 Transitional//EN"
    "http://www.w3.org/TR/xhtml1/DTD/xhtml1-transitional.dtd">
2   <html xmlns="http://www.w3.org/1999/xhtml">
3   <head>
4   <meta http-equiv="Content-Type" content="text/html; charset=utf-8" />
5   <title>Welcome to the Striped Umbrella</title>
6   <style type="text/css">
7   <!--
8   .style1 {
9       font-family: Arial, Helvetica, sans-serif;
10      font-size: 10px;
11  }
12  .style2 {font-family: Arial, Helvetica, sans-serif;
13      font-size: 18px; }
14  body {
15      background-color: #99CCCC;
16  }
17  a:link {
18      color: #990000;
19  }
20  -->
21  </style>
22  </head>
23
```

Add a style to a Cascading Style Sheet

1. Click the **New CSS Rule button** 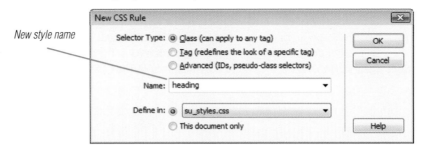 in the CSS Styles panel.

2. Type **heading** in the Name text box, as shown in Figure 20, then click **OK**.

3. Set the Font to **Arial**, **Helvetica**, **sans-serif**, set the Size to **16**, set the Style to **normal**, set the Weight to **bold**, set the Color to **#000066**, compare your screen to Figure 21, then click **OK**.

4. Click the **Edit Style button** 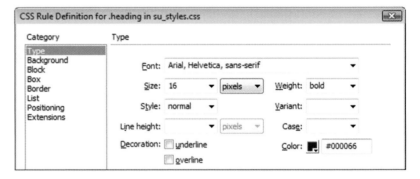.

5. Click the **Block category** in the CSS Rule Definition for .heading in su_styles.css dialog box, click the **Text align list arrow**, click **center**, as shown in Figure 22, then click **OK**.

6. Select the heading text "Spa Services," then use the Property inspector to set the Format to **None** and the Font to **Default Font**.

7. With the heading still selected, click the **Text Color button** to open the color picker, then click the **Default Color button**.

8. Click the **Style list arrow** in the Property inspector, then click **heading** to apply it to the Spa Services heading.

9. Repeat Steps 1 through 3 to add another style called **body_text** with the **Arial**, **Helvetica**, **sans-serif** font, size **14**, and **normal** style.

10. Repeat Steps 6 through 8 to apply the body_text style to the all the text on the page except for the blue text that already has the bullets style applied to it and the heading text "Questions you may have."

FIGURE 20
Adding a style to a CSS Style sheet

New style name

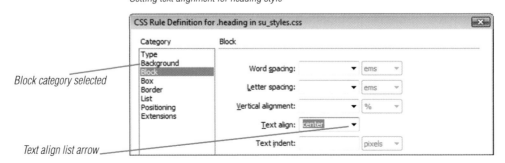

FIGURE 21
Formatting options for heading style

FIGURE 22
Setting text alignment for heading style

Block category selected

Text align list arrow

FIGURE 23

Spa page with styles applied

heading
style applied

body_text
style applied

Spa Services

Our spa services include numerous skin care treatments, body treatments, and massages. We also have
some spa packages that combine several spa services into economical packages.

Skin Care Treatments

- **Revitalizing Facial**
  A light massage that moisturizes the skin and restores circulation.
- **Gentlemen's Facial**
  A cleansing facial that includes a neck and shoulder massage.
- **Milk Mask**
  A mask applied to soften and moisturize the face.

FIGURE 24

Attaching a style sheet to a page

su_styles.css

Link option
button

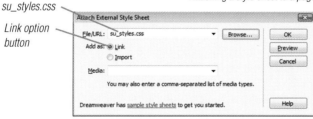

FIGURE 25

Viewing the code to link the CSS style sheet file

```
8   <link href="su_styles.css" rel="stylesheet" type="text/css" />
9   </head>
10
11  <body bgcolor="#FFFFFF">
12  <div align="center">
13    <h4><img src="assets/su_banner.gif" alt="The Striped Umbrella"
    "125" /><br />
14      <font face="Arial, Helvetica, sans-serif"><a href="index.ht
    "about_us.html">About Us</a> - <a href="spa.html">Spa</a> - <a hr
    - <a href="activities.html">Activities</a></font> </h4>
15  </div>
16  <hr width="75%" />
17  <p class="body_text">  Welcome to The Striped Umbrella - a full-s
    just steps from the Gulf of Mexico and ten miles east of Crab Key
    the best of both worlds, a secluded sandy beach populated with be
```

Code linking external style
sheet file to the index page

Code that applies the body_text
style to the paragraph

11. Click **File** on the menu bar, then click **Save
    All**, to save both the spa page and the
    su_styles.css file.

    The styles are saved and applied to the text,
    as shown in Figure 23.

    TIP You must save the open su_styles.css
    file after editing it, or you will lose your
    changes.

*You added two new styles called heading and
body_text to the su_styles.css file. You then
applied the two styles to selected text.*

Attach a style sheet

1. Close the spa page and open the index page.
2. Click the **Attach Style Sheet button** ⊕ on
   the CSS Styles panel.
3. Browse to select the file su_styles.css (if
   necessary), click **Choose** (Mac) verify that
   the **Link option button** is selected, as shown
   in Figure 24, then click **OK**.
4. Select the opening paragraph text, then set
   the Font to **Default Font** and the Size to
   None to clear prior formatting.
5. Click the **Style list arrow**, then click
   body_text.
6. Click the **Show Code view button** ⟨⟩ Code
   and view the code that links the su_styles.css
   file to the index page, as shown in Figure 25.
7. Click the **Show Design view button**
   ⬚ Design , save your work, then close the
   index page.

*You attached the su_styles.css file to the
index.html page.*

INSERT AND ALIGN
GRAPHICS

What You'll Do

In this lesson, you will insert five graphics on the about us page in The Striped Umbrella Web site. You will then stagger the alignment of the images on the page to make the page more visually appealing.

Understanding Graphic File Formats

When you add graphics to a Web page, it's important to choose the appropriate graphic file format. The three primary graphic file formats used in Web pages are **GIF** (Graphics Interchange Format), **JPEG** (Joint Photographic Experts Group), and **PNG** (Portable Network Graphics). GIF files download very quickly, making them ideal to use on Web pages. Though limited in the number of colors they can represent, GIF files have the ability to show transparent areas. JPEG files can display many colors. Because they often contain many shades of the same color, photographs are often saved in JPEG format. Files saved with the PNG format can display many colors and use various degrees of transparency, called **opacity**. While the GIF format is subject to licensing restrictions, the PNG format is free to use. However, not all browsers support the PNG format.

QUICKTIP
The status bar displays the download time for the page. Each time you add a new graphic to the page, you can see how much additional time is added to the total download time.

Understanding the Assets Panel

When you add a graphic to a Web site, it is automatically added to the Assets panel. The **Assets panel**, located in the Files panel group, displays all the assets in a Web site. The Assets panel contains nine category buttons that you use to view your assets by category. These include Images, Colors, URLs, Flash, Shockwave, Movies, Scripts, Templates, and Library. To view a particular type of asset, click the appropriate category button. The Assets panel is split into two panes. When you click the Images button, as shown in Figure 26, the lower pane displays a list of all the images in your site and contains four columns. The top pane displays a thumbnail of the selected image in the list. You can view assets in each category in two ways. You can use the Site option button to view all the assets in a Web site, or you can use the Favorites option button to view those assets that you have designated as **favorites**, or assets that you expect to use repeatedly while you work on the site. You can use the Assets panel to add an asset to a Web page by dragging the asset from the Assets panel to the page or by using the Insert button on the Assets panel.

QUICKTIP

You might need to resize the Assets panel to see all four columns when it is docked. To resize the Assets panel, undock the Files panel group and drag a side or corner of the panel border.

Inserting Files with Adobe Bridge

You can manage project files, including video and Camera Raw files, with a file-management tool called Adobe Bridge. Bridge is an easy way to view files outside the Web site before bringing them into the Web site. It is an integrated application, working with other Adobe programs such as Photoshop and Illustrator. You can also use Bridge to add meta tags and search text to your files. To open Bridge, click the Browse in Bridge command on the File menu or click the Browse In Bridge button on the Standard toolbar.

Aligning Images

When you insert an image on a Web page, you need to position it in relation to other elements on the page. Positioning an image is referred to as **aligning** an image. By default, when you insert an image in a paragraph, its bottom edge aligns with the baseline of the first line of text or any other element in the same paragraph. When you select an image, the Align text box in the Property inspector displays the alignment setting for the image. You can change the alignment setting using the options in the Align menu in the Property inspector.

QUICKTIP

The Align menu options function differently from the Align buttons in the Property inspector. You use the Align buttons to center, left-align, or right-align an element without regard to how the element is aligned in relation to other elements.

FIGURE 26
The Assets panel

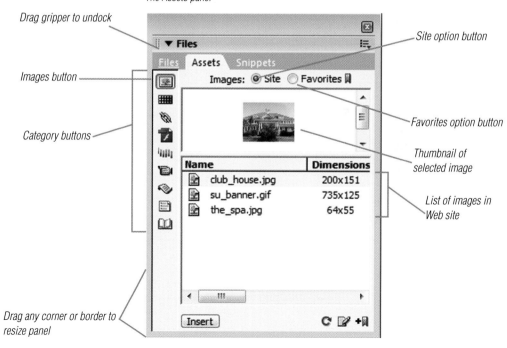

Drag gripper to undock

Images button

Category buttons

Site option button

Favorites option button

Thumbnail of selected image

List of images in Web site

Drag any corner or border to resize panel

Insert a graphic

1. Open dw3_1.html from where you store your Data Files, then save it as **about_us.html** in the striped_umbrella root folder.

2. Click **Yes** (Win) or **Replace** (Mac) to overwrite the existing file, then click **No** to Update Links.

3. Click the **Attach Style Sheet button** in the CSS Styles panel, attach the su_styles.css style sheet, then apply the body_text style to all of the paragraph text on the page.

4. Place the insertion point before "When" in the first paragraph, click the **Common tab** on the Insert bar (if necessary), click the **Images list arrow**, then click **Image** to open the Select Image Source dialog box.

5. Navigate to the assets folder where you store your Data Files, double-click **club_house.jpg,** type the alternate text **Club House** if prompted, click **OK,** then verify that the file was copied to your assets folder in the striped_umbrella root folder.

   Compare your screen to Figure 27.

6. Click the **Assets panel tab** in the Files panel group, click the **Images button** on the Assets panel (if necessary), then click the **Refresh Site List button** on the Assets panel to update the list of images in The Striped Umbrella Web site.

   The Assets panel displays a list of all the images in The Striped Umbrella Web site, as shown in Figure 28.

You inserted one image on the about_us page and copied it to the assets folder of the Web site.

FIGURE 27

The Striped Umbrella about us page with inserted image

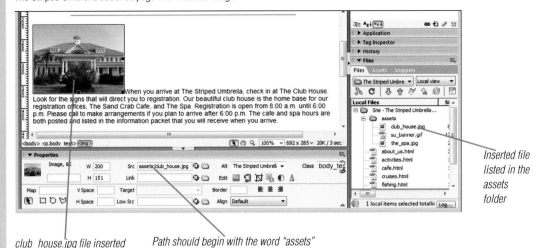

club_house.jpg file inserted   *Path should begin with the word "assets"*

Inserted file listed in the assets folder

FIGURE 28

Image files for The Striped Umbrella Web site listed in Assets panel

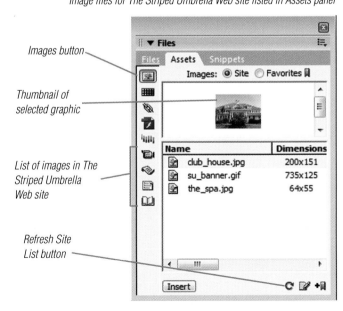

Images button

Thumbnail of selected graphic

List of images in The Striped Umbrella Web site

Refresh Site List button

FIGURE 29
Using Adobe Bridge

boardwalk.jpg
image is selected

FIGURE 30
Assets panel with seven images

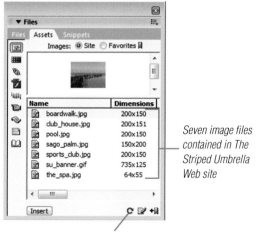

Seven image files
contained in The
Striped Umbrella
Web site

Click Refresh Site List button to refresh file list

Use Adobe Bridge

1. Click to place the insertion point before the word "After" at the beginning of the second paragraph.

2. Click **File** on the menu bar, click **Browse in Bridge,** navigate to where you store your Data Files, then click the thumbnail image **boardwalk.jpg** in the assets folder, as shown in Figure 29.

   Bridge is divided into several panels; files and folders are listed in the Folders Panel. The files in the selected folder appear in the Content Panel. A picture of the file appears in the Preview Panel. The Metadata and Keywords Panels list any tags that have been added to the file.

3. Click **File** on the menu bar, point to **Place,** then click **In Dreamweaver**.

4. Type the alternate text **Boardwalk to the beach,** if prompted.

   The image appears on the page.

   TIP: You can also click the Browse in Bridge button [icon] on the Standard toolbar to open Bridge.

5. Repeat Steps 1–4 to place the **pool.jpg,** **sago_palm.jpg**, and **sports_club.jpg** files at the beginning of each of the succeeding paragraphs, adding appropriate alternate text if prompted for the pool, sago palm, and sports club images.

   After refreshing, your Assets panel should resemble Figure 30.

You inserted four images using Adobe Bridge on the about_us page and copied each image to the assets folder of The Striped Umbrella Web site.

Align an image

1. Scroll to the top of the page, click the **club house image**, then expand the Property inspector (if necessary).

   Because an image is selected, the Property inspector displays tools for setting the properties of an image.

2. Click the **Align list arrow** in the Property inspector, then click **Left**.

   The club house photo is now left-aligned with the text and the paragraph text flows around its right edge, as shown in Figure 31.

   (continued)

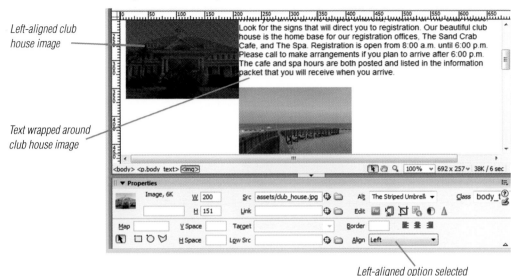

FIGURE 31
Left-aligned club house image

Left-aligned club house image

Text wrapped around club house image

Left-aligned option selected

Using Favorites in the Assets panel

The assets in the Assets panel can be listed two ways: Site and Favorites. The Site option lists all of the assets in the Web site in the selected category in alphabetical order. As your list of assets grows, you can designate some of the assets that are used more frequently as Favorites for quicker access. To add an asset to the Favorites list, right-click (Win) or [control]-click (Mac) the asset name in the Site list, and then click Add to Favorites. When an asset is placed in the Favorites list, it is still included in the Site list. To delete an asset from the Favorites list, select the asset you want to delete, and then press [Delete] or the Remove from Favorites button on the Assets panel. You can further organize your Favorites list by creating folders for similar assets and grouping them inside the folders.

FIGURE 32

Aligned images on the about us page

3. Select the boardwalk image, click the **Align list arrow** in the Property inspector, then click **Right**.

4. Align the pool image, using the **Left Align** option.

5. Align the sago palm image, using the **Right Align** option.

6. Align the sports club image, using the **Left Align** option.

7. Save your work.

8. Preview the Web page in your browser, compare your screen to Figure 32, then close your browser.

9. Close Adobe Bridge.

You used the Property inspector to set the alignment for the five images. You then previewed the page in your browser.

Graphics versus images

Two terms that sometimes seem to be used interchangeably are graphics and images. For the purposes of discussion in this text, we will use the term **graphics** to refer to the appearance of most non-text items on a Web page such as photographs, logos, navigation bars, Flash animations, graphs, background images, and drawings. A file that produces any of these page elements is called a graphic file. Files that produce images on a page are referred to by their file type, or graphic file format, such as JPEG (Joint Photographic Experts Group), GIF (Graphics Interchange Format), or PNG (Portable Network Graphics). We will refer to the actual pictures that you see on the pages as images. Don't worry about which term to use. Many people use one term or the other according to habit or region, or use them interchangeably.

ENHANCE AN IMAGE AND
USE ALTERNATE TEXT

What You'll Do

 In this lesson, you will add borders to images, add horizontal and vertical space to set them apart from the text, and then add alternate text to each image on the page.

Enhancing an Image

After you place an image on a Web page, you have several options for **enhancing** it, or improving its appearance. To make changes to the image itself, such as removing scratches from it, or erasing parts of it, you need to use an image editor such as Adobe Fireworks or Adobe Photoshop. To edit an image directly in Fireworks from Dreamweaver, first select the image, and then click Edit on the Property inspector. This will open the Fireworks program.

Complete your editing, and then click Done to return to Dreamweaver.

QUICKTIP

You can copy a Photoshop PSD file directly into Dreamweaver. After inserting the image, Dreamweaver will prompt you to optimize the image for the Web.

You can use Dreamweaver to enhance certain aspects of how images appear on a page. For example, you can add borders around an image or add horizontal and

---

DESIGNTIP **Resizing graphics using an external editor**

Each image on a Web page takes a specific number of seconds to download, depending on the size of the file. Larger files (in kilobytes, not width and height) take longer to download than smaller files. It's important to determine the smallest acceptable size for an image on your Web page. Then, if you need to resize an image to reduce the file size, use an external image editor to do so, *instead* of resizing it in Dreamweaver. Although you can adjust the width and height settings of an image in the Property inspector to change the size of the image as it appears on your screen, these settings do not affect the file size. Decreasing the size of an image using the H (height) and W (width) settings in the Property inspector does *not* reduce the time it will take the file to download. Ideally you should use images that have the smallest file size and the highest quality possible, so that each page downloads as quickly as possible.

vertical space. **Borders** are frames that surround an image. Horizontal and vertical space is blank space above, below, and on the sides of an image that separates the image from text or other elements on the page. Adding horizontal or vertical space is the same as adding white space, and helps images stand out on a page. In the Web page shown in Figure 33, the horizontal and vertical space around the images in the center column helps make these images more prominent. Adding horizontal or vertical space does not affect the width or height of the image. Spacing around Web page objects can also be created by using "spacer" images, or clear images that act as placeholders.

Using Alternate Text

One of the easiest ways to make your Web page viewer-friendly and accessible to people of all abilities is to use alternate text. **Alternate text** is descriptive text that appears in place of an image while the image is downloading or when the mouse pointer is placed over it. You can program some browsers to display only alternate text and to download images manually. Alternate text can be "read" by a **screen reader**, a device used by persons with visual impairments to convert written text on a computer monitor to spoken words. Screen readers and alternate text make it possible for viewers who have visual impairments to have an image described to them in detail. One of the

default preferences in Dreamweaver is to prompt you to enter alternate text whenever you insert an image on a page.

The use of alternate text is the first checkpoint listed in the World Wide Web Consortium (W3C) list of Priority 1 checkpoints. The Priority 1 checkpoints

dictate the most basic level of accessibility standards to be used by Web developers today. The complete list of these and the other priority-level checkpoints are listed on the W3C Web site, *www.w3.org*. You should always strive to meet these criteria for all Web pages.

FIGURE 33
Lands' End Web site

Lands' End Web site used with permission from Lands' End, Inc. - www.landsend.com

Add a border

1. Select the club house image, then expand the Property inspector (if necessary).

2. Type **1** in the Border text box, then press **[Tab]** to apply the border to the club house image, as shown in Figure 34.

   The border setting is not visible until you preview the page in a browser.

3. Repeat Step 2 to add borders to the other four images.

You added a 1-pixel border to each image on the about_us page.

Add horizontal space

1. Select the club house image, type **7** in the V Space text box in the Property inspector, press **[Tab]**, type **7** in the H Space text box, then compare your screen to Figure 35.

   The text is more evenly wrapped around the image and is easier to read, because it is not so close to the edge of the image.

2. Repeat Step 1 to set the V Space and H Space to 7 for the other four images.

   The spacing under each picture differs because of the difference in the lengths of the paragraphs.

You added horizontal spacing and vertical spacing around each image on the about_us page.

FIGURE 34
Using the Property inspector to add a border

Selected image with 1-pixel border

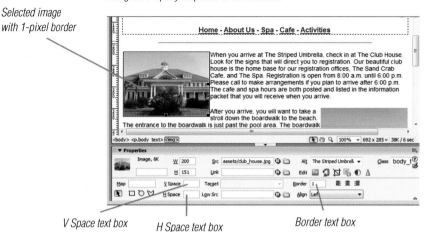

V Space text box   H Space text box   Border text box

FIGURE 35
Comparing images with and without horizontal and vertical space

Image with horizontal and vertical space

Image without horizontal and vertical space

Working with Text and Images

FIGURE 36

Brightness and contrast settings for the boardwalk image

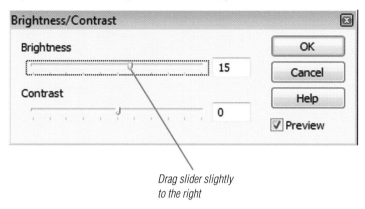

Drag slider slightly
to the right

Apply the Brightness/Contrast feature to graphics

1. Select the **boardwalk image**.

2. Click the **Brightness and Contrast button** in the Property inspector, then click **OK** to close the warning dialog box to open the Brightness/Contrast dialog box.

3. Drag the **Brightness slider** to the right until **15** appears in the text box, as shown in Figure 36, then click **OK**.

   The image is now lighter.

4. Repeat Step 3 to adjust any of the other images if desired.

   TIP   In addition to using brightness and contrast features, you can also scale an image. First, select the image, then drag one of the borders toward the center of the image to reduce it, or drag away from the center of the image to enlarge it.

You used the Brightness/Contrast dialog box to lighten an image.

Integrating Photoshop CS3 with Dreamweaver

Dreamweaver has many functions integrated with Photoshop CS3. This new partnership includes the ability to copy and paste a Photoshop PSD file directly from Photoshop into Dreamweaver. After using the Paste command, Dreamweaver will prompt you to optimize the image by choosing a file format and settings for the Web. After optimization, Dreamweaver will then paste the image on the page. If you want to edit the image later, simply double-click the image in Dreamweaver and it will open in Photoshop.

Photoshop users can set Photoshop as the default image editor in Dreamweaver. Click Edit on the menu bar, click Preferences, click Dreamweaver (Mac), click File Types/Editors, click the Editors plus sign button to add Photoshop, (if you don't see it listed already) and then click Make Primary. You can view a tutorial for Photoshop and Dreamweaver integration on the Adobe Web site at *www.adobe.com/go/vid0200*.

Edit alternate text

1. Select the club house image, select any existing text in the Alt text box in the Property inspector (if necessary), type **The Striped Umbrella Club House** as shown in Figure 37, then press **[Enter]** (Win) or **[return]** (Mac).

2. Save your work, preview the page in your browser, then point to the **club house image** until the alternate text appears, as shown in Figure 38.

3. Close your browser.

4. Select the boardwalk image, type **The board-walk to the beach** in the Alt text box, replacing any existing text, then press **[Enter]** (Win) or **[return]** (Mac).

5. Repeat Step 4 to add the alternate text **The pool area** to the pool image.

6. Repeat Step 4 to add the alternate text **Sago palm** to the sago palm image.

7. Repeat Step 4 to add the alternate text **The Sports Club** to the sports club image.

8. Save your work.

9. Preview the page in your browser, view the alternate text for each image, then close your browser.

You edited the alternate text for five images on the page, then you viewed the alternate text in your browser.

FIGURE 37
Alternate text setting in the Property inspector

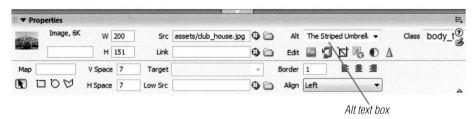

Alt text box

FIGURE 38
Alternate text displayed in browser

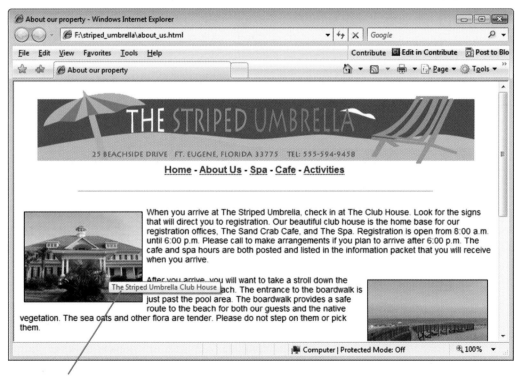

Alternate text appears when triggered by the mouse pointer

FIGURE 39

Preferences dialog box with Accessibility category selected

Accessibility category

Check boxes for Form objects, Frames, Media, and Images

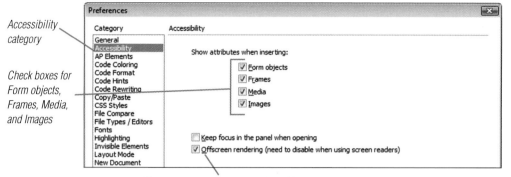

This option is not available in Mac OS X

Set the alternate text accessibility option

1. Click **Edit** (Win) or **Dreamweaver** (Mac) on the menu bar, click **Preferences** to open the Preferences dialog box, then click the **Accessibility category**.

2. Verify that the four check boxes are checked, as shown in Figure 39, check them if they are not checked, then click **OK**.

   TIP Once you set the Accessibility preferences, they will be in effect for all Web sites that you develop, not just the one that's open when you set them.

You set the Accessibility preferences to prompt you to enter alternate text each time you insert a form object, frame, media, image, or object on a Web page.

POWER USER SHORTCUTS

To do this:	Use this shortcut:
Switch views	[Ctrl][`] (Win) or [control][`] (Mac)
Insert image	[Ctrl][Alt][I] (Win) or [[⌘]][option][I] (Mac)
Indent text	[Ctrl][Alt][]] (Win) or [[⌘]][option][]] (Mac)
Outdent text	[Ctrl][Alt][[] (Win) or [[⌘]][option][[] (Mac)
Align Left	[Ctrl][Alt][Shift][L] (Win) or [[⌘]][option][shift][L] (Mac)
Align Center	[Ctrl][Alt][Shift][C] (Win) or [[⌘]][option][shift][C] (Mac)
Align Right	[Ctrl][Alt][Shift][R] (Win) or [[⌘]][option][shift][R] (Mac)
Align Justify	[Ctrl][Alt][Shift][J] (Win) or [[⌘]][option][shift][J] (Mac)
Bold	[Ctrl][B] (Win) or [[⌘]][B] (Mac)
Italic	[Ctrl][I] (Win) or [[⌘]][I] (Mac)
Refresh	[F5]
Browse in Bridge	[Ctrl][At][O] (Win) or [[⌘]][option][O] (Mac)

INSERT A BACKGROUND IMAGE
AND PERFORM SITE
MAINTENANCE

What You'll Do

 In this lesson, you will insert two types of background images. You will then use the Assets panel to delete them both from the Web site. You will also check for Non-Websafe colors in the Assets panel.

Inserting a Background Image

You can insert a background image on a Web page to provide depth and visual interest to the page, or to communicate a message or mood. **Background images** are image files used in place of background colors. Although you can use background images to create a dramatic effect, you should avoid inserting them on Web pages where they would not provide the contrast necessary for reading a well-designed page. Even though they might seem too plain, standard white backgrounds are usually the best choice for Web pages. If you choose to use a background image on a Web page, it should be small in file size. You can insert either a small image file that is tiled, or repeated, across the page or a larger image that is not repeated across the page. A tiled image will download much faster than a large image. A **tiled image** is a small image that repeats across and down a Web page, appearing as individual squares or rectangles. When you create a Web page, you can use either a background color or a background image, but

not both, unless you have a need for the background color to be displayed while the background image finishes downloading. The background in the Web page shown in Figure 40 is a gray-green color, along with an image faded to become the background for a large portion of the page.

Managing Images

As you work on a Web site, you might find that you accumulate files in your assets folder that the Web site does not use. To avoid accumulating unnecessary files, it's a good idea to look at an image first, before you place it on the page and copy it to the assets folder. If you inadvertently copy an unwanted file to the assets folder, you should delete it or move it to another location. This is a good Web-site management practice that will prevent the assets folder from filling up with unwanted image files.

Removing an image from a Web page does not remove it from the assets folder in the local root folder of the Web site. To remove an asset from a Web site, you first locate the file you want to remove in the Assets panel. You then use the Locate in Site command to open the Files panel with the unwanted file selected. You can then use the Delete command to remove the file from the site.

Removing Colors from a Web Site

You can use the Assets panel to locate Non-Websafe colors in a Web site. **Non-Websafe** colors are colors that may not be displayed uniformly across computer platforms. After you replace a Non-Websafe color with another color, you should use the Refresh Site List button on the Assets panel to verify that the color has been removed. Sometimes it's necessary to press [Ctrl] (Win) or ⌘ (Mac) while you click the Refresh Site List button. If refreshing the Assets panel does not work, try re-creating the site cache, and then refreshing the Assets panel again.

FIGURE 40
The Mansion on Turtle Creek

The Mansion on Turtle Creek Web site used with permission from The Mansion on Turtle Creek, A Rosewood Hotel - www.mansiononturtlecreek.com

Insert a background image

1. Click **Modify** on the menu bar, then click **Page Properties** to open the Page Properties dialog box.

2. Click the **Appearance category**, if necessary.

3. Click **Browse** next to the Background image text box, navigate to the assets folder where you store your Data Files, then double-click **umbrella_back.gif**.

   The umbrella_back.gif file is automatically copied to The Striped Umbrella assets folder.

4. Click **OK** to close the Page Properties dialog box, then click the **Refresh Site List button** to refresh the file list in the Assets panel.

   A file with a single umbrella forms a background made up of individual squares, replacing the white background, as shown in Figure 41. It is much too busy and makes it difficult to read the page.

5. Repeat Steps 1–4 to replace the umbrella_back.gif background image with stripes_back.gif, located in the chapter_3 assets folder.

   As shown in Figure 42, the striped background is also tiled, but with vertical stripes, so you aren't aware of the small squares making up the pattern. It is still too busy, though.

You applied a tiled background to the about us page. Then you replaced the tiled background with another tiled background that was not as busy.

FIGURE 41
The about_us page with a busy tiled background

Each umbrella is a small square that forms a tiled background

FIGURE 42
The about_us page with a more subtle tiled background

It is harder to tell where each square ends

FIGURE 43
Removing a background image

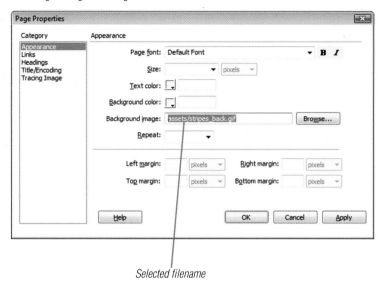

Selected filename

Understanding HTML body tags

When you are setting page preferences, it is helpful to understand the HTML tags that are being generated. Sometimes it's much easier to make changes to the code, rather than use menus and dialog boxes. The <body> </body> tags define the beginning and end of the body section of a Web page. The page content falls between these two tags. If you want to change the page properties, additional codes must be added to the <body> tag. The tag to add a color to the page background is bgcolor, so the tag will read <body bgcolor="#000000">, where the numbers following the pound sign indicate a color. If you insert an image for a background, the code will read <body background="assets/stripes.gif">. The filename between the quotation marks is the name of the image file used for the background.

Remove a background image from a page

1. Click **Modify** on the menu bar, click **Page Properties**, then click **Appearance**.

2. Select the text in the Background image text box, as shown in Figure 43, press **[Delete]**, then click **OK**.

   The background of the about us page is white again.

You deleted the link to the background image file to change the about us page background back to white.

Delete files from a Web site

1. Click the **Assets panel tab**, then click the **Images button** 🖼 (if necessary).

2. Right-click (Win) or [control]-click (Mac) **stripes_back.gif** in the Assets panel, click **Locate in Site** to open the Files panel, select **stripes_back.gif** in the Files panel (if necessary), press **[Delete]**, then click **Yes** in the dialog box that appears.

   TIP Refresh the Assets panel if you still see the file listed.

3. Repeat Step 2 to remove umbrella_back.gif from the Web site, open the Assets panel, then refresh the Assets panel.

   TIP If you delete a file in the Files panel that has an active link to it, you will receive a warning message. If you rename a file in the Files panel that has a link to it, the Files panel will update the links to correctly link to the renamed file. To rename a file, right-click (Win) or [control]-click (Mac) the file you want to rename, point to Edit, click Rename, then type the new name.

   Your Assets panel should resemble Figure 44.

You removed two image files from The Striped Umbrella Web site, then refreshed the Assets panel.

FIGURE 44
Images listed in Assets panel

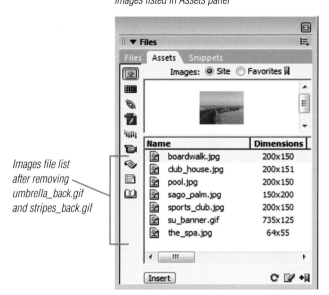

Images file list after removing umbrella_back.gif and stripes_back.gif

Managing image files

It is a good idea to store original unedited copies of your Web site image files in a separate folder, outside the assets folder of your Web site. If you edit the original files, save them again using different names. Doing this ensures that you will be able to find a file in its original, unaltered state. You may have files on your computer that you are currently not using at all, however, you may need to use them in the future. Storing currently unused files also helps keep your assets folder free of clutter. Storing copies of original Web site image files in a separate location also ensures that you have backup copies in the event that you accidentally delete a file from the Web site.

FIGURE 45

Colors listed in Assets panel

Both colors
are Websafe

Drag the border to the left
to expand panel width

1. Click the **Colors button** [⊞] in the Assets panel to display the colors used in the Web site, then drag the left border of the Assets panel (if necessary) to display the second column, as shown in Figure 45.

   The Assets panel does not list any Non-Websafe colors.

2. Save your work, preview the page in your browser, close your browser, then close all open files.

   TIP If previewing the page in Internet Explorer 7, click the Information bar when prompted to allow blocked content.

You checked for Non-Websafe colors in the Assets panel list of colors.

Using color in compliance with accessibility guidelines

The second guideline listed in the World Wide Web Consortium (W3C) list of Priority 1 Checkpoints is to not rely on the use of color alone. This means that if your Web site content is dependent on your viewer correctly seeing a color, then you are not providing for those people who cannot distinguish between certain colors or do not have monitors that display color.

Be especially careful when choosing color used with text to provide a good contrast between the text and the background. It is better to reference colors as numbers, rather than names. For example, use "#FFFFFF" instead of "white." Using style sheets for specifying color formats is the preferred method for coding. For more information, see the complete list of priority level checkpoints listed on the W3C Web site, *www.w3.org*.

Create unordered and ordered lists.

1. Open the blooms & bulbs Web site.
2. Open the tips page.
3. Select the four lines of text below the Seasonal Gardening Checklist heading and format them as an unordered list. (*Hint*: If each line does not become a separate list item, enter a paragraph break between each line, then remove any extra spaces.)
4. Select the lines of text below the Basic Gardening Tips heading and format them as an ordered list.
5. Save your work.

Create, apply, and edit Cascading Style Sheets.

1. Create a new CSS rule named **seasons**, making sure that the Class option button is selected in the Selector Type section and that the (New Style Sheet File) option button is selected in the Define in section of the New CSS Rule dialog box.
2. Click OK, name the style sheet file **blooms_styles** in the Save Style Sheet File As dialog box, then click Save.
3. Choose the following settings for the seasons style: Font = Arial, Helvetica, sans-serif, Size = medium, Style = normal, Weight = bold, and Color = #003366.
4. Change the Font setting to Default Font and the Size setting to None for the following words in the Seasonal Gardening Checklist: "Fall," "Winter," "Spring," and "Summer."

Apply the seasons style to Fall, Winter, Spring, and Summer.

5. Edit the seasons style by changing the font size to 16 pixels.

Add styles and attach cascading style sheets.

1. Add an additional style called **headings** in the blooms_styles.css file and define this style choosing the following type settings: Font = Arial, Helvetica, sans-serif, Size = large Style = normal, Weight = bold, and Color = #003366.
2. Apply the headings style to the two sub-headings on the page: Seasonal Gardening Checklist and Basic Gardening Tips. (*Hint:* Make sure you remove any manual formatting before applying the style.)
3. Click File on the menu bar, click Save All, then view the page in the browser. (*Hint:* If previewing the page in Internet Explorer 7, click the Information bar when prompted to allow blocked content.)
4. Close the browser and all open pages.

Insert and align graphics.

1. Open dw3_2.html from where you store your Data Files, then save it as **plants.html** in the blooms & bulbs Web site, overwriting the existing plants.html. Do not update links.
2. Verify that the path of the blooms & bulbs banner is set correctly to the assets folder in the blooms root folder.
3. Set the Accessibility preferences to prompt you

to add alternate text to images (if necessary).

4. Use Adobe Bridge to insert the petunias.jpg file from the assets folder where you store your Data Files to the left of the words "Pretty petunias" and add **Petunias** as alternate text.
5. Insert the verbena.jpg file from assets folder where you store your Data Files in front of the words "Verbena is one" and add **Verbena** as alternate text.
6. Insert the lantana.jpg file from the assets folder where you store your Data Files in front of the words "Dramatic masses" and add **Lantana** as alternate text.
7. Refresh the Files panel to verify that all three images were copied to the assets folder.
8. Left-align the petunias image.
9. Right-align the verbena image.
10. Left-align the lantana image.
11. Save your work.

Enhance an image and edit alternate text.

1. Apply a 1-pixel border and horizontal spacing of 20 pixels around the verbana image.
2. Apply a 1-pixel border and horizontal spacing of 20 pixels around the verbana image.
3. Apply a 1-pixel border and horizontal spacing of 20 pixels around the lantana image.
4. Save your work, preview it in the browser, then compare your screen to Figure 46.
5. Close the browser and open the tips page and add H Space of 10 and V Space of 10 to the garden_tips.jpg image.

6. Left-align the garden tips image, then compare your screen to Figure 47.
7. Save your work.

Insert a background image and manage graphics.

1. Switch to the plants page, then insert the **daisies.jpg** file as a background image from the assets folder where you store your Data Files.
2. Save your work.
3. Preview the Web page in your browser, then close your browser.
4. Remove the daisies.jpg file from the background.
5. Open the Assets panel, then refresh the Files list.
6. Use the Files panel to delete the daisies.jpg file from the list of images.
7. Refresh the Assets panel, then verify that the daisies.jpg file has been removed from the Web site.
8. View the colors used in the site in the Assets panel, then verify that all are Websafe.
9. Save your work, then close all open pages.

FIGURE 46
Completed Skills Review

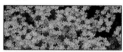

Drop by to see our Featured Spring Plants

Pretty petunias blanket your beds with lush green leaves and bright blooms in assorted colors. Shown is the Moonlight White Petunia (Mini-Spreading). This variety is fast-growing and produces spectacular blooms. Cut them back in July for blooms that will last into the fall. Full sun to partial shade. Great for border plants or hanging baskets.

Verbena is one of our all-time favorites. The variety shown is Blue Silver. Verbena grows rapidly and is a good choice for butterfly gardens. The plants can spread up to two feet wide, so it makes excellent ground cover. Plant in full sun. Heat resistant. Beautiful also in rock gardens. We have several other varieties equally as beautiful.

Dramatic masses of Lantana display summer color for your beds or containers. The variety shown is Golden Dream. Blooms late spring through early fall. This variety produces outstanding color. Plant in full sun with well-drained soil. We carry tall, dwarf, and trailing varieties. You can also overwinter with cuttings.

Stop by to see us soon. We will be happy to help you with your selections.

FIGURE 47
Completed Skills Review

We have some planting tips we would like to share with you as you prepare your gardens this season. Remember, there is always something to be done for your gardens, no matter what the season. Our experienced staff is here to help you plan your gardens, select your plants, prepare your soil, assist you in the planting, and maintain your beds. Check out our calendar for a list of our scheduled classes. All classes are free of charge and on a first-come, first-served basis!

Seasonal Gardening Checklist:

- **Fall** – The time to plant trees and spring blooming bulbs.
- **Winter** – The time to prune fruit trees and finish planting your bulbs.
- **Spring** – The time to prepare your beds, plant annuals, and apply fertilizer to established plants.
- **Summer** – The time to supplement rainfall so that plants get one inch of water per week.

Basic Gardening Tips

1. Select plants according to your climate.
2. In planning your garden, consider the composition, texture, structure, depth, and drainage of your soil.
3. Use compost to improve the structure of your soil.
4. Choose plant foods based on your garden objectives.
5. Generally, plants should receive one inch of water per week.
6. Use mulch to conserve moisture, keep plants cool, and cut down on weeding.

Use Figures 48 and 49 as guides to continue your work on the TripSmart Web site that you began in Project Builder 1 in Chapter 1, and continued to work on in Chapter 2. You are now ready to format text on the newsletter page and begin work on the destinations page that showcases one of the featured tours to Kenya. You want to include some colorful pictures and attractively formatted text on the page.

1. Open the TripSmart Web site.
2. Open dw3_3.html from where you store your Data Files and save it in the tripsmart root folder as **newsletter.html**, overwriting the existing newsletter.html file and not updating the links.
3. Verify that the path for the banner is correctly set to the assets folder of the TripSmart Web site. Create an unordered list from the text beginning "Expandable clothesline" to the end of the page.
4. Create a new CSS rule called **body_text** making sure that the Class option button is selected in the Selector Type section and that

the (New Style Sheet File) option button is selected in the Define in section of the New CSS Rule dialog box.

5. Save the style sheet file as **tripsmart_styles.css** in the TripSmart Web site root folder.
6. Choose a font, size, style, color, and weight of your choice for the body_text style.
7. Apply the **body_text** style to all of the text on the page except the "Ten Packing Essentials" heading on the newsletter page.
8. Create another style called **heading** with a font, size, style, color, and weight of your choice and apply it to the "Ten Packing Essentials" heading.
9. Type **Travel Tidbits** in the Title text box on the Document toolbar, then save and close the newsletter page.
10. Open dw3_4.html from where you store your Data Files and save it in the tripsmart root folder as **destinations.html**, overwriting the existing destinations.html file. Do not update links.
11. Insert **zebra_mothers.jpg** from the assets folder where you store your Data Files to the

left of the sentence beginning "Our next," then add appropriate alternate text.
12. Insert **lion.jpg** from the assets folder where you store your Data Files to the left of the sentence beginning "This lion," then add appropriate alternate text.
13. Align both images using the Align list arrow in the Property inspector with alignments of your choice, then add horizontal spacing, vertical spacing, or borders if desired.
14. Apply the **heading** style to the "Destination: Kenya" heading and the **body_text** style to the rest of the text on the page.
15. Apply any additional formatting to enhance the page appearance, then add the page title **Destination: Kenya**.
16. Verify that the Accessibility Preference option is turned on.
17. Save your work, then preview the destinations page in your browser. (*Hint:* If previewing the page in Internet Explorer 7, click Information bar when prompted to allow blocked content.)
18. Close your browser, then close all open files.

FIGURE 48
Sample Project Builder 1

Ten Packing Essentials

The next time you are packing for a trip, whether it is for an adventure-backpacking trip to the jungles of Panama or for a weekend in New York , consider our list of "can't do without these" items:

- Expandable clothesline and clothespins – These are handy after you have hand-washed your clothes in the river or hotel sink.
- Paperback book – A book will help pass the time on a long plane trip or a wait in a customs line.
- Small hotel-size shampoo bottle – Shampoo is actually a mild detergent, handy for washing your hair, of course, but also for washing your clothes.
- Travel alarm clock – Don't depend on wake-up calls or a hotel clock to keep you from an important meeting time.
- Small flashlight – You never know when a flashlight will come in handy. Even five-star hotels have been known to lose power at times. Invaluable for snake spotting at night in the woods!
- Zippered plastic bags – These are so handy for storing a number of things: snacks, dirty clothes, wet clothes, small items that would get "lost" in your bag, like pens, tape, and your expandable clothesline and clothespins!
- Guidebook – There are many great guidebooks that range from guides for students on a shoestring budget to guides on shopping for fine antiques in Italy . Take advantage of available research to obtain general background knowledge of your destination.
- Backpack – Backpacks are versatile, easy to carry, and have enough style variations to appeal to all ages and sexes. They hold a lot of your essential items!
- Packing cubes – Packing cubes are zippered nylon bags that are great for organizing your packed items. You can squeeze the air out of the packed cubes, conserving space in your bag.

FIGURE 49
Sample Project Builder 2

Destination: Kenya

Our next Photo Safari to Kenya has now been scheduled with a departure date of May 5 and a return date of May 23. Come join us and take some beautiful pictures like these two Grevy's zebras nursing their young at Samburu National Reserve. Our flight will leave New York for London, where you will have dayrooms reserved before flying all night to Nairobi, Kenya. To provide the finest in personal attention, this tour will be limited to no more than sixteen persons. Game drives will take place early each morning and late afternoon to provide maximum opportunity for game viewing, as the animals are most active at these times. We will visit five game reserves to allow for a variety of animal populations and scenery.

This lion is relaxing in the late afternoon sun. Notice the scar under his right ear. He might have received that when he was booted out of his pride as a young lion. We will be spending most nights in tented camps listening to the night sounds of hunters such as this magnificent animal. Enjoy visiting native villages and trading with the local businessmen. Birding enthusiasts will enjoy adding to their bird lists with Kenya's over 300 species of birds. View the beginning of the annual migration of millions of wildebeest, a spectacular sight. The wildebeest are traveling from the Serengeti Plain to the Mara in search of water and grass. Optional excursions include ballooning over the Masai Mara, fishing on Lake Victoria, camel rides at Amboseli Serena Lodge, and golfing at the Aberdare Country Club. Lake Victoria is the largest freshwater lake

In this exercise, you continue your work on the Carolyne's Creations Web site that you started in Project Builder 2 in Chapter 1, and continued to build in Chapter 2. You are now ready to add two new pages to the Web site. One page will display featured items in the kitchen store and one will be used to showcase a recipe. Figures 50 and 51 show possible solutions for this exercise. Your finished pages will look different if you choose different formatting options.

1. Open the Carolyne's Creations Web site.
2. Open dw3_5.html from where you store your Data Files, save it to the Web site root folder as **recipes.html**, overwriting the existing file and not updating the links.
3. Format the list of ingredients as an unordered list.
4. Create a CSS rule named **body_text** and save the style sheet file as **cc_styles.css** in the Web site root folder. Use any formatting options that you like, and then apply the body_text style to all text except the text "Cranberry Ice" and "Directions."
5. Create another style called **headings** using appropriate formatting options and apply it to the text "Cranberry Ice" and "Directions."
6. Insert the file **cranberry_ice.jpg** from where you store your Data Files, then place it on the page, using alignment, horizontal space, and vertical space settings. (*Hint*: In Figure 50 the align setting is set to left, H space is set to 30, and V space is set to 10.
7. Add appropriate alternate text to the banner, then save and close the file.
8. Open dw3_6.html from where you store your Data Files and save it as **shop.html**, overwriting the existing file and not updating the links.
9. Attach the **cc_styles.css** style sheet and create a new style named **sub_head** to use in formatting the text "January Specials - Multifunctional Pot and Cutlery Set." Use any formatting options that you like. Apply the **body_text** style to the rest of the text on the page.
10. Insert the **pot_knives.jpg** image from the assets folder where you store your Data Files next to the paragraph beginning "We try," choosing your own alignment and spacing settings and adding appropriate alternate text.
11. Save all pages, then preview both new pages in the browser, (*Hint:* If previewing the page in Internet Explorer 7, click the Information bar when prompted to allow blocked content.)
12. Close your browser, then close all open pages.

FIGURE 50

Completed Project Builder 2

Home | Shop | Classes | Catering | Recipes

This is one of our most requested desserts. It is simple, elegant, and refreshing. You will need a small electric ice cream maker to produce the best results.

Cranberry Ice

- 3 pts. fresh cranberries
- 1 1/2 pts. sugar
- juice of 1 1/2 lemons
- 1 cup whipping cream
- dash salt

Directions:

Boil cranberries in 3 pints of water. When soft, strain. Add the sugar to the juice and bring to a brisk boil. Cool. Add the lemon juice and freeze to a soft mush. Stir in whipping cream and freeze in an ice cream maker. Serves 14.

This recipe was given to us by Cosie Simmons, who served it as one of her traditions at Thanksgiving and Christmas family gatherings.

FIGURE 51

Completed Project Builder 2

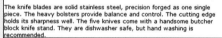
Home | Shop | Classes | Catering | Recipes

Our small storefront is filled with wonderful kitchen accessories and supplies. We also have a large assortment of gourmet items from soup mixes to exotic teas and coffee — perfect for gift baskets for any occasion. We deliver to homes and offices, as well as dorms and hospitals.

January Specials: Multifunctional Pot and Cutlery Set

We try to feature special items each month and love to promote local foods. This month's features: A large multifunctional pot for tempting soups and stews and a professional grade cutlery set.

The pot is made of polished stainless steel with a tempered glass lid so you can peak without lifting the lid to monitor progress. A pasta insert lifts out for draining. Each piece is dishwasher safe. The handles remain cool to the touch while the pot is heating on the stovetop.

The knife blades are solid stainless steel, precision forged as one single piece. The heavy bolsters provide balance and control. The cutting edge holds its sharpness well. The five knives come with a handsome butcher block knife stand. They are dishwasher safe, but hand washing is recommended.

Don Chappell is a new sixth-grade history teacher. He is reviewing educational Web sites for information he can use in his classroom.

1. Connect to the Internet, then navigate to the Library of Congress Web site at *www.loc.gov*. The Library of Congress Web site is shown in Figure 52.
2. Which fonts are used for the main content on the home—serif or sans-serif? Are the same fonts used consistently on the other pages in the Web site?
3. Do you see ordered or unordered lists on any pages in the Web site? If so, how are they used?
4. Use the Source command on the View menu to view the source code to see if a style sheet was used.
5. Do you see the use of Cascading Style Sheets noted in the source code?
6. Select another site from the list and compare the use of text on the two sites.

FIGURE 52
Design Project

Library of Congress Web site - www.loc.gov

In this assignment, you will continue to work on the Web site that you started in Chapter 1, and continued to build in Chapter 2. No Data Files are supplied. You are building this Web site from chapter to chapter, so you must do each Portfolio Project assignment in each chapter to complete your Web site.

You continue building your Web site by designing and completing a page that contains a list, headings, body text, images, and a background. During this process, you will develop a style sheet and add several styles to it. You will insert appropriate images on your page and enhance them for maximum effect. You will also check for Non-Websafe colors and remove any that you find.

1. Consult your storyboard and decide which page to create and develop for this chapter.
2. Plan the page content for the page and make a sketch of the layout. Your sketch should include at least one ordered or unordered list, appropriate headings, body text, several images, and a background color or image. Your sketch should also show where the body text and headings should be placed on the page and what styles should be used for each type of text. You should plan on creating at least two styles.

3. Create the page using your sketch for guidance.
4. Create a Cascading Style Sheet for the Web site and add to it the styles you decided to use. Apply the styles to the appropriate content.
5. Access the images you gathered in Chapter 2, and place them on the page so that the page matches the sketch you created in Step 2. Add a background image if you want, and appropriate alternate text for each image.
6. Remove any Non-Websafe colors.
7. Identify any files in the Assets panel that are currently not used in the Web site. Decide which of these assets should be removed, then delete these files.

8. Preview the new page in a browser, then check for page layout problems and broken links. Make any necessary corrections in Dreamweaver, then preview the page again in the browser. Repeat this process until you are satisfied with the way the page looks in the browser. (*Hint:* If previewing the page in Internet Explorer 7, click the Information bar when prompted to allow blocked content.)
9. Use the checklist in Figure 53 to check all the pages in your site.
10. Close the browser, then close the open pages.

FIGURE 53
Portfolio Project check list

Web Site Checklist

1. Does each page have a page title?
2. Does the home page have a description and keywords?
3. Does the home page contain contact information?
4. Does every page in the Web site have consistent navigation links?
5. Does the home page have a last updated statement that will automatically update when the page is saved?
6. Do all paths for links and images work correctly?
7. Do all images have alternate text?
8. Are all colors Websafe?
9. Are there any unnecessary files you can delete from the assets folder?
10. Is there a style sheet with at least two styles?
11. Did you apply the styles to all text blocks?
12. Do all pages view well using at least two different browsers?

chapter

4 WORKING WITH LINKS

1. Create external and internal links

2. Create internal links to named anchors

3. Insert rollovers with Flash text

4. Create, modify, and copy a navigation bar

5. Create an image map

6. Manage Web site links

4 WORKING WITH
LINKS

Introduction

What makes Web sites so powerful are the links that connect one page to another within a Web site or to any page on the Web. Although you can add graphics, animations, movies, and other enhancements to a Web site to make it visually attractive, the links you include are often a site's most essential components. Links that connect the pages within a Web site are always very important because they help viewers navigate between the pages of the site. However, if one of your goals is to keep viewers from leaving your Web site, you might want to avoid including links to other Web sites. For example, most e-commerce sites include only links to other pages in the site to discourage shoppers from leaving the site. In this chapter, you will create links to other pages in The Striped Umbrella Web site and to other sites on the Web. You will also insert a navigation bar that contains images instead of text, and check the links in The Striped Umbrella

Web site to make sure they all work correctly.

Understanding Internal and External Links

Web pages contain two types of links: internal links and external links. **Internal links** are links to Web pages in the same Web site, and **external links** are links to Web pages in other Web sites or to e-mail addresses. Both internal and external links have two important parts that work together. The first part of a link is the element that viewers see and click on a Web page, for example, text, an image, or a button. The second part of a link is the **path**, or the name and location of the Web page or file that will open when the element is clicked. Setting and maintaining the correct paths for all your links is essential to avoid having broken links in your site, which can easily cause a visitor to click away immediately.

Tools You'll Use

Named anchor button

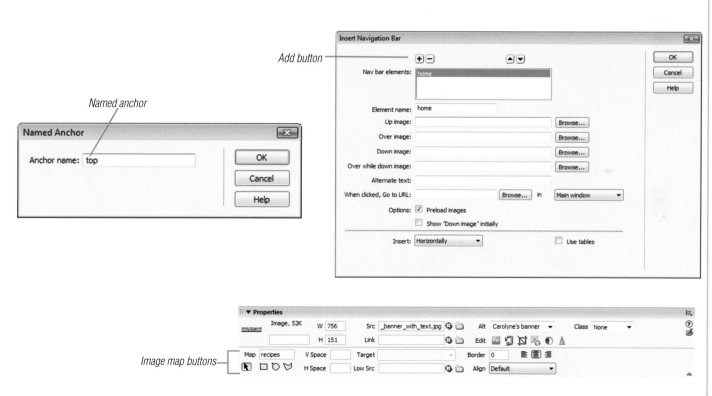

Named anchor

Add button

Image map buttons

CREATE EXTERNAL AND
INTERNAL LINKS

What You'll Do

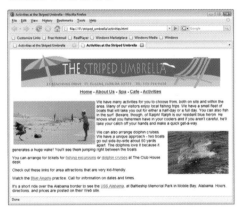

In this lesson, you will create external links on The Striped Umbrella activities page that link to Web sites related to area attractions. You will also create internal links to other pages within The Striped Umbrella Web site.

Creating External Links

A good Web site usually includes a variety of external links to other related Web sites so that viewers can get more information on a particular topic. To create an external link, you first select the text or object that you want to serve as a link, then you type the absolute path to the destination Web page in the Link text box in the Property inspector. An **absolute path** is a path used for external links that includes the complete address for the destination page, including the protocol (such as http://)

and the complete **URL** (Uniform Resource Locator), or address, of the destination page. When necessary, the Web page filename and folder hierarchy are also part of an absolute path. Figure 1 shows an example of an absolute path showing the protocol, URL, and filename. After you enter external links on a Web page, you can view them in the site map. An example for the code for an external link would be <a href="http://www.adobe.com" Adobe Web site </a>.

FIGURE 1
An example of an absolute path

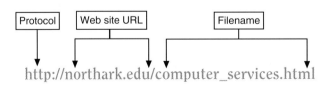

http://northark.edu/computer_services.html

Creating Internal Links

Each page in a Web site usually focuses on an individual category or topic. You should make sure that the home page provides links to each major page in the site, and that all pages in the site contain numerous internal links so that viewers can move easily from page to page. To create an internal link, you first select the text element or image that you want to use to make a link, and then use the Browse for File icon next to the Link text box in the Property inspector to specify the relative path to the destination page. A **relative path** is a type of path used to reference Web pages and image files within the same Web site. Relative paths include the filename and folder location of a file. Figure 2 shows an example of a relative path. Table 1 describes absolute paths and relative paths. Relative paths can either be site-root relative or document-relative. You can also use the Point to File icon in the Property inspector to point to the file you want to use for the link, or drag the file you want to use for the link from the Files panel into the Link text box on the Property inspector.

You should take great care in managing your internal links to make sure they work correctly and are timely and relevant to the page content. You should design the navigation structure of your Web site so that viewers are never more than three or four clicks away from the page they are seeking. An example for the code for an internal link would be
<a href="activities.html" Activities page </a>.

FIGURE 2
An example of a relative path

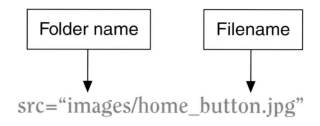

src="images/home_button.jpg"

TABLE 1: Description of absolute and relative paths

type of path	description	examples
Absolute path	Used for external links and specifies protocol, URL, and filename of destination page	*http://www.yahoo.com/recreation*
Relative path	Used for internal links and specifies location of file relative to the current page	spa.html or assets/heron.gif
Root-relative path	Used for internal links when publishing to a server that contains many Web sites or where the Web site is so large it requires more than one server	/striped_umbrella/activities.html
Document-relative path	Used in most cases for internal links and specifies the location of file relative to current page	cafe.html or assets/heron.gif

Create an external link

1. Open The Striped Umbrella Web site, open dw4_1.html from where you store your Data Files, then save it as **activities** in the striped_umbrella root folder, overwriting the existing activities page, but not updating links.

2. Attach the su_style.css file, then apply the **body_text style** to the paragraphs of text on the page (not to the navigation bar).

3. Select the first broken image, click the **Browse for File icon** next to the Src text box, then select the **heron_waiting_small.jpg** in the Data Files folder to save the image in your assets folder.

4. Repeat Step 3 for the second image, **two_dolphins_small.jpg**.

5. Scroll down, then select the text "Blue Angels."

6. Click in the Link text box in the Property inspector, type **http://www.blueangels. navy.mil**, press **[Enter]** (Win) or **[return]** (Mac), then compare your screen to Figure 3.

7. Repeat Steps 5 and 6 to create a link for the USS Alabama site in the next paragraph: **http://www.ussalabama.com.**

8. Save your work, preview the page in your browser, test all the links to make sure they work, then close your browser.

> TIP You must have an active Internet connection to test the links. If clicking a link does not open a page, make sure you typed the URL correctly in the Link text box.

You opened The Striped Umbrella Web site, replaced the existing activities page, attached the su_styles.css.file, applied the body_text style to the text, then added two external links to other sites on the page. You also tested each link in your browser.

FIGURE 3

Creating an external link to the Blue Angels Web site

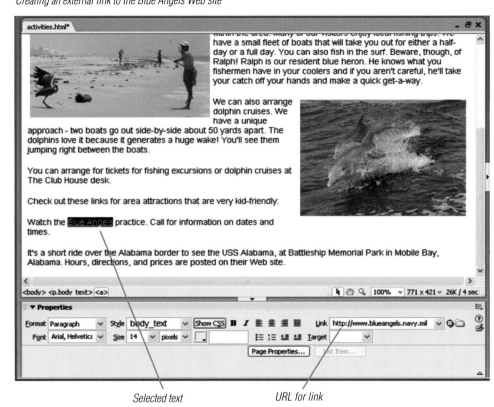

Selected text   URL for link

Typing URLs

Typing URLs in the Link text box in the Property inspector can be very tedious. When you need to type a long and complex URL, it is easy to make mistakes and create a broken link. You can avoid such mistakes by copying and pasting the URL from the Address text box (Internet Explorer) or Location bar (Mozilla Firefox) to the Link text box in the Property inspector. Copying and pasting a URL ensures that the URL is entered correctly.

FIGURE 4
Site map displaying external links on the activities page

Click button to collapse window

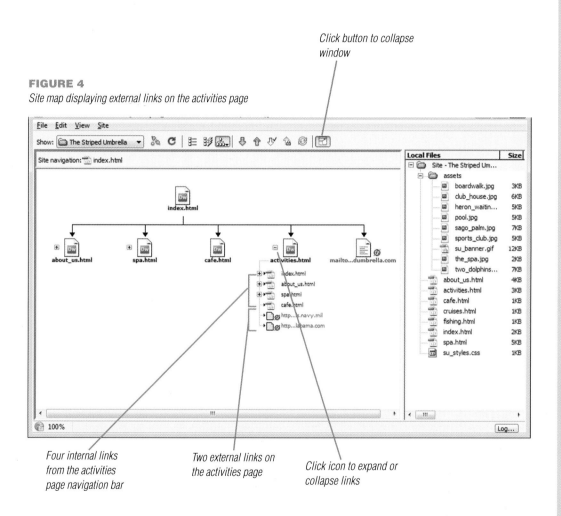

Four internal links from the activities page navigation bar

Two external links on the activities page

Click icon to expand or collapse links

1. Click the **Expand to show local and remote sites button** 🗗 on the Files panel to expand the Files panel.

2. Click the **Site Map list arrow** on the toolbar, then click **Map and Files**.

    Four links from the navigation bar appear as internal links.

    > TIP If you want to view or hide page titles in the site map, click View on the menu bar, point to Site Map Options, then click Show Page Titles (Win) or click the Options button in the Files panel group title bar, point to View, then click Show Page Titles (Mac).

3. Click the **plus sign** to the left of the activities page icon in the site map (if necessary) to view a list of the two external links you created, as shown in Figure 4.

4. Click the **minus sign** to the left of the activities page icon in the site map to collapse the list of links.

5. Click the **Collapse to show only local or remote site button** 🗗 on the toolbar.

    You viewed The Striped Umbrella site map and expanded the view of the activities page to display the two external links you added.

Create an internal link

1. Select the text "fishing excursions" in the third paragraph.

2. Click the **Browse for File icon** next to the Link text box in the Property inspector, then double-click **fishing.html** in the Select File dialog box to set the relative path to the fishing page.

    Notice that fishing.html appears in the Link text box in the Property inspector, as shown in Figure 5.

    TIP To collapse all open panels below the Document window, such as the Link Checker or the Property inspector, click the expander arrow in the center of the bottom border of the Document window. Pressing [F4] will hide all panels, including the ones on the right side of the screen.

3. Select the text "dolphin cruises" in the same sentence.

4. Click the **Browse for File icon** next to the Link text box in the Property inspector, then double-click **cruises.html** in the Select File dialog box to specify the relative path to the cruises page.

    The words "dolphin cruises" are now a link to the cruises page.

5. Save your work, preview the page in your browser to verify that the internal links work correctly, then close your browser.

    The fishing and cruises pages do not have page content yet, but serve as placeholders until they do.

You created two internal links on the activities page, and then tested the links in your browser.

FIGURE 5
Creating an internal link on the activities page

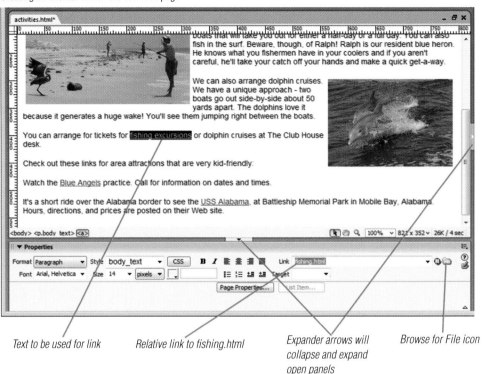

Text to be used for link   Relative link to fishing.html   Expander arrows will collapse and expand open panels   Browse for File icon

Using case-sensitive links

When text is said to be "case sensitive," it means that the text will be treated differently when it is typed using uppercase letters rather than lowercase letters, or vice-versa. With some operating systems, such as Windows, it doesn't matter which case you use when you enter URLs. However, with other systems, such as UNIX, it does matter. To be sure that your links will work with all systems, use lowercase letters for all links. This is another good reason to select and copy a URL from the browser address bar, and then paste it in the link text box or code in Dreamweaver when creating an external link. You won't have to worry about missing a case change.

FIGURE 6

Site map displaying external and internal links on the activities page

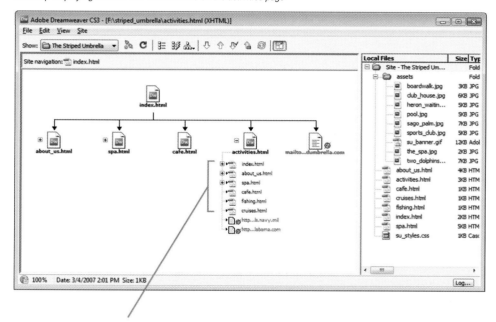

Six internal links, four from the navigation
bar and two from text links

1. Click the **Expand to show local and remote sites button** ⊡ on the Files panel.

2. Click the **Site Map list arrow**, then click **Map and Files** (if necessary).

   TIP Under Site Map Options on the View menu, verify that Show Page Titles is not selected.

3. Click the **plus sign** to the left of the activities page icon.

   A list of eight links appears below the activities page icon, as shown in Figure 6. Two are external links, and six are internal links.

   TIP If your links do not display correctly, re-create the site cache. To re-create the site cache, click Site on the menu bar, click Advanced, then click Re-create Site Cache.

4. Click the **Collapse to show only local or remote site button** ⊡.

5. Close the activities page.

You viewed the links on the activities page in the site map.

CREATE INTERNAL LINKS
TO NAMED ANCHORS

What You'll Do

In this lesson, you will insert five named anchors on the spa page: one for the top of the page and four for each of the spa services lists. You will then create internal links to each named anchor.

Inserting Named Anchors

Some Web pages have so much content that viewers must scroll repeatedly to get to the bottom of the page and then back up to the top of the page. To make it easier for viewers to navigate to specific areas of a page without scrolling, you can use a combination of internal links and named anchors. A **named anchor** is a specific location on a Web page that has a descriptive name. Named anchors act as targets for internal links and make it easy for viewers to jump to a particular place on the same page quickly. A **target** is the location on a Web page that a browser displays when an internal link is clicked. For example, you can insert a named anchor called "top" at the top of a Web page, and then create a link to it from the bottom of the page. You can also insert named anchors in strategic places on a Web page, such as at the beginning of paragraph headings.

You insert a named anchor using the Named Anchor button in the Common category of the Insert bar, as shown in Figure 7. You then enter the name of the anchor in the Named Anchor dialog box. You should choose short names that describe the named anchor location on the page. Named anchors are represented by yellow anchor icons on a Web page. Selected anchors are represented by blue icons. You can show or hide named anchor icons by clicking View on the menu bar, pointing to Visual Aids, and then clicking Invisible Elements.

Creating Internal Links to Named Anchors

Once you create a named anchor, you can create an internal link to it using one of two methods. You can select the text or image on the page that you want to use to make a link, and then drag the Point to File icon from the Property inspector to the named anchor icon on the page. Or, you can select the text or image to which you want to use to make a link, then type # followed by the named anchor name (such as "#top") in the Link text box in the Property inspector.

QUICKTIP

To avoid possible errors, you should create a named anchor before you create a link to it.

FIGURE 7

Named Anchor button on the Insert bar

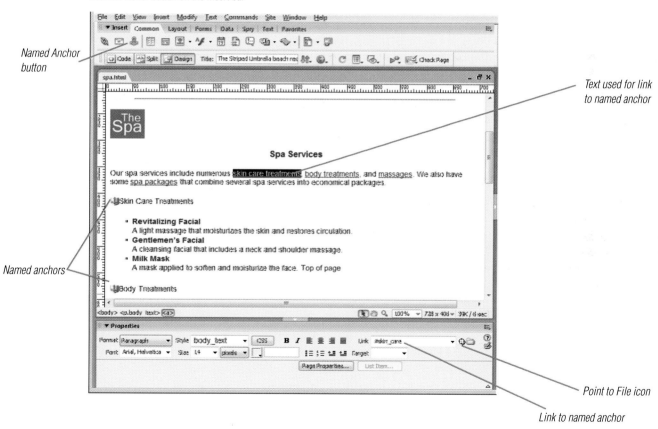

Named Anchor button

Text used for link to named anchor

Named anchors

Point to File icon

Link to named anchor

Insert a named anchor

1. Open the spa page, click the **banner image** to select it, then press [←] to place the insertion point to the left of the banner.

2. Click **View** on the menu bar, point to **Visual Aids**, then verify that Invisible Elements is checked.

   TIP If there is no check mark next to Invisible Elements, this feature is turned off. Click Invisible Elements to turn this feature on.

3. Click the **Common tab** on the Insert bar (if necessary).

4. Click the **Named Anchor button** ⚓ on the Insert bar to open the Named Anchor dialog box, type **top** in the Anchor name text box, compare your screen with Figure 8, then click **OK**.

   An anchor icon now appears before The Striped Umbrella banner.

   TIP Use lowercase letters, no spaces, and no special characters in named anchor names. You should also avoid using a number as the first character in a named anchor name.

   (continued)

FIGURE 8
Named Anchor dialog box

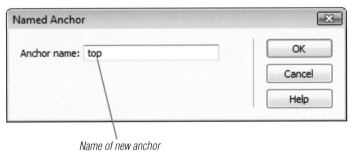

Name of new anchor

Working with Links

5. Click to the left of the Skin Care Treatments heading, then insert a named anchor named **skin_care**.

6. Insert named anchors to the left of the Body Treatments, Massages, and Packages headings using the following names: **body_treatments**, **massages**, and **packages**.

Your screen should resemble Figure 9.

You created five named anchors on the activities page; one at top of the page, and four that will help viewers quickly access the Spa Services headings on the page.

FIGURE 9

Named anchors on the activities page

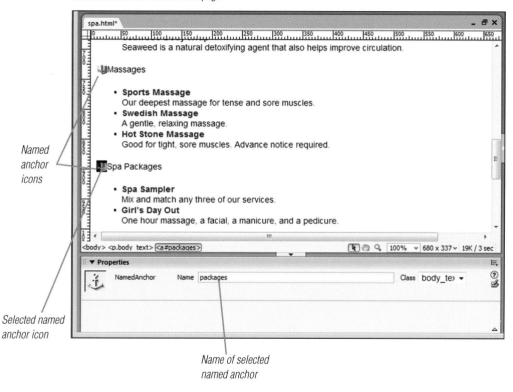

Named anchor icons

Selected named anchor icon

Name of selected named anchor

Create an internal link to a named anchor

1. Select the words "skin care treatments" in the first paragraph, then drag the **Point to File icon** ⊕ from the Property inspector to the anchor named skin_care, as shown in Figure 10.

   The words "skin care treatments" are now linked to the skin_care named anchor. When viewers click the words "skin care treatments" the browser will display the Skin Care Treatments heading at the top of the browser window.

   TIP The name of a named anchor is always preceded by a pound (#) sign in the Link text box in the Property inspector.

2. Create internal links for body treatments, massages, and spa packages in the first paragraph by first selecting each of these words or phrases, then dragging the **Point to File icon** ⊕ to the appropriate named anchor icon.

   The words "body treatments," "massages," and "spa packages" are now links that connect to the Body Treatments, Massages, and Spa Packages headings.

   TIP Once you select the text on the page you want to link, you might need to scroll down to view the named anchor on the screen. Once you see the named anchor on your screen, you can drag the Point to File icon on top of it.

   (continued)

FIGURE 10

Dragging the Point to File icon to a named anchor

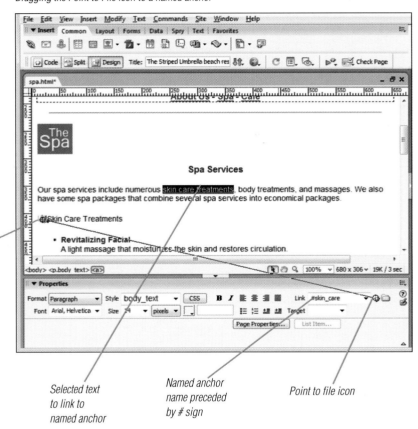

Point to File icon dragged to named anchor

Selected text to link to named anchor

Named anchor name preceded by # sign

Point to file icon

FIGURE 11

Spa page in Mozilla Firefox with internal links to named anchors

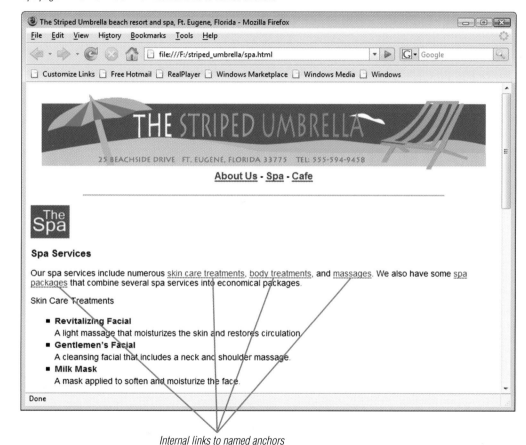

Internal links to named anchors

3. Save your work, preview the page in your browser, as shown in Figure 11, then test the links to each named anchor.

   Notice that when you click the spa packages link in the browser, the associated named anchor appears in the middle of the page instead of at the top. This happens because the spa page is not long enough to position this named anchor at the top of the page.

4. Close your browser.

You created internal links to the named anchors next to the Spa Services headings on the spa page. You then previewed the page in your browser and tested each link.

INSERT ROLLOVERS
WITH FLASH TEXT

What You'll Do

In this lesson, you will use the Insert Flash Text dialog box to create a button that links to the top named anchor on the spa page. You will copy this button to several locations on the spa page, and then change the alignment of each button.

Understanding Flash Text

Flash is an Adobe software application that you can use to create vector-based graphics and animations. **Vector-based graphics** are graphics that are based on mathematical formulas, as opposed to other types of graphic files such as JPG and GIF which are based on pixels. Vector-based graphics have a smoother look and are smaller in file size than pixel-based graphics. Because they download quickly, vector-based graphics are ideal for Web sites. **Flash text** is a vector-based graphic file that contains text. You can insert Flash text to add visual interest to an otherwise dull Web page or to help deliver or reinforce a message. You can use Flash text to create internal or external links. Flash text files are saved with the .swf filename extension.

When Flash text is inserted on a Web page, JavaScript code is added to the page to control the rollover. Dreamweaver automatically creates a folder named Scripts in the root folder, which stores the new JavaScript code

file, AC-RunActiveContent.js. When a viewer views a Web page with Flash text, the JavaScript that runs is stored on the user's, or client's, computer.

QUICKTIP

To view Flash animations, you must have the Flash player installed on your computer. The Flash player is free software that lets you play streaming video and audio.

Inserting Flash Text on a Web Page

You can create Flash text in Dreamweaver without opening the Flash program. To insert Flash text on a Web page, you choose the Common tab on the Insert bar, click the Media list arrow, and then click Flash Text, as shown in Figure 12. Clicking this button opens the Insert Flash Text dialog box, which you use to specify the settings for the Flash text. You first need to specify the text you want to create as Flash text by typing it in the Text text box. You can then specify the font, size, and color of the Flash text, apply bold or italic styles to it, and align it using left, center, or right alignment options. You can also specify a **rollover color,** or the color in which the text will appear when the mouse pointer is placed on it. You also need to enter the path for the destination link in the Link text box. The destination link can be an internal link to another page in the site, to a named anchor on the same page, or to an external link to a page on another Web site. You then use the Target list to specify how to open the destination page. The four options are described in Table 2.

QUICKTIP

Notice that the _parent option in the table displays the page in the parent frameset. A **frameset** is a group of Web pages displayed using more than one **frame** or window.

Before you close the Insert Flash Text dialog box, you need to type a descriptive name for your Flash text file in the Save as text box. Because Flash text files must be saved in the same folder as the page that contains the Flash text, you should save your Flash text files in the root folder of the Web site.

Using Flash Player

To play Flash movies in Dreamweaver and in your browser, you must have the Flash Player installed on your computer. If the Flash Player is not installed, you can download it from the Adobe Web site at *www.adobe.com.* In addition, you need to choose a specific setting in your browser. If you are using Internet Explorer, click Tools on the menu bar, click Internet Options, click the Advanced tab, click the Allow active content to run in files on my computer check box, and then click OK. If you are using another browser, look for a similar setting in your Options or Preferences dialog boxes.

FIGURE 12

Media menu on the Common group

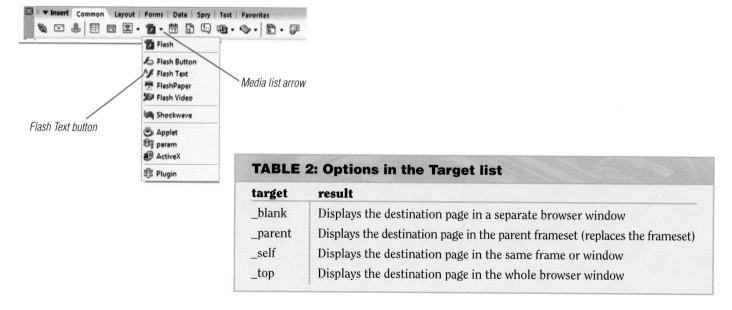

Media list arrow

Flash Text button

TABLE 2: Options in the Target list	
target	**result**
_blank	Displays the destination page in a separate browser window
_parent	Displays the destination page in the parent frameset (replaces the frameset)
_self	Displays the destination page in the same frame or window
_top	Displays the destination page in the whole browser window

Create Flash text

1. Click after the last sentence on the spa page, then press **[Enter]** (Win) or **[return]** (Mac) twice to end the ordered list.

2. Click the **Common tab** on the Insert bar (if necessary), click the **Media list arrow**, then click **Flash Text** to open the Insert Flash Text dialog box.

3. Set the Font to **Arial,** set the Size to **14,** set the Color to **#000066,** set the Rollover color to **#66CCFF,** type **Top of page** in the Text text box, type **spa.html#top** in the Link text box, use the Target list arrow to set the Target to **_top,** type **top.swf** in the Save as text box, as shown in Figure 13, then click **OK**.

4. Type **Link to top of page** in the Flash Accessibility Attributes dialog box, then click **OK**.

   The Top of page Flash text appears as a button at the bottom of the page. When clicked, the browser will display the top of the page.

5. Click **Assets** in the Files panel group, click the **Flash button** on the Assets panel, as shown in Figure 14, click the **Refresh button** (if necessary), click the **top.swf** file, then click the **Play button** to see the Flash text preview.

6. Drag **top.swf** from the Assets panel to the end of the last bulleted entry in each of the spa services groups to insert four top links adding **Link to top of page** in the Object Tag Accessibility Attributes dialog box.

7. Click the **Files panel tab**, then refresh the Files panel (if necessary).

8. Switch to Show Code and Design views to view the JavaScript code shown in Figure 15, then switch back to Design view.

(continued)

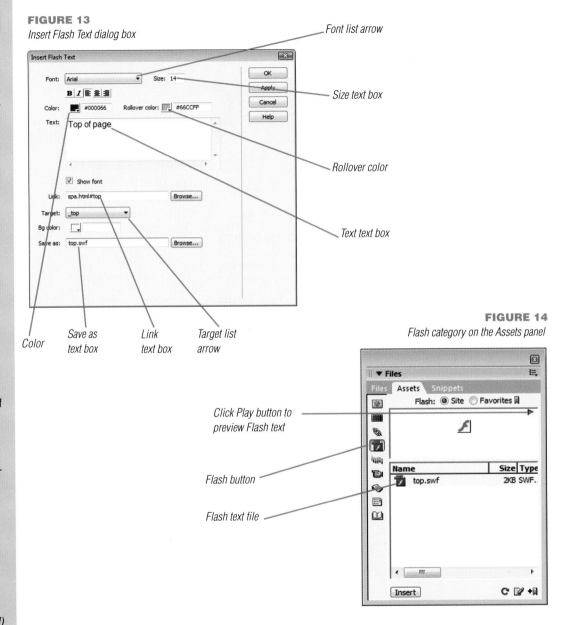

FIGURE 13
Insert Flash Text dialog box

Font list arrow
Size text box
Rollover color
Text text box
Color
Save as text box
Link text box
Target list arrow

FIGURE 14
Flash category on the Assets panel

Click Play button to preview Flash text
Flash button
Flash text file

FIGURE 15

Script added to code and script file added to root folder

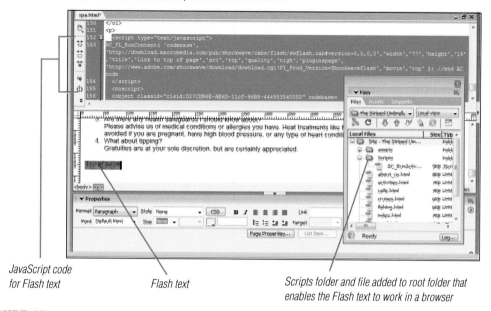

JavaScript code
for Flash text

Flash text

Scripts folder and file added to root folder that
enables the Flash text to work in a browser

FIGURE 16

Flash text aligned to top

Flash text aligned with top of
paragraph text line

9. Save your work, click **OK** in the Copy
Dependent Files dialog box to copy the script
to the root folder, preview the spa page in
your browser, test each Top of page link, then
close your browser.

Dreamweaver added the file
AC_RunActiveContent.js in a new Scripts
folder to the root folder. This file enables the
Flash file to be viewed in a browser. See
Figure 15.

> TIP If the top of the page is already dis-
> played, the window will not move when you
> click the Flash text.

*You used the Insert Flash Text dialog box to create
a Top of page Flash text button that links to the top
named anchor on the spa page. You also inserted
the Top of page button at the end of each spa
service.*

Align Flash text

1. Click the **Top of page button** at the end of the
Skin Care Treatments section, expand the
Property inspector, click the **Align list arrow**
in the Property inspector, then click **Top**.

The Top of page button is now aligned with the
top of the line of text. See Figure 16.

2. Apply the Top alignment setting to the Top of
page button located at the end of the Body Treatments, Massages, and Spa Packages sections.

3. Collapse the Property inspector, turn off
Invisible Elements, then save your work.

4. Preview the spa page in a browser, test each
Top of page button, then close the browser.

You aligned the Flash text.

CREATE, MODIFY, AND COPY
A NAVIGATION BAR

What You'll Do

 In this lesson, you will create a navigation bar on the spa page that can be used to link to each major page in the Web site. The navigation bar will have five elements: home, about us, cafe, spa, and activities. You will also copy the new navigation bar to other pages in the Web site. On each page you will modify the appropriate element state to reflect the current page.

Creating a Navigation Bar Using Images

To make your Web site more visually appealing, you can create a navigation bar with images rather than text. Any images you use in a navigation bar must be created in a graphics software program, such as Adobe Fireworks or Adobe Illustrator. For a browser to display a navigation bar correctly, all image links in the navigation bar must be exactly the same size. You insert a navigation bar by clicking Insert on the menu bar, pointing to Image Objects, then clicking Navigation Bar. The Insert Navigation Bar dialog box appears. You use this dialog box to specify the appearance of each link, called an **element**, in each of four possible states. A **state** is the condition of the element relative to the mouse pointer. The four states are as follows: **Up image** (the state when the mouse pointer is not on top of the element), **Over image** (the state when the mouse pointer is positioned on top of the element), **Down image** (the state when you click the element), and **Over while down image** (the state when the

mouse pointer is positioned over an element that has been clicked). You can create a rollover effect by using different colors or images to represent each element state. You can add many special effects to navigation bars or to links on a Web page. For instance, the Web site shown in Figure 17 contains a navigation bar that uses rollovers and also contains images that link to featured items in the Web site.

When a navigation bar is inserted on a Web page using the Insert Navigation Bar command, JavaScript code is added to the page to make the interaction work with the navigation bar elements. Dreamweaver also creates a Scripts folder and adds it to the root folder to store the newly created AC-RunActiveContent.js file.

> **QUICK**TIP
> You can insert only one navigation bar using the Insert Navigation Bar dialog box or by clicking the Common tab and then selecting Navigation Bar from the Images menu.

Copying and Modifying a Navigation Bar

After you create a navigation bar, you can reuse it and save time by copying and pasting it to the other main pages in your site. Make sure you place the navigation bar in the same position on each page. This practice ensures that the navigation bar will look the same on each page, making it much easier for viewers to navigate to all the pages in a Web site. If you are even one line or one pixel off, the navigation bar will "jump" as it changes position from page to page.

You can then use the Modify Navigation Bar dialog box to customize the appearance of the copied navigation bar on each page. For example, you can change the appearance of the spa navigation bar element on the spa page so that it appears in a different color. Highlighting the navigation element for the current page provides a visual reminder so that viewers can quickly tell which page they are viewing. This process ensures that the navigation bar will not only look consistent across all pages, but will be customized for each page.

FIGURE 17
Ohio Historical Society Web site

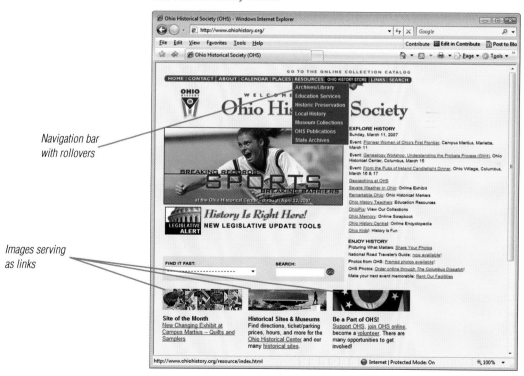

Navigation bar
with rollovers

Images serving
as links

*Ohio Historical Society Web site used with permission from Ohio Historical Society -
www.ohiohistory.org*

Create a navigation bar using images

1. Select the navigation bar (About Us - Spa - Cafe) on the spa page, then delete it.

   The insertion point is now positioned between the banner and the horizontal rule.

2. Click the **Common** tab on the Insert bar (if necessary), click the **Images list arrow**, then click **Navigation Bar**.

3. Type **home** in the Element name text box, click the **Insert list arrow** in the dialog box, click **Horizontally** (if necessary), to specify that the navigation bar be placed horizontally on the page, then remove the check mark in the Use tables check box.

   Be sure to choose Horizontally for the navigation bar orientation and uncheck the Use tables check box. These two options (below the horizontal rule) will not be available in the Modify Navigation Bar dialog box. If you miss these settings now, you will either have to make your corrections directly in the code or start over.

4. Click **Browse** next to the Up image text box, navigate to the assets folder where you store your Data Files, then double-click **home_up.gif**.

   The path to the file home_up.gif appears in the Up image text box, as shown in Figure 18.

5. Click **Browse** next to the Over image text box to specify a path to the file home_down.gif located in the chapter_4 assets folder.

6. Click **Browse** next to the Down image text box to specify a path to the file home_down.gif

   (continued)

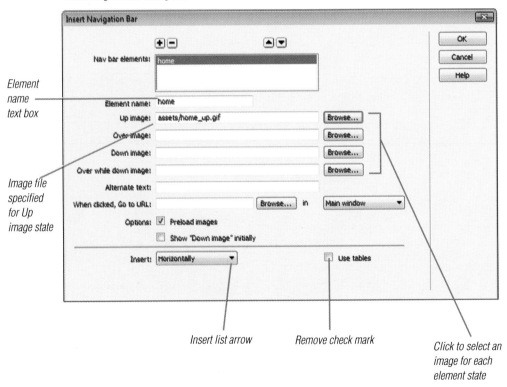

FIGURE 18
Insert Navigation bar dialog box

Element name text box

Image file specified for Up image state

Insert list arrow

Remove check mark

Click to select an image for each element state

FIGURE 19

Insert Navigation bar dialog box

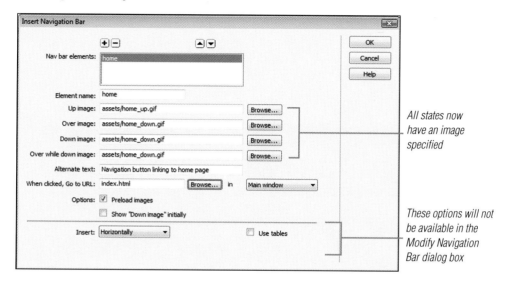

All states now
have an image
specified

These options will not
be available in the
Modify Navigation
Bar dialog box

FIGURE 20

Home element of the navigation bar

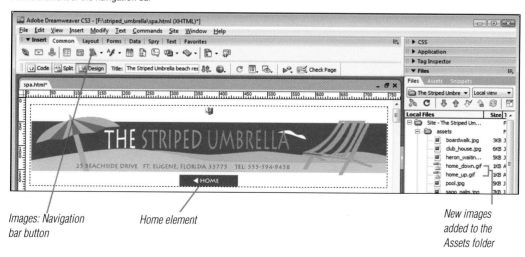

Images: Navigation
bar button

Home element

New images
added to the
Assets folder

located in the chapter_4 assets folder, overwriting the existing file.

Because this is a simple navigation bar, you
use the home_down.gif image for the Over,
Down, and Over while down image states.

> TIP   Instead of clicking Browse in Steps
> 6 and 7, you could copy the path of the
> home_down.gif file in the Over image text
> box and paste it to the Down image and
> Over while down image text boxes. You
> could also reference the home_down.gif file
> in The Striped Umbrella assets folder once it
> is copied there in Step 5.

7. Click **Browse** next to the Over while down
   image text box to specify a path to the
   file home_down.gif located in the chapter_4
   assets folder, overwriting the existing file.

   By specifying one graphic for the Up image
   state, and another graphic for the Over
   image, Down image, and Over while down
   image states, you will create a rollover effect.

8. Type **Navigation button linking to home page**
   in the Alternate text text box, click **Browse** next
   to the When clicked, Go to URL text box, double-
   click **index.html** in the striped_umbrella root
   folder, then compare your screen to Figure 19.

9. Click **OK**, refresh the Files panel to view the
   new images you added to The Striped Umbrella
   assets folder, deselect the button, place the
   insertion point in front of the button, press
   [Backspace] (Win) or **[delete]** (Mac), press
   [Shift][Enter] (Win) or **[Shift][return]** (Mac),
   compare your screen to Figure 20, then save
   your work.

*You used the Insert Navigation Bar dialog box to
create a navigation bar for the spa page and added
the home element to it. You used one image for
the Up state and one for the other three states.*

Add elements to a navigation bar

1. Click **Modify** on the menu bar, then click **Navigation Bar**.

2. Click the **Add button** + in the Modify Navigation Bar dialog box, then type **about_us** in the Element name text box.

   TIP You use the Add button + to add a new navigation element to the navigation bar, and the Delete button − to delete a navigation element from the navigation bar.

3. Click **Browse** next to the Up image text box, navigate to the chapter_4 assets folder, click **about_us_up.gif**, then click **OK** (Win) or **Choose** (Mac).

   TIP If a dialog box appears asking if you would like to copy the file to the root folder, click Yes, then click Save (Mac).

4. Click **Browse** next to the Over image text box to specify a path to the file **about_us_down.gif** located in the chapter_4 assets folder.

5. Click **Browse** next to the Down image text box to specify a path to the file **about_us_down.gif** located in the chapter_4 assets folder, overwriting the existing file.

6. Repeat Step 5 for the **Over while down** image.

7. Type **Navigation button linking to about_us page** in the Alternate text text box, click **Browse** next to the When clicked, Go to URL text box, double-click **about_us.html**, then compare your screen to Figure 21.

   (continued)

FIGURE 21
Add elements to a navigation bar

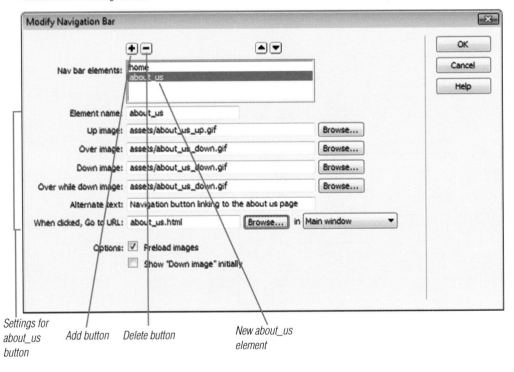

Settings for about_us button

Add button

Delete button

New about_us element

FIGURE 22
Navigation bar with all elements added

TABLE 3: Settings to use in the Modify Navigation Bar dialog box for each new element

dialog box item	cafe element	spa element	activities element
Up image file	cafe_up.gif	spa_up.gif	activities_up.gif
Over image file	cafe_down.gif	spa_down.gif	activities_down.gif
Down image file	cafe_down.gif	spa_down.gif	activities_down.gif
Over while down image file	cafe_down.gif	spa_down.gif	activities_down.gif
Alternate text	Navigation button linking to cafe page	Navigation button linking to the spa page	Navigation button linking to activities page
When clicked, Go to URL	cafe.html	spa.html	activities.html

8. Using the information provided in Table 3, add three more navigation bar elements in the Modify Navigation Bar dialog box called **cafe**, **spa**, and **activities.**

   TIP   All files listed in the table are located in the assets folder of the chapter_4 folder where you store your Data Files.

9. Click **OK** to close the Modify Navigation Bar dialog box.

10. Save your work, preview the page in your browser, compare your screen to Figure 22, check each link to verify that each element works correctly, then close your browser.

   TIP   If you see spaces between each button in your browser, select the first button, press [→], then press delete. Continue for each button to remove each space after the button.

You completed The Striped Umbrella navigation bar by adding four more elements to it, each of which contain links to four pages in the site. All images added to the navigation bar are now stored in the assets folder of The Striped Umbrella Web site.

Copy and paste a navigation bar

1. Place the insertion point to the left of the navigation bar, press and hold **[Shift]**, then click to the right of the navigation bar.

2. Click **Edit** on the menu bar, then click **Copy**.

3. Double-click **activities.html** in the Files panel to open the activities page.

4. Select the original navigation bar on the page, click **Edit** on the menu bar, click **Paste**, then compare your screen to Figure 23.

5. Click in front of the navigation bar, press **[Backspace]** (Win) or **[delete]** (Mac), then press **[Shift][Enter]** (Win) or **[shift][return]** (Mac).

You copied the navigation bar from the spa page and pasted it on the activities page.

Customize a navigation bar

1. Click **Modify** on the menu bar, then click **Navigation Bar** to open the Modify Navigation Bar dialog box.

2. Click **activities** in the Nav bar elements text box, then click the **Show "Down image" initially check box**, as shown in Figure 24.

   An asterisk appears next to activities in the Nav bar elements text box, indicating that this element will be displayed in the Down image state initially. The sand-colored activities navigation element normally used for the Down image state of the activities navigation bar element will remind viewers that they are on the activities page.

   (continued)

FIGURE 23
Navigation bar copied to the activities page

FIGURE 24
Changing settings for the activities element

Asterisk is placed next to the element name

Show "Down image" initially is selected

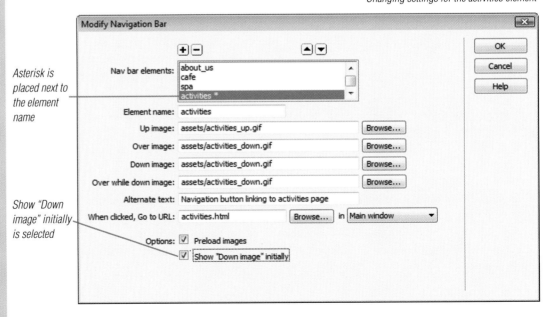

FIGURE 25

about_us page with the modified navigation bar

When you arrive at The Striped Umbrella, check in at The Club House. Look for the signs that will direct you to registration. Our beautiful club house is the home base for our registration offices, The Sand Crab Cafe, and The Spa. Registration is open from 8:00 a.m. until 6:00 p.m. Please call to make arrangements if you plan to arrive after 6:00 p.m. The cafe and spa hours are both posted and listed in the

3. Click **OK** to save the new settings and close the Modify Navigation Bar dialog box, then save and close the activities page.

4. Repeat Steps 1 through 3 to modify the navigation bar on the spa page to show the Down image initially for the spa element, then save and close the spa page.

    TIP The Show "Down image" initially check box should be checked only for the element that links to the current page.

5. Open the home page, paste the navigation bar on top of the original navigation bar, remove any spaces before the navigation bar, add a line break, then modify the navigation bar to show the Down image initially for the home element.

6. Save and close the home page.

7. Open the about us page, paste the navigation bar on top of the original navigation bar, then use the Modify Navigation Bar dialog box to specify that the Down image be displayed initially for the about_us element, then compare your screen to Figure 25.

8. Save your work, preview the current page in your browser, test the navigation bar on the home, about us, spa, and activities pages, then close your browser.

    The cafe page is blank at this point, so use the Back button when you test the spa link to return to the page you were viewing previously.

You modified the navigation bar on the activities page to show the activities element in the Down state initially. You then copied the navigation bar to two additional pages in The Striped Umbrella Web site, modifying the navigation bar elements each time to show the Down image state initially.

CREATE AN
IMAGE MAP

What You'll Do

 In this lesson, you will create an image map by placing a hotspot on The Striped Umbrella banner that will link to the home page.

Another way to create links for Web pages is to combine them with images by creating an image map. An **image map** is an image that has one or more hotspots placed on top of it. A **hotspot** is a clickable area on an image that, when clicked, links to a different location on the page or to another Web page. For example, a map of the United States could have a hotspot placed on each individual state so that viewers could click a state to link to information about that state. The National Park Service Web site is shown in Figure 26. As you place your mouse over a state, the state name, a photo, and introductory sentences from that state's page are displayed. When you click a state, you will be linked to information about national parks in

that state. You can create hotspots by first selecting the image on which you want to place a hotspot, and then using one of the hotspot tools in the Property inspector to define its shape.

There are several ways to create image maps to make them more user-friendly and accessible. One way is to be sure to include alternate text for each hotspot. Another is to draw the hotspot boundaries a little larger than they need to be to cover the area you want to set as a link. This allows viewers a little leeway when they place their mouse over the hotspot by creating a larger target area for them.

The hotspot tools in Dreamweaver make creating image maps a snap. In addition to the Rectangular Hotspot tool, there is an Oval Hotspot tool and a Polygon Hotspot tool for creating different shapes. These tools can be used to create any shape hotspot that you need. For instance, on a map of the United States, you can draw an outline around each state with the Polygon Hotspot tool. You can then make each state "clickable." Hotspots can be easily changed and rearranged on the image. Use the Pointer Hotspot tool to select the hotspot you would like to edit. You can drag one of the hotspot selector handles to change the size or shape of a hotspot. You can also move the hotspot by dragging it to a new position on the image. It is a good idea to limit the number of complex hotspots in an image because the code can become too lengthy for the page to download in a reasonable length of time.

FIGURE 26

Viewing an image map on the National Park Service Web site

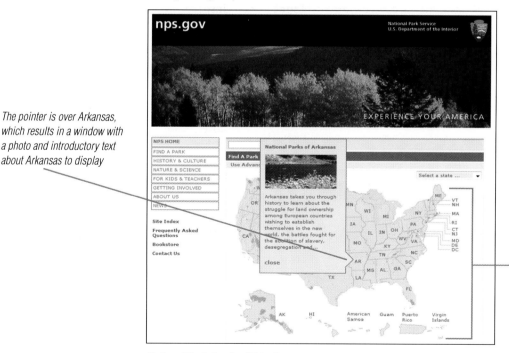

The pointer is over Arkansas, which results in a window with a photo and introductory text about Arkansas to display

Clicking an individual state will link to information about parks in that state

National Park Service Web site: www.nps.gov

Create an image map

1. Open or switch to the activities page, if necessary, select the banner, then click the **Rectangular Hotspot tool** ☐ in the Property inspector.

2. Drag the **pointer** to create a rectangle over the umbrella in the banner, as shown in Figure 27, then click **OK** to close the dialog box that reminds you to supply alternate text for the hotspot.

   TIP To adjust the shape of a hotspot, click the Pointer Hotspot tool ▶ in the Property inspector, then drag a sizing handle on the hotspot.

3. Use the **Point to File icon** ⊕ in the Property inspector to link the index page to the hotspot.

4. Type **home** in the Map text box in the Property inspector to give the image map a unique name.

5. Click the **Target list arrow** in the Property inspector, then click **_top**.

   When the hotspot is clicked, the home page will open in the same window.

   (continued)

(continued)

FIGURE 27
Properties of the rectangular hotspot on the banner

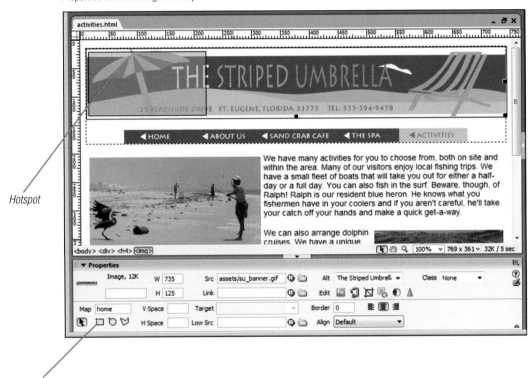

Hotspot

Rectangular
Hotspot tool

FIGURE 28

Properties of the hotspot

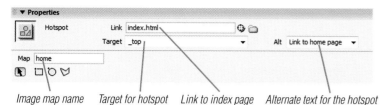

Image map name   Target for hotspot   Link to index page   Alternate text for the hotspot

6. Type **Link to home page** in the Alt text box in the Property inspector, as shown in Figure 28. then press **[Enter]** (Win) or **[return]** (Mac).

7. Save your work, then preview the page in your browser to test the link on the image map.

   As you place the pointer over the hotspot, you see the alternate text displayed and the pointer indicates the link (Win), as shown in Figure 29.

8. Close the browser, then close all open pages.

You created an image map on the banner of the activities page using the Rectangular Hotspot tool. You then linked the hotspot to the home page.

FIGURE 29

Preview of the image map on the activities page in the browser

Alternate text for hotspot

MANAGE WEB SITE
LINKS

What You'll Do

In this lesson, you will use some of Dreamweaver's reporting features to check The Striped Umbrella Web site for broken links and orphaned files.

Managing Web Site Links

Because the World Wide Web changes constantly, Web sites may be up one day and down the next. If a Web site changes server locations or goes down due to technical difficulties or a power failure, the links to it become broken. Broken links, like misspelled words on a Web page, indicate that a Web site is not being maintained diligently.

Checking links to make sure they work is an ongoing and crucial task you need to perform on a regular basis. You must check external links manually by reviewing your Web site in a browser and clicking each link to make sure it works correctly. The Check Links Sitewide feature is a helpful tool for managing internal links. You can use it to check your entire Web site for the total number of links and the number of links that are okay, external, or broken, and then view the results in the Link Checker panel. The Link Checker panel also provides a list of all of the files used in a Web site, including those that are **orphaned files**, or files that are not linked to any pages in the Web site.

DESIGNTIP   **Considering navigation design issues**

As you work on the navigation structure for a Web site, you should try to limit the number of links on each page to no more than is necessary. Too many links may confuse visitors to your Web site. You should also design links so that viewers can reach the information they want within a few clicks. If finding information takes more than three or four clicks, the viewer may become discouraged or lost in the site. It's a good idea to provide visual clues on each page to let viewers know where they are, much like a "You are here" marker on a store directory at the mall, or a bread crumbs trail. A **bread crumbs trail** is a list of links that provides a path from the initial page you opened in a Web site to the page that you are currently viewing.

FIGURE 30

Link Checker panel displaying external links

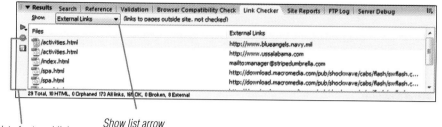

List of external links

Show list arrow

FIGURE 31

Link Checker panel displaying no orphaned files

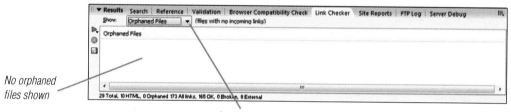

No orphaned files shown

Show list arrow

FIGURE 32

Assets panel displaying links

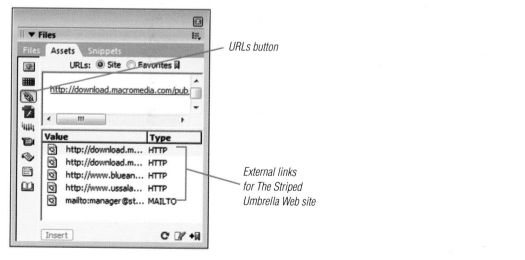

URLs button

External links for The Striped Umbrella Web site

Manage Web site links

1. Click **Site** on the menu bar, point to **Advanced**, then click **Re-create Site Cache**.

2. Click **Site** on the menu bar, then click **Check Links Sitewide**.

   The Results panel group opens with the Link Checker panel displayed. By default, the Link Checker panel initially displays any broken internal links found in the Web site. The Striped Umbrella Web site has no broken links.

3. Click the **Show list arrow** in the Link Checker panel, click **External Links**, then compare your screen to Figure 30.

   Some external links are listed more than once because the Link Checker displays each instance of an external link.

4. Click the **Show list arrow**, then click **Orphaned Files** to view the orphaned files in the Link Checker panel, as shown in Figure 31.

   The Striped Umbrella Web site has no orphaned files.

5. Click the **Options button** 📧 in the Results panel group title bar, then click **Close panel group**.

6. Display the Assets panel (if necessary), then click the **URLs button** 📎 in the Assets panel to display the list of links in the Web site.

   The Assets panel displays the external links used in the Web site, as shown in Figure 32.

You used the Link Checker panel to check for broken links, external links, and orphaned files in The Striped Umbrella Web site.

Update a page

1. Open dw4_2.html from where you store your Data Files, then save it as **fishing.html** in the striped_umbrella root folder, overwriting the existing fishing page, but not updating the links.

2. Click the broken link image placeholder, click the **Browse for File icon**  next to the Src text box on the Property inspector, then browse to the chapter_4 assets folder and select the file **heron_small.jpg** to copy the file to the striped_umbrella assets folder.

3. Deselect the image placeholder and the image will appear as shown in Figure 33.

   Notice that the text is automatically updated with the body_text style. The code was already in place on the page linking the su_styles.css to the file.

4. Save and close the page.

FIGURE 33
Fishing page updated

POWER USER SHORTCUTS

to do this:	use this shortcut:
Close a file	[Ctrl][W] (Win) or ⌘[W] (Mac)
Close all files	[Ctrl][Shift][W] (Win) or ⌘[Shift][W] (Mac)
Print Code	[Ctrl][P] (Win) or ⌘[P] (Mac)
Check page links	[Shift][F8]
Undo	[Ctrl][Z], [Alt][BkSp] (Win) or ⌘[Z], [option][delete] (Mac)
Redo	[Ctrl][Y], [Ctrl][Shift][Z] (Win) or ⌘[Y], ⌘[Shift][Z] (Mac)
Refresh Design View	[F5]
Hide all Visual Aids	[Ctrl][Shift][I] (Win) or ⌘[Shift][I] (Mac)
Insert a Flash file	[Ctrl][Alt][F] (Win) or ⌘[option][F] (Mac)
Insert a Named Anchor	[Ctrl][Alt][A] (Win) or ⌘[option][A] (Mac)
Make a Link	[Ctrl][L] (Win) or ⌘[L] (Mac)
Remove a Link	[Ctrl][Shift][L] (Win) or ⌘[Shift][L] (Mac)
Check Links Sitewide	[Ctrl][F8] (Win) or ⌘[F8] (Mac)
Show Assets panel	[F11]
Show Files panel	[F8]

Working with Links

FIGURE 34

Cruises page updated

THE STRIPED UMBRELLA

25 BEACHSIDE DRIVE   FT. EUGENE, FLORIDA 33775   TEL: 555-594-9458

◀ HOME   ◀ ABOUT US   ◀ SAND CRAB CAFE   ◀ THE SPA   ◀ ACTIVITIES

This is the Dolphin Racer at dock. We leave daily at 4:00 p.m.and 6:30 p.m. for 1
1/2 hour cruises. There are snacks and restrooms available on board. We
welcome children of all ages. Our ship is a U.S. Coast Guard approved vessel
and our captain is a former member of the Coast Guard. Call The Club desk for
reservations.

5. Open dw4_3.html from where you store your Data Files, then save it as **cruises.html** in the striped_umbrella root folder, overwriting the existing cruises page, but not updating the links.

6. Click the broken link graphic placeholder, click the **Browse for File icon** 📁 next to the Src text box on the Property inspector, then browse to the chapter_4 assets folder and select the file **boats.jpg** to copy the file to the striped_umbrella assets folder.

7. Deselect the image placeholder and the image will appear as shown in Figure 34.

   Notice that the text is automatically updated with the body_text style. The code was already in place on the page linking the su_styles.css to the file.

8. Save and close the page.

Create external and internal links.

1. Open the blooms & bulbs Web site.
2. Open dw4_4.html from where you store your Data Files, then save it as **newsletter.html** in the blooms & bulbs Web site, overwriting the existing file without updating the links.
3. Verify that the banner path is set correctly to the assets folder in the Web site and correct it, if it is not.
4. Scroll to the bottom of the page, then link the National Gardening Association text to *http://www.garden.org*.
5. Link the Better Homes and Gardens Gardening Home Page text to *http://bhg.com/gardening*.
6. Link the Southern Living text to *http://www.southernliving.com/southern*.
7. Save the file, then preview the page in your browser, verifying that each link works correctly.
8. Close your browser, then return to the newsletter page in Dreamweaver.
9. Scroll to the paragraph about gardening issues, select the gardening tips text in the last sentence, then link the selected text to the tips.html file in the blooms root folder.
10. Add a new rule to the blooms_styles.css file called **bodytext** using the following formatting choices: Font: **Arial**, Helvetica, **sans-serif**; Style: **normal**; Weight: **normal**; and Size: **medium**.

11. Apply the headings style to the text "Gardening Matters," the seasons style to the subheadings on the page, and the bodytext style to the descriptions under each subheading and the three external links.
12. Center the "Gardening Matters" text.
13. Change the page title to **Gardening Matters**, then save your work.
14. Open the plants page and add the following sentence to the end of the last paragraph: **We have many annuals, perennials, and water plants that have just arrived**.
15. Link the "annuals" text to the annuals.html file, link the "perennials" text to the perennials.html file, and the "water plants" text to the water_plants.html file.
16. Save your work, test the links in your browser, then close your browser.

Create internal links to named anchors.

1. Show Invisible Elements (if necessary).
2. Click the Common tab on the Insert bar.
3. Switch to the newsletter page, then insert a named anchor in front of the Grass heading named **grass**.
4. Insert a named anchor in front of the Plants heading named **plants**.

5. Insert a named anchor in front of the Trees heading named **trees**.
6. Insert a named anchor at the top of the page named **top**.
7. Use the Point to File icon in the Property inspector to create a link from the word "grass" in the Gardening Issues paragraph to the anchor named "grass."
8. Create a link from the word "trees" in the Gardening Issues paragraph to the anchor named "trees."
9. Create a link from the word "plants" in the Gardening Issues paragraph to the anchor named "plants."
10. Save your work, view the page in your browser, test all the links to make sure they work, then close your browser.

Insert Flash text.

1. Insert Flash text at the bottom of the page that will take you to the top of the page. Use the following settings: Font: **Arial**, Size: **16**, Color: **#000066**, Rollover color: **#3366FF**, Text: **Top of page**, Link: **newsletter.html#top,** Target: **_top.**
2. Save the Flash text file as **top.swf** and enter the title **Link to top of page** in the Flash Accessibility Attributes dialog box.
3. Save all open files, view the page in your browser, test the Flash text link, then close your browser.

Create, modify, and copy a navigation bar.

1. Place your insertion point right under the banner, click the Images list arrow on the Insert bar, then click Navigation Bar to insert a horizontal navigation bar at the top of the newsletter page below the banner. Uncheck the option to use tables.

2. Type **home** as the first element name, then use the b_home_up.jpg file for the Up image state. This file is in the assets folder where you store your Data Files.

3. Specify the file **b_home_down.jpg** for the three remaining states. This file (and all files for the remainder of this exercise) are in the assets folder where you store your Data Files.

4. Enter **Link to home page** as the alternate text, then set the **index.html** file as the link for the home element.

5. Create a new element named **plants** and use the **b_plants_up.jpg** file for the Up image state and the **b_plants_down.jpg** file for the remaining three states.

6. Enter **Link to plants page** as the alternate text, then set the **plants.html** file as the link for the plants element.

7. Create a new element named **tips** and use the **b_tips_up.jpg** file for the Up image state and the **b_tips_down.jpg** file for the remaining three states.

8. Enter **Link to tips page** as the alternate text, then set the **tips.html** file as the link for the tips element.

9. Create a new element named **classes** and use the **b_classes_up.jpg** file for the Up image state and the **b_classes_down.jpg** file for the remaining three states.

10. Enter **Link to classes page** as the alternate text, then set the **classes.html** file as the link for the classes element.

11. Create a new element named **newsletter**, then use the **b_newsletter_up.jpg** file for the Up image state and the **b_newsletter_down.jpg** file for the remaining three states.

12. Enter the alternate text **Link to newsletter page**, then set the **newsletter.html** file as the link for the newsletter element.

13. Center the navigation bar (if necessary), save the page and test the links in your browser, then close the browser.

14. Select and copy the navigation bar, then open the home page.

15. Delete the current navigation bar on the home page, then paste the new navigation bar under the banner. (*Hint*: Insert a line break after the banner before you paste so that the navigation bar is directly below the banner.)

16. Modify the home element on the navigation bar to show the Down image state initially.

17. Save the page, test the links in your browser, then close the browser and the page.

18. Modify the navigation bar on the newsletter page so the Down image is shown initially for the newsletter element, then save and close the newsletter page.

19. Paste the navigation bar on the plants page and the tips page, making the necessary modifications so that the Down image is shown initially for each element.

20. Save your work, preview all the pages in your browser, compare your newsletter page to Figure 35, test all the links, then close your browser.

Create an image map

1. Use the Rectangular Hotspot tool to draw an image map across the left side of the banner on the newsletter page that will link to the home page.

2. Name the image map **home** and set the target to **_top**.

3. Add the alternate text **Link to home page**, save the page, then preview it in the browser to test the link.

4. Close the page.

Manage Web site links.

1. Use the Link Checker panel to view and fix broken links, external links, and orphaned files in the blooms & bulbs Web site.

2. Open **dw4_5.html** from where you store your Data Files, then save it as **annuals.html**, replacing the original file. Do not update links, but save the file **fuschia.jpg** in the assets folder of the Web site.

3. Repeat Step 2 using **dw4_6.html** to replace **perennials.html,** saving the **iris.jpg** file in the assets folder and using **dw4_7.html** to replace **water_plants.html,** saving the **water_hyacinth.jpg** file in the assets folder.

4. Save your work, then close all open pages.

FIGURE 35
Completed Skills Review

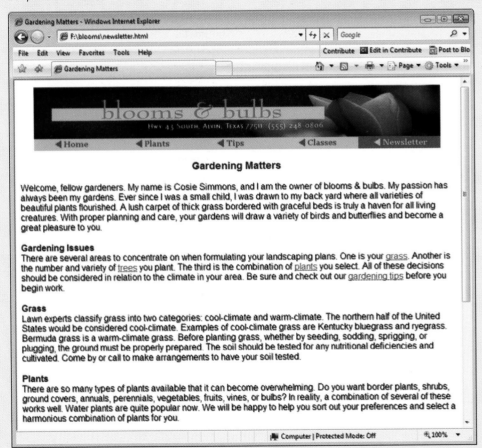

Use Figure 36 as a guide to continue your work on the TripSmart Web site that you began in Project Builder 1 in Chapter 1 and developed in the previous chapters. You have been asked to create a new page for the Web site that lists helpful links for customers. You will also add content to the destinations, kenya, and amazon pages.

1. Open the TripSmart Web site.
2. Open **dw4_8.html** from where you store your Data Files, then save it as **services.html** in the TripSmart Web site root folder, not updating links.
3. Verify that the TripSmart banner is in the assets folder of the root folder.
4. Apply the **body_text** style to the paragraphs of text and the heading style to the paragraph headings.
5. Create named anchors named **reservations, outfitters, tours**, and **links** in front of the respective headings on the page, then link each named anchor to "Reservations,"

"Travel Outfitters," "Escorted Tours," and "Helpful Links in Travel Planning" in the first paragraph.
6. Link the text "on-line catalog" in the Travel Outfitters paragraph to the catalog.html page.
7. Link the text "CNN Travel Channel" under the heading Travel Information Sites to *http://www.cnn.com/TRAVEL*.
8. Repeat Step 7 to create links for the rest of the Web sites listed:
   US Department of State:
   http://travel.state.gov
   Yahoo! : *http://yahoo.com/Recreation/Travel*
   MapQuest:
   http://www.mapquest.com
   Rand McNally:
   http://www.randmcnally.com
   AccuWeather:
   http://www.accuweather.com
   The Weather Channel:
   http://www.weather.com
9. Save the services page, then open the index page.

10. Attach the style sheet to the index page and assign a style to all text. Create new styles if you need them.
11. Reformat the navigation bar on the home page with a style of your choice, then place it on each completed page of the Web site. If you decide to use graphics for the navigation bar, you will have to create your own graphic files using a graphics program. There are no data files for you to use. (*Hint*: If you create your own graphic files, be sure to create two graphic files for each element: one for the Up image state and one for the Down image state.) To design a navigation bar using text, you simply type the text for each navigation bar element, format the text appropriately, and insert links to each text element as you did in Chapter 2. The navigation bar should contain the following elements: Home, Catalog, Services, Destinations, and Newsletter.

Working with Links

12. Save each page, then check for broken links and orphaned files. (*Hint*: The two orphaned files will be removed after completing the next steps.)

13. Open the destinations.html file in your root folder and save it as **kenya.html**, overwriting the existing file, then close the file.

14. Open dw4_9.html from where you store your Data Files, then save it as **amazon.html**, overwriting the existing file. Do not update links, but save the **water_lily.jpg** and **sloth.jpg** files in the assets folder of the Web site, then save and close the file.

15. Open dw4_10.html from where you store your Data Files, then save the file as **destinations.html**, overwriting the existing file. Do not update links, but save the **parrot.jpg** and **giraffe.jpg** files in the assets folder of the Web site.

16. Link the text "Amazon" in the second sentence of the first paragraph to the **amazon.html** file.

17. Link the text "Kenya" in the first sentence in the second paragraph to the **kenya.html** file.

18. Copy your customized navigation bar to the two new pages so they will match the other pages.

19. Check all text on all pages to make sure each text block uses a style for formatting. Correct those that don't.

20. Save all files.

21. Test all links in your browser, close your browser, then close all open pages.

FIGURE 36
Sample Project Builder 1

Working with Links

You are continuing your work on the Carolyne's Creations Web site that you started in Project Builder 2 in Chapter 1 and developed in the previous chapters. Chef Carolyne has asked you to create a page describing her cooking classes offered every month. You will create the content for that page and individual pages describing the children's classes and the adult classes. Refer to Figures 37–40 for possible solutions.

1. Open the Carolyne's Creations Web site.
2. Open **dw4_11.html** from where you store your Data Files, save it as **classes.html** in the root folder of the Carolyne's Creations Web site, overwriting the existing file and not updating the links.
3. Check the path of the banner to make sure it is linking to the banner in the assets folder of the Web site. Notice that styles have already been applied to the text, because the CSS code was already in the Data File.
4. Select the text "adults' class" in the last paragraph, then link it to the adults.html page. (*Hint*: This page has not been developed yet.)
5. Select the text "children's class" in the last paragraph and link it to the children.html page. (*Hint*: This page has not been developed yet.)

6. Create an e-mail link from the text "Sign me up!" that links to **carolyne@carolynes-creations.com**
7. Insert the file **fish.jpg** from the assets folder where you store your Data Files at the beginning of the second paragraph, add

appropriate alternate text, then choose your own alignment and formatting settings.
8. Add the file **children_cooking.jpg** from the assets folder where you store your Data Files at the beginning of the third paragraph.

FIGURE 37

Completed Project Builder 2

Cooking Classes are fun!

Chef Carolyne loves to offer a fun and relaxing cooking school each month in her newly refurbished kitchen. She teaches an **adult class** on the fourth Saturday of each month from 6:00 to 8:00 pm. Each class will learn to cook a complete dinner and then enjoy the meal at the end of the class with a wonderful wine pairing. This is a great chance to get together with friends for a fun evening. .

 Chef Caroline also teaches a **children's class** on the second Tuesday of each month from 4:00 to 5:30 pm. Our young chefs will learn to cook two dishes that will accompany a full meal served at 5:30 pm. Kids aged 5–8 years accompanied by an adult are welcome. We also host small birthday parties where we put the guests to work baking and decorating the cake! Call for times and prices.

We offer several special adult classes throughout the year. The **Valentine Chocolate Extravaganza** is a particular favorite. You will learn to dip strawberries, make truffles, and bake a sinful Triple Chocolate Dare You Torte. We also host the **Not So Traditional Thanksgiving** class and the **Super Bowl Snacks** class each year with rave reviews. Watch the Web site for details!

Prices are $40.00 for each adult class and $15.00 for each children's class. Sign up for classes by calling 555-963-8271 or by emailing us: Sign me up!

See what's cooking this month for the adults' class and children's class.

9. Compare your work to Figure 37 for a possible solution, then save and close the file.

10. Open dw4_12.html from where you store your Data Files, then save it as **children.html**, overwriting the existing file and not updating links. Save the image **cookies_oven.jpg** from the assets folder where you store your Data Files to the Web site assets folder.

11. Add your own alignment and formatting settings, compare your work to Figure 38 for a possible solution, then save and close the file.

12. Repeat Steps 10 and 11 to open the dw4_13.html file and save it as **adults.html**, overwriting the existing file and saving the files **dumplings1.jpg**, **dumplings2.jpg**, and **dumplings3.jpg** in the assets folder, then use alignment settings of your choice. Compare your work to Figure 39 for a possible solution, then save and close the file.

13. Open the **index** page and delete the banner and navigation bar.

14. Insert the file **cc_banner_with_text.jpg** from where you store your Data Files in its place, adding appropriate alternate text.

15. Create an image map for each word at the bottom of the navigation bar to be used as a link to that page, as shown in Figure 40. Use **_top** as the target, the names of the "buttons" as the image map names, and appropriate alternate text. Link each image map to its corresponding page.

16. Copy the new navigation bar to each completed page, deleting existing navigation bars and banners.

17. Save all the pages, then check for broken links and orphaned files.

18. Preview all the pages in your browser, check to make sure the links work correctly, close your browser, then close all open pages.

FIGURE 38

Completed Project Builder 2

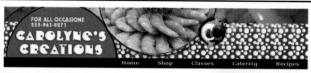

Children's Cooking Class for March: Oven Chicken Fingers, Chocolate Chip Cookies

This month we will be baking oven chicken fingers that are dipped in a milk and egg mixture, then coated with breadcrumbs. The chocolate chip cookies are based on a famous recipe that includes chocolate chips, M&Ms, oatmeal, and pecans. Yummy! We will be learning some of the basics like how to cream butter and crack eggs without dropping shells into the batter.

We will provide French fries, green beans, fruit salad, and a beverage to accompany the chicken fingers.

FIGURE 39

Completed Project Builder 2

Adult Cooking Class for March: Chinese Cuisine

The class in March will be cooking several traditional Chinese dishes: Peking dumplings, wonton soup, fried rice, Chinese vegetables, and shrimp with lobster sauce. For dessert: banana spring rolls.

This looks easier than it is! Chef Carolyne is demonstrating the first steps in making Chinese dumplings, known as *jiaozi* (pronounced geeow dz). Notice that she is using a traditional wooden rolling pin to roll out the dough. These dumplings were stuffed with pork and then steamed, although other popular fillings are made with chicken and leeks or vegetables with spiced tofu and cellophane noodles. Dumplings can be steamed, boiled, or fried, and have unique names depending on the preparation method.

FIGURE 40

Completed Project Builder 2

Let Carolyne's Creations be your personal chef, your one stop shop for the latest in kitchen items and fresh ingredients, and your source for new and innovative recipes. We enjoy planning and executing special events for all occasions - from children's birthday parties to corporate retreats. Feel like a guest at your own party. Give us a call or stop by our shop to browse through our selections.

Carolyne's Creations
496 Maple Avenue
Seven Falls, Virginia 52404
555.963.8271
E-mail Carolyne Kate

Copyright 2001 - 2010
Last updated on March 14, 2007

Grace Keiko is a talented young water-color artist who specializes in botanical works. She wants to develop a Web site to advertise her work, but isn't sure what she would like to include in a Web site or how to tie the pages together. She decides to spend several hours looking at other artists' Web sites to help her get started.

1. Connect to the Internet, then navigate to the Kate Nessler Web site pictured in Figure 41, *www.katenessler.com.*

2. Spend some time looking at several of the pages in the site to get some ideas.

3. What categories of page content would you include on your Web site if you were Grace?

4. What external links would you consider including?

5. Describe how you would place external links on the pages and list examples of ones you would use.

6. Would you use text or images for your navigation bar?

7. Would you include rollover effects on the navigation bar elements? If so, describe how they might look.

8. How could you incorporate named anchors on any of the pages?

9. Would you include an image map on a page?

10. Sketch a Web site plan for Grace, including the pages that you would use as links from the home page.

11. Refer to your Web site sketch, then create a home page for Grace that includes a navigation bar, a short introductory paragraph about her art, and a few external links.

FIGURE 41
Design Project

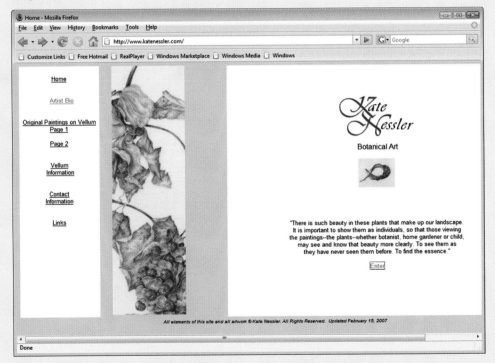

Kate Nessler Web site used with permission from Kate Nessler - www.katenessler.com

In this assignment, you will continue to work on the Web site that you started in Chapter 1 and developed in the previous chapters.

You will continue building your Web site by designing and completing a page with a navigation bar. After creating the navigation bar, you will copy it to each completed page in the Web site. In addition to the navigation bar, you will add several external links and several internal links to other pages as well as to named anchors. You will also link Flash text to a named anchor. After you complete this work, you will check for broken links and orphaned files.

1. Consult your storyboard to decide which page or pages you would like to develop in this chapter. Decide how to design and where to place the navigation bar, named anchors, Flash text, and any additional page elements you decide to use. Decide which reports should be run on the Web site to check for accuracy.

2. Research Web sites that could be included on one or more of your pages as external links of interest to your viewers. Create a list of the external links you want to use. Using your storyboard as a guide, decide where each external link should be placed in the site.

3. Add the external links to existing pages or create any additional pages that contain external links.

4. Create named anchors for key locations on the page, such as the top of the page, then link appropriate text on the page to them.

5. Insert at least one Flash text object that links to either a named anchor or an internal link.

6. Decide on a design for a navigation bar that will be used on all pages of the Web site.

7. Create the navigation bar and copy it to all finished pages on the Web site. If you decided to use graphics for the navigation bar, create the graphics that will be used.

8. Think of a good place to incorporate an image map, then add it to a page.

9. Use the Link Checker panel to check for broken links and orphaned files.

10. Use the checklist in Figure 42 to make sure your Web site is complete, save your work, then close all open pages.

FIGURE 42
Portfolio Project checklist

Web Site Checklist

1. Do all pages have a page title?
2. Does the home page have a description and keywords?
3. Does the home page contain contact information?
4. Does every page in the Web site have consistent navigation links?
5. Does the home page have a last updated statement that will automatically update when the page is saved?
6. Do all paths for links and images work correctly?
7. Do all images have alternate text?
8. Are all colors Websafe?
9. Are there any unnecessary files that you can delete from the assets folder?
10. Is there a style sheet with at least two styles?
11. Did you apply the style sheet to page content?
12. Does at least one page contain links to one or more named anchors?
13. Does at least one page contain Flash text that links to either a named anchor or an internal link?
14. Do all pages view well using at least two different browsers?

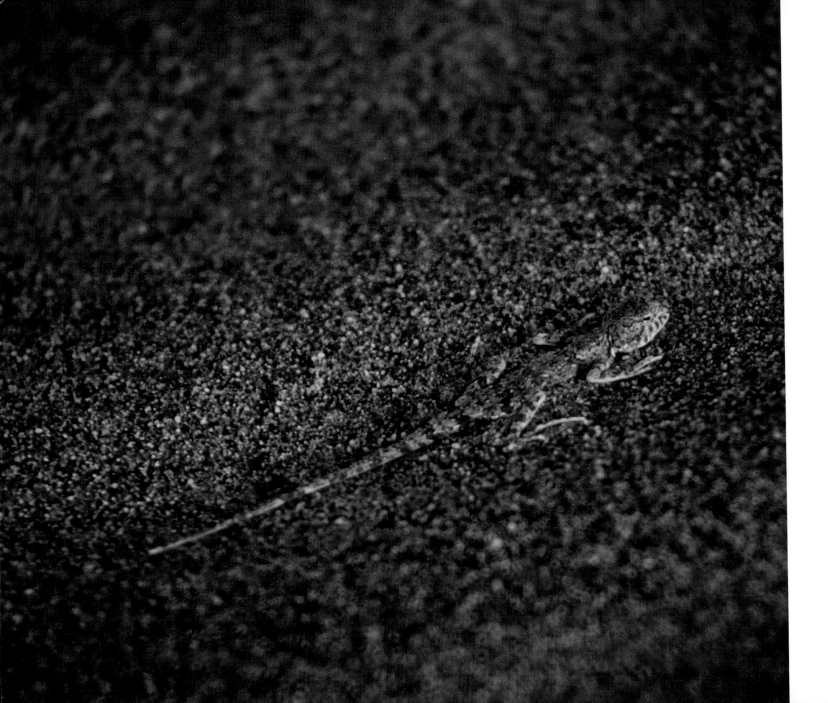

USING HTML TABLES
TO LAY OUT
A PAGE

1. Create a table

2. Resize, split, and merge cells

3. Insert and align images in table cells

4. Insert text and format cell content

5 USING HTML TABLES
TO LAY OUT
A PAGE

Introduction

You have learned how to place and align elements on a page and enhance them using various formatting options. However, page layout options are fairly limited without the use of tables, AP Elements, or Cascading Style Sheets. Tables offer one solution for organizing text and graphics on a page. **Tables** are placeholders made up of small boxes called **cells**, into which you can insert text and graphics. Cells in a table are arranged horizontally in **rows** and vertically in **columns**. Using tables on a Web page gives you total control over the placement of each object on the page. In this chapter, you will learn how to create and format tables, work with table rows and columns, and format the contents of table cells. You will also learn how to select and format table cells using table tags on the tag selector. Clicking a table tag on the tag selector selects the table element associated with that tag. In later chapters, we will use AP Elements and Cascading Style Sheets for page layout.

Inserting Graphics and Text in Tables

Once you insert a table on a Web page, it becomes very easy to place text and graphics exactly where you want them on the page. You can use a table to control both the placement of elements in relation to each other and the amount of space between them. Before you insert a table, however, you should always plan how you would like your table to look with all the text and graphics in it. Even a rough sketch before you begin will save you time as you add content to the page.

Tools You'll Use

Table properties
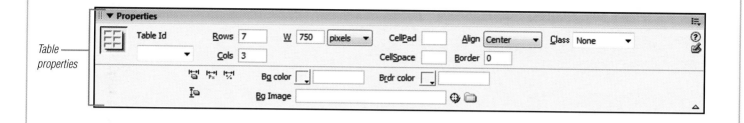

Cell properties
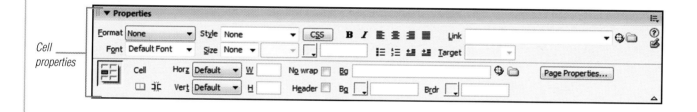

Row properties

CREATE A TABLE

What You'll Do

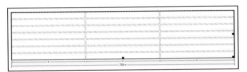

In this lesson, you will create a table for the cafe page in The Striped Umbrella Web site to provide the framework for the page layout.

Understanding Table Modes

There are two ways to create a table in Dreamweaver. Each method requires working in Design view. The first method is to click the Table button on the Insert bar. The Table button is available in the Common category of the Insert bar and in the Layout category of the Insert bar, whenever the Standard mode button is enabled. The second method is to click View, Table Mode, Layout Mode; then click the Draw Layout Table button or the Draw Layout Cell button. When the Layout category of the Insert bar is displayed, you can choose Standard mode or Expanded Table mode by clicking the appropriate button on the Insert bar.

Creating a Table in Standard Mode

Creating a table in Standard mode is useful when you want to create a table with a specific number of columns and rows. To create a table in Standard mode, click the Table button on the Insert bar to open the Table dialog box. Enter values for the number of rows and columns, the border thickness, table width, cell padding, and cell spacing. The **border** is the outline or frame around the table and the individual cells and is measured in pixels. The table width can be specified in pixels or as a percentage. When the table width is specified as a percentage, the table width will adjust to the width of the browser window. Figure 1 could either be a page based on a table set to 100% width (of the browser window), or it could be a page that is not based on a table at all. The content spreads across the entire browser window, without a container to set boundaries. When the table width is specified in pixels, the table width stays the same, regardless of the size of the browser window. The page in Figure 2 is an example of a page based on a table with a fixed width of 750 pixels. The content will not spread outside the table borders unless it contains images that are wider than the table. **Cell padding** is the distance between the cell content and the **cell walls**, the lines inside the cell borders. **Cell spacing** is the distance between cells.

Planning a Table

Before you create a table, you should sketch a plan for it that shows its location on the Web page and the placement of text and graphics in its cells. You should also decide whether to include borders around the tables and cells. Setting the border value to 0 causes the table to appear invisible, so that viewers will not realize that you used a table for the page layout unless they look at the code. Figure 3 shows a sketch of the table you will create on The Striped Umbrella cafe page to organize graphics and text.

Setting Table Accessibility Preferences for Tables

You can make a table more accessible to visually handicapped viewers by adding a table caption and a table summary that screen readers can read. The table caption appears on the screen. The table summary does not. These features are especially useful for tables that are used for tabular data. **Table headers** are another way to provide accessibility. Table headers can be placed at the top or sides of a table with data. They are automatically centered and bold and are used by screen readers to help viewers identify the table content. Table captions, summaries, and headers are all created in the Table dialog box.

Drawing a Table in Layout Mode

You use Layout mode when you want to draw your own table. Drawing a table is ideal when you want to place page elements on a Web page and have no need for a specific number of rows and columns. You can use the Draw Layout Cell button or the Draw Layout Table button in the Layout category of the Insert bar to draw a cell or a table. After you draw the first cell, Dreamweaver plots a table for you automatically.

FIGURE 1

Page shown without using tables or using a table based on a 100% width

Content spreads across the browser window

FIGURE 2

Same page shown using a fixed-width table for layout

Table confines content; leftover white space displayed outside table borders

FIGURE 3

Sketch of table on cafe page

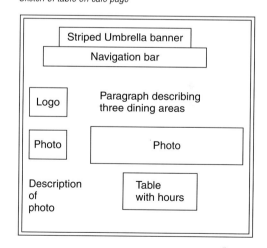

Create a table

1. Open The Striped Umbrella Web site that you completed in Chapter 4.

2. Double-click **cafe.html** in the Files panel to open the cafe page in Design view.

   The cafe page is blank.

3. Click the **Layout tab** on the Insert bar, click the **Standard mode button** `Standard`, then click the **Table button** ⊞.

   The Table dialog box opens.

4. Type **7** in the Rows text box, type **3** in the Columns text box, type **750** in the Table width text box, click the **Table width list arrow**, click **pixels**, then type **0** in the Border thickness text box, as shown in Figure 4.

   > TIP It is better to add more rows than you think you will need when you create your table. After they are filled with content, it is far easier to delete rows than to add rows if you decide later to split or merge cells in the table.

   (continued)

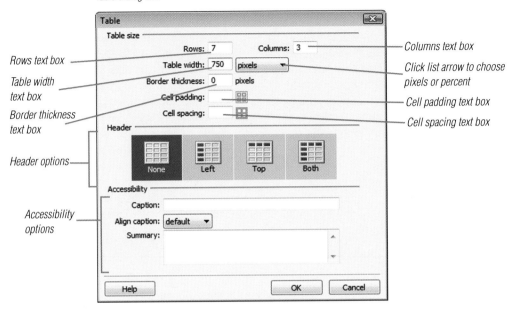

FIGURE 4
Table dialog box

Rows text box
Columns text box
Click list arrow to choose pixels or percent
Table width text box
Border thickness text box
Cell padding text box
Cell spacing text box
Header options
Accessibility options

Expanded Tables mode

Expanded Tables mode is a feature that allows you to change to a table view with expanded table borders and temporary cell padding and cell spacing. This mode makes it much easier to actually see how many rows and columns you have in your table. Many times, especially after splitting empty cells, it is difficult to place the insertion point precisely in a table cell. The Expanded Tables mode allows you to see each cell clearly. However, most of the time you will want to work in Standard mode to maintain the WYSIWYG environment. **WYSIWYG** is the acronym for What You See Is What You Get. This means that your Web page should look the same in the browser as it does in the Web editor. You can toggle between Expanded Tables mode and Standard mode by pressing [F6]. You can access Layout mode by holding the [Ctrl] (Win) or [option] (Mac) key and then pressing [F6].

FIGURE 5
Table dialog box

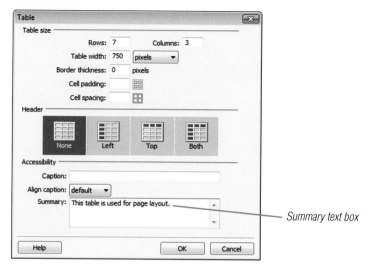

Summary text box

FIGURE 6
Expanded Tables mode

Click to exit
Expanded
Tables mode

Expanded Tables
mode displays more
space between cells
for easier editing

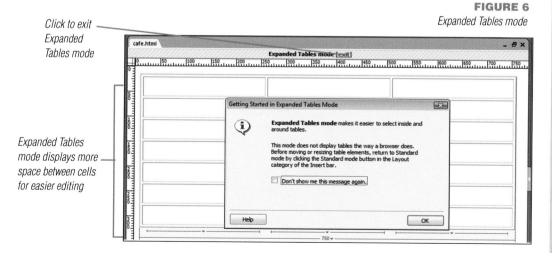

5. Type **This table is used for page layout.** in the Summary text box, then compare your screen to Figure 5.

6. Click **OK**.

The table appears on the page, but the table summary is not visible. The summary will not appear in the browser but will be read by screen readers.

> TIP To edit accessibility preferences for a table, switch to Code view to edit the code directly.

7. Click the **Expanded Tables mode button** Expanded on the Layout tab, then click **OK** in the Getting Started in Expanded Tables Mode dialog box, as shown in Figure 6.

The Expanded Tables mode makes it easier to select and edit tables.

8. Click the **Standard mode button** Standard to return to Standard mode.

> TIP You can also return to Standard mode by clicking [exit] at the top of the table.

You opened the cafe page in The Striped Umbrella Web site. You then created a table containing seven rows and three columns and set the width to 750 pixels so it will appear in the same size regardless of the browser window size. Finally, you entered a table summary that will be read by screen readers.

Set table properties

1. Move the pointer slowly to the top or bottom
   edge of the table until you see the pointer
   change to a Table pointer ⌗ , then click
   the **table border** to select the table.

   TIP   You can also select a table by: (1) clicking the insertion point in the table, then
   clicking Modify, Table, Select Table;
   (2) selecting a cell in the table, then clicking
   Edit, Select All twice; or (3) clicking the table
   tag <table> on the tag selector.

2. Expand the Property inspector (if necessary) to
   display the current properties of the new table.

   TIP   The Property inspector will display
   information about the table only when the
   table is selected.

3. Click the **Align list arrow** on the Property
   inspector, then click **Center** to center the
   table on the page, as shown in Figure 7.

   The center alignment formatting ensures
   that the table will be centered in all browser
   windows, regardless of the screen size.

   TIP   The position of the left edge of the
   table on the ruler will depend on the size
   of the Document window.

You selected and center-aligned the table.

FIGURE 7
Property inspector showing properties of selected table

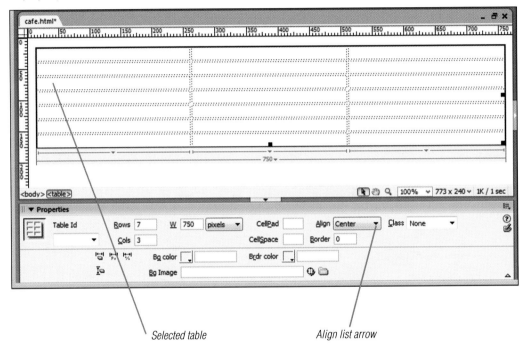

Selected table   Align list arrow

FIGURE 8
Table in Layout mode

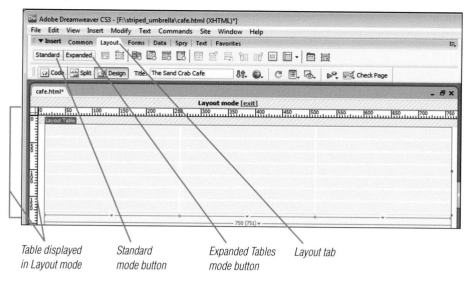

Table displayed   Standard   Expanded Tables   Layout tab
in Layout mode   mode button   mode button

View the table in Layout mode

1. Click **View** on the menu bar, point to **Table Mode,** then click **Layout Mode.**

   The table appears in Layout mode, as shown in Figure 8.

   TIP   The Getting Started in Layout Mode dialog box might open, providing instructions on creating and editing a table in Layout mode.

2. Click **OK** (if necessary) to close the Getting Started in Layout Mode dialog box.

3. Click the **Standard mode button** [Standard] to return to Standard mode.

4. Click the **Common tab** on the Insert bar.

You viewed the table in Layout mode, then returned to Standard mode.

DESIGNTIP   **Setting table and cell widths**

If you use a table to place all the text and graphics contained on a Web page, it is wise to set the width of the table in pixels. This ensures that the table will not resize itself proportionally if the browser window size is changed. If you set the width of a table using pixels, the table will remain one size, regardless of the browser window size. For instance, if the width of a table is set to slightly less than 800, the table will stretch across the whole width of a browser window set at a resolution of 800×600. The same table would be the same size on a screen set at 1024×768 and therefore would not stretch across the entire screen. Most designers use a resolution of 800×600 or higher. Be aware, however, that if you set the width of your table at 800 pixels, your table will be too wide to print the entire width of the page, and part of the right side of the page will be cut off. If you are designing a table layout for a page that is likely to be printed by the viewer, you should make your table narrower to fit on a printed page. If you set a table width as a percentage, however, the table would resize itself proportionally in any browser window, regardless of the resolution. You can also set each cell width as either a percentage of the table or as fixed pixels.

RESIZE, SPLIT, AND
MERGE CELLS

What You'll Do

In this lesson, you will set the width of the table cells to be split across the table in predetermined widths. You will then split one cell. You will also merge some cells to provide space for the banner.

Resizing Table Elements

You can resize the rows or columns of a table manually. To resize a table, row, or column, you must first select the table, then drag one of the table's three selection handles. To change all the columns in a table so that they are the same size, drag the middle-right selection handle. To resize the height of all rows simultaneously, drag the middle-bottom selection handle. To resize the entire table, drag the right-corner selection handle. To resize a row or column individually, drag the interior cell borders up, down, to the left, or to the right. You can also resize selected columns, rows, or individual cells by entering specific measurements in the W and H text boxes in the Property inspector specified either in pixels or as a percentage. Cells whose width or height is specified as a percentage will maintain that percentage in relation to the width or height of the entire table if the table is resized.

Adding or deleting a row

As you add new content to your table, you might find that you have too many or too few rows or columns. You can add or delete one row or column at a time or several at once. You use commands on the Modify menu to add and delete table rows and columns. When you add a new column or row, you must first select the existing column or row to which the new column or row will be adjacent. The Insert Rows or Columns dialog box lets you choose how many rows or columns you want to insert or delete, and where you want them placed in relationship to the selected row or column. The new column or row will have the same formatting and number of cells as the selected column or row.

Splitting and Merging Cells

Using the Table button creates a new table with evenly spaced columns and rows. Sometimes you might want to adjust the cells in a table by splitting or merging them. To split a cell means to divide it into multiple rows or columns. To merge cells means to combine multiple cells into one cell. Using split and merged cells gives you more flexibility and control in placing page elements on a page and can help you create a more visually exciting layout. When you merge cells, the HTML tag used to describe the merged cell changes from a width size tag to a column span or row span tag. For example, <td colspan="2"> is the code for two cells that have been merged into one cell that spans two columns.

QUICKTIP
You can split merged cells and merge split cells.

DESIGNTIP   **Using nested tables**

A nested table is a table inside a table. To create a nested table, you place the insertion point in the cell where you want to insert the nested table, then click the Table button on the Insert bar. The nested table is a separate table that can be formatted differently from the table in which it is placed. Nested tables are useful when you want part of your table data to have visible borders and part to have invisible borders. For example, you can nest a table with red borders inside a table with invisible borders. You need to plan carefully when you insert nested tables. It is easy to get carried away and insert too many nested tables, which makes it more difficult to apply formatting and rearrange table elements. Before you insert a nested table, consider whether you could achieve the same result by adding rows and columns or by splitting cells.

Resize columns

1. Click inside the **first cell** in the bottom row, then click **<td>** on the tag selector, as shown in Figure 9.

   Clicking the cell tag <td> (the HTML tag for that cell) selects the corresponding cell in the table.

   > TIP You can also click inside a cell to select it. To select the entire table, click the <table> tag on the tag selector.

2. Type **30%** in the W text box in the Property inspector, then press **[Enter]** (Win) or **[return]** (Mac) to change the width of the cell to 30 percent of the table width.

   Notice that the column width is shown as a percentage at the bottom of the first column in the table, along with the table width of 750 pixels.

   > TIP You need to type the % sign next to the number you type in the W text box. Otherwise, the width will be expressed in pixels.

3. Repeat Steps 1 and 2 for the next two cells in the last row, using **30%** for the middle cell and **40%** for the last cell.

   The combined widths of the three cells add up to 100 percent. As you add content to the table, the columns will remain in this proportion unless you insert a graphic that is larger than the table cell. If a larger graphic is inserted, the cell width will expand to display it.

   > TIP Changing the width of a single cell changes the width of the entire column.

   You set the width of each of the three cells in the bottom row to set the column sizes for the table. This will keep the table from resizing when you add content.

FIGURE 9
Selecting a cell

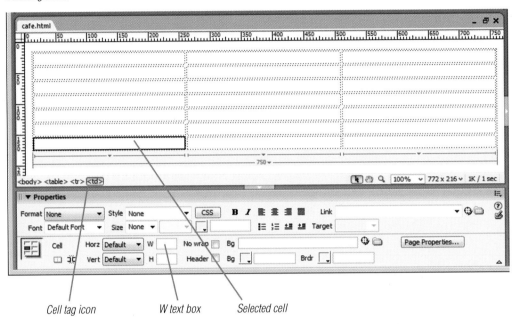

Cell tag icon   W text box   Selected cell

Resetting table widths and heights

After resizing columns and rows in a table, you might want to change the sizes of the columns and rows back to their previous sizes. To reset columns and rows to their previous widths and heights, click Modify on the menu bar, point to Table, then click Clear Cell Heights or Clear Cell Widths. Using the Clear Cell Heights command also forces the cell border to snap to the bottom of any inserted graphics, so you can also use this command to tighten up extra white space in a cell.

FIGURE 10

Resizing the height of a row

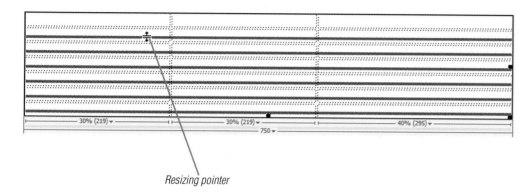

Resizing pointer

1. Place the pointer over the bottom border of the first row until it changes to a resizing pointer ⇌, as shown in Figure 10, then click and drag down about ¼ of an inch (approximately 24 pixels on the vertical ruler) to increase the height of the row.

   The border turns darker when you select and drag it.

2. Click **Window** on the menu bar, click **History**, then drag the **slider** in the History panel up one line to the **Set Height: 40%** mark to return the row to its original height. (Explanatory text for under step 2)

   The percentage shown in the Set Height state in the History panel will depend on how much you resized the row.

3. Close the History panel group.

You changed the height of the top row, then used the History panel to change it back it to its original height.

HTML table tags

When formatting a table, it is important to understand the basic HTML table tags. The tags used for creating a table are <table> </table>. The tags used to create table rows are <tr></tr>. The tags used to create table cells are <td></td>. Dreamweaver places the   code into each empty table cell at the time it is created. The   code represents a nonbreaking space, or a space that a browser will display on the page. Some browsers will collapse an empty cell, which can ruin the look of a table. The nonbreaking space will hold the cell until content is placed in it, at which time it will be automatically removed.

Split cells

1. Click inside the first cell in the fifth row, then click the **<td>** in the tag selector.

2. Click the **Splits cell into rows or columns button** ⌶Ɛ in the Property inspector.

3. Click the **Split cell into Rows option button** (if necessary), type **2** in the Number of rows text box (if necessary), as shown in Figure 11, click **OK,** then click in the cell to deselect it.

   The cell is split, as shown in Figure 12.

   | TIP To create a new row identical to the one above it, place the insertion point in the last cell of a table, then press [Tab].

You split a cell into two rows.

FIGURE 11
Splitting a cell into two rows

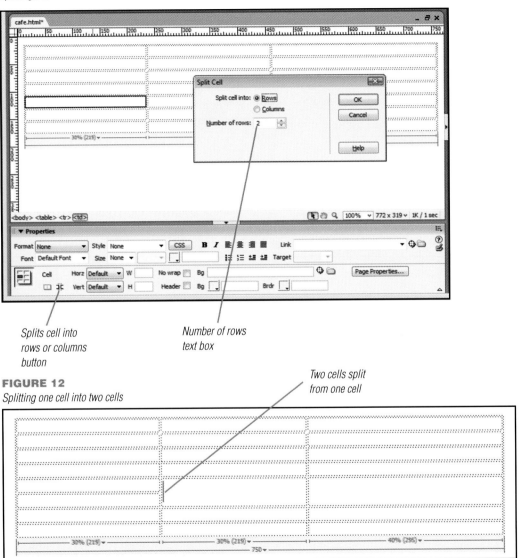

Splits cell into
rows or columns
button

Number of rows
text box

Two cells split
from one cell

FIGURE 12
Splitting one cell into two cells

Working with Tables

FIGURE 13
Merging selected cells into one cell

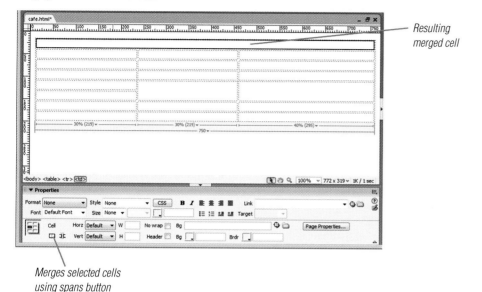

Resulting merged cell

Merges selected cells using spans button

FIGURE 14
Code view for merged cells

```
1   <!DOCTYPE html PUBLIC "-//W3C//DTD XHTML 1.0 Transitional//EN"
    "http://www.w3.org/TR/xhtml1/DTD/xhtml1-transitional.dtd">
2   <html xmlns="http://www.w3.org/1999/xhtml">
3   <head>
4   <meta http-equiv="Content-Type" content="text/html; charset=utf-8" />
5   <title>The Sand Crab Cafe</title>
6   </head>
7
8   <body>
9   <table width="750" border="0" align="center" summary="This table is used for page layout.">
10
11  <tr>
12      <td colspan="3"> </td>
13  </tr>
14  <tr>
15      <td> </td>
16      <td> </td>
17      <td> </td>
18  </tr>
19  <tr>
```

colspan tag

Merge cells

1. Click the insertion point in the first cell in the top row, then drag to the right to select the second and third cells in the top row.

2. Click the **Merges selected cells using spans button** ▣ in the Property inspector.

   The three cells are merged into one cell, as shown in Figure 13. Merged cells are good placeholders for banners or page headings.

   TIP You can only merge cells that are adjacent to each other.

3. Click the **Show Code view button** ‹› Code , then view the code for the merged cells, as shown in Figure 14.

   Notice the table tags denoting the column span (td colspan="3") and the nonbreaking spaces ( ) inserted in the empty cells.

   TIP The nonbreaking space is a special character that is inserted automatically in an empty cell to serve as a placeholder until content is added. A nonbreaking space will override automatic word wrap, or prevent a line break from being inserted in HTML code.

4. Click the **Show Design view button** ▣ Design , then save your work.

You merged three cells in the first row to make room for The Striped Umbrella banner.

INSERT AND ALIGN
IMAGES IN TABLE CELLS

What You'll Do

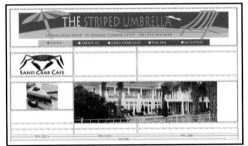

 In this lesson, you will insert The Striped Umbrella banner in the top row of the table. You will then insert three images in three different cells. After placing the three images, you will align them within their cells.

Inserting Images in Table Cells

You can insert images in the cells of a table using the Image command in the Images menu on the Insert bar. If you already have images saved in your Web site that you would like to insert in a table, you can drag them from the Assets panel into the table cells. When you add a large image to a cell, the cell expands to accommodate the inserted image. If you select the Show attributes when inserting Images check box in the Accessibility category of the Preferences dialog box, the Image Tag Accessibility Attributes dialog box will open after you insert an image, prompting you to enter alternate text. Figure 15 shows the John Deere Web site, which uses several tables for page layout and contains several images in its table cells. Notice that some images appear in cells by themselves, and some appear in cells containing text or other graphics. Some cells have a white background, and some have a green background.

Aligning Images in Table Cells

You can align images both horizontally and vertically within a cell. You can align an image horizontally using the Horz (horizontal) alignment options in the Property inspector. This option is used to align the entire contents of the cell, whether there is one object or several. You can also align an image vertically by the top, middle, bottom, or baseline of a cell. To align an image vertically within a cell, use the Vert (vertical) Align list arrow in the Property inspector, then choose an alignment option, as shown in Figure 16. To control spacing between cells, you can use cell padding and cell spacing. Cell padding is the space between a cell's border and its contents. Cell spacing is the distance between adjacent cells.

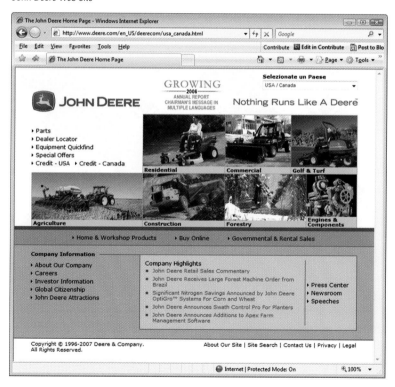
FIGURE 16

Vertically aligning cell contents

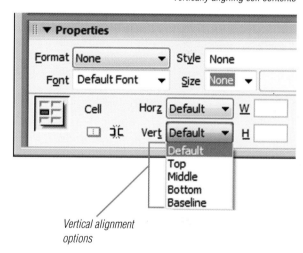

Vertical alignment options

Insert images in table cells

1. Open the index page, click the **banner image** to select it, press and hold **[Shift]**, then click to the right of the navigation bar to select both the banner and the navigation bar.

2. Click **Edit** on the menu bar, click **Copy**, then close the index page.

3. Click in the top cell on the cafe page, click **Edit** on the menu bar, then click **Paste**.

4. Compare your screen to Figure 17.

   The banner and navigation bar are copied to the page. We will adjust the alignment in the next lesson.

   (continued)

FIGURE 17
Banner and navigation bar copied from the home page into table

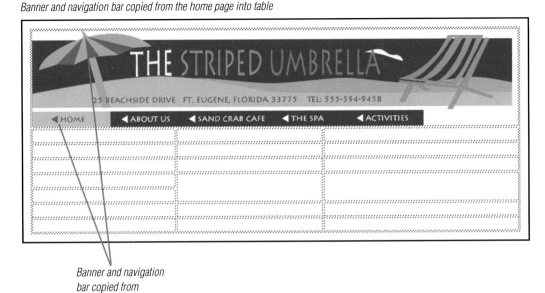

Banner and navigation bar copied from index page

Using visual aids

Dreamweaver has an option for turning on and off various features, such as table borders, that are displayed in Design view but are not displayed in the browser. This tool is called Visual Aids and can be accessed through the View menu or through the Visual Aids button on the Document toolbar. Most of the time, these features are very helpful while you are editing and formatting a page. However, turning them off is a quick way to see how the page will be viewed in the browser without having to open it in the browser window.

Working with Tables

FIGURE 18
Images inserted into table cells

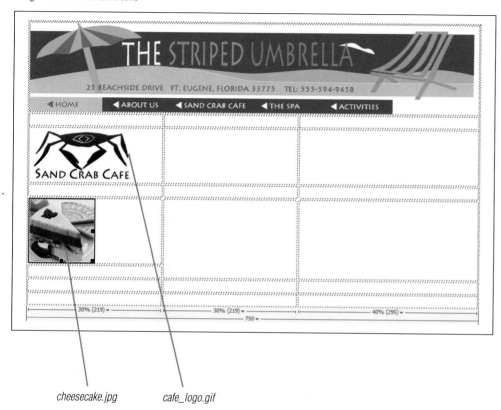

cheesecake.jpg   cafe_logo.gif

5. Click inside the first cell in the third row and insert **cafe_logo.gif** from the assets folder where you store your Data Files, then type **Sand Crab Cafe logo** as the alternate text.

   | TIP   Remember to count the banner and nav bar as the first row.

6. Repeat Step 5 to insert **cheesecake.jpg** in the first cell in the fifth row (the top row in the set of split cells), using **Banana Chocolate Cheesecake** for the alternate text.

7. Compare your screen to Figure 18.

(continued)

8. Merge the two cells to the right of the cheesecake graphic, repeat Step 5 to insert the **cafe_photo.jpg** in the newly merged cells, using **The Sand Crab Cafe** as the alternate text, then compare your screen to Figure 19.

> TIP Press [Tab] to move the insertion point to the next cell in a row. Press [Shift][Tab] to move the insertion point to the previous **cell**.

9. Refresh the Assets panel to verify that the three new images were copied to The Striped Umbrella Web site assets folder.

10. Save your work, then preview the page in your browser.

> Notice that the page would look better if the new images had better placement on the **page.**

11. Close your browser.

You inserted images into four cells of the table on the cafe page.

FIGURE 19
Cafe photo inserted into table cell

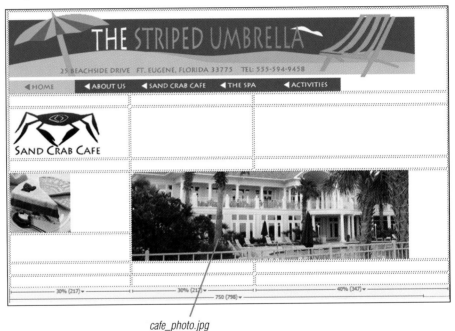

cafe_photo.jpg

Working with Tables

FIGURE 20

Aligning images in cells

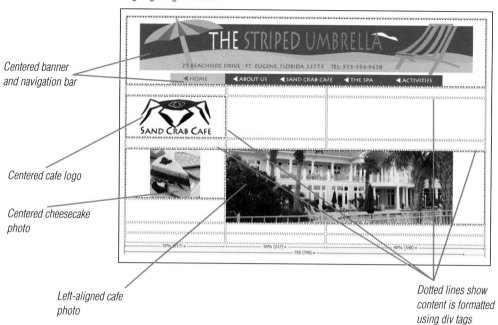

Centered banner
and navigation bar

Centered cafe logo

Centered cheesecake
photo

Left-aligned cafe
photo

Dotted lines show
content is formatted
using div tags

1. Click the **banner**, then click the **Align Center button** 🖹 in the Property inspector.

   The banner and navigation bar move together to become centered in the cell. You may have copied the center alignment tag when you copied the banner and navigation bar from the index page. In that case, the banner and navigation bar will already be centered on the cafe page.

2. Center-align the logo and cheesecake images, then left-align the cafe photo, as shown in Figure 20.

   Notice the extra dotted lines surrounding the four images. Each one represents a div tag that was generated when the alignment button was applied to the image.

3. Save your work.

4. Preview the page in your browser, view the aligned images, then close your browser.

You center-aligned The Striped Umbrella banner and two other images within their respective cells. You left-aligned the fourth image.

Working with div tags

Div tags are used for formatting blocks of content, similar to the way P tags are used to format paragraphs of text. Div tags, however, are more flexible in that they can be used as a container for any type of block content. They are used in various ways, such as centering content on a page or applying color to an area of a Web page. One of the benefits of using div tags is that they are combined easily with Cascading Style Sheets for formatting and positioning. When alignment is assigned to a block of content, Dreamweaver will automatically add a div tag. They are frequently used in style sheets to specify formatting attributes.

INSERT TEXT AND FORMAT
CELL CONTENT

What You'll Do

 In this lesson, you will insert text that describes the restaurant in a cell, type text in two cells, and then type the cafe hours in a nested table. You will also format the text to enhance its appearance on the page. Last, you will add formatting to some of the cells and cell content.

Inserting Text in a Table

You can enter text in a table either by typing it in a cell, copying it from another source and pasting it into a cell, or importing it from another program. Once you place text in a table cell, you can format it to make it more readable and more visually appealing on the page.

Formatting Cell Content

Making modifications and formatting changes to a table and its contents is easier to do in Standard mode than in Layout mode. To format the contents of a cell in Standard mode, select the contents in the cell, then apply formatting to it. For example, you can select an image in a cell and center it, add a border, or add V space.

Or, you can select text in a cell and apply a style or use the Text Indent or Text Outdent buttons in the Property inspector to move the text farther away from or closer to the cell walls.

If a cell contains multiple objects of the same type, such as text, you can either format each item individually or select the entire cell and apply formatting that will be applied identically to all items. You can tell whether you have selected the cell contents or the cell by looking to see what options are showing in the Property inspector. Figure 21 shows a selected image in a cell. Notice that the Property inspector displays options for formatting the object, rather than options for formatting the cell.

Formatting Cells

Formatting a cell is different from formatting a cell's contents. Formatting a cell can include setting properties that visually enhance the cell's appearance, such as setting a cell width and assigning a background color. You can also set global alignment properties for the cell content, using the Horz or Vert list arrows on the Property inspector. These options set the alignment for cell content horizontally or vertically. To format a cell, you need to either select the cell or place the insertion point inside the cell you want to format, then choose the cell formatting options you want in the Property inspector. For example, to choose a fill color for a selected cell, click the Background Color button in the Property inspector, then choose a color from the color picker. To set a background image for a cell, use the Browse for file button or the Point to file button in the Property inspector next to the Background URL of cell button to link to an image. To format a cell, you must expand the Property inspector to display the cell formatting options. In Figure 22, notice that the insertion point is positioned in the cafe logo cell, but the logo is not selected. The Property inspector displays the formatting options for cells.

FIGURE 21

Property inspector showing options for formatting cell contents

FIGURE 22

Property inspector showing options for formatting a cell

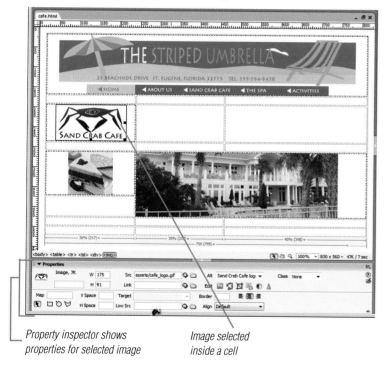

Property inspector shows properties for selected image

Image selected inside a cell

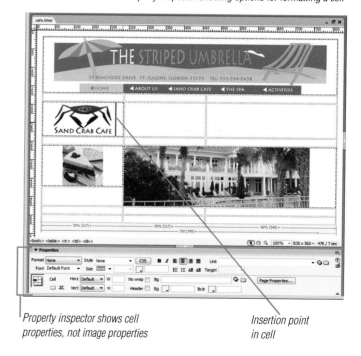

Property inspector shows cell properties, not image properties

Insertion point in cell

Insert text

1. Merge the two cells to the right of the cafe logo, click in the newly merged cell, then import the Word document, cafe.doc, from where you store your Data Files (Win) or copy and paste (Mac).

2. Click in the cell below the cheesecake photo, type **Banana Chocolate**, press **[Shift][Enter]** (Win) or **[shift][return]** (Mac), type **Cheesecake**, press **[Shift][Enter]** (Win) or **[shift][return]** (Mac), then type **Our signature dessert**.

3. Click in the next cell down and type **Reservations are recommended for The Dining Room during the peak summer season.**, as shown in Figure 23.

4. Use the Clean Up Word HTML command to correct the code from the cafe.doc file.

You imported a Word document describing the restaurant into one cell and typed two descriptive paragraphs into two cells.

FIGURE 23
Importing and typing text into cells

Imported text describing the cafe

Text typed into cells

Importing and exporting data from tables

You can import and export tabular data into and out of Dreamweaver. Tabular data is data that is arranged in columns and rows and separated by a **delimiter**: a comma, tab, colon, semicolon, or similar character. **Importing** means to bring data created in another software program into Dreamweaver, and **exporting** means to save data created in Dreamweaver in a special file format that can be inserted into other programs. Files that are imported into Dreamweaver must be saved as delimited files. **Delimited files** are database or spreadsheet files that have been saved as text files with delimiters such as tabs or commas separating the data. Programs such as Microsoft Access and Microsoft Excel offer many file formats for saving files. To import a delimited file, click File on the menu bar, point to Import, then click Tabular Data. The Import Tabular Data dialog box opens, offering you formatting options for the imported table. To export a table that you created in Dreamweaver, click File on the menu bar, point to Export, then click Table. The Export Table dialog box opens, letting you choose the type of delimiter you want for the delimited file.

FIGURE 24

Table dialog box settings for nested table

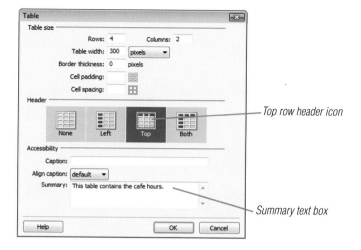

Top row header icon

Summary text box

FIGURE 25

Adding a nested table

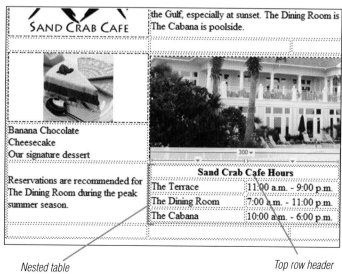

Nested table

Top row header

Insert text using a nested table

1. Merge the two empty cells below the cafe photo.

2. Place the insertion point inside the newly merged cells, then click the **Table button** [icon] on the Common tab to open the Table dialog box.

3. Type **4** in the Rows text box, type **2** in the Columns text box, type **300** in the Table width text box, click the **Table width list arrow**, click **pixels**, type **0** in the Border thickness text box, click the **Top row header icon** [icon] in the Header section, type **This table contains the cafe hours.** in the Summary text box, compare your Table dialog box to Figure 24, then click **OK**.

   The Top row header option will automatically center and bold the text that is typed into the top cells of the table. The header will be read by screen readers, providing more accessibility for the table.

4. Merge the two cells in the top row of the nested table, click in the cell, then type **Sand Crab Cafe Hours**.

5. Enter the cafe dining area names and hours, as shown in Figure 25.

You inserted a nested table and entered a schedule for the cafe hours.

Format cell content

1. Expand the CSS panel group (if necessary).
2. Click the **Attach Style Sheet button** 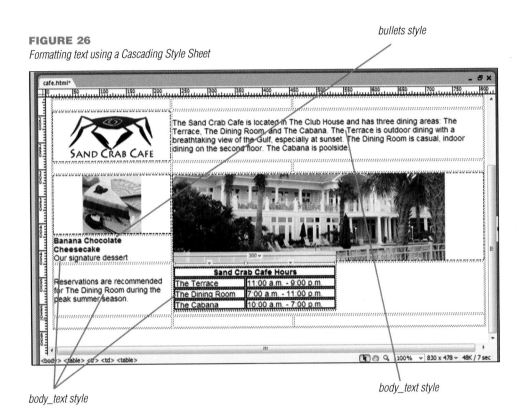 to attach the **su_styles.css** file to the cafe page.
3. Select the paragraph next to the cafe logo, then use the Property inspector to apply the **body_text style**.
4. Select the text "Banana Chocolate Cheesecake," then apply the bullets style.
5. Select the text "Our Signature dessert" and apply the **body_text style**, then select all of the text about reservations in the cell below and apply the **body_text style**.
6. Repeat Step 5 to apply the **body_text** style to the nested table text.

   Your screen should resemble Figure 26.

You formatted text in table cells using a Cascading Style Sheet.

FIGURE 26
Formatting text using a Cascading Style Sheet

bullets style

body_text style

body_text style

FIGURE 27
Formatting cells using horizontal alignment

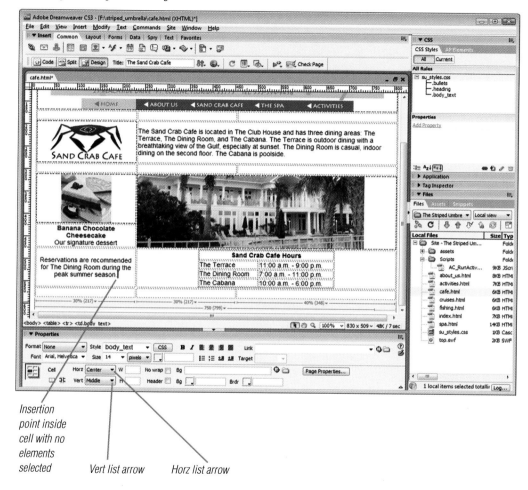

Insertion point inside cell with no elements selected

Vert list arrow

Horz list arrow

Format cells

1. Click to place the insertion point in the cell with the cheesecake name.

2. Click the **Horz list arrow** in the Property inspector, then click **Center** to center the cell contents.

   You do not need to select the text because you are setting the alignment for all contents in the cell.

3. Repeat Steps 1 and 2 for the cell with the reservations text and the cell with the nested table.

   TIP Click to the right of the nested table to easily select the cell.

4. Click in the cell with the reservations text, click the **Vert list arrow**, then click **Middle**, as shown in Figure 27.

   TIP Setting alignment can be helpful if you need to troubleshoot a page later.

5. Save your work.

You formatted table cells by adding horizontal and vertical alignment.

Modify cell content

1. Click **Modify** on the menu bar, then click **Navigation Bar** to open the Modify Navigation Bar dialog box.

2. Click the **Show "Down image" initially check box** to remove the check mark for the home button.

3. Click **cafe** in the Nav bar elements box, click the **Show "Down image" initially check box** to add a check mark, then click **OK**.

   The button now shows viewers that they are on the cafe page by displaying the down state when the page is open, as shown in Figure 28.

4. Save your work.

You edited the navigation bar to show the correct initial down state.

FIGURE 28
Edited navigation bar on the cafe page

Correct button is shown in the down state

Power User Shortcuts	
To do this:	**Use this shortcut:**
Toggle between table modes	F6
Access layout mode	[Ctrl][F6] (Win) or [option][F6] (Mac)
Insert table	[Ctrl][Alt][T] (Win) or ⌘[option][T] (Mac)
Select table	[Ctrl][A] (Win) or ⌘[A] (Mac)
Merge cells	[Ctrl][Alt][M] (Win) or ⌘[option][M] (Mac)
Split cell	[Ctrl][Alt][S] (Win) or ⌘[option][S] (Mac)
Insert row	[Ctrl][M] (Win) or ⌘[M] (Mac)
Insert column	[Ctrl][Shift][A] (Win) or ⌘[Shift][A] (Mac)
Delete row	[Ctrl][Shift][M] (Win) or ⌘[Shift][M] (Mac)
Delete column	[Ctrl][Shift][-] (Win) or ⌘[Shift][-] (Mac)
Increase column span	[Ctrl][Shift][]] (Win) or ⌘[Shift][]] (Mac)
Decrease column span	[Ctrl][Shift][[] (Win) or ⌘[Shift][[] (Mac)

FIGURE 29

Hiding visual aids

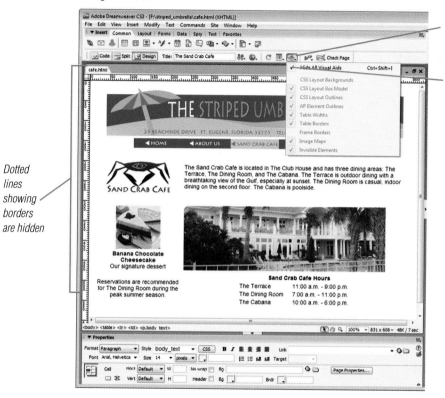

Visual Aids button

Hide All Visual Aids option

Dotted lines showing borders are hidden

Use visual aids to check layout

1. Click the **Visual Aids button** 🗔 on the Document toolbar, then click **Hide All Visual Aids**, as shown in Figure 29.

   The borders around the table, table cells, and div tags (where you used alignment options) are all hidden, allowing you to see more clearly how the page will look in the browser.

2. Repeat Step 1 to show the visual aids again.

3. Save your work, preview the cafe page in the browser, then close the browser.

You used the Hide All Visual Aids command to hide the table borders and layout block outlines, then showed them again.

Using grids and guides for positioning page content

There are some other options available to help you position your page content that are available through the View menu. **Grids** provide a graph paper-like view of a page. Horizontal and vertical lines fill the page when this option is turned on. You can edit the colors of the lines, the distance they are apart, whether they are displayed using lines or dots, and whether or not objects "snap" to them. **Guides** are horizontal or vertical lines that you drag onto the page from the rulers. You can edit both the colors of the guides and the color of the distance, a feature that shows you the distance between two guides. You can lock the guides so you don't accidentally move them and you can set them either to snap to page elements or have page elements snap to them. To display either feature, click View on the menu bar, then click Grids or Guides.

Create a table.

1. Open the blooms & bulbs Web site.
2. Open classes.html from the Web site.
3. Insert a table on the page with the following settings: Rows: **5**, Columns: **3**, Table width: **750 pixels**, Border thickness: **0**, Cell padding: **5**, and Cell spacing: **5**.
4. Enter the text **This table is used for page layout.** in the Summary text box.
5. Center-align the table on the page, then use Figure 30 as a guide for completing this exercise.
6. Replace the existing page title with the title **Master Gardener classes begin soon!**, then save your work.

Resize, split, and merge cells.

1. Select the first cell in the first row, then set the cell width to **25%**.
2. Select the second cell in the first row, then set the cell width to **40%**.
3. Select the third cell in the first row, then set the cell width to **35%**.
4. Merge the three cells in the first row.
5. Merge the first two cells in the second row.
6. Merge the third cell in the third row with the third cell in the fourth row.
7. Split the first cell in the fourth row into two columns.
8. Merge the three cells in the last row.
9. Save your work.

Insert and align graphics in table cells.

1. Copy the banner and the navigation bar together from the home page and paste them into the first row of the table.
2. Center the banner and the navigation bar.
3. Modify the navigation bar to show the classes element in the Down image state and the home element in the Up image state.
4. Use the Insert bar to insert **flower_bed.jpg** in the last row. You can find the flower_bed.jpg file in the assets folder where you store your Data Files. Add the alternate text **Flower bed in downtown Alvin** to the flower_bed.jpg image when prompted, then center the image in the cell.
5. Use the tag selector to select the cell containing the flower_bed.jpg image, then set the vertical alignment to **Top**.
6. Save your work.

Insert text and format cell content.

1. Type **Master Gardener Classes Beginning Soon!** in the first cell in the second row.
2. Type **Who are Master Gardeners?** in the second cell in the second row.
3. Type **Schedule** in the first cell in the third **row**.
4. Type **Registration** in the second cell in the third row.
5. Type the dates and times for the classes from Figure 30 in the first and second cells in the fourth row. (*Hint*: You can drag the border between columns to adjust the cells to display the hours correctly.)
6. Use the Import Word Document command on the File menu to import the file **registration.doc** into the third cell in the fourth row, (or use copy and paste) then use the Clean up Word HTML command on the Commands menu to remove any unnecessary code.
7. Repeat Step 6 to place the text from the **gardeners.doc** file into the next empty cell.
8. Attach the **blooms_styles.css** file, then apply the **bodytext** style to the dates, times, and two paragraphs of text describing the program.
9. Create a new style in the blooms_styles.css style sheet named **subheadings** with the following settings: Font: **Arial, Helvetica, sans-serif**; Size: **14**; Style: **normal**; Weight: **bold**; Color: **#003366**.
10. Create another new style in the blooms_styles.css style sheet named **reverse_text** with the following settings: Font: **Arial, Helvetica, sans-serif**; Size: **14**; Style: **normal**; Weight: **bold**; Color: **#FFFFFF**.
11. Select each cell that contains text and set the vertical alignment to **Top**.
12. Center-align the four headings (Master Gardener Classes Beginning Soon!, Who are Master Gardeners?, Schedule, and Registration).

Working with Tables

13. Set the horizontal alignment for the cell with the dates to **Center**.

14. Set the horizontal alignment for the cell with the times and the cells describing registration and Master Gardeners to **Left**.

15. Select the cell with the word "Registration" in it, then change the cell background color to **#000099**.

16. Apply the **subheadings style** to the text "Schedule" and "Who are Master Gardeners?"

17. Apply the **reverse_text** style to the heading "Registration," then apply the seasons style to the text "Master Gardener Classes Beginning Soon!"

18. Save your work, preview the page in your browser, then close your browser.

19. Close all open pages.

FIGURE 30
Completed Skills Review

In this exercise, you will continue your work on the TripSmart Web site that you began in Project Builder 1 in Chapter 1 and developed in the previous chapters. You are ready to begin work on a page that will feature catalog items. You plan to use a table for page layout.

1. Open the TripSmart Web site.
2. Open catalog.html from the Web site.
3. Insert a table with the following settings: Rows: **6**, Columns: **3**, Table width: **750 pixels**, Border thickness: **0**. Enter an appropriate table summary, then center-align the table.
4. Set the cell widths in the bottom row to **33%**, **33%**, and **34%**.
5. Merge the cells in the top row, copy the TripSmart banner and navigation bar from the home page, then paste them into the resulting merged cell. Add the following alternate text to the image: **TripSmart banner**, then center the banner.
6. Center the navigation bar, if necessary.
7. Merge the three cells in the second row, type **Our products are backed with a 100% guarantee.**, then center the text.
8. Type **Protection from harmful UV rays, Cool, light-weight, versatile**, and **Pockets for everything** in the three cells in the third row.
9. Place the files hat.jpg, pants.jpg, and vest.jpg from the assets folder where you store your Data Files in the three cells in the fourth row, add the following alternate text to the images: **Safari hat, Kenya convertible pants**, and **Photographer's vest,** then center the three images.
10. Type **Safari Hat, Kenya Convertible Pants**, and **Photographer's Vest** in the three cells in the fifth row, then center each label.
11. Type **Item number 50501** and **$29.00** with a line break between them in the first cell in the sixth row.
12. Repeat Step 11 to type **Item number 62495** and **$39.50** in the second cell in the sixth row.
13. Repeat Step 11 to type **Item number 52301** and **$54.95** in the third cell in the sixth row.
14. Attach the **tripsmart_styles.css** file to the page, apply the **body_text style** to the three descriptions in the third row, then center each description.
15. Create a new style in the tripsmart_styles.css style sheet named **reverse_text** with the following settings: Font, **Verdana, Arial, Helvetica, sans-serif**; Size, **14 px**; Style, **normal**; Weight, **bold**; Color, **#FFFFFF**.
16. Apply the **reverse_text style** to the text "Our products are backed by a 100% guarantee.", then change the cell background color to **#666666**.

17. Apply the **reverse_text style** to the three item names under the images, then change the cell background color to **#999999**.
18. Create a new style called **item_numbers** with the following settings: Font: **Verdana, Arial, Helvetica, sans-serif**; Size: **10 px**; Style: **normal**; Weight: **bold**.
19. Apply the **item_numbers style** to the three items' numbers and prices.
20. Save your work, view the page in your browser, compare your screen with Figure 31, then close the browser.
21. Save your work, then close all open pages.

FIGURE 31
Sample Project Builder 1

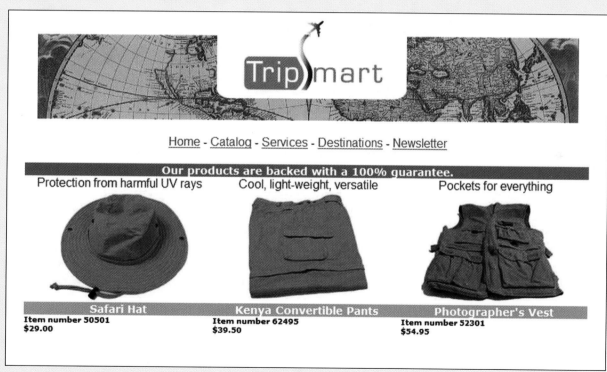

Use Figure 32 as a guide to continue your work on the Carolyne's Creations Web site that you started in Chapter 1 and developed in the previous chapters. You are now ready to begin work on a page that will showcase the catering services. You decide to use a table to lay out the page.

1. Open the Carolyne's Creations Web site, then open catering.html.
2. Type **Carolyne's Catering** for the page title, replacing the original title.
3. Create a table on the page with the following settings: Rows: **11**, Columns: **3**, Table width: **770 pixels**, Cell Pad: **3**, Cell Space: **0**, Border thickness: **0**, adding an appropriate table summary.
4. Center-align the table and set the width of the three cells to **33%** each.
5. Merge the cells in the first row, then insert the banner with links from another page in the site. Enter appropriate alternate text for the banner, then center-align the banner (if necessary).
6. Type **Catering for All Occasions** in the second cell in the third row and **Dinner to Go** in the second cell in the seventh row.
7. Attach the **cc_styles.css** file to the page, then apply the **sub_head** style to the text you typed in Step 6 and center the text.
8. Merge the cells in the 6th and 10th rows, then Insert rules that are 100% wide. (*Hints*: Change the view to Expanded Tables mode to be able to see the cells easier and use the Insert, HTML, Horizontal Rule command to insert a horizontal rule.)
9. Type **Lunch Boxes**, **Brunch Boxes**, and **Gift Baskets** in the three cells in the fourth row.
10. Type **Soups**, **Entrees**, and **Desserts** in the three cells in the eighth row.
11. Apply the **sub_head** style to the text you typed in Steps 9 and 10, then center each heading.
12. Use the file cell_back.jpg from your Data Files folder to serve as the background for each cell in the fourth and eighth rows. (*Hint*: Use the Browse for File icon next to the Bg text box.)

Working with Tables

13. Type the text **Call/fax by 9:00 a.m. for lunch orders, Call/fax by 1:00 p.m. for dinner orders, Fax number: 555-963-5938** in the first cell in the last row using a line break to separate the first two lines and a paragraph break to separate the last line.

14. Apply the **body_text style** to the text you typed in Step 13.

15. Open the file menu items.doc from your Data Files folder. Copy and paste each text block into the cells in the fifth and ninth rows, then apply the **body_text style** to each text block, using Figure 32 as a guide.

16. Merge the last two cells in the last row, then insert the image muffins.jpg with any additional formatting of your choice.

17. Save your work, preview the page in your browser, then close all open files.

FIGURE 32
Completed Project Builder 2

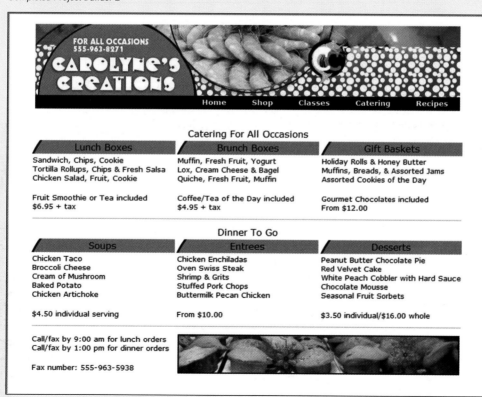

Vesta Everitt has opened a new shop called CollegeFandz, an online source for college clothing and collectibles. She is considering creating a Web site to promote her services and products and would like to gather some ideas before she hires a Web designer. She decides to visit retail Web sites to look for design ideas. Figures 33 and 34 show the Teva and L.L. Bean Web sites.

1. Connect to the Internet, then go to *www.teva.com*.
2. Click View on your browser's menu bar, then click the Source or View Source command to view the source code for the Web site you selected.
3. Search the code for table tags. Note the number that you find.
4. Browse to *www.llbean.com* next and repeat Steps 2 and 3.
5. Using a word processor or paper, list five design ideas that you like from either of these pages. Be sure to specify which page was the source of each idea.

FIGURE 33
Design Project

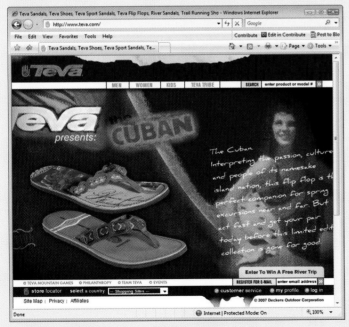

Teva Web site used with permission from Deckers Outdoor Corporation – www.teva.com

FIGURE 34
Design Project

LL. Bean Web site used with permission from L.L. Bean – www. llbean.com

In this assignment, you will continue to work on the Web site that you started in Chapter 1 and developed in Chapters 2 through 4. There will be no data files supplied. You are building this Web site from chapter to chapter, so you must do each Portfolio Project assignment in each chapter to complete your Web site.

You will continue building your Web site by designing and completing a page that contains a table used for page layout. After completing your page, you will run several reports to test the Web site.

1. Take a few minutes to evaluate your storyboard. Choose a page or pages to develop in which you will use a table for page layout.
2. Plan the content for the new page (or pages) by making a sketch of the table that shows where the content will be placed in the table cells. Split and merge cells and align each element as necessary to create a visually attractive layout.
3. Create the table and place the content in the cells using the sketch for guidance.
4. After you complete the pages, run a report that checks for broken links in the Web site. Correct any broken links that appear in the report.
5. Run a report on the Web site for orphaned files and correct any if found.
6. Check for any Non-Websafe colors in the Web site. If any are found, replace them with Websafe colors.
7. Preview all the pages in your browser and test all links. Evaluate the pages for both content and layout, then use the checklist in Figure 35 to make sure your Web site is completed.
8. Make any modifications necessary to improve the pages.

FIGURE 35
Portfolio Project checklist

Web Site Checklist

1. Title any pages that have no page titles.
2. Check to see that all pages have consistent navigation links.
3. Check to see that all links work correctly.
4. Check to see that all images have alternate text.
5. Remove any Non-Websafe colors.
6. Delete any unnecessary files.
7. Remove any orphaned files.
8. Use tables for layout when possible.
9. View all pages using at least two different browsers.
10. Verify that the home page has keywords, a description, and a point of contact.

Working with Tables

6

MANAGING A WEB
SERVER AND FILES

1. Perform Web site maintenance

2. Publish a Web site and transfer files

3. Check files out and in

4. Cloak files

5. Import and export a site definition

6. Evaluate Web content for legal use

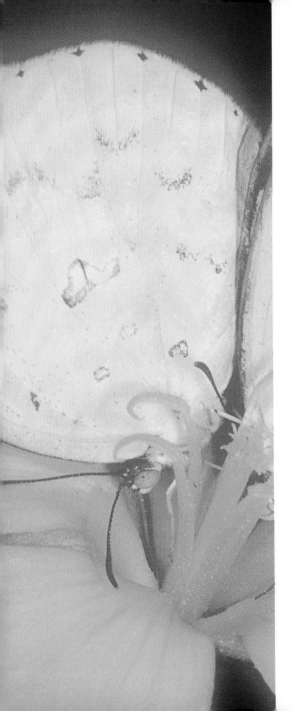

chapter **6** MANAGING A WEB
SERVER AND FILES

Introduction

Once you have created all the pages of your
Web site, finalized all the content, and performed site maintenance, you are ready to
publish your site to a remote server so the
rest of the world can access it. In this chapter, you will start by running some reports to
make sure the links in your site work properly, that the colors are Websafe, and that
orphaned files are removed. Next, you will
set up a connection to the remote site for
The Striped Umbrella Web site. You will then
transfer files to the remote site and learn
how to keep them up to date. You will also
check out a file so that it is not available to
other team members while you are editing it
and you will learn how to cloak files. When a
file is **cloaked**, it is excluded from certain
processes, such as being transferred to the
remote site. Next, you will export the site
definition file from The Striped Umbrella
Web site so that other designers can import
the site. Finally, you will research important
copyright issues that affect all Web sites.

Preparing to Publish a Site

Before you publish a site to a remote
server so that it is available to others, it is

extremely important that you test it regularly to make sure the content is accurate
and up to date and that everything is
functioning properly. When viewing
pages over the Internet, it is very frustrating to click a link that doesn't work or
have to wait for pages that load slowly
because of large graphics and animations.
Remember that a typical Web viewer has
a short attention span and limited
patience. Before you publish your site,
make sure to use the Link Checker panel
to check for broken links and orphaned
files. Make sure that all image paths are
correct and that all images load quickly
and have alternate text. Verify that all
pages have titles, and remove all Non-
Websafe colors. View the pages in at least
two different browsers and different versions of the same browser to ensure that
everything works correctly. The more frequently you test, the better the chance
that your viewers will have a positive experience at your site and want to return. All
content must be original to the Web site,
have been obtained legally, or used properly without violating the copyright of
someone else's work.

6-2

Tools You'll Use

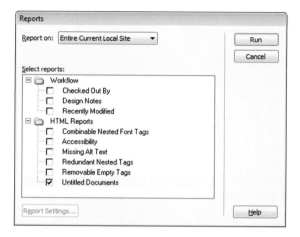

PERFORM WEB SITE MAINTENANCE

What You'll Do

 In this lesson, you will use some of Dreamweaver's site management tools to check for broken links, orphaned files, and missing alternate text. You will also verify that all colors are Websafe. You will then correct any problems that you find.

Maintaining a Web Site

As you add pages, links, and content to a Web site, it can quickly become difficult to manage. It's important to perform maintenance tasks frequently to make sure your Web site operates smoothly and remains "clean." You have already learned about some of the tools described in the following paragraphs. Although it is important to use them as you create and modify your pages, it is also important to run them at periodic intervals after publishing your Web site to make sure your Web site is always error-free.

Using the Assets Panel

You should use the Assets panel to check the list of images and colors used in your Web site. If you see images listed that are not being used, you should move them to a storage folder outside the Web site until you need them. If you are concerned about using only Websafe colors, you should also check the Colors list to make sure that all colors in the site are Websafe. If there are non-Websafe colors in the list, locate the elements to which

these colors are applied and apply Websafe colors to them.

Checking Links Sitewide

Before and after you publish your Web site, you should use the Link Checker panel to make sure all internal links are working. If the Link Checker panel displays any broken links, you should repair them. If the Link Checker panel displays any orphaned files, you should evaluate whether to delete them or link them with existing pages.

Using Site Reports

You can use the Reports command in the Site menu to generate six different HTML reports that can help you maintain your Web site. You choose the type of report you want to run in the Reports dialog box, shown in Figure 1. You can specify whether to generate the report for the current document, the entire current local site, selected files in the site, or a selected folder. You can also generate Workflow reports to see files that have been checked out by others or recently modified or you can view the Design Notes attached to files.

Design Notes are separate files in a Web site that contain additional information about a page file or a graphic file. In a collaborative situation, designers can record notes to exchange information with other designers. Design Notes can also be used to record sensitive information that would not be included in files that could be viewed on the Web site. Information about the source files for graphic files, such as Flash files or Fireworks files, are also stored in Design Notes.

Using the Site Map

You can use the site map to check your navigation structure. Does the site map show that you have followed the file hierarchy in the storyboard and flow chart? Does the navigation structure shown in the site map reflect a logically organized flowchart? Is each page three or four clicks from the home page? If the answer is no to any of these questions, make adjustments to improve the navigation structure.

Validating Markup

One of the report features in Dreamweaver is the ability to validate markup. This means that Dreamweaver will go through the code to look for errors that could occur with different language versions, such as XHTML or XML. To validate code for a page, click File on the menu bar, point to Validate, and then click Markup. The Results panel opens and lists any pages with errors, the line numbers where the errors occur, and an explanation of the errors. The Validate button on the

Results panel offers the choice of validating a single document, an entire local Web site, or selected files in a local Web site.

Testing Pages

Finally, you should test your Web site using many different types and versions of browsers, platforms, and screen resolutions. You can use the Check Page button on the Document toolbar to check browser compatibility. This feature lists issues with the pages in your site that may cause problems when the pages are viewed using certain browsers, such as the rendering of square bullets in Mozilla Firefox. If you find such issues, you then have the choice to make changes to your page to eliminate the problems. The Reports panel includes a URL that you can visit to find the solutions to problems. You should test every link to make sure it connects to valid, active Web sites. Pages that download slowly should be reduced in size to improve performance. You should analyze all feedback on the Web site objectively, saving both positive and negative comments for future reference to help you make improvements to the site.

FIGURE 1
Reports dialog box

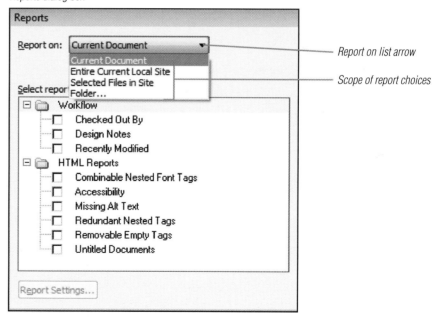

Report on list arrow

Scope of report choices

Check for broken links

1. Open The Striped Umbrella Web site.

2. Show the Files panel (if necessary).

3. Click **Site** on the menu bar, point to **Advanced**, then click **Recreate Site Cache**.

4. Click **Site** on the menu bar, then click **Check Links Sitewide**.

   No broken links are listed in the Link Checker panel of the Results panel group, as shown in Figure 2.

You verified that there are no broken links in the Web site.

Check for orphaned files

1. In the Link Checker panel, click the **Show list arrow**, then click **Orphaned Files**.

   As Figure 3 shows, there are no orphaned files.

2. Close the Results panel group.

You verified that there are no orphaned files in the Web site.

FIGURE 2
Link Checker panel displaying no broken links

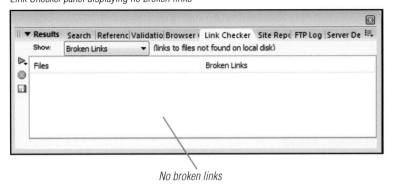

No broken links

FIGURE 3
Link Checker panel displaying no orphaned files

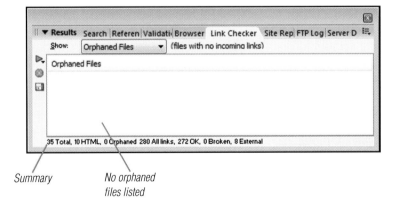

Summary

No orphaned
files listed

FIGURE 4

Assets panel displaying Websafe colors

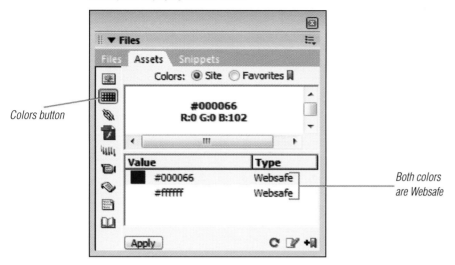

Colors button

Both colors
are Websafe

1. Click the **Assets tab**, then click the **Colors button** ▦ to view the Web site colors, as shown in Figure 4.

   The Assets panel shows that all colors used in the Web site are Websafe.

You verified that the Web site contains all Websafe colors.

Using Find and Replace to Locate Non-Websafe Colors

As with many software applications, Dreamweaver has a Find and Replace feature that can be used both in Design view and in Code view under the Edit menu. If you are looking for a non-Websafe color, you will probably save time by using the Find and Replace feature to locate the hexadecimal color code in Code view. If a site has very many pages, this will be the fastest way to locate it. The Find and Replace feature can also be used to locate other character combinations, such as a phrase that begins or ends with a particular word or tag. These patterns of character combinations are referred to as **regular expressions**. To find out more, search for "regular expressions" in Dreamweaver Help.

Check for untitled documents

1. Click **Site** on the menu bar, then click **Reports** to open the Reports dialog box.

2. Click the **Untitled Documents check box**, click the **Report on list arrow**, click **Entire Current Local Site**, as shown in Figure 5, then click **Run**.

   The Site Reports panel opens in the Results panel group, and shows no files, indicating that all documents in the Web site contain titles.

You verified that the Web site contains no untitled documents.

FIGURE 5

Reports dialog box with Untitled Documents option selected

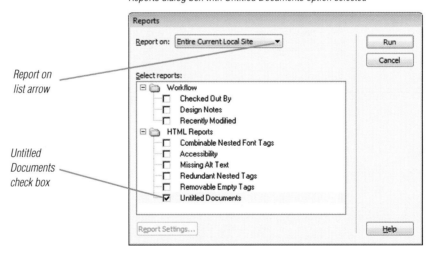

Report on list arrow

Untitled Documents check box

FIGURE 6

Reports dialog box with Missing Alt Text option selected

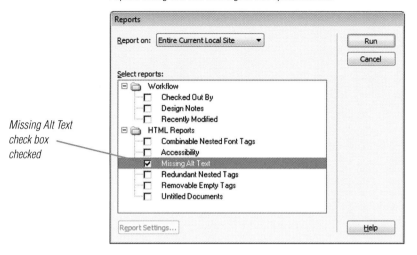

Missing Alt Text check box checked

1. Using Figure 6 as a guide, run another report that checks the entire current local site for missing alternate text.

   The results show that the spa page contains images that are missing alternate text, as shown in Figure 7.

2. Open the spa page, then find the images that are missing alternate text.

   TIP   The Site Reports panel documents the code line numbers where the missing alt tags occur. Sometimes it is faster to locate the errors in Code view, rather than in Design view.

3. Add appropriate alternate text to the images.

4. Save your work, then run the report again to check the entire site for missing alternate text.

   No files should appear in the Site Reports panel.

5. Close the Results panel group, then close all open pages.

You ran a report to check for missing alternate text in the entire site. You then added alternate text to two images and ran the report again.

FIGURE 7

Site Reports panel displaying missing "alt" tags

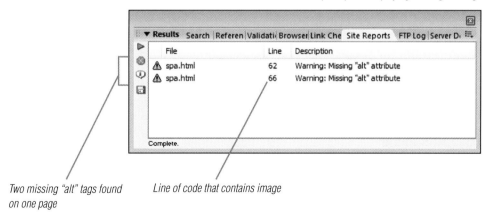

Two missing "alt" tags found on one page

Line of code that contains image

Enable Design Notes

1. Click **Site** on the menu bar, point to **Manage Sites**, click **Edit**, click the **Advanced tab** (if necessary), then click the **Design Notes category**.

2. Click the **Maintain Design Notes check box**, to select it (if necessary), as shown in Figure 8.

3. Click the **File View Columns category**, then click **Notes** in the File View Columns list.

4. Click the **Options**: **Show check box**, to select it (if necessary), click **OK**, then click **Done** in the Manage Sites dialog box.

   The Notes column now displays the word "Show" in the Show column, as shown in Figure 9, indicating that the Notes column will be visible in the Files panel.

You set the preference to use Design Notes in the Web site. You also set the option to display the Notes column in the Files panel.

FIGURE 8

Site Definition for The Striped Umbrella

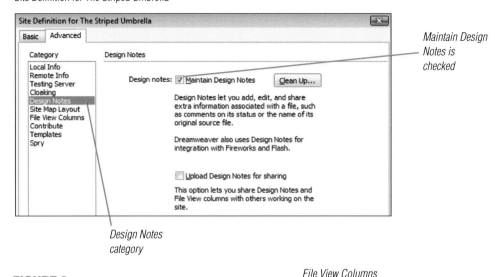

Maintain Design Notes is checked

Design Notes category

FIGURE 9

Site Definition for The Striped Umbrella

File View Columns category

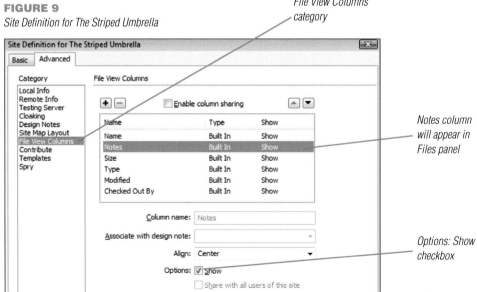

Notes column will appear in Files panel

Options: Show checkbox

Managing a Web Server and Files

FIGURE 10

Design Notes dialog box

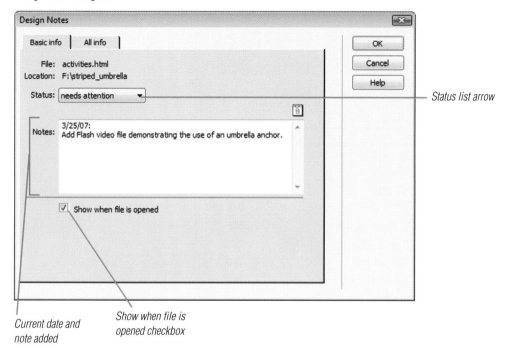

Status list arrow

Current date and
note added

Show when file is
opened checkbox

Associate a Design Note with a file

1. Open the activities page, click **File** on the menu bar, click **Design Notes**, then click the **Basic Info tab** (if necessary).

   The Design Notes dialog box opens with a text box to record a note related to the open file, the option to display the note each time the file is opened, an option to include the current date, and a status indicator.

2. Click the **Date icon** 🗓 above the Notes text box on the right.

   The current date is added to the Notes text box.

3. Type **Add Flash video file demonstrating the use of an umbrella anchor**. in the Notes text box beneath the date.

4. Click the **Status list arrow**, then click **needs attention**.

5. Click the **Show when file is opened** check box to select it, as shown in Figure 10, then click **OK**.

You added a design note to the activities page with the current date and a status indicator. The note will open each time the file is opened.

Using Version Cue to Manage Assets

Another way to collaborate with team members is through Adobe Version Cue, a workgroup collaboration system that is included in Adobe Creative Suite 3. You can perform such functions such as managing security, backing up data, and using metadata to search files. **Metadata** includes information about a file such as keywords, descriptions, and copyright information. Adobe Bridge also organizes files with metadata.

Edit a Design Note

1. Click **File** on the menu bar, then click **Design Notes** to open the Design Note associated with the activities page.

   You can also right-click (Windows) or control-click (Mac) the filename in the Files panel, then click Design Notes, or double-click the yellow Design Notes icon in the Files panel next to the filename to open a Design Note, as shown in Figure 11.

2. Edit the note by adding the sentence **Ask Jane Pinson to send the files.** beneath the existing text in the Notes section, then click **OK** to close it.

   A file named activities.html.mno has been created in a new folder called_notes. This folder and file will not display in the Files panel unless you have the option to show hidden files and folders selected. However, you can switch to Windows Explorer to see them without selecting this option.

FIGURE 11
Files panel with Notes icon displayed

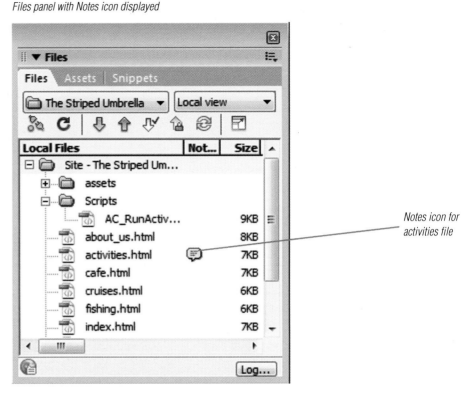

Notes icon for activities file

Deleting a Design Note

There are two steps to deleting a design note that you don't need anymore. The first step is to delete the file. To delete a Design Note, right-click the filename in the Files panel that is associated with the Design Note you want to delete, and then click Explore (Win) or Reveal in Finder (Mac) to open your file management system. Delete the .mno file in the files list, and then close Explorer (Win) or Finder (Mac). The second step is done in Dreamweaver. Click Site on the menu bar, click Manage Sites, click Edit, and then select the Design Notes category. Click the Clean Up button. (*Note*: Don't do this if you deselect Maintain Design Notes first or it will delete all of your design notes!) The Design Notes icon will be removed from the Notes column in the Files panel.

FIGURE 12

Windows Explorer displaying the notes file and folder

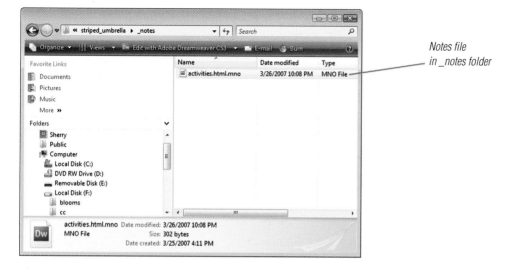

Notes file
in _notes folder

3. Right-click (Win) or control-click (Mac) **activities.html** in the Files panel, then click **Explore** (Win) or **Reveal in Finder** (Mac).

4. Double-click the folder **_notes** to open it, then double-click the file **activities.html.mno**, shown in Figure 12, to open the file in Dreamweaver.

   The notes file opens in Code view in Dreamweaver, as shown in Figure 13.

5. Read the file, close it, then close Explorer (Win) or Finder (Mac).

You opened the Design Notes dialog box and edited the note in the Notes text box. Next, you viewed the .mno file that Dreamweaver created when you added the Design Note.

FIGURE 13

Code for the activities.html.mno file

```
1  <?xml version="1.0" encoding="utf-8" ?>
2  <info>
3      <infoitem key="notes" value="3/25/07: &#xD;Add Flash video file
   demonstrating the use of an umbrella anchor. Ask Jane Pinson to send the
   files." />
4      <infoitem key="showOnOpen" value="true" />
5      <infoitem key="status" value="needs attention" />
6  </info>
7
```

PUBLISH A WEB SITE
AND TRANSFER FILES

What You'll Do

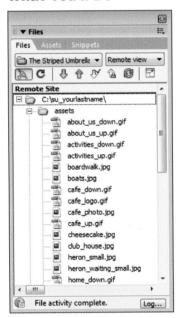

 In this lesson, you will set up remote access to either an FTP folder or a local/network folder for The Striped Umbrella Web site. You will also view a Web site on a remote server, upload files to it, and synchronize the files.

Defining a Remote Site

As you learned in Chapter 1, publishing a site means transferring all the site's files to a Web server. A **Web server** is a computer that is connected to the Internet with an IP (Internet Protocol) address so that it is available on the Internet. Before you can publish a site to a Web server, you must first define the remote site by specifying the Remote Info settings in the Advanced section of the Site Definition dialog box. You can specify remote settings when you first create a new site and define the root folder (as you did in Chapter 1 when you defined the remote access settings for The Striped Umbrella Web site), or you can do it after you have completed all of your pages and are confident that your site is ready for public viewing. To specify the remote settings for a site, you must first choose an Access setting, which specifies the type of server you will use. The most common Access setting is FTP (File Transfer Protocol). If you specify FTP, you will need to specify an address for the server and the name of the folder on the FTP site in which your root folder will be stored. You will also need to enter login and password information. Figure 14 shows an example of FTP settings in the Remote Info category of the Site Definition dialog box.

> **QUICK**TIP
>
> If you do not have access to an FTP site, you can publish a site to a local/network folder. This is referred to as a **LAN**, or a Local Area Network. Use the alternate steps provided in this lesson to publish your site to a local/network folder.

Viewing a Remote Site

Once you have defined a site to a remote location, you can then view the remote folder in the Files panel by choosing Remote view from the View list. If your remote site is located on an FTP server, Dreamweaver will connect to it. You will see the File Activity dialog box showing the progress of the connection. You can also use the Connects to remote host button on the Files panel toolbar to connect to the remote site. If you defined your site on a local/network folder, then you don't need to use the Connects to remote host button; the root folder and any files and folders it contains will appear in the Files panel when you switch to Remote view.

Transferring Files to and from a Remote Site

After you define a remote site, you will need to transfer or **upload** your files from the local version of your site to the remote host. To do this, view the site in Local view, select the files you want to upload, and then click the Put File(s) button on the Files panel toolbar. Once you click this button, the files will be transferred to the remote site. To view the uploaded files, switch to Remote view, as shown in Figure 15. Or, you can expand the Files panel to view both the Remote Site and the Local Files panes.

If a file you select for uploading requires additional files, such as graphics, a dialog box will open after you click the Put File(s) button and ask if you want those files (known as **dependent files**) to be uploaded. By clicking Yes, all dependent files in the selected page will be uploaded to the appropriate folder in the remote site. If a file that you want to upload is located in a folder in the local site, the entire folder will be automatically transferred to the remote site.

QUICKTIP

To upload an entire site to a remote host, select the root folder, then click the Put File(s) button. Sometimes you will need to move the files you want to upload to an intermediary folder before transferring them to the remote site.

If you are developing or maintaining a Web site in a group environment, there might be times when you want to transfer or **download** files that other team members have created from the remote site to your local site. To do this, switch to Remote view,

FIGURE 14

FTP settings in the Site Definition for The Striped Umbrella dialog box

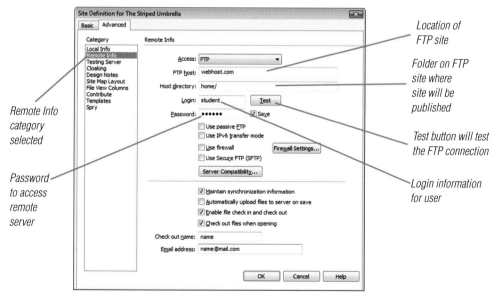

Remote Info category selected

Password to access remote server

FIGURE 15

Files panel with Remote view selected

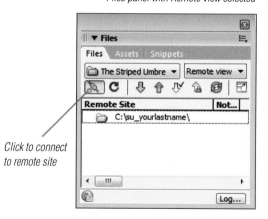

Location of FTP site

Folder on FTP site where site will be published

Test button will test the FTP connection

Login information for user

Click to connect to remote site

select the files you want to download, then click the Get File(s) button on the Files panel toolbar.

Synchronizing Files

To keep a Web site up to date—especially one that contains several pages and involves several team members—you will need to update and replace files. Team members might make changes to pages on the local version of the site or make additions to the remote site. If many people are involved in maintaining a site, or if you are constantly making changes to the pages, ensuring that both the local and remote sites have the most up-to-date files could get confusing. Thankfully, you can use the Synchronize command to keep things straight. The Synchronize command instructs Dreamweaver to compare the dates of the saved files in both versions of the site, then transfers only the files that have changed. To synchronize files, use the Synchronize Files dialog box, as shown in Figure 16. You can synchronize an entire site or just selected files. You can also specify whether to upload newer files to the remote site, download newer files from the remote site, or both.

FIGURE 16
Synchronize Files dialog box

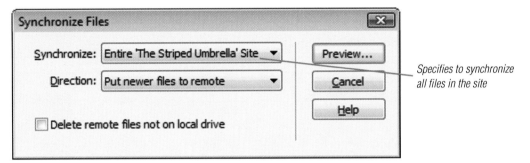

Specifies to synchronize all files in the site

Understanding Dreamweaver connection options for transferring files

The connection types with which you are probably the most familiar are FTP and Local/Network. Other connection types that you can use with Dreamweaver are VSS, WebDav, and RDS. **VSS** refers to Microsoft Visual SafeSource, and is used only with the Windows operating system with Microsoft Visual SafeSource Client version 6. **WebDav** stands for Web-based Distributed Authoring and Versioning. This type of connection is used with the WebDav protocol. An example would be a Web site residing on an Apache Web server. **RDS** stands for Remote Development Services, and is used with Web servers using Cold Fusion.

FIGURE 17

FTP settings specified in the Site Definition for The Striped Umbrella dialog box

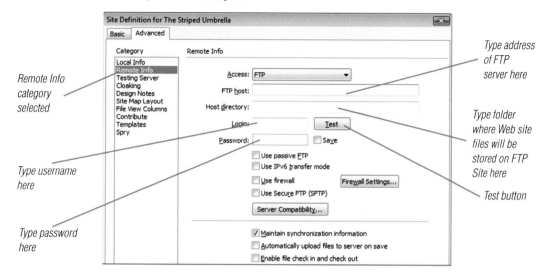

Remote Info category selected

Type username here

Type password here

Type address of FTP server here

Type folder where Web site files will be stored on FTP Site here

Test button

Comparing two files for differences in content

There are situations where it would be helpful to be able to compare the contents of two files, such as a local file and the remote version of the same file; or an original file and the same file that has been saved with a different name. Once the two files are compared and differences are detected, you can merge the information in the files. A good time to compare files is before you upload them to a remote server to prevent accidentally writing over a file with more recent information. To compare files, you must first locate and install a third-party file comparison utility, or "dif" tool, such as FileMerge or BBEdit. (Dreamweaver does not have a file comparison tool included as part of the software. You will have to download one. If you are not familiar with these tools, find one using your favorite search engine.)

After installing the files comparison utility, use the Preferences command on the Edit menu, and then select the File Compare category. Next, browse to select the application to compare files. After you have set your Preferences, click the Compare with Remote command on the File menu to compare an open file with the remote version.

Set up Web server access on an FTP site

NOTE: Complete these steps only if you know you can store The Striped Umbrella files on an FTP site and you know the login and password information. If you do not have access to an FTP site, complete the exercise called Set up Web server access on a local or network folder on Page 6-18.

1. Click **Site** on the menu bar, then click **Manage Sites**.

2. Click **The Striped Umbrella** in the Manage Sites dialog box (if necessary), then click **Edit**.

3. Click the **Advanced tab**, click **Remote Info** in the Category list, click the **Access list arrow**, click **FTP**, then compare your screen to Figure 17.

4. Enter the FTP host, Host directory, Login, and Password information in the dialog box.

   TIP You must have file and folder permissions to use FTP.

5. Click the **Test button** to test the connection to the remote site.

6. If the connection is successful, click **Done** to close the dialog box; if it is not successful, repeat Step 4.

7. Click **OK**, then click **Done** to close the Manage Sites dialog box.

You set up remote access information for The Striped Umbrella Web site using an FTP site folder.

Set up Web server access on a local or network folder

NOTE: Complete these steps if you do not have the ability to post files to an FTP site and could not complete the previous objective.

1. Using Windows Explorer (Win) or Finder (Mac), create a new folder on your hard drive or on a shared drive named **su_yourlastname** (e.g., if your last name is Jones, name the folder **su_jones**.)

2. Switch back to Dreamweaver, open The Striped Umbrella Web site, click **Site** on the menu bar, then click **Manage Sites** to open the Manage Sites dialog box.

3. Click **The Striped Umbrella**, click **Edit** to open the Site Definition for The Striped Umbrella dialog box, click the **Advanced tab**, then click **Remote Info** in the Category list.

4. Click the **Access list arrow**, then click **Local/Network**.

5. Click the **Browse for File icon** 🗀 next to the Remote folder text box to open the Choose remote root folder for site The Striped Umbrella dialog box, navigate to the folder you created in Step 1, select the folder, click **Open**, then click **Select** (Win) or **Choose** (Mac).

6. Compare your screen to Figure 18, click **OK**, click **OK** in the message window about the site cache, then click **Done**.

You created a new folder and specified it as the remote location for The Striped Umbrella Web site, then set up remote access to a local or network folder.

FIGURE 18

Local/Network settings specified in the Site Definition for The Striped Umbrella dialog box

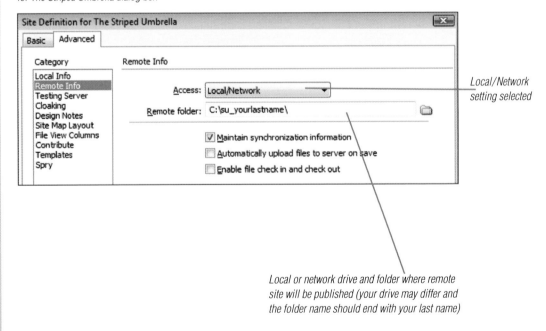

Local/Network setting selected

Local or network drive and folder where remote site will be published (your drive may differ and the folder name should end with your last name)

FIGURE 19
Connecting to the remote site

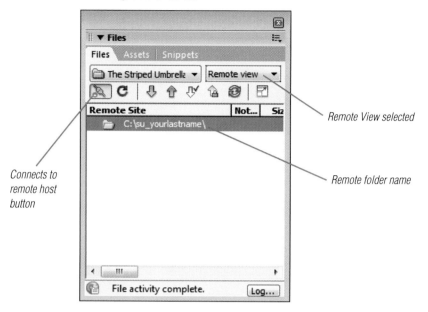

Connects to
remote host
button

Remote View selected

Remote folder name

View a Web site on a remote server

1. Click the **View list arrow** in the Files panel, then click **Remote view**, as shown in Figure 19.

   If you specified your remote access to a local or network folder, then the su_yourlastname folder will now appear in the Files panel. If your remote access is set to an FTP site, Dreamweaver will connect to the host server to see the remote access folder.

2. Click the **Expand to show local and remote sites button** to view both the Remote Site and Local Files panes. The su_yourlast-name folder appears in the Remote Site portion of the Files panel.

   TIP If you don't see your remote site files, click the Connects to remote host button or the Refresh button .

3. Click the **Collapse to show only local or remote site button** to return to Design view.

You used the Files panel to set the view for The Striped Umbrella site to Remote view. You then connected to the remote server to view the contents of the remote folder you specified.

Using a site usability test to test your site

Once you have at least a prototype of the Web site ready to evaluate, it is a good idea to conduct a site usability test. This is a process that involves asking unbiased people, who are not connected to the design process, to use and evaluate the site. A comprehensive usability test will include pre-test questions, participant tasks, a post-test interview, and a post-test survey. This will provide much-needed information as to how usable the site is to those unfamiliar with it. Typical questions include: "What are your overall impressions?"; "What do you like the best and the least about the site?"; and "How easy is it to navigate inside the site?" For more information, go to *www.w3.org* and search for "site usability test."

Upload files to a remote server

1. Click the **about_us.html file**, then click the **Put File(s) button** ⬆ on the Files panel toolbar.

   The Dependent Files dialog box opens, asking if you want to include dependent files.

2. Click **Yes**.

   The about_us file and the other image files used in the about_us page are copied to the remote server. The Status dialog box appears and flashes the names of each file as they are uploaded.

3. Expand the assets folder (if necessary), then compare your screen to Figure 20.

   The remote site now contains the about_us page as well as several images, and the striped_umbrella external style sheet file, all of which are needed by the about_us page.

   TIP   You might need to expand the su_yourlastname folder in order to view the assets folder.

You used the Put File(s) button to upload the about_us file and all files that are dependent files of the about_us page.

FIGURE 20
Remote view of The Striped Umbrella Web site after uploading the about_us page

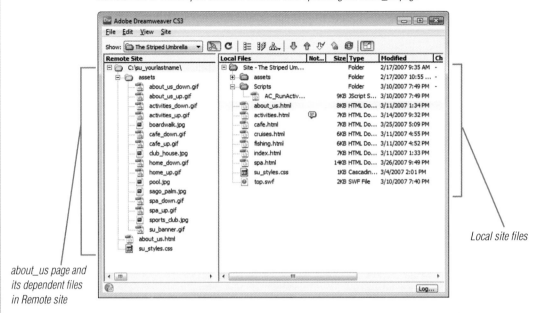

about_us page and its dependent files in Remote site

Local site files

Continuing to work while transferring files to a remote server

During the process of uploading files to a remote server, there are many Dreamweaver functions that you can continue to use while you wait. For example, you can create a new site, create a new page, edit a page, add files and folders, and run reports. However, there are some functions that you cannot use while transferring files, many of which involve accessing files on the remote server or using Check In/Check Out.

FIGURE 21
Synchronize Files dialog box

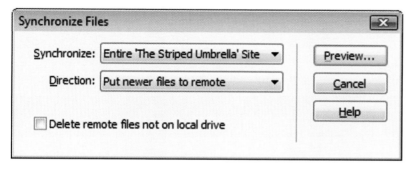

FIGURE 22
Files that need to be uploaded to the remote site

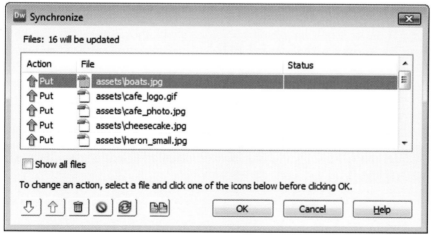

Synchronize files

1. Click **Site** on the menu bar, click **Synchronize Sitewide** to open the Synchronize Files dialog box (Win) or click the **Options list arrow**, point to **Site**, then click **Synchronize** to open the Synchronize Files dialog box (Mac).

2. Click the **Synchronize list arrow**, then click **Entire 'The Striped Umbrella' Site**.

3. Click the **Direction list arrow**, click **Put newer files to remote** (if necessary), then compare your screen to Figure 21.

4. Click **Preview**.

   The Status dialog box might appear and flash the names of all the files from the local version of the site that need to be uploaded to the remote site. The dialog box shown in Figure 22 then opens and lists all the files that need to be uploaded to the remote site.

5. Click **OK**.

   All the files from the local The Striped Umbrella Web site are now contained in the remote version of the site. The dialog box changes to show the files that were uploaded.

   TIP   If you want to keep a record of your synchronizations, click Save Log, specify a location and name for the synchronization log, then click Save.

6. Refresh the Files panel to place the files and folders in alphabetical order.

You synchronized The Striped Umbrella Web site files to copy all remaining files from the local root folder to the remote root folder.

CHECK FILES
OUT AND IN

What You'll Do

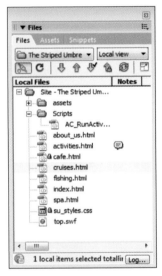

 In this lesson, you will use the Site Definition dialog box to enable the Check In/Check Out feature. You will then check out the cafe page, make a change to it, and then check it back in.

Managing a Web Site with a Team

When you work on a large Web site, chances are that many people will be involved in keeping the site up to date. Different individuals will need to make changes or additions to different pages of the site by adding or deleting content, changing graphics, updating information, and so on. If everyone had access to the pages at the same time, problems could arise. For instance, what if you and another team member both made edits to the same page at the same time? If you post your edited version of the file to the site after the other team member posts his edited version of the same file, the file that you upload will overwrite his version and none of his changes will be incorporated.

Not good! Fortunately, you can avoid this scenario by using Dreamweaver's collaboration tools.

Checking Out and Checking In Files

Checking in and out files is similar to checking in and out library books or video/DVD rentals. No one else can read the same copy that you have checked out. Using Dreamweaver's Check In/Check Out feature ensures that team members can not overwrite each other's pages. When this feature is enabled, only one person can work on a file at a time. To check out a file, click the file you want to work on in the Files panel, and then click the Check Out File(s) button on the Files panel toolbar. Files that you have checked out are marked with green check marks in the Files panel. Files that have been checked in are marked with padlock icons.

After you finish editing a checked-out file, you need to save and close the file, and then click the Check In button to check the file back in and make it available to other users.

When a file is checked in, you cannot make edits to it unless you check it out again. Figure 23 shows the Check Out File(s) and Check In buttons on the Files panel toolbar.

Enabling the Check In/Check Out Feature

To use the Check In /Check Out feature with a team of people, you must first enable it. To turn on this feature, check the Enable file check in and check out check box in the Remote Info settings of the Site Definition dialog box.

FIGURE 23

Check Out File(s) and Check in buttons on the Files Panel toolbar

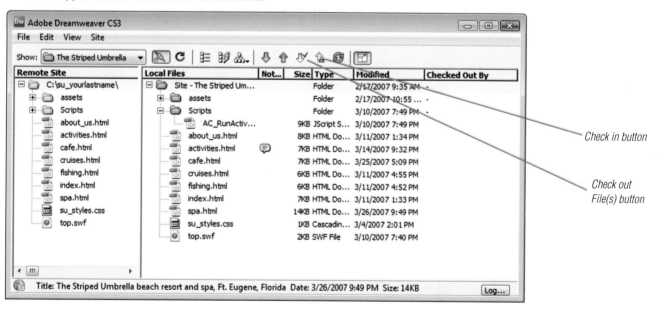

Enable the Check In/Check Out feature

1. Verify that the Site panel is in expanded view, click **Site** on the menu bar, click **Manage Sites** to open the Manage Sites dialog box, click **The Striped Umbrella** in the list, then click **Edit** to open the Site Definition for The Striped Umbrella dialog box.

2. Click **Remote Info** in the Category list, then click the **Enable file check in and check out check box** to select it.

3. Check the **Check out files when opening check box** to select it (if necessary).

4. Type **your name** using lowercase letters and no spaces in the Check out name text box.

5. Type your **e-mail address** in the Email address text box.

6. Compare your screen to Figure 24, click **OK** to close the Site Definition for The Striped Umbrella dialog box, then click **Done** to close the Manage Sites dialog box.

You used the Site Definition for The Striped Umbrella dialog box to enable the Check In/Check Out feature to let site collaborators know when you are working with a file in the site.

Check out a file

1. Click the **cafe page** in the Local Files list in the Files panel to select it.

(continued)

FIGURE 24
Enabling the Check In/Check Out feature

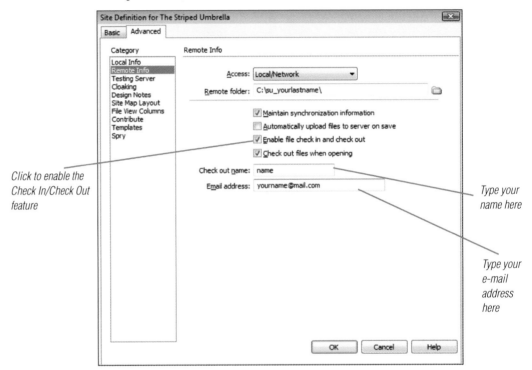

Click to enable the Check In/Check Out feature

Type your name here

Type your e-mail address here

FIGURE 25

Files panel in Local view after checking out cafe page

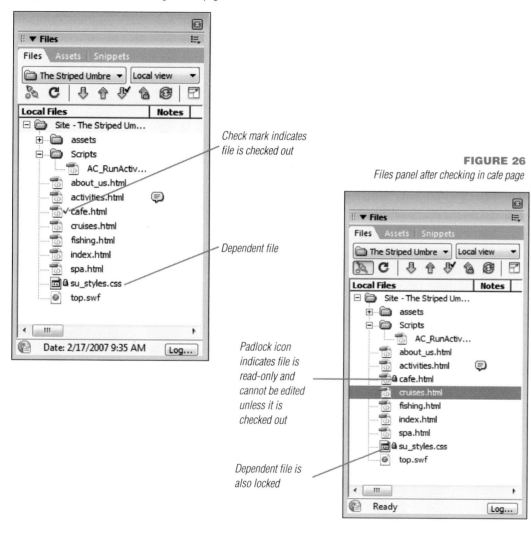

Check mark indicates file is checked out

Dependent file

Padlock icon indicates file is read-only and cannot be edited unless it is checked out

Dependent file is also locked

FIGURE 26

Files panel after checking in cafe page

2. Click the **Check Out File(s) button** on the Files panel toolbar.

The Dependent Files dialog box appears, asking if you want to include all files that are needed for the cafe page.

3. Click **Yes**, click another file in the Files panel to deselect the cafe page, collapse the Files panel, switch to Local view, then compare your screen to Figure 25.

The cafe file has a check mark next to it indicating you have checked it out. The dependent file has a padlock icon.

TIP   If a dialog box appears asking "Do you wish to overwrite your local copy of cafe.html?", click Yes.

You checked out the cafe page so that no one else can use it.

Check in a file

1. Open the cafe page, change the closing hour for the The Cabana in the nested table to **7:00 p.m.**, then save your changes.

2. Close the cafe page, then click the **cafe page** in the Files panel to select it.

3. Click the **Check In button** on the Files panel toolbar.

The Dependent Files dialog box opens, asking if you want to include dependent files.

4. Click **Yes**, click another file in the Files panel to deselect the cafe page, then compare your screen to Figure 26.

A padlock icon appears instead of a green check mark next to the cafe page on the Files panel.

You made a content change on the cafe page, then checked in the cafe page, making it available for others to check it out.

CLOAK
FILES

What You'll Do

 In this lesson, you will cloak the assets folder so that it is excluded from various operations, such as the Put, Get, Check In, and Check Out commands. You will also use the Site Definition dialog box to cloak all .gif files in the site.

Understanding Cloaking Files

There may be times when you want to exclude a particular file or files from being uploaded to a server. For instance, suppose you have a page that is not quite finished and needs more work before it is ready to be viewed by others. You can exclude such files by **cloaking** them, which marks them for exclusion from several commands, including Put, Get, Synchronize, Check In, and Check Out. Cloaked files are also excluded from site-wide operations, such as checking for links or updating a template or library item. You can cloak a folder or specify a type of file to cloak throughout the site.

QUICKTIP

By default, the cloaking feature is enabled. However, if for some reason it is not turned on, open the Site Definition dialog box, click the Advanced tab, click the Cloaking category, then click the Enable cloaking check box.

Cloaking a Folder

There may be times when you want to cloak an entire folder. For instance, if you are not concerned with replacing outdated image files, you might want to cloak the assets folder of a Web site to save time when synchronizing files. To cloak a folder, select the folder, click the Options list arrow in the Files panel, point to site, point to Cloaking, and then click Cloak. The folder you cloaked and all the files it contains appear with red slashes across them, as shown in Figure 27. To uncloak a folder, click the Options list arrow in the Files panel, point to Site, point to Cloaking, and then click Uncloak.

QUICKTIP

To uncloak all files in a site, click the Files panel Options list arrow, point to Site, point to Cloaking, then click Uncloak All.

Cloaking Selected File Types

There may be times when you want to cloak a particular type of file, such as a .swf file. To cloak a particular file type, open the Site Definition dialog box, click the Cloaking category, click the Cloak files ending with check box, and then type a file extension in the text box below the check box. All files throughout the site that have the specified file extension will be cloaked.

FIGURE 27
Cloaked assets folder in the Files panel

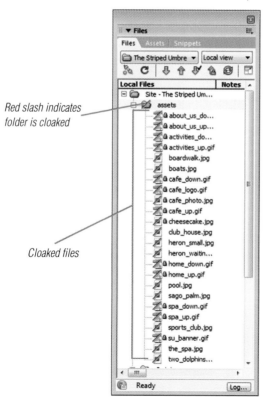

Red slash indicates folder is cloaked

Cloaked files

Cloak and uncloak a folder

1. Verify that Local view is displayed in the Files panel, click **Site** on the menu bar, then click **Manage Sites**.

2. Click **The Striped Umbrella** (if necessary), click **Edit** to open the Site Definition for The Striped Umbrella dialog box, click **Cloaking** in the Category list, verify that the Enable cloaking check box is checked, click **OK**, then click **Done**.

3. Click the **assets folder** in the Files panel, click the **Options list arrow** [icon], point to **Site**, point to **Cloaking**, click **Cloak**, expand the assets folder (if necessary), then compare your screen to Figure 28.

    A red slash now appears on top of the assets folder in the Files panel, indicating that all files in the assets folder are cloaked and will be excluded from putting, getting, checking in, checking out, and many other operations.

    TIP   You can also cloak a folder by right-clicking (Win) or [control]-clicking (Mac) the folder, pointing to Cloaking, then clicking Cloak.

4. Right-click (Win) or [control]-click (Mac) the **assets folder**, point to **Cloaking**, then click **Uncloak**.

    The assets folder and all the files it contains no longer appear with red slashes across them, indicating they are no longer cloaked.

You cloaked the assets folder so that this folder and all the files it contains would be excluded from many operations, including uploading and downloading files. You then uncloaked the assets folder.

FIGURE 28
Assets folder after cloaking

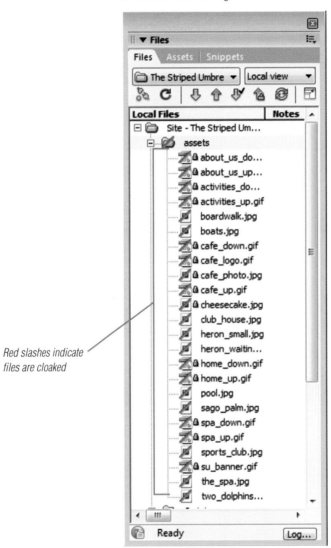

Red slashes indicate
files are cloaked

FIGURE 29

Specifying a file type to cloak

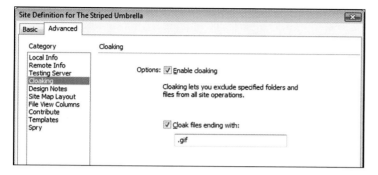

FIGURE 30

Assets folder in Files panel after cloaking .gif files

Assets folder
is not cloaked

All .gif files
are cloaked

Dependent
file for the
cafe page
still shows
padlock
icon

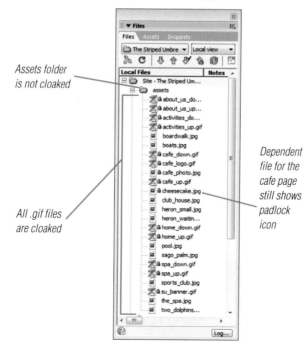

Cloak selected file types

1. Right-click (Win) or [control]-click (Mac) the **assets folder** in the Files panel, point to **Cloaking**, then click **Settings** to open the Site Definition for The Striped Umbrella dialog box with the Cloaking category selected.

2. Click the **Cloak files ending with check box**, select the text in the text box that appears, type **.gif** in the text box, then compare your screen to Figure 29.

3. Click **OK**.

   A dialog box opens, indicating that the site cache will be re-created.

4. Click **OK**, open the assets folder (if necessary), then compare your screen to Figure 30.

   All of the .gif files in the assets folder appear with red slashes across them, indicating that they are cloaked. Notice that the assets folder is not cloaked.

You cloaked all the .gif files in The Striped Umbrella Web site.

IMPORT AND EXPORT
A SITE DEFINITION

What You'll Do

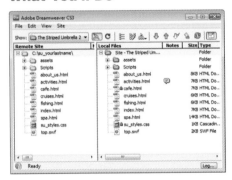

In this lesson, you will export the site definition file for The Striped Umbrella Web site. You will then import The Striped Umbrella Web site.

Exporting a Site Definition

When you work on a Web site for a long time, it's likely that at some point you will want to move it to another machine or share it with other collaborators who will help you maintain it. The site definition for a Web site contains important information about the site, including its URL, preferences that you've specified, and other secure information, such as login and password information. You can use the Export command to export the site definition file to another location. To do this, click Site on the menu bar, click Manage Sites, click the site you want to export, and then click Export. Because the site definition file contains password information that you will want to keep secret from other site users, you should never save the site definition file in the Web site. Instead, save it in an external file.

Importing a Site Definition

If you want to set up another user with a copy of your Web site, you can import the site definition file. To do this, click Import in the Manage Sites dialog box to open the Import Site dialog box, navigate to the .ste file you want to import, then click Open.

FIGURE 31

Saving The Striped Umbrella.ste file in the su_site_definition folder

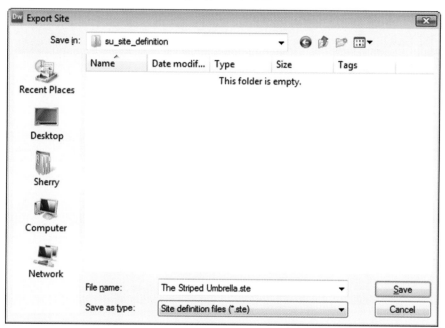

1. Use Windows Explorer (Win) or Finder (Mac) to create a new folder on your hard drive or external drive named **su_site_definition**.

2. Switch back to Dreamweaver, click **Site** on the menu bar, click **Manage Sites**, click **The Striped Umbrella**, then click **Export** to open the Export Site dialog box.

3. Navigate to and select the **su_site_definition folder** that you created in Step 1, as shown in Figure 31, click **Save**, then click **Done**.

You used the Export command to create the site definition file and saved it in the su_site_definition folder.

Import a site definition

1. Click **Site** on the menu bar, click **Manage Sites**, click **The Striped Umbrella**, then click **Import** to open the Import Site dialog box.

2. Navigate to the su_site_definition folder, compare your screen to Figure 32, select **The Striped Umbrella.ste**, then click **Open**.

   A dialog box opens and says that a site named The Striped Umbrella already exists. It will name the imported site The Striped Umbrella 2 so that it has a different name.

3. Click **OK**.

4. Click **The Striped Umbrella 2** (if necessary), click **Edit**, then compare your screen to Figure 33.

   The settings show that the The Striped Umbrella 2 site has the same root folder and default images folder as the The Striped Umbrella site. Both of these settings are specified in the The Striped Umbrella.ste file that you imported. Importing a site in this way makes it possible for multiple users with different computers to work on the same site.

   > TIP Make sure you know who is responsible for which files to keep from overwriting the wrong files when they are published. The Synchronize Files and Check In/Check Out features are good procedures to use with multiple designers.

5. Click **OK**, click **OK** to close the warning message, then click **Done**.

   > TIP If a dialog box opens warning that the root folder chosen is the same as the folder for the site "The Striped Umbrella," click OK.

You imported The Striped Umbrella.ste file and created a new site, The Striped Umbrella 2.

FIGURE 32
Import Site dialog box

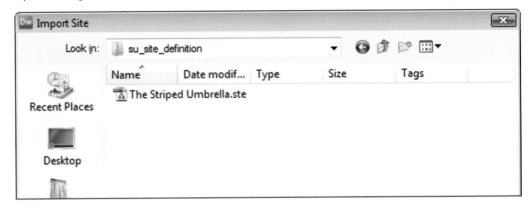

FIGURE 33
Site Definition for the The Striped Umbrella 2 dialog box

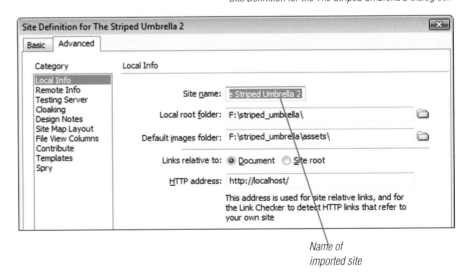

Name of
imported site

FIGURE 34

Viewing The Striped Umbrella 2 Web site files

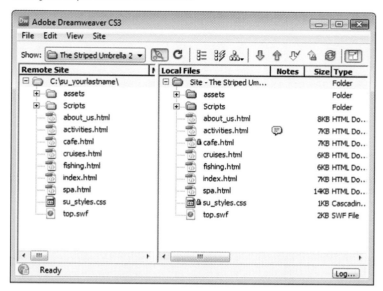

1. Click the **Expand to show local and remote sites button** on the Files panel toolbar to expand the Files panel.

2. Expand the Site root folder to view the contents (if necessary).

3. Click the **Refresh button** to view the files in the Remote Site pane.

   As shown in Figure 34, the site looks identical to the original The Striped Umbrella site, except the name has been changed to The Striped Umbrella 2.

   TIP If you don't see your remote site files, click the Connects to remote host button.

4. Click the **Collapse to show only local or remote site button** to collapse the Files panel.

5. Click **Site** on the menu bar, click **Manage Sites**, click **Remove**, click **Yes** to clear the warning dialog box, then click **Done** to delete The Striped Umbrella 2 Web site.

You viewed the expanded Files panel for The Striped Umbrella 2 Web site and then deleted The Striped Umbrella 2 Web site.

Power User Shortcuts

To do this:	Use this shortcut:
Validate Markup	[Shift][F6]
Get	[Ctrl][Shift][D] (Win) or ⌘[Shift][D] (Mac)
Check Out	[Ctrl][Alt][Shift][D] (Win) or ⌘[option][Shift][D] (Mac)
Put	[Ctrl][Shift][U] (Win) or ⌘[Shift][U] (Mac)
Check In	[Ctrl][Alt][Shift][U] (Win) or ⌘[option][U] (Mac)
Check Links	[Shift][F8]
Check Links Sitewide	[Ctrl][F8] (Win) or ⌘[F8] (Mac)

EVALUATE WEB CONTENT FOR
LEGAL USE

What You'll Do

In this lesson, you will examine copyright issues in the context of using content gathered from sources such as the Internet.

Can You Use Downloaded Media?

The Internet has made it possible to locate compelling and media-rich content to use in Web sites. A person who has learned to craft searches can locate a multitude of interesting material, such as graphics, animations, sounds, and text. Just because you can find it easily does not mean that you can use it however you want or under any circumstance. Learning about copyright law can help you decide whether or how to use content created and published by someone other than yourself.

Understanding Intellectual Property

Intellectual property is a product resulting from human creativity. It can include inventions, movies, songs, designs, clothing, and so on.

Understanding Copyright Law

The purpose of copyright law is to promote progress in society, not expressly to protect the rights of copyright owners. However, the vast majority of work you might want to download is protected by either copyright or trademark law.

Copyright protects the particular and tangible *expression* of an idea, not the idea itself. If you wrote a story using the idea about aliens crashing in Roswell, New Mexico, no one could copy or use your story without permission. However, anyone could write a story using a similar plot or characters—the idea of aliens crashing in Roswell is not copyright-protected. Copyright attaches to a work as soon as you create it; you do not have to register it with the U.S. Copyright Office.

Trademark protects an image, word, slogan, symbol, or design used to identify goods or services. For example, the Nike swoosh, Disney characters, or the shape of a classic Coca-Cola bottle are works protected by trademark.

What Exactly Does the Copyright Owner Own?

The Copyright Act of 1976 provided the copyright owner with a "bundle" of six rights, consisting of:

1) reproduction (including downloading)
2) creation of **derivative works** (for example, a movie version of a book)
3) distribution to the public
4) public performance
5) public display
6) public performance by digital audio transmission of sound recordings.

By default, only a copyright holder can create a derivative work of his or her original by transforming or adapting it. For example, the film *Hairspray* has gone from movie to musical play back to movie musical, all under the creative guidance of its writer, John Waters.

Understanding Fair Use

The law builds in limitations to copyright protection. One limitation to copyright is **fair use**. Fair use allows limited use of copyright-protected work. For example, you could excerpt short passages of a film or song for a class project or parody a television show. Determining if fair use applies to a work depends on the *purpose* of its use, the *nature* of the copyrighted work, *how much* you want to copy, and the *effect* on the market or value of the work. However, there is no clear formula on what constitutes fair use. It is always decided on a case by case basis.

How Do I Use Work Properly?

Being a student doesn't mean you can use any amount of any work for class. On the other hand, the very nature of education means you need to be able to use or reference different work in your studies. There are many situations that allow you to use protected work.

In addition to applying a fair use argument, you can obtain permission, pay a fee, use work that does not have copyright protection, or use work that has a flexible copyright license, where the owner has given the public permission to use the work in certain ways. For more information about open-access licensing, visit *www.creativecommons.org*. Work that is no longer protected by copyright is in the **public domain**; anyone can use it however they wish for any purpose. In general, the photos and other media on federal government Web sites are in the public domain.

For example, say you need to create a presentation about volcanoes for a class. Because your topic is about volcanoes, it makes sense that you would insert photos or video about volcanoes, quote from articles or books, and of course give proper credit for all your sources.

However, if you were designing a Web page for a client and wanted to insert a volcano photo that fit the site's design, you couldn't just insert your favorite volcano photo. In this case, you would need to obtain permission or pay a fee to use it, find a photo that is in the public domain, or find a photo with a Creative Commons license that permits commercial use.

Understanding Licensing Agreements

Before you decide whether to use a work you find on a Web site, such as an image or a sound file, you must decide whether you can comply with its licensing agreement. A **licensing agreement** is the permission given by a copyright holder that conveys the right to use the copyright holder's work under certain conditions.

Web sites have rules that govern how a user may use its text and media, known as **terms of use**. Figures 35 and 36 are great examples of clear terms of use for the Library of Congress Web site.

A site's terms of use do not override your right to apply fair use. Also, someone cannot compile public domain images in a Web site and then claim they own them or dictate how the images can be used. Conversely, someone can erroneously state in their terms of use that you can use work on the site freely, but they may not know the work's copyright status. The burden is on you to research the veracity of anyone claiming you can use work.

Obtaining Permission or a License

The **permissions process** is specific to what you want to use (text, photographs, music, trademarks, merchandise, and so on) and how you want to use it (school term paper, personal Web site, fabric pattern). And, getting permission from an amateur photographer whose work you found on a photo-sharing Web site may prove to be quite different from getting permission from a large corporation. How you want to use the work will determine the level and scope of permissions you need to secure. The fundamentals, however, are the same. Your request should contain the following:

- Your full name, address, and complete contact information.
- A specific description of your intended use. Sometimes including a sketch, storyboard, or link to a Web site is helpful.
- A signature line for the copyright holder.
- A target date when you would like the copyright holder to respond. This can be important if you're working under deadline.

Posting a Copyright Notice

The familiar © symbol or "Copyright" is no longer required to indicate copyright, nor does it automatically register your work, but it does serve a useful purpose. When you post or publish it, you are stating clearly to those who may not know anything about copyright law that this work is claimed by you and is not in the public domain. Your case is made even stronger if someone violates your copyright and your notice is clearly visible. A violator can never

FIGURE 35

The Library of Congress home page

Link to legal information regarding the use of content on the Web site

Library of Congress Web site: www.loc.gov

claim ignorance of the law as an excuse for infringing. Common notification styles include:

Copyright 2010
Thomson Course Technology
or © **2010 Thomson Course Technology**
Giving proper attribution for text excerpts is a must; giving attribution for media is excellent practice, but is never a substitute for applying a fair use argument, buying a license, or simply getting permission.

References
Waxer, Barbara M., and Baum, Marsha L. 2006. **Internet Surf and Turf - The Essential Guide to Copyright**, **Fair Use**, and **Finding Media**. Boston: Thomson Course Technology.

You must provide proper citation for the Web materials you incorporate into your own material. This expectation applies even to unsigned material and material that does not display the copyright symbol (©). Moreover, the expectation applies just as certainly to ideas you summarize or paraphrase as to words you quote verbatim.

Here's a list of the elements that make up an APA-style citation of Web-based resources:
- Author's name (if known)
- Date of publication or last revision (if known), in parentheses
- Title of document
- Title of complete work or Web site (if applicable), underlined
- URL, in angled brackets
- Date of access, in parentheses

Here are a few examples as they might appear on a references page in your paper:

References
Citation Guides. (1996). UMUC Information and Library Services. **www.umuc.edu/library/citation guides.html** (19 Feb. 2004).

Harnack, A. and Kleppinger, E. (1996). Beyond the MLA handbook. **http://english.ttu.edu/kairos/1.2/inbox/ mla_archive.html** (19 Feb. 2004).

Walker, J. R. and Taylor, T. (1998). *The Columbia Guide to Online Style.* **www.columbia.edu/cu/cup/cgos/ idx_basic.html** (19 Feb. 2004).

FIGURE 36
Library of Congress Web site Legal page

Library of Congress Web site: www.loc.gov

About Copyright and the Collections

Whenever possible, the Library of Congress provides factual information about copyright owners and related matters in the catalog records, finding aids and other texts that accompany collections. As a publicly supported institution, the Library generally does not own rights in its collections. Therefore, it does not charge permission fees for use of such material and generally does not grant or deny permission to publish or otherwise distribute material in its collections. Permission and possible fees may be required from the copyright owner independently of the Library. It is the researcher's obligation to determine and satisfy copyright or other use restrictions when publishing or otherwise distributing materials found in the Library's collections. Transmission or reproduction of protected items beyond that allowed by fair use requires the written permission of the copyright owners. Researchers must make their own assessments of rights in light of their intended use.

The Library of Congress wants to hear from any copyright owners who are not properly identified on this Web site so that we may make the necessary corrections.

Perform Web site maintenance.

1. Open the blooms & bulbs Web site, then re-create the site cache.

2. Use the Link Checker panel to check for broken links, then fix any broken links that appear.

3. Use the Link Checker to check for orphaned files. If any orphaned files appear in the report, take steps to link them to appropriate pages or remove them.

4. Use the Assets panel to check for Non-Websafe colors.

5. Run an Untitled Documents report for the entire local site. If the report lists any pages that have no titles, add page titles to the untitled pages. Run the report again to verify that all pages have page titles.

6. Run a report to look for missing alternate text. Add alternate text to any graphics that need it, then run the report again to verify that all images contain alternate text.

7. Enable the Design Notes preference and add a design note to the classes page as follows: **Shoot a video of the hanging baskets class to add to the page**. Add the status **needs attention** and check the **Show when file is opened** option.

Publish a Web site and transfer files.

1. Set up Web server access for the blooms & bulbs Web site on an FTP server or a local/network server (whichever is available to you) using appropriate settings.

2. View the blooms & bulbs remote site in the Files panel.

3. Upload the iris.jpg file to the remote site, then view the remote site.

4. Synchronize all files in the blooms & bulbs Web site, so that all files from the local site are uploaded to the remote site.

Check files out and in.

1. Enable the Check In/Check Out feature.

2. Check out the plants page and all dependent pages.

3. Open the plants page, change the heading style of "Drop by to see our Featured Spring Plants" to **seasons**, center the heading, then save your changes. (*Hint*: You will have to attach the style sheet to the page.)

4. Check in the plants page and all dependent files.

Cloak files.

1. Verify that cloaking is enabled in the blooms & bulbs Web site.

2. Cloak the assets folder, then uncloak it.

3. Cloak all the .jpg files in the blooms & bulbs Web site.

Import and export a site definition.

1. Create a new folder named **blooms_site_ definition** on your hard drive or external drive.

2. Export the blooms & bulbs site definition to the blooms_site_definition folder.

3. Import the blooms & bulbs site definition to create a new site called **blooms & bulbs 2**.

4. Make sure that all files from the blooms & bulbs Web site appear in the Files panel for the imported site, then compare your screen to Figure 37.

5. Remove the blooms & bulbs 2 site.

FIGURE 37
Completed Skills Review

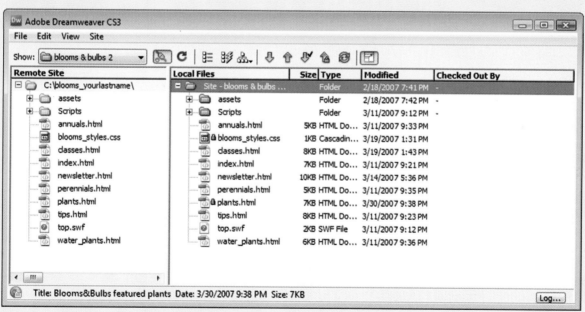

In this Project Builder, you will publish the TripSmart Web site that you have developed throughout this book to a remote server or local/network folder. Mike Andrew has provided the password and login information to publish the site on a remote server. You will first run several reports on the site, specify the remote settings for the site, upload files to the remote site, check files out and in, and cloak files. Finally, you will export and import the site definition.

1. Use the TripSmart Web site that you began in Project Builder 1 in Chapter 1 and developed in previous chapters.

2. Use the Link Checker panel to check for broken links, then fix any broken links that appear.

3. Use the Link Checker to check for orphaned files. If any orphaned files appear in the report, take steps to link them to appropriate pages or remove them.

4. Use the Assets panel to check for non-Websafe colors.

5. Run an Untitled Documents report for the entire local site. If the report lists any pages that lack titles, add page titles to the untitled pages. Run the report again to verify that all pages have page titles.

6. Run a report to look for missing alternate text. Add alternate text to any graphics that need it, then run the report again to verify that all images contain alternate text.

7. Enable the Design Notes preference, if necessary, and add a design note to the newsletter page as follows: **Add a short video demonstrating how to pack clothing wrinkle-free in a suitcase**. Add the status **needs attention** and check the **Show when file is opened** option.

8. If you did not do so in Project Builder 1 in Chapter 1, use the Site Definition dialog box to set up Web server access for a remote site using either an FTP site or a local or network folder.

9. Upload the index page and all dependent files to the remote site.

10. View the remote site to make sure that all files uploaded correctly.

11. Synchronize the files so that all other files on the local TripSmart site are uploaded to the remote site.

12. Enable the Check In/Check Out feature.

13. Check out the index page and all dependent files.

14. Open the index page, close the index page, then check in the index page and all dependent pages.

15. Cloak all .jpg files in the Web site.

16. Export the site definition to a new folder named **tripsmart_site_definition**.

17. Import the **TripSmart.ste** file to create a new site named TripSmart 2.

18. Expand the assets folder in the Files panel (if necessary), then compare your screen to Figure 38.

19. Remove the TripSmart 2 site.

FIGURE 38
Sample Project Builder 1

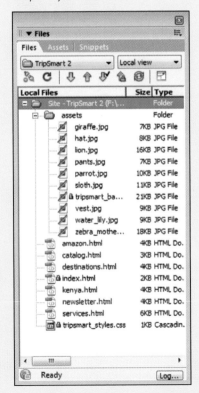

In this Project Builder, you will finish your work on the Carolyne's Creations Web site. You are ready to publish the Web site to a remote server and transfer all the files from the local site to the remote site. First, you will run several reports to make sure the Web site is in good shape. Next, you will enable the Check In/Check Out feature so that other staff members may collaborate on the site. Finally, you will export and import the site definition file.

1. Use the Carolyne's Creations Web site that you began in Project Builder 1 in Chapter 1 and developed in previous chapters.

2. If you did not do so in Project Builder 2 in Chapter 1, use the Site Definition dialog box to set up Web server access for a remote site using either an FTP site or a local or network folder.

3. Run reports for broken links and orphaned files, correcting any errors that you find. The cc_banner.jpg is no longer needed, so delete the file.

4. Run reports for untitled documents and missing alt text, correcting any errors that you find.

5. Check for non-Websafe colors.

6. Upload the classes.html page and all dependent files to the remote site.

7. View the remote site to make sure that all files uploaded correctly.

8. Synchronize the files so that all other files on the local Carolyne's Creations site are uploaded to the remote site.

9. Enable the Check In/Check Out feature.

10. Check out the classes page and all its dependent files.

11. Open the classes page, then change the price of the adult class to **$45.00**.

12. Save your changes, close the page, then check in the classes page and all dependent pages.

13. Export the site definition to a new folder named **cc_site_definition**.

14. Import the Carolyne's Creations.ste file to create a new site named Carolyne's Creations 2.

15. Expand the root folder in the Files panel (if necessary), compare your screen to Figure 39, then remove the Carolyne's Creations2 site.

FIGURE 39

Completed Project Builder 2

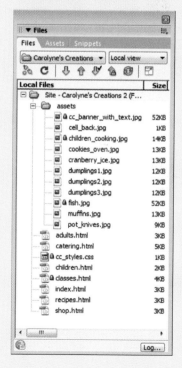

Throughout this book you have used Dreamweaver to create and develop several Web sites that contain different elements, many of which are found in popular commercial Web sites. For instance, Figure 40 shows the National Park Service Web site, which contains photos and information on all the national parks in the United States. This Web site contains many types of interactive elements, such as image maps, Flash content, and tables—all of which you learned to create in this book.

1. Connect to the Internet, then go to the National Park Service Web site at *www.nps.gov*.

2. Spend some time exploring the pages of this site to familiarize yourself with its elements.

3. Type a list of all the elements in this Web site that you have learned how to create in this book. After each item, write a short description of where and how the element is used in the site.

4. Print the home page and one or two other pages that contain some of the elements you described and attach it to your list.

FIGURE 40
Design Project

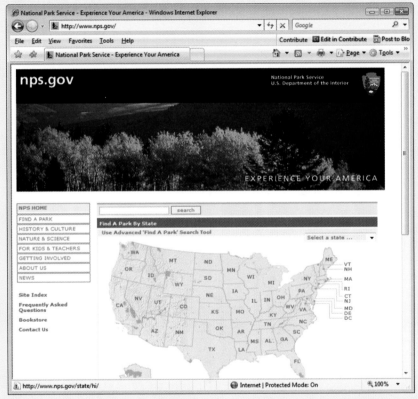

National Park Service Web site: www.nps.gov

In this project, you will finish your work on the Web site that you created and developed throughout this book.

You will publish your site to a remote server or local or network folder.

1. Before you begin the process of publishing your Web site to a remote server, make sure that it is ready for public viewing. Use Figure 41 to assist you in making sure your Web site is complete. If you find problems, make the necessary changes to finalize the site.

2. Decide where to publish your site. The folder where you will publish your site can be either an FTP site or a local/network folder. If you are publishing to an FTP site, be sure to write down all the information you will need to publish to the site, including the URL of the FTP host, the directory on the FTP server where you will publish your site's root folder, and the login and password information.

3. Use the Site Definition dialog box to specify the remote settings for the site using the information that was decided upon in Step 2.

4. Transfer one of the pages and its dependent files to the remote site, then view the remote site to make sure the appropriate files were transferred.

5. Synchronize the files so that all the remaining local pages and dependent files are uploaded to the remote site.

6. Enable the Check In/Check Out feature.

7. Check out one of the pages. Open the checked-out page, make a change to it, save the change, close the page, then check the page back in.

8. Cloak a particular file type.

9. Export the site definition for the site to a new folder on your hard drive or on an external drive.

10. Import the site to create a new version of the site.

11. Close the imported site, save and close all open pages (if necessary), then exit Dreamweaver.

FIGURE 41
Portfolio Project checklist

Web Site Checklist

1. Are you satisfied with the content and appearance of every page?
2. Are all paths for all links and images correct?
3. Does each page have a title?
4. Do all images appear?
5. Are all colors Websafe?
6. Do all images have appropriate alternate text?
7. Have you eliminated any orphaned files?
8. Have you deleted any unnecessary files?
9. Have you viewed all pages using at least two different browsers?
10. Does the home page have keywords and a description?

chapter

7 USING STYLES AND STYLE SHEETS FOR DESIGN

1. Create and use embedded styles

2. Modify embedded styles

3. Work with external CSS style sheets

4. Work with conflicting styles

5. Use coding tools to view and edit styles

7 USING STYLES AND
STYLE SHEETS
FOR DESIGN

Introduction

In Chapter 3, you learned how to create, apply, and edit Cascading Style Sheets. Using CSS styles is the best and most powerful way to ensure that all elements in a Web site are formatted consistently. The advantage of using CSS styles is that all of your formatting rules are kept in a separate or **external** style sheet file, so that you can change the appearance of every page to which the style sheet is attached by modifying the style sheet file. For instance, suppose your external style sheet contains a style called headings that is applied to all top-level headings in your Web site. If you want to change the heading color to blue, you simply change the color attribute to blue in the style sheet file, and all headings in the Web site are updated instantly. Because style sheets separate the formatting from the content, the site is formatted automatically from the style sheet information.

You can also create **embedded** CSS styles, which are styles whose code is located within the head section of the HTML code of a Web page. The advantage of embedded styles is that you can use them to override an external style. For instance, if all headings in your Web site are blue because the external style applied to them specifies blue as the color attribute, you could change the color of one of those headings to a different color by creating and applying an embedded style that specifies a different color as the color attribute. However, in general, you should avoid using embedded styles to format all the pages of a Web site; it is a better practice to keep formatting rules in a separate file from the content. CSS styles also reduce the overall file sizes of your pages; most formatting code can be stored in a single file, rather than in individual page files.

In this chapter, you will import a redesigned Striped Umbrella Web site. Each page has been redesigned using tables for page layout to provide better consistency. You will replace your current Web site with this new one. You will then create and apply embedded styles and work with external CSS style sheets to format the pages in the site.

Tools You'll Use

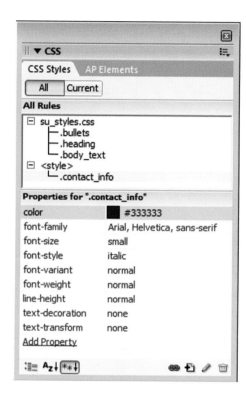

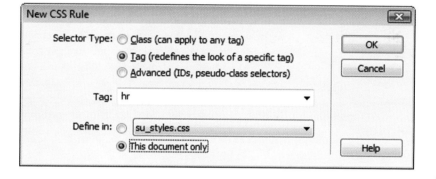

CREATE AND USE
EMBEDDED STYLES

What You'll Do

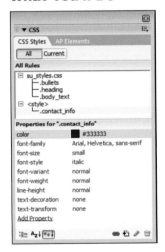

In this lesson, you will replace your Striped Umbrella files by importing a revised Web site. Next, you will create and apply an embedded style to the home page.

Understanding Embedded Styles

In Chapter 3, you learned how to create and use an external style sheet to apply consistent formatting to the elements of a Web site. An external style sheet is a separate file with a .css extension that contains a collection of rules for formatting elements of a Web site. External style sheets can be applied to multiple pages, and are, therefore, a great tool to help ensure formatting consistency across all pages of a Web site. Sometimes, however, you might want to create a style that is used only on a single page of your Web site. You can do this using embedded styles, or styles whose code is embedded in the code of a particular page. Embedded styles are handy when you want a particular page in your Web site to contain formatting that is different from the rules specified in an external style sheet. If both an external style and embedded style are applied to a single element, the embedded style overrides the external style. There is also a type of style similar to an embedded style called an inline style. Like an embedded style, the **inline style** is part of the individual page code, but

it is written in the body section, rather than the head section. Inline styles refer to a specific instance of a tag, rather than a global tag style on a page.

Creating and Applying a Custom Style

To create an embedded style, you use the New CSS Rule button in the CSS Styles panel to open the New CSS Rule dialog box, as shown in Figure 1. You use this dialog box to create both embedded styles as well as styles that are added to external style sheets. To specify the new style as an embedded style, click the This document only option button in the Define in section. If you click the New Style Sheet File option button, you will need to name and save a new CSS style sheet using the Save Style Sheet File As dialog box. You also have the choice of creating a new style in an existing CSS style sheet, such as the one you have already created for The Striped Umbrella Web site.

You use the New CSS Rule dialog box to create a **custom style** (also known as a **class style**), which contains a combination of formatting attributes that can be applied to a block of text or other page elements. When you name a custom style, you begin the name with a period (.).

After you name the style and click OK, the CSS Rule Definition dialog box will open with settings for the Type category displayed, as shown in Figure 2. This dialog box contains eight different categories whose settings can be defined. To specify the settings for a category, click the category, then enter the settings. When you finish specifying settings for all of the desired categories, click OK.

Once you create a custom style, it appears in the CSS Styles panel and as a choice in the list of Styles in the Property inspector. To apply a custom style to an element on a Web page, select the element, and then click the style from the Style list in the Property inspector.

FIGURE 1
New CSS Rule dialog box

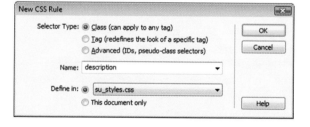

FIGURE 2
CSS Rule Definition for .heading in su_styles.css

Choose a category to see property options for that category

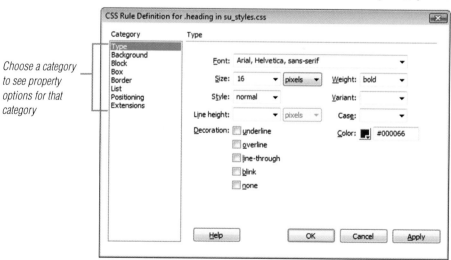

Import the revised Striped Umbrella Web site (Win)

1. Open Windows Explorer, then navigate to where you store your Data Files for this chapter, so that the files appear in the right pane.

2. In the left pane, navigate to where you store your striped_umbrella folder, as shown in Figure 3, right-click it, then click **Delete**.

3. Drag the **striped_umbrella folder** from the Chapter_7 Data Files folder in the right pane to the folder where you save your files in the left pane.

   The redesigned pages in the new folder replace your previous root folder.

4. Close Windows Explorer, then start Dreamweaver.

5. Click **Site** on the menu bar, click **Manage Sites**, verify that The Striped Umbrella Web site is selected, click **Remove,** then click **Yes** in the warning dialog box.

   It is better to remove the previous site, because the site you will be importing has the same name. Remember that deleting a Web site in the Manage Sites dialog box does not actually delete the files. It just deletes the site definition.

6. Click **Import**.

   The Import Site dialog box opens.

7. Click the **Look in list arrow** to navigate to the chapter_7 Data Files folder, click **The Striped Umbrella.ste**, as shown in Figure 4, then click **Open**.

   (continued)

FIGURE 3

Dragging the striped_umbrella folder to create a folder with revised files

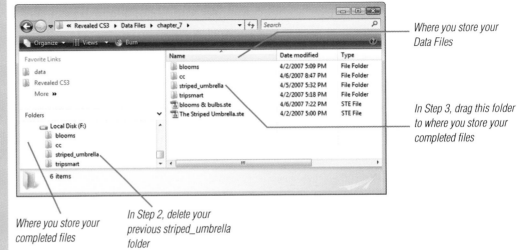

Where you store your Data Files

In Step 3, drag this folder to where you store your completed files

Where you store your completed files

In Step 2, delete your previous striped_umbrella folder

FIGURE 4

Import Site dialog box

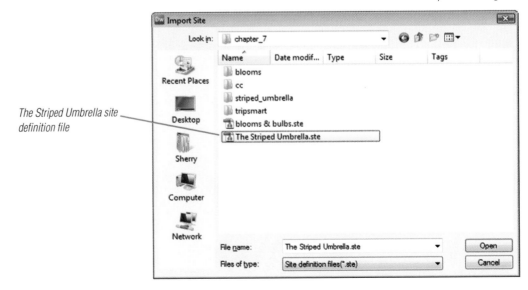

The Striped Umbrella site definition file

The .ste file is an XML file that contains information about the Web site, including any information entered in the Manage Sites dialog box.

8. Verify that The Striped Umbrella site is selected in the Manage Sites dialog box, then click **Edit**.

9. Verify that the striped_umbrella folder is the root folder for the Web site and the assets folder under the striped_umbrella folder is the default location for images, as shown in Figure 5.

   TIP If you receive a warning that the selected folder does not contain the current site's home page, click Edit again to return to the Site Definition dialog box, click Site Map Layout in the Category column, click the Browse for File icon 🗀 next to the Home page text box, then double-click index.html in the striped_umbrella root folder.

10. Click **OK**, then click **Done**.

   TIP If you do not see the files listed in the Files panel, click the plus sign next to the root folder.

You copied the striped_umbrella folder from the chapter_7 Data Files folder to a different folder on your computer or external drive. You then imported the revised Striped Umbrella site and verified that the root folder was set to the striped_umbrella folder that you copied. You also verified that the default images folder is still the assets folder of the striped_umbrella folder.

FIGURE 5

Site Definition for The Striped Umbrella dialog box (Win)

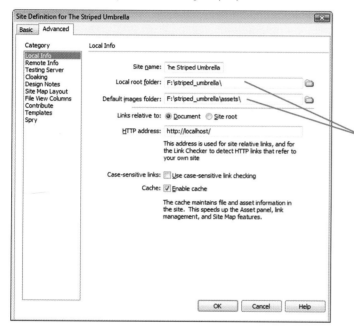

Your paths will be different depending on the location you chose for the striped_umbrella folder and will probably be the same locations you chose for the original files

Import the revised Striped Umbrella Web site (Mac)

1. Open Finder, then navigate to the folder where you want to store the revised Striped Umbrella Web site, then delete your original root folder..

2. Click **File** on the menu bar, click **New Finder Window** to open another instance of Finder, then open the chapter_7 Data Files folder.

3. Drag the **striped_umbrella folder** from the chapter_7 folder to where you want to store The Striped Umbrella Web site, as shown in Figure 6.

4. Close the Finder windows, start Dreamweaver (if necessary), click **Site** on the menu bar, click **Manage Sites**, verify that The Striped Umbrella Web site is selected, click **Remove**, then click **Yes** in the Warning dialog box.

    It is better to remove the previous site, since the site you will be importing has the same name. Remember that deleting a Web site in the Manage Sites dialog box does not actu-ally delete the files. It just deletes the site definition.

5. Click **Import**.

    The Import Site dialog box opens.

6. Click **The Striped Umbrella.ste** in the chapter_7 folder, then click **Open**.

    The Choose Local Root Folder for Site The Striped Umbrella opens.

    (continued)

FIGURE 6

Dragging the striped_umbrella folder to replace the old folder (Mac)

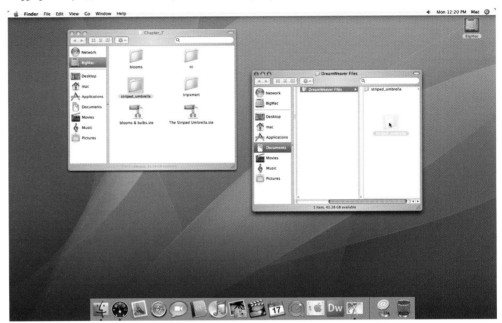

Using Styles and Style Sheets for Design

FIGURE 7

Site Definition for The Striped Umbrella dialog box (Mac)

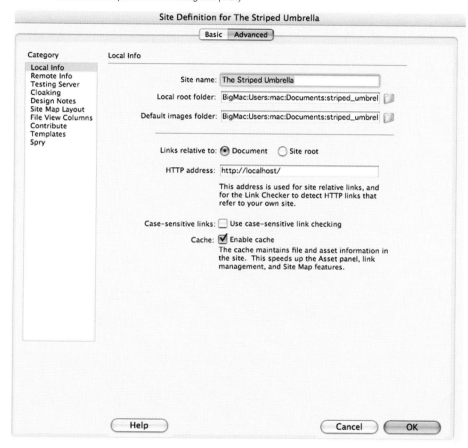

7. Navigate to the striped_umbrella folder that you moved in Step 3, then click **Choose**.

   The Choose local images folder for site The Striped Umbrella dialog box opens.

8. Click the **assets folder** in the striped_umbrella folder, then click **Choose**.

   This sets the Default Images Folder path to the assets folder located in the striped_umbrella folder.

9. Verify that The Striped Umbrella site is selected in the Manage Sites dialog box, then click **Edit**.

10. Click the **Advanced tab** (if necessary), then click the **Local Info category** (if necessary).

11. Compare your screen with Figure 7, click **OK**, then click **Done**.

   TIP   If you receive a warning that the selected folder does not contain the current site's home page, click Edit again to return to the Site Definition dialog box, click Site Map Layout in the Category column, click the Browse for File icon next to the Home page text box, then double-click index.html in the striped_umbrella root folder.

You copied the striped_umbrella folder from the chapter_7 Data Files folder to a different folder on your computer or external drive. You then imported The Striped Umbrella site and verified that the default images folder is still the assets folder of the striped_umbrella folder.

Create a custom style

1. Open the home page in The Striped Umbrella Web site, expand the CSS Styles panel, then click the **Switch to All (Document) Mode button** `All` (if necessary).

   TIP   Notice that the new, redesigned home page is now based on a table layout.

2. Click the **New CSS Rule button** in the CSS Styles panel to open the New CSS Rule dialog box.

3. Type **contact_info** in the Name text box, verify that the Class option button is selected, click the **This document only option button**, then compare your screen to Figure 8.

4. Click **OK** to open the CSS Rule definition for .contact_info dialog box, and verify that the Type category is selected.

5. Set the Font to **Arial, Helvetica, sans-serif**; set the Size to **small**; set the Style to **italic**; set the Line height to **normal**; set the Decoration to **none**; set the Weight to **normal**; set the Variant to **normal**; set the Case to **none**; set the Color to **#333333**, then compare your screen to Figure 9.

6. Click **OK**.

   The contact_info style appears in the CSS Styles panel.

   TIP   If you do not see the contact_info style, click the plus sign (Win) or the triangle (Mac) next to <style> in the CSS Styles panel.

You created a new custom style named contact_info and set the properties for it.

FIGURE 8
New CSS Rule dialog box with settings for contact_info style

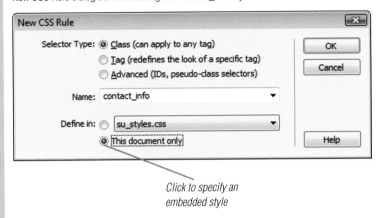

Click to specify an embedded style

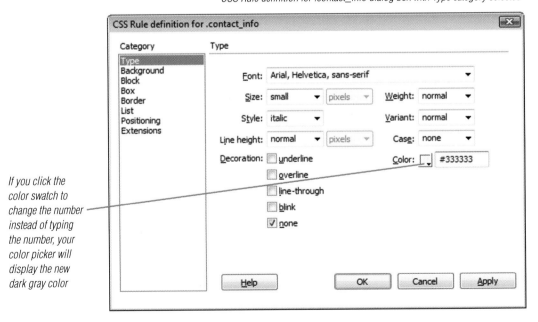

If you click the color swatch to change the number instead of typing the number, your color picker will display the new dark gray color

FIGURE 10

Applying the contact_info style using the Property inspector

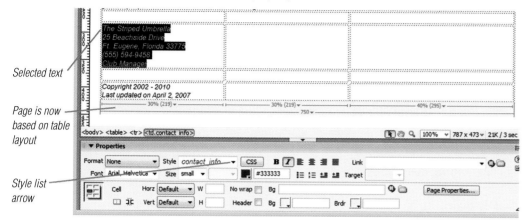

Selected text

Page is now based on table layout

Style list arrow

Apply a custom style

1. Select the paragraph with The Striped Umbrella contact information.

2. Use the Property inspector to change the Font to **Default Font** and the Size to **None**, then click the **Italic button** *I* to remove the italic formatting.

   You must remove manual formatting before applying a CSS style.

3. Click the **Style list arrow** in the Property inspector, click **contact_info** as shown in Figure 10, then deselect the text.

   The selected text now appears with the contact_info style applied as dark gray.

4. Select the copyright and last updated statements, then repeat Step 2 to remove any prior formatting.

5. Apply the contact_info style to the copyright and last updated statements, then compare your screen to Figure 11.

   Notice how the contact_info style is displayed in the CSS Styles panel, but not as a part of the su_styles.css style sheet. The contact_info style is an embedded style. The rest of the styles are external styles that reside in the su_styles.css file.

6. Save your work.

You used the Property inspector to apply the contact_info style to selected text.

FIGURE 11

Copyright and date with contact_info style applied

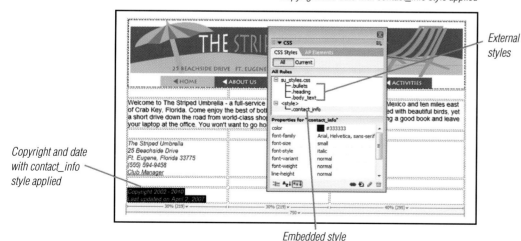

External styles

Copyright and date with contact_info style applied

Embedded style

MODIFY EMBEDDED
STYLES

What You'll Do

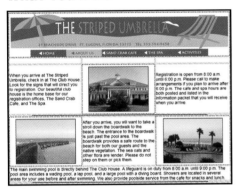

 In this lesson, you will modify the contact_info style, redefine an HTML tag, edit an embedded style, and then delete an embedded style.

Editing Embedded Styles

To edit a custom style, click the style you want to edit in the CSS Styles panel, click the Edit Style button in the CSS Styles panel, then use the CSS Rule Definition dialog box to change the settings as you wish, or simply enter the new settings in the CSS properties panel. Any changes that you make to the style are automatically reflected on the page; all elements to which the style is attached will update to reflect the change.

Redefining HTML Tags

When you use the Property inspector to format a Web page element, a predefined HTML tag is added to that element. Sometimes, you might want to change the definition of an HTML tag to add more "pizzazz" to elements that have that tag. For instance, perhaps you want all text that has the <em> tag, which is the tag used for italic formatting, to appear in purple bold. To change the definition of an HTML tag, click the Tag option button in the New CSS Rule dialog box, click the Tag

list arrow to view all available HTML tags, click the tag you want to redefine, then click OK to open the CSS Rule Definition dialog box, where you specify the desired formatting settings. Once you save the style and apply that tag, selected text will be formatted according to the altered settings you specified. To edit a setting, click the setting in the CSS Styles panel to display the list of customized HTML tags. Select the HTML tag you want to change, then click the Edit Style button to open the CSS Rule Definition dialog box where you can make any changes you want, or use the CSS properties panel to quickly enter the changes. There are two modes in the CSS Styles panel: All (document mode) and Current (selection mode). When All is selected, you will see style sheet rules listed in the top half of the panel, which is called the All Rules pane. When you click one of the rules, the bottom half, which is called the Properties pane, lists that rule's properties, as shown in Figure 12.

Using Styles and Style Sheets for design

When Current mode is selected, the top half of the panel is called the Summary for Selection pane. When an object with a style is selected on an open Web page, the Summary for Selection pane will display the properties for that style. If the object is not associated with a style, the Summary for Selection pane will show other formatting properties, as shown in Figure 13. The bottom half of the CSS Styles panel is called the Properties pane in either mode.

FIGURE 12
CSS Styles panel in All mode

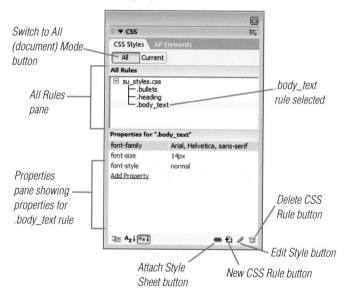

Switch to All (document) Mode button

All Rules pane

.body_text rule selected

Properties pane showing properties for .body_text rule

Delete CSS Rule button

Edit Style button

Attach Style Sheet button

New CSS Rule button

FIGURE 13
CSS Styles panel in Current mode

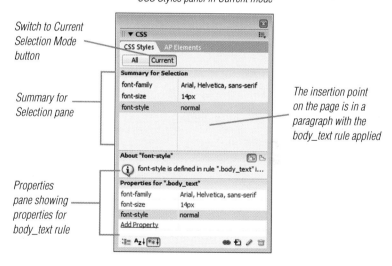

Switch to Current Selection Mode button

Summary for Selection pane

Properties pane showing properties for body_text rule

The insertion point on the page is in a paragraph with the body_text rule applied

Modify a custom style

1. Click the **contact_info style** in the CSS Styles panel, then click the **Edit Style button** .

2. Change the Color to **#000066,** then compare your screen to Figure 14.

3. Click **OK**, compare your screen to Figure 15, then save and close the index page.

   The text with the contact_info style applied to it automatically changed to reflect the changes that you made to the style.

You made formatting changes to the Type category of the contact_info style. You then saw these formatting changes reflected in text with the contact_info style applied to it.

FIGURE 14

CSS Rule definition for .contact_info dialog box with modified type settings

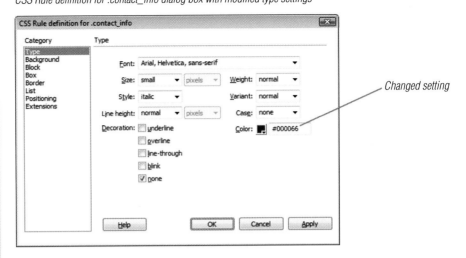

Changed setting

FIGURE 15

Text with contact_info style has been modified

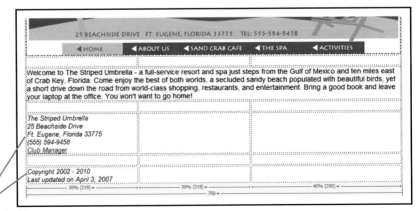

Text with contact_info style now appears in blue

FIGURE 16

Creating a new CSS Rule to redefine the hr HTML tag

Tag selector type

This document only option

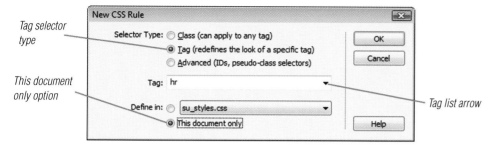

Tag list arrow

FIGURE 17

Redefining the hr HTML tag

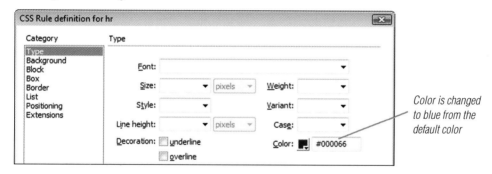

Color is changed to blue from the default color

FIGURE 18

Redefining the body HTML tag

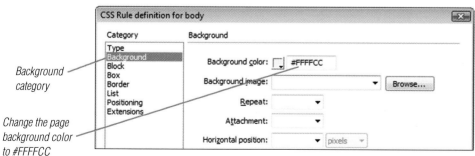

Background category

Change the page background color to #FFFFCC

Redefine an HTML tag

1. Open the about_us page, then click the **New CSS Rule button** 🔁 in the CSS Styles panel to open the New CSS Rule dialog box.

2. Click the **Tag option button**, click the **Tag list arrow**, scroll down, click **hr**, then click the **This document only option button**, as shown in Figure 16.

   The hr tag is the tag that creates a horizontal rule.

   TIP   To scroll quickly to the tags that begin with the letter h, type h after you click the Tag list arrow.

3. Click **OK** to open the CSS Rule definition for hr dialog box, set the Color to **blue (#000066)**, compare your screen to Figure 17, then click **OK**.

   Notice that the two horizontal rules on the page changed to blue because the rule definition has changed the way a horizontal rule is rendered.

4. Using Steps 1 through 3 as a guide, create a new CSS style that redefines the body HTML tag, by using the Background category rather than the Type category to set the Background color to **#FFFFCC**, as shown in Figure 18, then click **OK**.

   Notice that the page now has a yellow background.

   (continued)

5. Switch to Code view to view the code changing the properties for the horizontal rule, as shown in Figure 19.

Because these are embedded styles, the code for the styles is embedded into the page in the head section of the code. Notice that the style changing the background page color to yellow overrode the white page background color that was defined earlier by using the Page Properties dialog box.

6. Scroll up in the code, if necessary, to find the code that links the external style sheet file, as shown in Figure 20.

You cannot see the individual rule properties, because the file is linked, not embedded. If you open the su_styles.css file, however, you will see the rules and properties listed.

TIP   You can tell which tag takes precedence by its position in the tag selector. Tags with greater precedence are positioned to the right of other tags in the tag selector.

You used the New CSS Rule dialog box to redefine the hr and body HTML tags. You also viewed the code for the new embedded styles and the code that links the external style sheet file.

FIGURE 19

Viewing the code for embedded styles

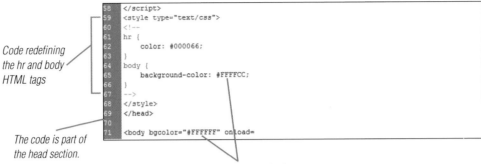

Code redefining the hr and body HTML tags

```
58  </script>
59  <style type="text/css">
60  <!--
61  hr {
62      color: #000066;
63  }
64  body {
65      background-color: #FFFFCC;
66  }
67  -->
68  </style>
69  </head>
70
71  <body bgcolor="#FFFFFF" onload=
```

The code is part of the head section.

The body style background color overrides the page background color set previously

FIGURE 20

Viewing the code linking an external style sheet file

The code linking the file resides in the head section of the code

```
1  <!DOCTYPE html PUBLIC "-//W3C//DTD XHTML 1.0 Transitional//EN"
   "http://www.w3.org/TR/xhtml1/DTD/xhtml1-transitional.dtd">
2  <html xmlns="http://www.w3.org/1999/xhtml">
3  <head>
4  <meta http-equiv="Content-Type" content="text/html; charset=iso-8859-1" />
5  <title>About our property</title>
6  <meta name="Keywords" content="beach resort, spa, Ft. Eugene, Florida, Gulf of Mexico, fishing,
   dolphin cruises" /><meta name="Description" content="The Striped Umbrella is a full-service resort and
   spa just steps from the Gulf of Mexico in Ft. Eugene, Florida." />
7  <link href="su_styles.css" rel="stylesheet" type="text/css" />
8  <script language="JavaScript" type="text/javascript">
9  <!--
```

Code linking the su_styles.css file to the about_us page

FIGURE 21

Changing the color property of the hr tag

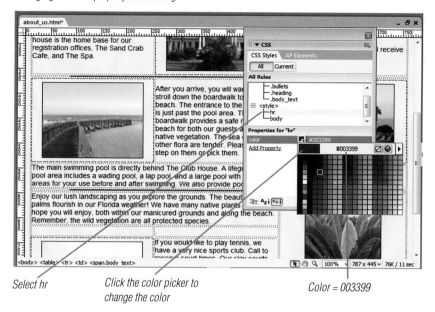

Select hr

Click the color picker to change the color

Color = 003399

FIGURE 22

CSS Styles panel after deleting body style

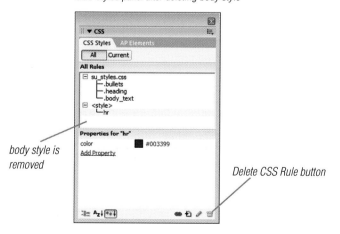

body style is removed

Delete CSS Rule button

Edit an embedded style

1. Switch to Design view, then view the styles for the about us page in the CSS Styles panel.

2. Click the **hr style** in the CSS Styles panel.

   The properties of the hr rule are displayed in the Properties pane.

3. Click the **color picker** in the Properties pane, click color swatch **#003399** to change the horizontal rule to a lighter blue, then compare your screen to Figure 21.

You used the CSS Styles panel to change the color settings for the hr embedded style.

Delete an embedded style

1. Click the **body style** in the CSS Styles panel to select it.

2. Click the **Delete CSS Rule button** 🗑 , then compare your screen to Figure 22.

   The body style is removed from the CSS Styles panel. The page background changes back to white.

   TIP   You can also delete an embedded style by right-clicking (Win) or [control]-clicking (Mac) the style in the CSS Styles panel, then clicking Delete.

3. Save your changes, then close the about us page.

You used the CSS Styles panel to delete the body style.

WORK WITH EXTERNAL
CSS STYLE SHEETS

What You'll Do

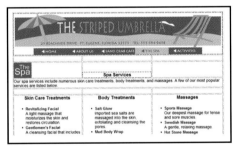

 In this lesson, you will make formatting changes in the style sheet and see those changes reflected on pages. You will also add hyperlink styles and custom code to the su_styles style sheet. Finally, you will delete a style from the su_styles style sheet.

Using External CSS Style Sheets

If you want to ensure consistent formatting across all elements of a Web site, it's a good idea to use external CSS style sheets instead of HTML styles or embedded styles. Most Web developers prefer to use external CSS style sheets so they can make changes to the appearance of a Web site without opening each page. Using embedded styles requires you to make changes to the styles on each page, which takes more time and leaves room for error and inconsistency.

Attaching an External CSS Style Sheet to a Page or Template

One of the big advantages of using external CSS style sheets is that you can attach them to pages that you've already created. When you do this, all of the rules specified in the style sheet are applied to the HTML tags on the page. So for instance, if your external style sheet specifies that all first-level headings are

formatted in Arial 14-point bold blue, then all text in your Web page that has the <h1> tag will change to reflect these settings when you attach the style sheet to the page. To attach an external style sheet to a page, open the page, and then use the Attach Style Sheet button in the CSS Styles panel to open the Attach External Style Sheet dialog box, as shown in Figure 23. Use this dialog box to browse for the external style sheet file you want to attach and to specify whether to link or import the file. In most cases, you should choose to link the file so that the content of the page is kept separate from the style sheet file.

If all the pages in your site are based on a template, you can save an enormous amount of time and development effort by attaching an external style sheet to the template. Doing this saves you from having to attach the style sheet to every page in the site; you have to attach it only to the template file. Then, when you make changes to the style sheet, those changes will be reflected in the template and will be updated in every page based on the template, when you save the template.

Adding Hyperlink Styles to a CSS Style Sheet

You can use an external style sheet to create styles for all links in a Web site. To do this, open the style sheet so it appears in the document window, and then click the New CSS Rule button to open the New CSS Rule dialog box. Click the Advanced option button, and then choose one of the selectors from the Selector list, as shown and described in Figure 24. After you choose a selector and click OK, the CSS Rule Definition dialog box opens, where you can specify the formatting of the selected link. Some older browsers may not recognize link styles.

Adding Custom Code to a CSS Style Sheet

You can make changes to a style sheet by changing its code or adding code directly into the style sheet file. To do this, open the style sheet file so that it appears in the document window, click to place the insertion point where you want to add code, and then type the code you want. For instance, you can add code to the body tag of the style sheet that changes the colors of a viewer's scroll bar to match the colors of your Web site.

FIGURE 23
Attach External Style Sheet dialog box

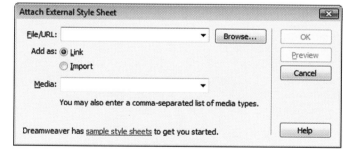

FIGURE 24
New CSS Rule dialog box with Advanced Selector Type displayed

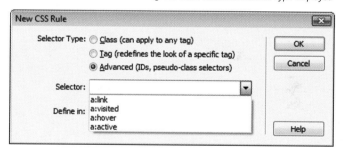

Modify an external CSS style sheet

1. Open the activities page.

2. Double-click the **su_styles.css file** in the root folder in the Files panel.

   The su_styles.css file opens in the Document window.

3. Switch back to the activities page, then click the **New CSS Rule button**  in the CSS Styles panel to open the New CSS Rule dialog box.

4. Click the **Advanced option button**, then click the **Define in su_styles.css option button** (if necessary).

5. Click the **Selector list arrow**, click **a:link**, then click **OK** to open the CSS Rule Definition for a:link in su_styles.css dialog box.

6. Set the Font to **Arial, Helvetica, sans-serif**; set the Size to **small**; set the Weight to **bold**; set the Color to **#003366**; compare your screen to Figure 25; then click **OK**.

7. Click the **su_styles.css tab** to view the file in the Document window.

   The su_styles.css page now contains new code that reflects the type settings you specified for the a:link style.

8. Save your changes, switch to the activities page, scroll down the page, then compare your screen to Figure 26.

   The fishing excursions and dolphin cruises page links in the paragraph text now appear in another shade of blue, reflecting the formatting changes that you made to the a:link style.

You opened the su_styles.css file and made modifications to the a:link style using the CSS Rule Definition dialog box.

FIGURE 25
Modifying the a:link style

FIGURE 26
About us page after modifying a:link style

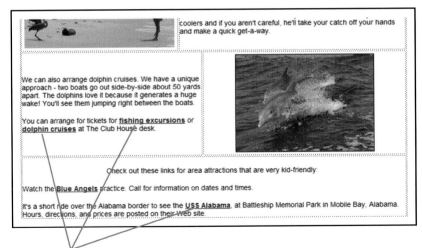

Links appear bold and dark blue

FIGURE 27

Activities page after modifying a:hover style

a:hover style changes link to bold blue when the mouse rolls over it

1. Switch to the su_styles.css file.

2. Click the **New CSS Rule button** 🔁 in the CSS Styles panel to open the New CSS Rule dialog box.

3. Click the **Advanced option button**.

4. Click the **Selector list arrow**, click **a:hover**, then click **OK** to open the CSS Rule definition for a:hover dialog box.

5. Set the Font to **Arial, Helvetica, sans-serif**; set the Size to **small**; set the Weight to **bold**; set the Color to **#0066CC**; then click **OK**.

   The su_styles.css page now contains new code that reflects the font specifications you set for the a:hover style.

6. Click **File** on the menu bar, then click **Save All** to save both pages, switch to the activities page, preview the page in your browser, position the mouse pointer over the dolphin cruises link, then compare your screen to Figure 27.

   The fishing excursions and dolphin cruises links in the paragraph text appear in medium blue when the mouse pointer rolls over them, reflecting the formatting changes that you made to the a:hover style.

7. Close your browser, then close the activities page.

You opened the su_styles.css file and then made modifications to the a:hover style using the CSS Rule Definition dialog box.

Add custom code to a style sheet

1. Open the spa page, then switch to the su_styles.css file.

2. Locate the bullets tag code on the page, then replace the font size with **small**, as shown in Figure 28.

3. Click **Refresh** on the CSS Styles panel to display the change you made in the code.

4. Switch to the spa page, then compare your screen to Figure 29.

   The text with the bullets style is smaller now and looks better on the page.

5. Close the spa page.

You opened the su_styles.css file and made changes to the bullets style directly in the code.

FIGURE 28

su_styles.css file after changing the font-size of the bullets style

```
1   .bullets {
2       font-family: Arial, Helvetica, sans-serif;
3       font-size: small;
4       font-style: normal;
5       font-weight: bold;
6       color: #000066;
7   }
8   .heading {
9       font-family: Arial, Helvetica, sans-serif;
10      font-size: 16px;
11      font-style: normal;
12      font-weight: bold;
13      color: #000066;
14      text-align: center;
```

Font-size changed to small

FIGURE 29

Spa page after style has been modified

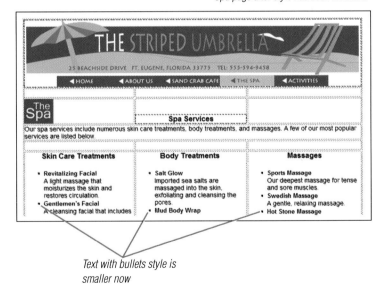

Text with bullets style is smaller now

FIGURE 30

Selected a:link code in su_styles.css file

```
1    .bullets {
2        font-family: Arial, Helvetica, sans-serif;
3        font-size: small;
4        font-style: normal;
5        font-weight: bold;
6        color: #000066;
7    }
8    .heading {
9        font-family: Arial, Helvetica, sans-serif;
10       font-size: 16px;
11       font-style: normal;
12       font-weight: bold;
13       color: #000066;
14       text-align: center;
15   }
16   .body_text {
17       font-family: Arial, Helvetica, sans-serif;
18       font-size: 14px;
19       font-style: normal;
20   }
21   a:link {
22       font-family: Arial, Helvetica, sans-serif;
23       font-size: small;
24       font-weight: bold;
25       color: #003366;
26   }
27   a:hover {
```

Selected a:link code

1. Select the **a:link tag** and the **five lines of code** below it, then compare your screen to Figure 30.

2. Press **[Delete]** (Win) or **[delete]** (Mac), save your changes, click **Refresh** on the CSS Styles panel, then save your changes again.

   Notice that the a:link style no longer appears in the CSS Styles panel.

3. Open the activities page, then preview it in your browser.

   Notice that the activities page text links no longer appear as bold, indicating that the a:link style has been deleted from the style sheet.

   TIP You can detach a style sheet from a template or Web page by clicking the style sheet file in the CSS Styles panel, then clicking the Delete CSS Rule button. When you do this, the file is no longer linked to the Web page, but it is not actually deleted; it remains in its original location on your hard drive.

4. Close the browser, then close all open files.

You deleted the a:link style from the su_styles.css file and then saved your changes.

WORK WITH
CONFLICTING STYLES

What You'll Do

 In this lesson, you will discover that embedded styles have precedence over styles redefining HTML tags.

When you have a mixture of embedded styles, external styles, and styles redefining HTML tags, you need to understand what happens when the styles conflict. In general, embedded styles override external styles and styles redefining HTML tags. Styles can also conflict with formatting applied using the Property inspector. If you try to use the Property inspector to format text that already has a style applied to it, Dreamweaver will automatically create an additional style based on the first style using the default naming convention (Style 1, Style 2, etc.). Using styles to format text is better than using the Property inspector. Styles ensure consistency, cleaner code, and allow you to work more efficiently. While you are just beginning to understand Cascading Style Sheets, it might be wise to stick to external style sheets until you build up your experience base and confidence.

FIGURE 31

Text with style applied from redefined body tag

With no style applied, the font family is applied from the redefined body tag

Style = None

1. Open the about_us page.

2. Click the **New CSS Rule button** on the CSS Styles panel, click the **Tag option button** in the Selector Type section, click the **This document only option button**, click the **Tag list arrow**, click **body**, then click **OK**.

3. Click the **Font list arrow**, click **Georgia, Times New Roman, Times, serif**, then click **OK**.

   The body style is listed in the CSS Styles panel as an embedded style, specifying that all text in the body of the page be displayed using the Georgia, Times New Roman, Times, serif font family. However, the text on the page did not change because the body_text style from the su_styles.css file takes precedence over the style that changed the body tag.

4. Select the last sentence on the page beginning "We can even. . .", click the **Style list arrow**, then click **None**.

   When the body_text style is removed, the style from the body tag is applied, as shown in Figure 31.

5. Click **Edit** on the menu bar, then click **Undo** to apply the body_text style again.

6. Delete the body style from the CSS Styles panel.

You found that an embedded style has precedence over a style redefining an HTML tag.

USE CODING TOOLS
TO VIEW AND EDIT STYLES

What You'll Do

```
<!DOCTYPE html PUBLIC "-//W3C//DTD XHTML 1.0 Transitional//EN"
"http://www.w3.org/TR/xhtml1/DTD/xhtml1-transitional.dtd">
<html xmlns="http://www.w3.org/1999/xhtml">
<head>
<meta http-equiv="Content-Type" content="text/html; charset=iso-8859-1" />
<title>About our property</title>
<meta name="Keywords" content="beach resort, spa, Ft. Eugene, Florida, Gulf of Mexico, fishing,
dolphin cruises" /><meta name="Description" content="The Striped Umbrella is a full-service resort
and spa just steps from the Gulf of Mexico in Ft. Eugene, Florida." />
<link href="su_styles.css" rel="stylesheet" type="text/css" />
<script>
<style type="text/css">
<!--
hr {
    color: #003399;
}
-->
```

 In this lesson, you will collapse, then expand the code for the about us page to view the code for the styles. You will then move the embedded style for the horizontal rule to the external style sheet file.

Coding Tools in Dreamweaver

There are several tools you can use with the Coding toolbar while you are in Code view. The Coding toolbar buttons include Open Documents, Collapse Full Tag, Collapse Selection, Expand All, Select Parent Tag, Balance Braces, Line Numbers, Highlight Invalid Code, Apply Comment, Remove Comment, Wrap Tag, Recent Snippets, Move or Convert CSS, Indent Code, Outdent Code, and Format Source Code, as shown in Figure 32. The

FIGURE 32
The Coding Toolbar

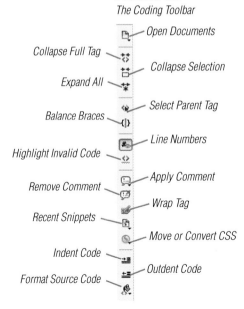

Using Styles and Style Sheets for Design

Coding toolbar is displayed on the left side of the Document window, and is designed to remain stationary. Although you cannot move it, you can hide it. Remember that you have several View options you can also use while viewing your code. These include Word Wrap, Line Numbers, Hidden Characters, Highlight Invalid Code, Syntax Coloring, and Auto Indent. These options can be turned on and off by checking the item. They are accessed by clicking the View options button on the Document toolbar.

Using Coding Tools to Navigate Code

As your pages get longer and the code more complex, it is helpful to collapse sections of code, similarly to the way you can collapse and expand panels, folders, and styles. To collapse lines of code, you can click the minus sign or plus sign next to the line

number. You can also use the Collapse Full Tag or Collapse Selection buttons on the Coding toolbar. This will allow you to look at two different sections of code that are not adjacent to each other in the code. Applying comments is an easy way to add comments to your code for documentation purposes. Comments are not visible in the browser. The Highlight Invalid Code is an easy way to spot code containing errors so you can fix it.

Using Code Hints to Streamline Coding

If you are typing code directly into Code view, one of the nice features Dreamweaver offers is the use of Code hints. Code hints are similar to other auto-complete features that you have probably used in other software applications. As you are typing code, Dreamweaver will recognize the tag name and offer you choices to complete the tag simply by clicking a tag choice in the

menu, as shown in Figure 33. You can also add your own code hints to the list using JavaScript. The code hints are stored in the file CodeHints.xml.

Converting styles

Several of the new features in Dreamweaver CS3 have improved the way you use and manage CSS rules. One of these features is the ability to convert one type of style to another. For instance, you can move an embedded style to an external style sheet or an inline style to either an embedded style or a style in an external style sheet. To do this, select the style in Code view, right-click the code, and then choose the action you want from the context menu. You can also convert styles in the CSS Styles panel by selecting the style, right-clicking the style, and choosing the action you want from the context menu.

FIGURE 33
Using Code Hints

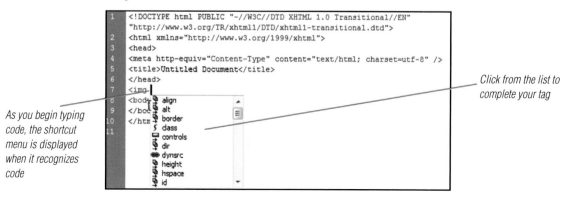

As you begin typing code, the shortcut menu is displayed when it recognizes code

Click from the list to complete your tag

Collapse code

1. Verify that the about_us page is open, then change to Code view.

2. Scroll up the page (if necessary), to display the code that links the external style sheet, su_styles.css, to the page.

   The code will probably be on or close to line 7 in the head section.

3. Select the line of code under the line with the su_styles.css link, then drag down to select all of the code down to the line of code that includes the style for the horizontal rule, as shown in Figure 34.

4. Click the **minus sign** (Win) or **vertical triangle** (Mac) in the last line of selected code to collapse all of the code that is selected.

   You can now see both code fragments—one in the head content and one in the body content. The head content fragment is shown in Figure 35. The plus sign (Win) or horizontal triangle (Mac) next to the line of code indicates that there is hidden code. You also see a gap in the line numbers where the hidden code resides.

You collapsed a block of code in Code view to be able to see two non adjacent sections of the code at the same time.

FIGURE 34
Selecting lines of code for the about us page to collapse

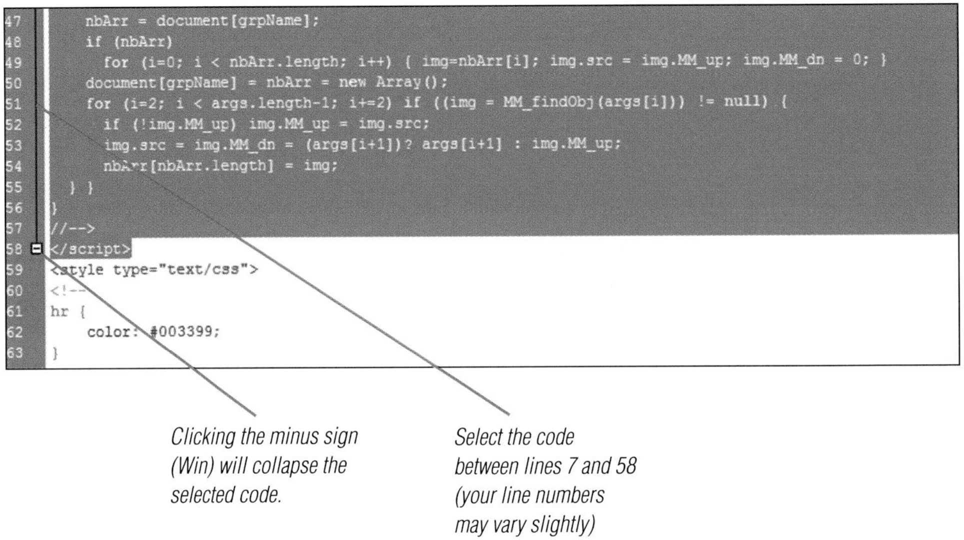

Clicking the minus sign (Win) will collapse the selected code.

Select the code between lines 7 and 58 (your line numbers may vary slightly)

FIGURE 35
Collapsed code in Code view

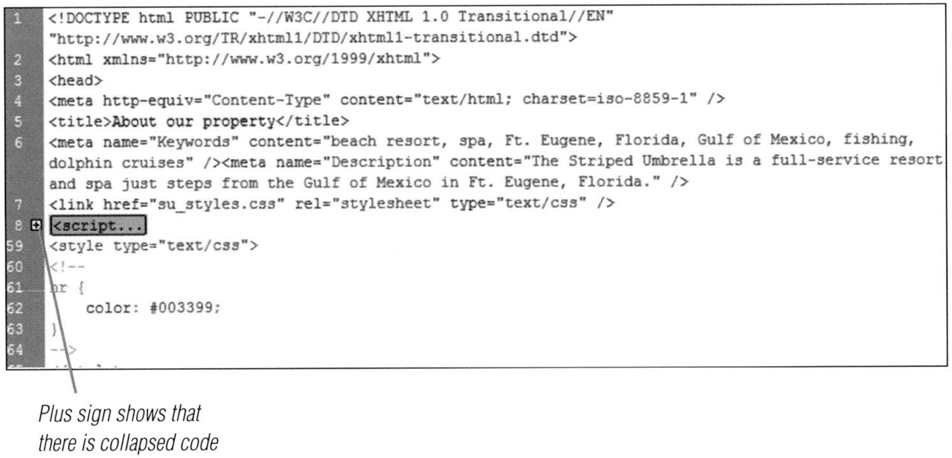

Plus sign shows that there is collapsed code

FIGURE 36
Expanded code for about us page

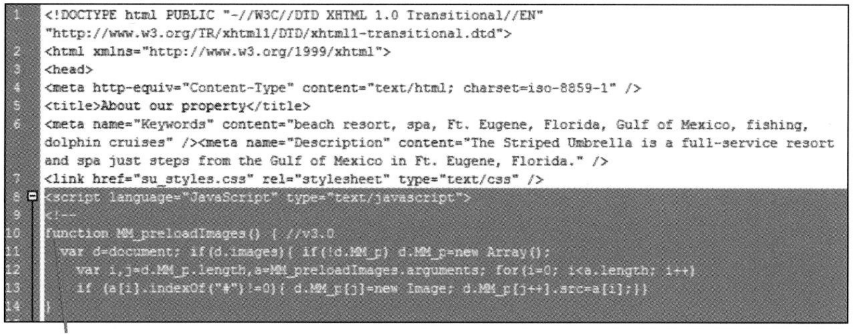

```
1    <!DOCTYPE html PUBLIC "-//W3C//DTD XHTML 1.0 Transitional//EN"
     "http://www.w3.org/TR/xhtml1/DTD/xhtml1-transitional.dtd">
2    <html xmlns="http://www.w3.org/1999/xhtml">
3    <head>
4    <meta http-equiv="Content-Type" content="text/html; charset=iso-8859-1" />
5    <title>About our property</title>
6    <meta name="Keywords" content="beach resort, spa, Ft. Eugene, Florida, Gulf of Mexico, fishing,
     dolphin cruises" /><meta name="Description" content="The Striped Umbrella is a full-service resort
     and spa just steps from the Gulf of Mexico in Ft. Eugene, Florida." />
7    <link href="su_styles.css" rel="stylesheet" type="text/css" />
8    <script language="JavaScript" type="text/javascript">
9    <!--
10   function MM_preloadImages() { //v3.0
11     var d=document; if(d.images){ if(!d.MM_p) d.MM_p=new Array();
12     var i,j=d.MM_p.length,a=MM_preloadImages.arguments; for(i=0; i<a.length; i++)
13     if (a[i].indexOf("#")!=0){ d.MM_p[j]=new Image; d.MM_p[j++].src=a[i];}}
14   }
```

Code is expanded

POWER USER SHORTCUTS

To do this:	Use this shortcut:
Collapse selection of code	[Ctrl][Shift][C] (Win) or [shift] ⌘ [C] (Mac)
Collapse outside selection of code	[Ctrl][Alt][C] (Win) or [option] ⌘ [C] (Mac)
Expand selection of code	[Ctrl[Shift][E] (Win) or [shift] ⌘ [E] (Mac)
Collapse full tag	[Ctrl][Shift][J] (Win) or [shift] ⌘ [J] (Mac)
Collapse outside full tag	[Ctrl][Alt][J] (Win) or [option] ⌘ [J] (Mac)
Expand all (code)	[Ctrl][Alt][E] (Win) or [option] ⌘ [E] (Mac)
Check links sitewide	[Ctrl][F8] (Win) or ⌘ [F8] (Mac)
Indent code	[Ctrl][Shift][>] (Win) or [shift] ⌘ [>] (Mac)
Outdent code	[Ctrl][Shift][<] (Win) or [shift] ⌘ [<] (Mac)
Balance braces	[Ctrl]['] (Win) or ⌘ ['] (Mac)
Go to line (of code)	[Ctrl][G] (Win) or ⌘ [,] (Mac)
Show code hints	[Ctrl][Spacebar] (Win) or [control][spacebar] (Mac)
Refresh code hints	[Ctrl][.] (Win) or [command][.] (Mac)

Expand code

1. Click the **plus sign** (Win) or **horizontal triangle** (Mac) on line 8 to expand the code.

2. Compare your screen to Figure 36, then click in the page to deselect the code.

   All line numbers are visible again and the plus sign (Win) or horizontal triangle (Mac) is replaced with a minus sign (Win) or vertical triangle (Mac).

You expanded the code to display all lines of the code again.

Move an embedded style to an external CSS style sheet

1. Select the **three lines of code** that format the style for the horizontal rule on the about_us page.

   The code will be on or close to lines 61 through 63.

2. Right-click (Win) or control-click (Mac) the **selected code**, point to **CSS Styles**, then click **Move CSS Rule**, as shown in Figure 37.

3. In the Move to External Style Sheet dialog box, verify that stu_styles.css appears in the Style Sheet text box, as shown in Figure 38, then click **OK**.

4. Compare your CSS Styles panel with Figure 39 to verify that the style has been moved to the style sheet external file, select <style> in the CSS Styles panel, then click the **Delete Embedded Style Sheet button** 🗑 to remove the remnants of code remaining for the embedded style.

   TIP The name of the trash can icon 🗑 in the CSS Rules panel changes depending on whether you have a style or a style sheet tag selected in the CSS Rules panel.

5. Save and close all open files.

You moved an embedded style for a horizontal rule to an external CSS style sheet.

FIGURE 37

Moving the embedded hr style to the style sheet file

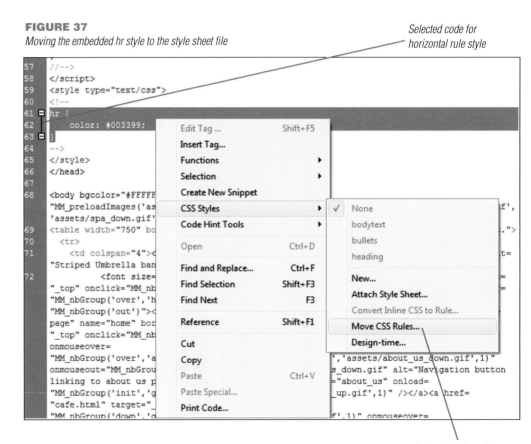

Selected code for horizontal rule style

In Step 2, select this option

Using Styles and Style Sheets for Design

FIGURE 38

Moving the embedded hr style to the style sheet file

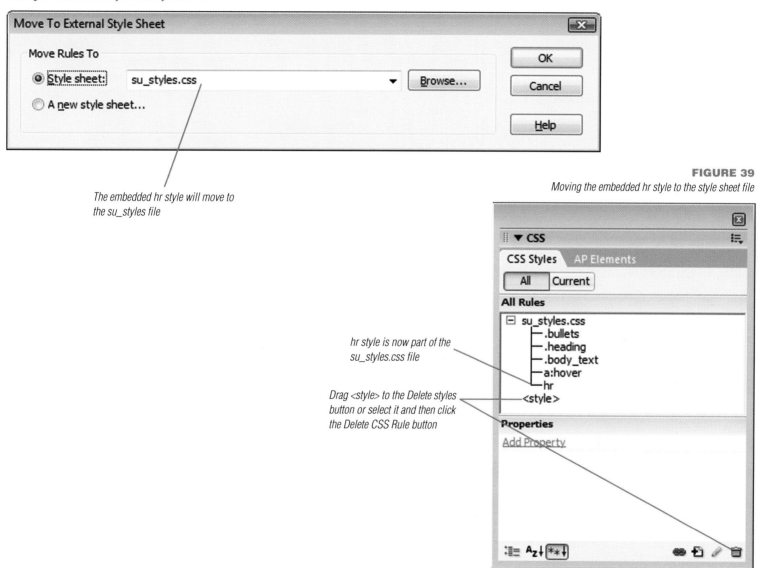

The embedded hr style will move to
the su_styles file

FIGURE 39

Moving the embedded hr style to the style sheet file

hr style is now part of the
su_styles.css file

Drag <style> to the Delete styles
button or select it and then click
the Delete CSS Rule button

Create and use embedded styles.

1. Delete the blooms & bulbs Web site and replace your blooms root folder with the blooms root folder where you store your Chapter 7 Data Files.
2. Import the **blooms & bulbs.ste** file and verify that the root folder and assets folder are linked correctly to your files.
3. Open the plants page.
4. Position the cursor to the right of the petunias image, then enter a line break to place the insertion point under the image. (*Hint*: The petunias image is the green and white photo.)
5. Type **Moonlight White Petunia (Mini-Spreading)**.
6. Create a new embedded style using the Class selector type and name it **flower_names**.
7. Choose the following type settings: Font: **Arial, Helvetica, sans-serif**, Size: **12 pixels**, Style: **italic**, and Color: **#003399**.
8. Apply the **flower_names style** to the text you typed in Step 5.

9. Repeat Steps 4 and 5 to label the verbena image **Silver Blue Verbena**.
10. Apply the **flower_names style** to the verbena label.
11. Type **Golden Dream Lantana** under the lantana image, then apply the **flower_names style** to the label.

Modify Embedded Styles

1. Modify the flower_names style to change the text size to **small**.
2. Save your changes, preview the plants page in your browser, compare your screen to Figure 40, close your browser, and close the page.

Work with external CSS style sheets.

1. Open the newsletter page.
2. Use the New CSS Rule dialog box to add the **a:link style** to the blooms_styles.css file.

Set the Font to **Arial, Helvetica, sans-serif**; set the Size to **14 pixels**; set the Weight to **normal**; then set the Color to **#003399**.
3. Save your changes, then make sure that the text links on the page now appear in a different shade of blue.
4. Use the New CSS Rule dialog box to add the **a:hover style** to the blooms_styles.css file. Set the Font to **Arial, Helvetica, sans-serif**; set the Size to **14 pixels**; set the Weight to **bold**; then set the Color to **#0066FF**.
5. Save your work, then preview the newsletter page in your browser and make sure that the links appear according to the settings you specified. (*Hint*: Visited links will remain a purple color.)

6. Edit the headings style to change the weight to **normal.**

7. Close the newsletter page.

Work with Conflicting Styles

1. Open the index page.

2. Create a new CSS rule to redefine the body tag in this document only.

3. Choose the **Georgia, Times New Roman, Times, serif font.**

4. Select the paragraph of text and remove the **bodytext** style.

5. Reapply the **bodytext style** and delete the **body style** from the CSS Styles panel.

Use Coding Tools to View and Edit Styles

1. Collapse all of the code for the head content.

2. Expand all code.

3. Convert the **flower_names** style on the plants page to an external style in the blooms_styles.css file. (*Hint:* Remember to remove any remaining code from the embedded style.)

4. Save and close all open pages.

FIGURE 40
Completed Skills Review

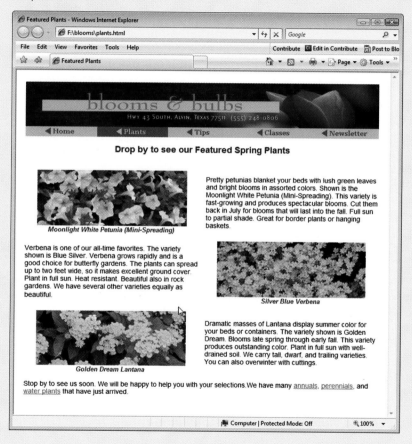

In this Project Builder you will continue your work on the TripSmart Web site. You have decided to add a few more styles to the style sheet to improve some of the page formatting.

1. Replace your tripsmart folder with the tripsmart folder from where you store your Chapter 7 Data Files.

2. Open the newsletter page.

3. Create a new embedded class style named **.bullets** with the following settings: Font: **Arial, Helvetica, sans-serif**, Size: **12 pixels**, Weight: **bold,** and Color: **#000033.**

4. Apply the **.bullets** custom style to the items listed at the beginning of each bullet, using Figure 41 as a guide.

5. Edit the heading style to change the color to **#000033.**

6. Add a horizontal rule under the list of items. (*Hint:* Remember to enter two paragraph breaks to end the unordered list. If you have difficulty ending the unordered list, click the Unordered List button.)

7. Create a new custom style in the tripsmart_styles.css file that redefines the hr tag as centered and with the color **#000033.** Notice how the horizontal rule on the page changes color slightly.

8. Change the horizontal rule width to **500 pixels.**

9. Convert the bullets style to an external style in the tripsmart_styles.css styles file.

10. Save all files.

11. Preview the newsletter page in your browser, then compare your screen to Figure 41.

12. Close your browser, then close all open files.

FIGURE 41
Sample Project Builder 1

Travel Tidbits

Ten Packing Essentials

The next time you are packing for a trip, whether it is for an adventure-backpacking trip to the jungles of Panama or for a weekend in New York , consider our list of "can't do without these" items:

- **Expandable clothesline and clothespins** – These are handy after you have hand-washed your clothes in the river or hotel sink.
- **Paperback book** – A book will help pass the time on a long plane trip or a wait in a customs line.
- **Small hotel-size shampoo bottle** – Shampoo is actually a mild detergent, handy for washing your hair, of course, but also for washing your clothes.
- **Travel alarm clock** – Don't depend on wake-up calls or a hotel clock to keep you from an important meeting time.
- **Small flashlight** – You never know when a flashlight will come in handy. Even five-star hotels have been known to lose power at times. Invaluable for snake spotting at night in the woods!
- **Zippered plastic bags** – These are so handy for storing a number of things: snacks, dirty clothes, wet clothes, small items that would get "lost" in your bag, like pens, tape, and your expandable clothesline and clothespins!
- **Guidebook** – There are many great guidebooks that range from guides for students on a shoestring budget to guides on shopping for fine antiques in Italy . Take advantage of available research to obtain general background knowledge of your destination.
- **Backpack** – Backpacks are versatile, easy to carry, and have enough style variations to appeal to all ages and sexes. They hold a lot of your essential items!
- **Packing cubes** – Packing cubes are zippered nylon bags that are great for organizing your packed items. You can squeeze the air out of the packed cubes, conserving space in your bag.
- **Bubble wrap and tape** – Keep a few feet of small-sized bubble wrap in your bag for wrapping breakable souvenirs you pick up along the way.

Using Styles and Style Sheets for Design

In this Project Builder, you will continue your work on the Carolyne's Creations Web site that you started in Project Builder 2 in Chapter 1. You will continue to work on the page formatting to include as much formatting as you can with the use of CSS styles.

1. Replace the Carolyne's Creations Web site root folder with the new folder from where you store your Chapter 7 Data Files.
2. Open the shop page.

3. Create a new custom style in the cc_styles.css file called **prices**.
4. Refer to Figure 42, then select the settings of your choice for the prices style that you will then use to format the prices of the two specials on the page.
5. Select each price and apply the **prices** style.
6. Create a new style for this page only, named **special_name**, selecting formatting settings of your choice.

7. Apply the **special_name style** to the Multifunctional Pot and Cutlery Set text.
8. Convert the **special_name style** to an external style in the cc_styles.css file.
9. Save your work, preview the shop page in your browser, then compare your screen to Figure 42.
10. Close your browser, then close all open files.

FIGURE 42
Completed Project Builder 2

Our small storefront is filled with wonderful kitchen accessories and supplies. We also have a large assortment of gourmet items from soup mixes to exotic teas and coffee — perfect for gift baskets for any occasion. We deliver to homes and offices, as well as dorms and hospitals.

January Specials: **Multifunctional Pot and Cutlery Set**

We try to feature special items each month and love to promote local foods. This month's features: A large multifunctional pot for tempting soups and stews and a professional grade cutlery set.

The knife blades are solid stainless steel, precision forged as one single piece. The heavy bolsters provide balance and control. The cutting edge holds its sharpness well. The five knives come with a handsome butcher block knife stand. They are dishwasher safe, but hand washing is recommended.

The pot is made of polished stainless steel with a tempered glass lid so you can peak without lifting the lid to monitor progress. A pasta insert lifts out for draining. Each piece is dishwasher safe. The handles remain cool to the touch while the pot is heating on the stovetop.

$109.00, regularly $135.00

$75.00, regularly $90.00

Many of today's leading Web sites use CSS style sheets to ensure consistent formatting and positioning of text and other elements. For instance, the United States Department of Justice Web site uses them. Figure 43 shows the Department of Justice home page.

1. Connect to the Internet, then go to the United States Department of Justice Web site at *www.usdoj.gov.*
2. Spend some time exploring the many pages of this site.
3. When you finish exploring all of the different pages, return to the home page. Click View on your browser's menu bar, then click Source to view the code for the page.
4. Look in the head content area for code relating to the CSS style sheet used. Note whether any styles are defined for a:link or a:hover and write down the specified formatting for those styles. Write down any other code you see that relates to styles.
5. Close the Source window, then look at the home page. Make a list of all the different text elements that you see on the page that you think should have CSS styles applied to them.

6. Print the home page of this site, along with the source code that contains CSS styles.

FIGURE 43
Design Project

In this assignment, you will continue to work on the Web site that you created in Chapters 1 through 6.

You will continue refining your Web site by using CSS style sheets and embedded styles to format the text in your Web site consistently.

1. Write a plan in which you define styles for all of the text elements in your site. Your plan should include how you will use an external style sheet as well as embedded styles. You can use either the external style sheet you created in Chapter 3 or create a new one. Your plan should include at least one custom style, one style that redefines an HTML tag, and one style that uses a selector.

2. Attach the completed style sheet to all individual pages in the site.

3. Create and apply the embedded styles you identified in your plan.

4. Create and apply the styles that will be added to the external style sheet.

5. Review the pages and make sure that all text elements appear as they should and look appropriate. Use the checklist in Figure 44 to make sure you have completed everything according to the assignment.

6. Make any necessary changes.

7. Save your work, then close all open pages.

FIGURE 44
Portfolio Project checklist

Web Site Checklist

1. Do all text elements in the site have a style applied to them?
2. Does your site have at least one embedded style?
3. Is the external style sheet attached to each page in the site?
4. Did you define and apply at least one custom style and one style that redefines an HTML tag?
5. Are you happy with the overall appearance of each page?

chapter

8 COLLECTING DATA
WITH FORMS

1. Plan and create a form

2. Edit and format a form

3. Work with form objects

4. Test and process a form

8 COLLECTING DATA
WITH FORMS

Introduction

Many Web sites have pages designed to collect information from viewers. You've likely seen such pages when ordering books online from Barnes & Noble or purchasing airline tickets from an airline Web site. Adding a form to a Web page provides interactivity between your viewers and your business. To collect information from viewers, you add forms for them to fill out and send to a Web server to be processed. Forms on a Web page are no different from forms in everyday life. Your checks are simple forms that ask for information: the date, the amount of the check, the name of the check's recipient, and your signature. A form on a Web page consists of **form objects** such as text boxes or radio buttons into which viewers type information or from which they make selections.

In this chapter, you will add a form to a page that provides a way for interested viewers to ask for more information about The Striped Umbrella resort. It will also give them the opportunity to comment on the Web site and make helpful suggestions.

Feedback is a vital part of a Web site and must be made easy for a viewer to submit.

Using Forms to Collect Information

Forms are just one of the many different tools that Web developers use to collect information from viewers. A simple form can consist of one form object and a button that submits information to a Web server, for example, a search text box that you fill out, and a button that you click to start the search. More complex forms can collect contact information, or even allow students to take exams online and receive grades after a short wait. You can use forms to insert information into databases, or to find a specific record in a database. The range of uses for forms is limited only by your imagination.

All forms need to be connected to an application that will process the information that the form collects. This application can store the form data in a database, or simply send it to you in an e-mail message. You need to specify how you want the information used, stored, and processed.

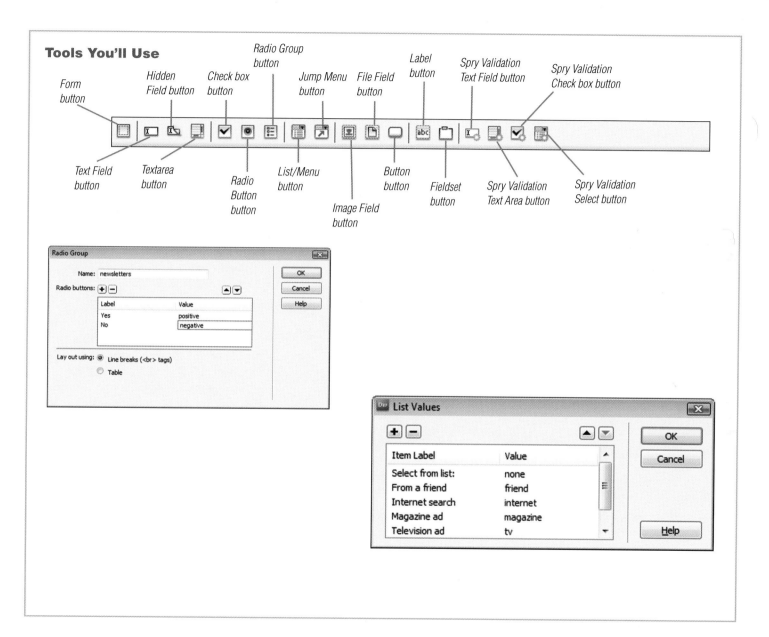

Tools You'll Use

PLAN AND
CREATE A FORM

What You'll Do

In this lesson, you will replace your Striped Umbrella files by importing a revised Web site. You will then add a new form to the feedback page in The Striped Umbrella Web site.

Planning a Form

Before you use Dreamweaver to create a form, it's a good idea to write down the information you want to collect and the order in which you want to collect it. It's also a good idea to make a sketch of the form. Planning your form content at the beginning saves you from spending time organizing the information when you create the form in Dreamweaver. The form you will create for The Striped Umbrella Web site will contain a form for viewers to request more information, sign up for an electronic newsletter, and submit their comments about the Web site. Figure 1 shows a sketch of the form that you will create in this chapter.

When planning your form content, you should organize the information in a logical order that will make sense to viewers. For instance, no one will expect to fill in their address before their name, simply because it isn't typically done that way.

Almost all forms, ranging from your birth certificate to your IRS tax forms, request your name before your address, so you should follow this standard. Placing information in an unusual order will only confuse your viewers.

People on the Internet are notoriously hurried and will often provide only information that is required or that is located on the top half of the form. Therefore, it's a good idea to put the most important information at the top of your form. In fact, this is a good rule to follow for Web pages in general. The most important information should be "above the fold" or on the part of the page that is visible before you have to scroll to see the rest.

Creating Forms

Once you have finished planning your form content, you are ready to create the form in Dreamweaver. To create a form on a Web page, you use the Form button in the Forms category of the Insert bar.

Clicking the Form button will insert a dashed red outline around the area of the form. To make your form function correctly, you then need to configure the form so that it "talks" to the scripts or e-mail server and processes the information submitted by the viewer. By itself, a form can do nothing. It has to have some type of script or program running behind it that will process the information to be used in a certain way.

There are two methods used to process the information your form collects: server-side scripting and client-side scripting. **Server-side scripting** uses applications that reside on your Web server and interact with the information collected in the form. The most common types of server-side applications are **Common Gateway Interface (CGI)** scripts, **Cold Fusion** programs, and **Active Server Pages (ASP)** applications. **Client-side scripting** means that the form is processed on the user's computer. The script resides on the Web page, rather than on the server. An example of this is a mortgage calculator that allows you to estimate mortgage payments. The data is processed on the user's computer. The most common types of scripts stored on a Web page are created with a scripting language called **JavaScript**, or **Jscript**. Server-side applications and scripts collect the information from the form, process the information, and react to the information the form contains.

You can process form information in a variety of ways. The easiest and most common way is to collect the information from the form and e-mail it to the owner of the Web site. You can also specify that form data be stored in a database for the Web site owner to use at a later date. You can even specify that the application do both: collect the form data in a database, as well as send it in an e-mail message.

You can also specify that the form data be processed instead of stored. For instance, you can create a form that totals the various prices and provides a total price to the site viewer on the order page, without recording any subtotals in a database or e-mail message. In this example, only the final total of the order would be stored in the database or sent in an e-mail message.

FIGURE 1

Sketch of Web form you will add to survey page

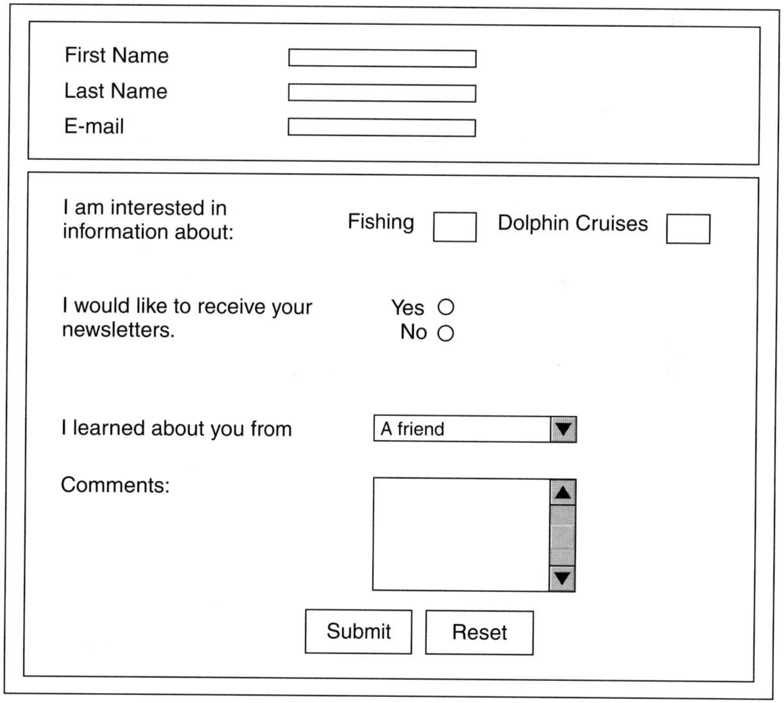

First Name

Last Name

E-mail

I am interested in information about: Fishing   Dolphin Cruises

I would like to receive your   Yes ○
newsletters.   No ○

I learned about you from   A friend ▼

Comments:

Submit   Reset

You can also create forms that make changes to your Web page based on information entered by viewers. For example, you could create a form that asks viewers to select a background color for a Web page. In this type of form, the information could be collected and sent to the processor. The processor could then compare the selected background color to the current background color and change the color if it is different from the viewer's selection.

Setting Form Properties

After you insert a form, use the Property inspector to specify the application that will process the form information and to specify how the information will be sent to the processing application. The **Action property** in the Property inspector specifies the application or script that will process the form data. Most of the time the Action property is the name and location of a CGI script, such as /cgi-bin/myscript.cgi; a Cold Fusion page, such as mypage.cfm; or an Active Server Page, such as mypage.asp. Figure 2 shows the properties of a selected form.

FIGURE 2
Form controls in the Property inspector

Form button

Form

Form properties

Form name property

Method property

Action property

Target property

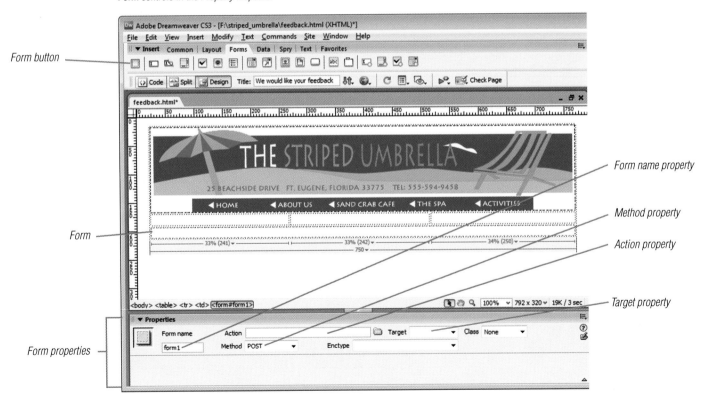

Collecting Data with Forms

The **Method property** specifies the **HyperText Transfer Protocol (HTTP)** method used to send the form data to the Web server. The **GET method** specifies that ASCII data collected in the form will be sent to the server appended to the URL or file included in the Action property. For instance, if the Action property is set to /cgi-bin/myscript.cgi, then the data will be sent as a string of characters after the address, as follows: /cgi-bin/myscript.cgi?a+collection+of+data+collected+by+the+form. Data sent with the GET method is usually limited to 8K or less, depending on the Web browser. The **POST method** specifies that the form data be sent to the processing script as a binary or encrypted file, allowing you to send data securely. When you specify the POST method, there is no limit to the amount of information that can be collected in the form, and the information is secure.

The **Form name property** specifies a unique name for the form. The name can be a string of any alphanumeric characters and cannot include spaces. The **Target property** lets you specify the window in which you want the form data to be processed.

Understanding CGI Scripts

CGI is one of the most popular tools used to collect form data. CGI allows a Web browser to work directly with the programs that are running on the server and also makes it possible for a Web site to change in response to user input. CGI programs can be written in Perl or in C, depending

on the type of server that is hosting your Web site. When a CGI script collects data from a Web form, it passes the data to a program running on a Web server, which in turn passes the data back to your Web browser, which then makes changes to the Web site in response to the form data. The

resulting data is then stored in a database or sent to an e-mail server, which then sends the information in an e-mail message to a designated recipient. Figure 3 illustrates how a CGI script processes information collected by a form.

FIGURE 3
Illustration of CGI process on Web server

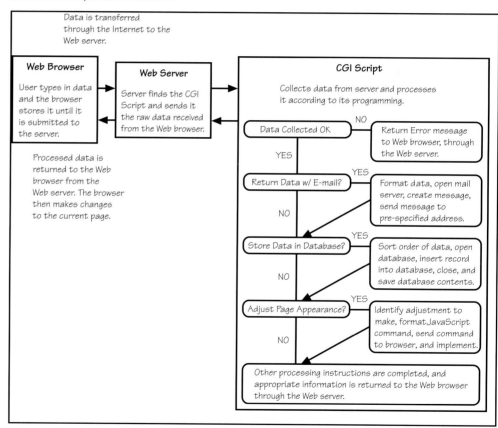

Lesson 1   Plan and Create a Form

DREAMWEAVER 8-7

Insert a form

1. Open the feedback page in The Striped Umbrella Web site.

2. Merge the three cells in the bottom row, then click inside the merged cell.

3. Click the **Forms tab** on the Insert bar, then click the **Form button** to insert a new form on the page.

   A dashed red rectangular outline appears on the page, as shown in Figure 4.

   TIP You will be able to see the form only if Invisible Elements are turned on. To turn on Invisible Elements, click View on the menu bar, point to Visual Aids, then click Invisible Elements.

You inserted a new form on the feedback page of The Striped Umbrella Web site.

FIGURE 4
New form in Design view

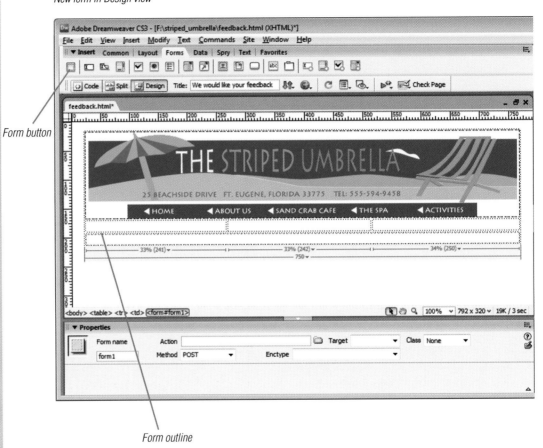

Form button

Form outline

FIGURE 5

Property inspector showing properties of selected form

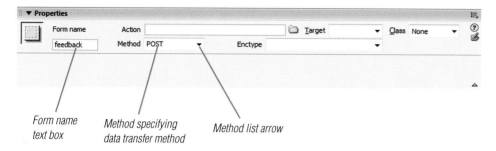

Form name
text box

Method specifying
data transfer method

Method list arrow

Set form properties

1. Click the **Form tag (<form#form1>)** in the tag selector on the status bar to select the form and display the form properties in the Property inspector.

2. Select **form1** in the Form name text box in the Property inspector, then type **feedback**.

3. Click the **Method list arrow** in the Property inspector, then click **POST** (if necessary), as shown in Figure 5.

   TIP   Leave the Action and Target text boxes blank unless you have the information necessary to process the form.

4. Save your work.

You configured the form on the feedback page.

Using CGI scripts

You can use CGI scripts to start and stop external programs or to specify that a page update automatically based on viewer input. You can use CGI scripts to create surveys, site search tools, and games. You can even use CGI to do basic tasks such as record entries to a guest book or count the number of people who have accessed a specific page of your site. CGI also lets you create dynamic Web documents "on the fly" so that pages can be generated in response to preferences specified by the viewer. Unless you have a specific application that you want your script applied to, you can probably find a low-priced script by searching on Google. Instructions for creating and modifying CGI scripts are not covered in this book.

EDIT AND FORMAT A FORM

What You'll Do

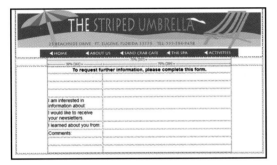

 In this lesson, you will insert a table to create a basic structure for the form on the feedback page. You will also add and format form labels.

Using Tables to Lay Out a Form

Just as you can use a table to help place page elements on a Web page, you can also use tables to help lay out a form. To make sure that your labels and form objects appear in the exact positions you want on a Web page, you can place them in table cells. When you use a table to lay out a form, you usually place labels in the first column and place form objects in the second column, as shown in Figure 6. Although there are different ways to lay out form elements, this two-column approach is probably the cleanest and simplest.

Using Fieldsets to Group Form Objects

If you are creating a long form on a Web page, you might want to organize your form elements in sections to make it easier for viewers to fill out the form. You can use fieldsets to group similar form elements together. A **fieldset** is an HTML tag used to group related form elements together. You can have as many fieldsets on a page as you want. To create a fieldset, use the Fieldset button on the Insert bar.

Adding Labels to Form Objects

When you create a form, you need to include form field labels so that viewers know what information you want them to enter in each field of the form. Because labels play such an important part in identifying the information that the form collects, you need to make sure to use labels that make sense to your viewers. For example, First Name and Last Name are good form field labels, because viewers understand clearly what information they should enter. However, a label such as Top 6 Directory Names might confuse viewers and cause them to leave the field blank or enter incorrect information. When you create a form field label, you should use a simple name that makes it obvious what information viewers should enter in the form field. If creating a simple and obvious label is not possible, then include a short paragraph that describes the information that should be entered into the form field. Figure 7 shows very clearly marked labels for both the form fields and the groups of related information.

You can add labels to a form using one of two methods. You can simply type a label in the appropriate table cell of your form or use the Label button on the Forms group of the Insert bar to link the label to the form object.

FIGURE 6

Web site that uses a table to lay out a form

Harvard Vanguard Web site used with permission from Harvard Vanguard: www.hardvardvanguard.com

Form objects in columns

FIGURE 7

Web site that uses clearly marked labels for form fields and groups of related information

Clearly labeled groups

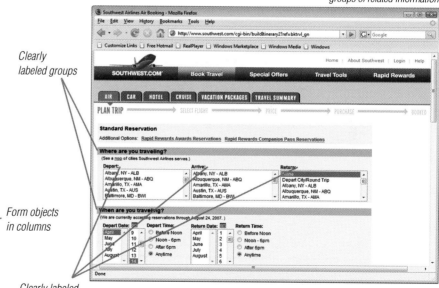

Clearly labeled options within groups

Southwest Airlines Web site used with permission from Southwest Airlines: www.southwest.com

Add a table to a form

1. Click to place the insertion point inside the form, as shown in Figure 8.

2. Click the **Common tab** on the Insert bar, then click the **Table button** .

3. In the Table dialog box, set the Rows to **10**, Columns to **2**, Table width to **75 percent**, Border thickness to **0**, Cell padding to **2**, and Cell spacing to **1**, then click the **Top row header icon** in the Header section.

4. Type **Table used for form layout.** in the Summary text box, compare your screen to Figure 9, then click **OK**.

   TIP The table may look like it is creeping over the bottom edge of the form. If it does, click the form tag on the Property inspector.

5. Center the table in the form, set the bottom-left cell width to **30%**, set the bottom-right cell width to **70%**, as shown in Figure 10, then save your work.

You added a table to the form on the feedback page.

FIGURE 8
Placing the insertion point inside the form

Insertion point placed inside form

FIGURE 9
Table dialog box

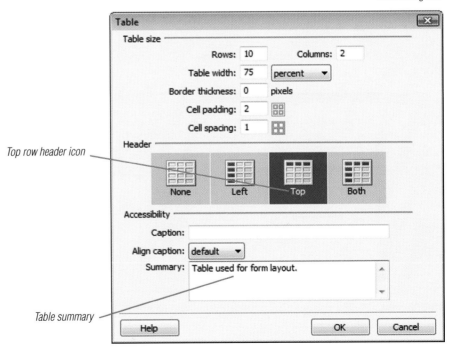

Top row header icon

Table summary

FIGURE 10
Setting table and cell properties

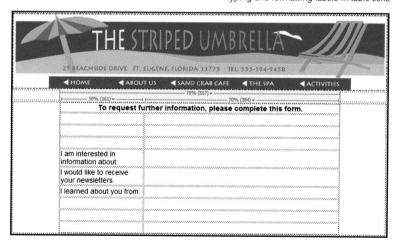

FIGURE 11
Typing and formatting labels in table cells

Add form labels to table cells

1. Merge the top two cells in the first row of the table, then type **To request further information**, **please complete this form.**, then apply the **body_text style** to the sentence.

   Because you designated a header for this table, the top row text is automatically centered and bolded. The header will be used by screen readers to assist viewers who have visual impairments to identify the table.

2. Click in the first cell in the fifth row, then type **I am interested in information about:**.

3. Press [↓], then type **I would like to receive your newsletters.**

4. Click [↓], type **I learned about you from:**, then press [↓].

5. Format each of the labels you entered with the **body_text style,** deselect the text, then compare your screen to Figure 11.

You added a header and three form labels to table cells in the form and formatted them with the body_text style.

Add form labels using the Label button

1. Click in the cell below the cell that contains the text "I learned about you from:".

2. Click the **Forms tab** on the Insert bar, then click the **Label button** [abc].

   | TIP You may need to scroll down in the Design pane to see the cell.

   The view changes to Code and Design view, as shown in Figure 12. The insertion point is positioned in the Code view pane between the tags <label> and </label>, which were added when you clicked the Label button.

   (continued)

FIGURE 12
Adding a label to a form using the Label button   Label button

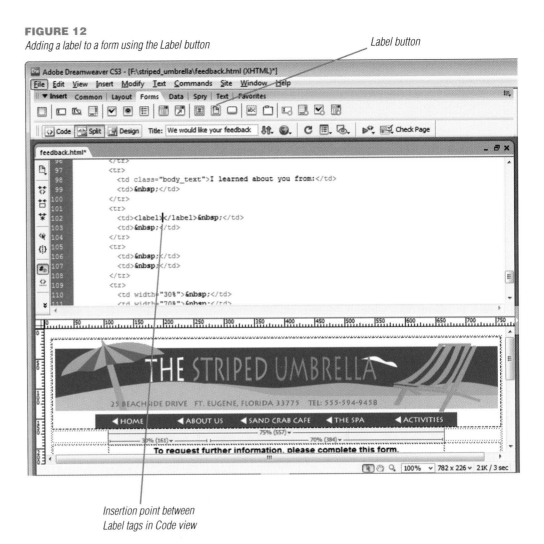

Insertion point between
Label tags in Code view

Collecting Data with Forms

FIGURE 13

New label added using the Label button

3. Type **Comments:**

   The label appears in the table cell in the Design view pane.

   > TIP You can also click Refresh in the Property inspector or press [F5] to refresh the page in Design view.

4. Format the new label as **body_text**, then compare your screen to Figure 13.

5. Click the **Show Design view button**
   [Design] , then save your work.

You added a new label to the form on the feedback page using the Label button, then formatted it with the body_text style.

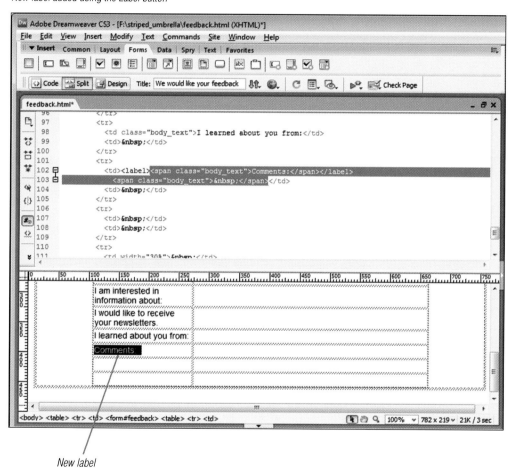

New label

WORK WITH
FORM OBJECTS

What You'll Do

In this lesson, you will add form objects to the form on the feedback page.

Understanding Form Objects

A form provides a structure in which you can place form objects. Form objects—which are also called **form elements**, **form controls**, or **fields**—are the components of a form such as check boxes, text boxes, and radio buttons that allow viewers to provide information and interact with the Web site. You can use form objects in any combination to collect the information you require. Figure 14 shows a form that contains a wide range of form objects.

Text fields are the most common type of form object and are used for collecting a string of characters, such as a name, address, password, or e-mail address. For some text fields, such as those collecting dollar amounts, you might want to set an initial value of 0. Use the Text Field button on the Insert bar to insert a text field.

A **text area field** is a text field that can store several lines of text. You can use text area fields to collect descriptions of

problems, answers to long questions, comments, or even a résumé. Use the Textarea button on the Insert bar to insert a text area.

You can use **check boxes** to create a list of options from which a viewer can make multiple selections. For instance, you could add a series of check boxes listing hobbies and ask the viewer to select the ones that interest him/her. You could also use a check box to answer a yes or no question.

You can use **radio buttons** to provide a list of options from which only one selection can be made. A group of radio buttons is called a **radio group**. Each radio group you create allows only one selection from within that group. You could use radio groups to ask viewers to select their annual salary range, their age group, or the T-shirt color they want to order. Use the Radio Group button on the Insert bar to insert a radio group.

You can insert a **menu** or **list** on a form using the List/Menu button on the Insert bar. You use menus when you want a viewer to select a single option from a list of choices. You use lists when you want a viewer to select one or more options from a list of choices. Menus are often used to provide navigation on a Web site, while lists are commonly used in order forms to let viewers choose from a list of possibilities. Menus must be opened to see all of the options they contain, whereas lists display some of their options all of the time. When you create a list, you need to specify the number of lines that will be visible on the screen by setting a value for the Height property in the Property inspector.

Using **hidden fields** makes it possible to provide information to the Web server and form-processing script without the viewer knowing that the information is being sent. For instance, you could add a hidden field that tells the server who should receive an e-mail message and what the subject of the message should be. You can also use hidden fields to collect information from a viewer without his/her knowledge. For instance, you can use a hidden field to send you the viewer's browser type or IP address.

You can insert an **image field** into a form using the Image Field button on the Insert bar. You can use the Image Field button to create buttons that contain custom graphics.

If you want your viewers to upload files to your Web server, you can insert a **file field**. You could insert a file field to let your viewers upload sample files to your Web site or to post photos to your Web site's photo gallery.

All forms must include a Submit button, which a viewer clicks to transfer the form data to the Web server. You can also insert a Reset button, which lets viewers clear data from a form and reset it to its default values, or a plain button to trigger an action that you specify on the page. You can insert a Submit, Reset, or plain button using the Button button on the Insert bar.

FIGURE 14

Web site displaying several form objects

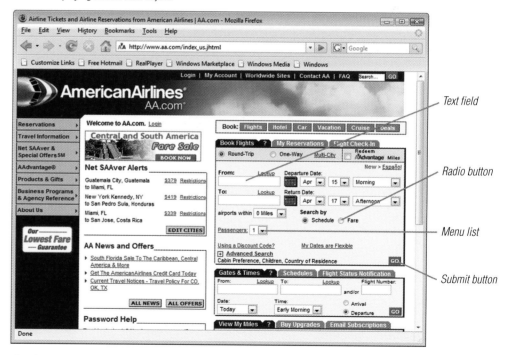

Text field

Radio button

Menu list

Submit button

American Airlines Web site used with permission from American Airlines: www.aa.com

Jump menus are navigational menus that let viewers go quickly to different pages in your site or to different sites on the Internet. You can create jump menus quickly and easily by using the Jump Menu button.

When you insert a form object in a form, you use the Property inspector to specify a unique name for it. You can also use the Property inspector to set other appropriate properties for the object, such as the number of lines or characters you want the object to display.

Using Dreamweaver Exchange

To obtain form controls designed for creating specific types of forms, such as online tests and surveys, you can visit Adobe Dreamweaver Exchange, shown in Figure 15. The Adobe Exchange site is a central storage location for program extensions, also known as add-ons. You can search the site by using keywords in a standard Search text box. You can also search by categories, highest rated, newest, and most downloaded (*www.adobe.com/ cfusion/exchange/index.cfm*).

FIGURE 15
Using Adobe Exchange

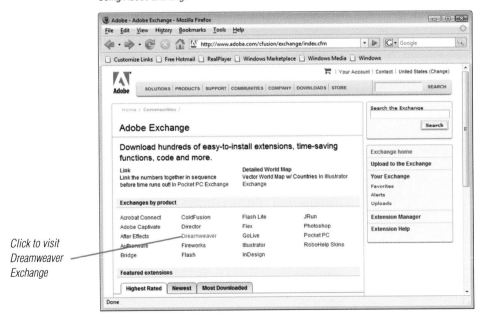

Click to visit
Dreamweaver
Exchange

Adobe Web site used with permission from Adobe Systems Incorporated: www.adobe.com

FIGURE 16
Input Tag Accessibility Attributes dialog box

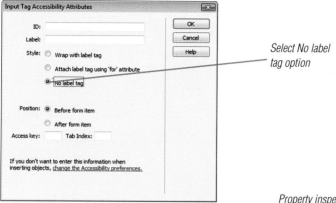

Select No label
tag option

FIGURE 17
Property inspector showing properties of selected text field

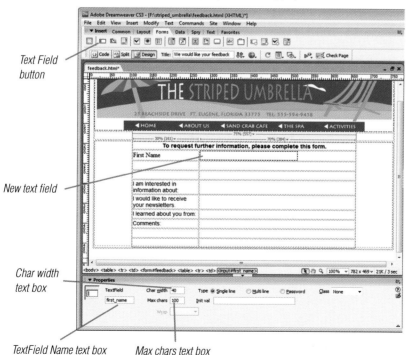

Text Field
button

New text field

Char width
text box

TextField Name text box   Max chars text box

Insert single-line text fields

1. Place the insertion point in the first cell under the header, then type **First Name**.

2. Press **[Tab]**, then click the **Text Field button** on the Insert bar.

3. Click the **No label tag option button** in the Style section, as shown in Figure 16, then click **OK**.

4. Select **textfield** in the TextField text box in the Property inspector, then type **first_name**.

   TIP You can also type the textfield name in the ID: text box in the Input Tag Accessibliity Attributes dialog box.

5. Type **40** in the Char width text box in the Property inspector.

   This specifies that 40 characters will be visible inside this text field when displayed in a browser.

6. Type **100** in the Max chars text box in the Property inspector.

   This specifies that a user can type no more than 100 characters in this field.

7. Click the **Single line option button** in the Property inspector (if necessary), then compare your screen to Figure 17.

(continued)

8. Repeat Steps 1 through 7 to create another label and single-line text field under the First Name label and text field, using **Last Name** for the label and **last_name** for the text field.

9. Repeat Steps 1 through 7 to create another label and single-line text field under the Last Name label and text field, using **E-mail** for the label and **email** for the TextField name.

10. Apply the **body_text style** to the three new labels in the first column.

> TIP Another way to apply styles to the text in a table is to apply the style to a selected cell, rather than selected text in a cell. You can also apply a single style to a table. That way, all text in the table will be formatted with the same style.

11. Save your changes, preview the page in your browser, compare your screen to Figure 18, then close your browser.

You added three single-line text fields to the form and previewed the page in your browser.

FIGURE 18
Form with single-line text fields added

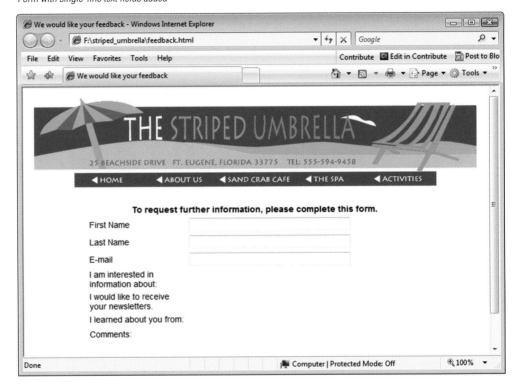

Collecting Data with Forms

FIGURE 19

Property inspector with properties of selected text area displayed

Textarea
button

New multiple-line
text field

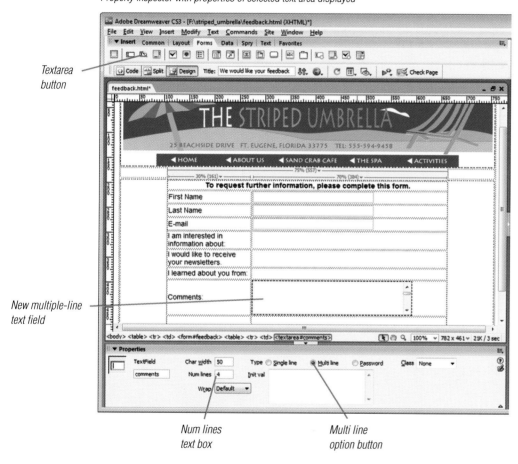

Num lines
text box

Multi line
option button

1. Click in the cell to the right of the Comments: label.

2. Click the **Textarea button** 🖵 on the Insert bar, click the **No label tag option button** on the Input Tag Accessibility Attributes dialog box, then click **OK**.

3. Select **textarea** in the TextField text box in the Property inspector, then type **comments**.

4. Click the **Multi line option button** in the Property inspector (if necessary).

5. Type **50** in the Char width text box in the Property inspector.

    This specifies that 50 characters will be visible inside this text field when the page is displayed in a browser.

6. Type **4** in the Num lines text box in the Property inspector, as shown in Figure 19.

    This specifies that the text box will display four lines of text.

You added a multiple-line text field to the form.

Insert check boxes

1. Place the insertion point in the empty table cell to the right of "I am interested in information about:".
2. Click the **Check box button** ☑ on the Insert bar to insert a check box in the form.
3. Type **Fishing** in the Label text box, click the **Wrap with label tag option button** in the Style section, click the **After form item option button** in the Position section, as shown in Figure 20, then click **OK**.
4. Select the check box, then type **fishing** in the Checkbox name text box in the Property inspector.
5. Type **fish** in the Checked value text box in the Property inspector.
   This is the value that will be sent to your script or program when the form is processed.
6. Click the **Unchecked option button** in the Property inspector (if necessary), as shown in Figure 21.
   Selecting the Checked option button would make a check mark appear in the check box by default.

(continued)

FIGURE 20
Input Tag Accessibility Attributes dialog box for Fishing label

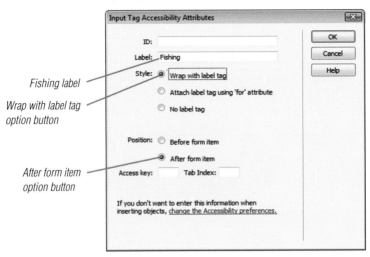

Fishing label

Wrap with label tag option button

After form item option button

FIGURE 21
Property inspector with check box properties displayed

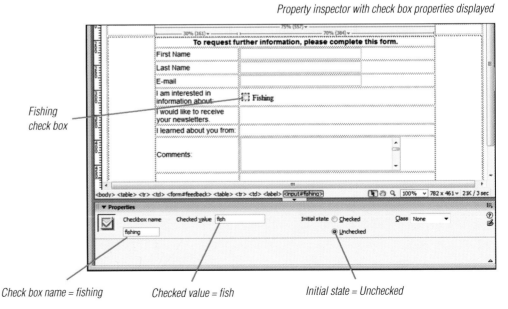

Fishing check box

Check box name = fishing

Checked value = fish

Initial state = Unchecked

Collecting Data with Forms

FIGURE 22

Feedback page in browser with check boxes added to the form

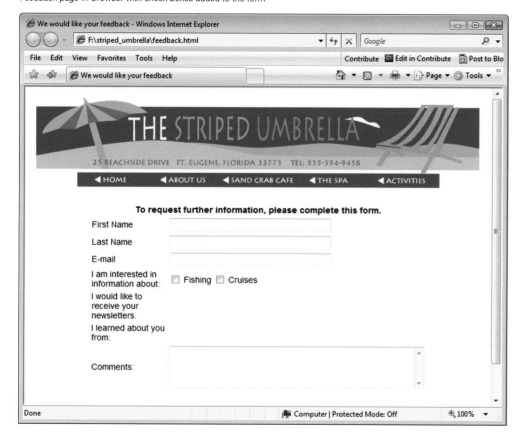

7. Format the Fishing text label with the **body_text** style.

8. Insert a space after the Fishing label, then repeat Steps 2 through 6 to place a check box to the right of the Fishing text box with the label **Cruises**, the Check box name **cruises**, a Checked value of **cruise**, and the Initial state of **Unchecked**.

9. Format the Cruises label with the **body_text** style (if necessary), save your changes, preview the page in your Web browser, compare your screen to Figure 22, then close your browser.

You added two check boxes to the form that will let viewers request more information about fishing and dolphin cruises.

Add radio groups to a form

1. Click in the empty table cell to the right of "I would like to receive your newsletters."

2. Click the **Radio Group button** 📋 on the Insert bar to open the Radio Group dialog box.

3. Type **newsletters** in the Name text box.

4. Click the **first instance of Radio** in the Label column of the Radio Group dialog box to select it, then type **Yes**.

5. Click the **first instance of Radio** in the Value column to select it, then type **positive**.

   You specified that the first radio button will be named Yes and set positive as the value that will be sent to your script or program when the form is processed.

6. Click the **Line breaks (
 tags) option button** (if necessary).

   TIP   If the Table option button is selected, then the radio buttons will appear in a separate table within the currently selected table.

7. Click the **second instance of Radio** to add another radio button named **No** with a value of **negative**.

8. Compare your screen with Figure 23, then click **OK** to close the Radio Group dialog box.

   (continued)

FIGURE 23
Radio Group dialog box

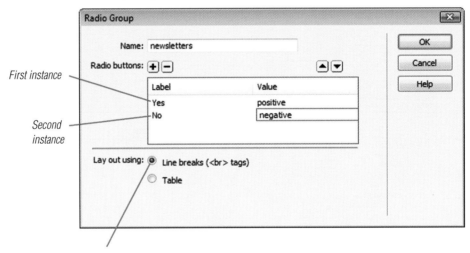

First instance

Second instance

Line breaks (
 tags) option button

FIGURE 24

Feedback page showing new radio group

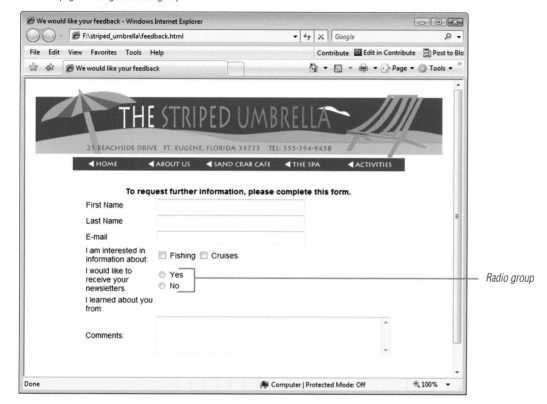

Radio group

9. Format the radio button labels using the **body_text** style.

10. Save your work, preview the page in your browser, compare your screen to Figure 24, then close your browser.

TIP To create radio buttons that are not part of a radio button group, click the Radio Button button ⦿ on the Insert bar.

You added a radio button group that will let viewers answer whether they would like to receive The Striped Umbrella newsletters.

Add a menu

1. Click in the cell to the right of the text "I learned about you from:".

2. Click the **List/Menu button** 📧 on the Insert bar, click the **No label tag option button** in the Input Tag Accessibility Attributes dialog box, then click **OK**.

3. Type **reference** in the List/Menu text box in the Property inspector.

4. Verify that the **Menu option button** in the Type section is selected in the Property inspector, as shown in Figure 25, then click **List Values** to open the List Values dialog box.

5. Click below the Item Label column heading (if necessary), type **Select from list:**, then press **[Tab]**.

6. Type **none** in the Value column.

   This value will be sent to the processing program when a viewer accidentally skips this menu. If one of the real choices was in the top position, it might return false positives when viewers really did not select it, but just skipped it.

7. Press **[Tab]**, type **From a friend** as a new Item Label, then type **friend** in the Value column.

(continued)

FIGURE 25

Property inspector showing properties of selected List/Menu

Menu option button   List Values button

FIGURE 26
List Values dialog box

Add button

New item labels

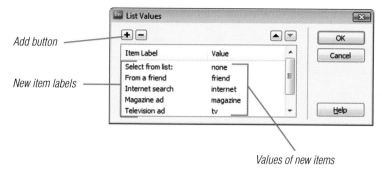

Values of new items

FIGURE 27
Feedback page with menu

Completed menu

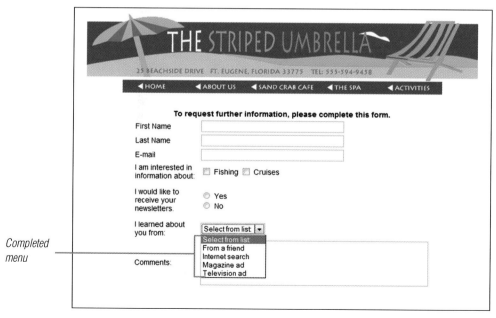

8. Use the **Add button** ➕ add the following three Item Labels: **Internet search**, **Magazine ad**, and **Television ad**, setting the Values as **internet**, **magazine**, and **tv**.

   TIP   You can also press [Tab] after entering an entry in the Value column to add a new item label.

9. Compare your screen to Figure 26, then click **OK**.

10. Save your work, preview the page in your browser, click the **list arrow** to view the menu, compare your screen to Figure 27, then close your browser.

You added a menu to the form on the feedback page.

Insert a hidden field

1. Click to the left of the First Name label at the top of the form to place the insertion point.

2. Click the **Hidden Field button** 📧 on the Insert bar.

   A Hidden Field icon appears at the insertion point.

   TIP If you do not see the Hidden Field icon, click View on the menu bar, point to Visual Aids, then click Invisible Elements.

3. Type **required** in the HiddenField text box, then type **first_name**, **last_name**, **email** in the Value text box in the Property inspector, as shown in Figure 28.

   Typing first_name, last_name, email in the Value text box specifies that viewers must enter text in the First Name, Last Name, and E-mail fields before the script can process the form. These names must match the names of other fields in your form exactly.

4. Save your work.

You added a hidden field to the form.

FIGURE 28
Property inspector showing properties of selected hidden field

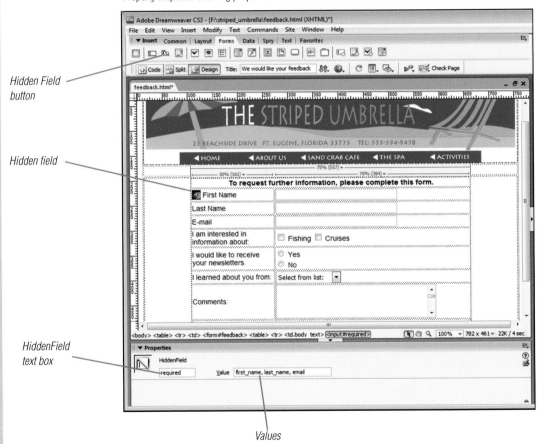

Hidden Field button

Hidden field

HiddenField text box

Values

FIGURE 29

New Submit and Reset buttons added to form

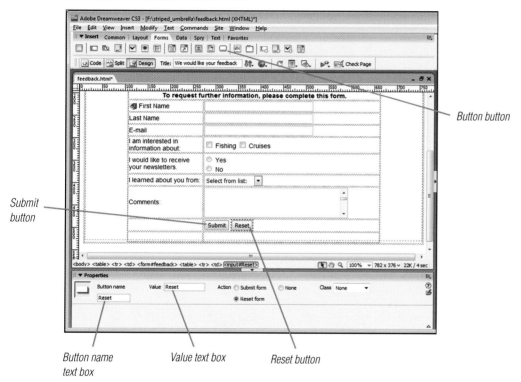

Submit button

Button name text box

Value text box

Reset button

Button button

1. Click in the **second cell** of the second to last row of the table.

2. Click the **Button button** ▭ on the Insert bar, click the **No label tag option button** in the Input Tag Accessiblity Attributes dialog box, then click **OK**.

3. Verify that the Submit form option button is selected in the Property inspector.

   When a viewer clicks this Submit button, the information in the form will be sent to the processing script.

4. Verify that "Submit" is entered in the Button name text box and the Value text box in the Property inspector.

   The name Submit is automatically set when you select the Submit form option in the Property inspector.

5. Click to the right of the Submit button, insert a space, then click the **Button button** ▭ on the Insert bar, click the **No label tag option button** in the Input Tag Accessibility Attributes dialog box, click **OK**, click the **Reset form option button** in the Property inspector, name the new button **Reset**, verify that the Value text box is set to **Reset**, then compare your screen to Figure 29.

   When a viewer clicks this Reset button, the form will remove any information typed by the viewer.

6. Save your work.

You added a Submit button and a Reset button to the form.

TEST AND PROCESS A
FORM

What You'll Do

 In this lesson, you will check the spelling on the feedback page and create a link to the feedback page on the about us page. You will then open the about us page in your browser, click the feedback link, and then test the form and reset it.

Creating User-Friendly Forms

After you create a form, you will want to test it to make sure that it works correctly and is easy to use.

When a form contains several required fields, fields that must be filled out before the form can be processed, it is a good idea to provide visual clues such as a different font color or other notation that label these fields as required fields. Many times you see an asterisk next to a required field with a corresponding note at either the top or the bottom of the form explaining that all fields marked with asterisks are required fields. This will encourage viewers to initially complete these fields rather than attempt to submit the form and then

receive an error message asking them to complete required fields that have been left blank. Using a different font color for the asterisks and notes is an easy way to call attention to them and make them stand out on the page.

As is true with all pages, your forms should have good contrast between the color of the text and the color of the table background. There should be a logical flow for the data fields, so the viewer is not confused about where to go next when completing the form. The Submit and Reset buttons should be at the end of the form. You should always have several people test your form before you publish it.

Understanding jump menus

If your Web site contains a large number of pages, you can add a jump menu to make it easier for viewers to navigate the site. Jump menus are menus that let viewers go directly from the current Web page to another page in the site with a single click. You can also use jump menus to provide links to other Web sites. You can create jump menus using the Jump Menu button on the Insert bar to open the Insert Jump Menu dialog box.

FIGURE 30
Adding visual clues for required fields

Hint for user   Asterisks added after labels

Using a testing server to test dynamic content

When a Web page contains content that allows the user to interact with the page by clicking or typing, and then responds to this input in some way, the page is said to contain **dynamic content**. A form is an excellent example of dynamic content, because as the user fills out the form, feedback can be returned, such as the availability of window seats on a particular airplane flight or whether or not certain colors or sizes of clothing items are available for purchase. This exchange of information is made possible through the use of a database, as you learned in Lesson 1. Once a form is developed and a database is tied to it, you should set up a **testing server** to evaluate how the form works and the data is processed. Your local computer or your remote server can serve as a testing server. You set up a testing server by filling out the relevant information in the Testing Server section of the Site Definition dialog box. The opposite of dynamic content is static content. **Static content** refers to page content that does not change or allow user interaction.

Creating visual clues for required fields

1. Click **Text** on the menu bar, then click **Check Spelling** to check the spelling on the form.

2. Correct any spelling errors you find using the Check Spelling dialog box.

3. Click after the text First Name, then type an **asterisk**.

   The asterisk will give viewers a clue that this is a required field.

4. Repeat Step 3 after the words "Last Name" and "E-mail."

5. Merge the two cells in the last row, type *** Required field**, as shown in Figure 30, then apply the **body_text style** to it.

6. Save and close the feedback page.

You checked the spelling on the feedback page, then added asterisks to the required fields on the page. Next, you typed text explaining what the asterisks mean and formatted the text with the body_text style.

Linking a file

1. Open the **about_us** page and add a row to the bottom of the page.

   TIP   Click in the cell with the text beginning "If you would like to play tennis . . ." in the bottom row, then press [Tab].

2. Merge the cells in the new row, then type **Please give us your feedback so that we may make your next stay the best vacation ever.**

3. Select the text you typed in Step 2, format it with the **body_text style**, then center-align the text in the newly merged cells.

4. Select the word "feedback," then use the **Point to File icon** to link the feedback text to the feedback page.

5. Compare your screen with Figure 31, save your work, then preview the page in the browser.

FIGURE 31

Viewing the feedback link

Link to feedback page

FIGURE 32

Feedback page in Mozilla Firefox

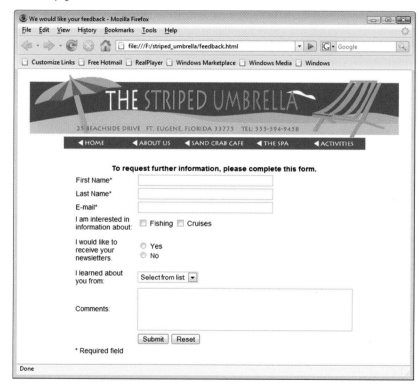

6. Click the **feedback link** to test it.

   The feedback page opens in a new window, as shown in Figure 32.

7. Test the form by filling it out, then clicking the **Reset button.**

   The Reset button will clear the form, but the Submit button will not work because this form has not been set up to send information to a database. Linking to a database is beyond the scope of this book. Refer to the information on page 8-7 to learn more about CGI scripts.

8. Close the browser and close all open pages.

You created a link on the about us page to link to the feedback form, and tested it in your browser.

Plan and create a form.

1. Open the blooms & bulbs Web site.
2. Open the tips page.
3. Scroll to the bottom of the page, insert two paragraph breaks to end the ordered list after the last line of text, then insert a form.
4. Set the Method to **POST** in the Property inspector.
5. Name the form **submit_tips**.
6. Set the Target to **_self**.
7. Save your work.

Format a form.

1. Insert a table within the form that contains **9** rows and **2** columns. Set the Table width to **75%**, set the Border thickness to **0**, the Cell padding to **2**, and the Cell spacing to **1**.
2. Choose the **Top row header** icon, then include an appropriate table summary that indicates that the table will be used for form layout purposes.
3. Merge the cells in the top row and type **Submit Your Favorite Gardening Tip** in the newly merged cell, then **left-align** the text.
4. Format the text you typed in Step 3 with the **seasons** style.
5. Type **E-mail** in the first cell in the second row.
6. Type **Category** in the first cell in the third row.
7. Type **Subject** in the first cell in the fourth row.
8. Type **Description** in the first cell in the fifth row.

9. Apply the **bodytext** style to the labels you typed in Steps 5 through 8.
10. Merge both cells in the sixth row of the table, then insert the label **How long have you been gardening?** in the resulting merged cell.
11. Merge both cells in the seventh row of the table, then insert the label **Receive notification when new tips are submitted?** in the resulting merged cell.
12. Apply the **bodytext** style to the text you typed in Steps 10 and 11, then save your work.

Work with form objects.

1. Click in the **second cell of the second row**. Insert a **text field**, click OK to close the Image Tag Accessibility Attributes dialog box, then name the new text field **email**. Set the Char width property to **30** and the Max chars property to **150**. (*Hint*: The Image Tag Accessibility Attributes dialog box will not appear if you do not have the accessibility preference set for adding form objects.)
2. Click in the **second cell of the fourth row**, then insert a **text field** with the name **subject**. (*Hint*: Each time the Image Tag Accessibility Attributes dialog box opens, click OK to close it.) Set the Char width to **30** and the Max chars to **150**.
3. Click in the **second cell of the fifth row**, then insert a textarea with the name **description**. Set the Char width to **40** and the Num lines to **5**.

4. Insert a **check box** to the right of the "Receive notification when new tips are submitted" label. Set the name of the check box to **receivetips**, then type **yes** in the Checked value text box.
5. Insert a **radio group** named **years_gardening** under the text "How long have you been gardening?" that contains the following labels: **1 - 5 years**, **5 - 10 years**, **Over 10 years**. Use the following **corresponding** values for each label: **1-5**, **5-10**, and **10+**. Apply the **bodytext** style to the labels.
6. Insert a list/menu named **category** in the empty cell to the right of Category. Set the Type to **List** and the Height to **3**. Use the List Values dialog box to add the following item labels: **Weed control**, **General growth**, and **Pest control**, and set the corresponding values for each to **weeds**, **growth**, and **pests**.
7. Insert a hidden field named **required** in the first cell of the eighth row that has the value **email**.
8. Insert a Submit button named **submit** in the second cell of the eighth row.
9. With your insertion point to the right of the Submit button, insert a Reset button named **reset** with the Reset form action.
10. Save your work.

Test and process a form.

1. Check the spelling on the form and correct any errors you find.
2. Type an **asterisk** after the label E-mail.
3. Merge the cells in the last row, then type ***Required field** in the last row.
4. Apply the **subheadings** style to the text you typed in Step 3.
5. Insert a horizontal rule that is **700 pixels** wide and **centered** both before and after the form.
6. Center the table in the form.
7. Save your work.
8. Preview the page in your browser, compare your form to Figure 33, then test the form by filling it out and using the Reset button.
9. Close your browser, then close all open pages.

FIGURE 33
Completed Skills Review

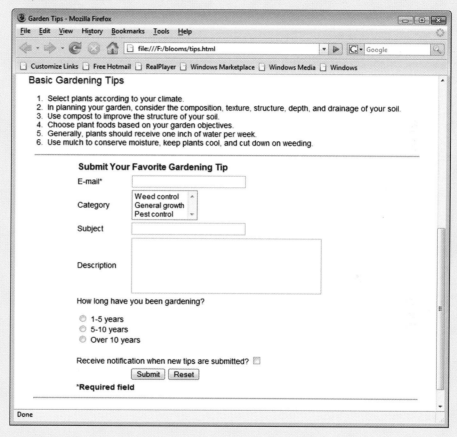

In this exercise, you will continue your work on the TripSmart Web site you created in Chapters 1 through 7. The owner, Thomas Howard, wants you to create a form to collect information from viewers who are interested in receiving more information on one or more of the featured trips.

1. Open the TripSmart Web site.
2. Open the destinations page.
3. Insert a form named **information** in the bottom row of the table.
4. Specify the Method as **POST.**

5. Insert a table in the form that contains **11** rows, **2** columns, a Table width of **75%,** a Border thickness of **0**, Cell padding of **1**, Cell spacing of **1**, and add an appropriate table summary.
6. Merge the cells in the top row, type **Please complete this form for additional information on these tours.**, apply the **reverse_text** style, then change the cell background color to **#666666.**
7. Beginning in the second row, type the following labels in the cells in the first column: **First Name**, **Last Name**, **Street**, **City**, **State**, **Zip Code**, **Phone**, **E-mail**, and

I am interested in:, then right-align them and apply the **bodytext** style to all of them.
8. Insert **single-line text fields** in the eight cells in the second column and assign the following names: **first_name**, **last_name**, **street**, **city**, **state**, **zip**, **phone**, and **email**.
9. Set the Char width to **30** and the Max chars to **100** for each of these text fields.
10. In the second cell of the tenth row, insert a check box with the label **The Amazon**, the name **amazon**, and a Checked value of **yes**.

11. Repeat Step 10 to add another check box under the Amazon check box with the label **Kenya**, the name **kenya**, and a Checked Value of **yes**.

12. Apply the **bodytext** style to the Amazon and Kenya labels.

13. **Left-align** the cells with the text boxes and check boxes, then set each cell's vertical alignment to **Top**.

14. Insert a Submit button and a **Reset button** in the second cell of the eleventh row.

15. Insert a horizontal rule that is **550 pixels** wide and centered below the form. (*Hint:* Select the form, press [right arrow] press [Enter], then insert the horizontal rule).

16. Save your work, preview the page in your browser, test the form, compare your screen to Figure 34, close your browser, then close the destinations page.

FIGURE 34

Completed Project Builder 1

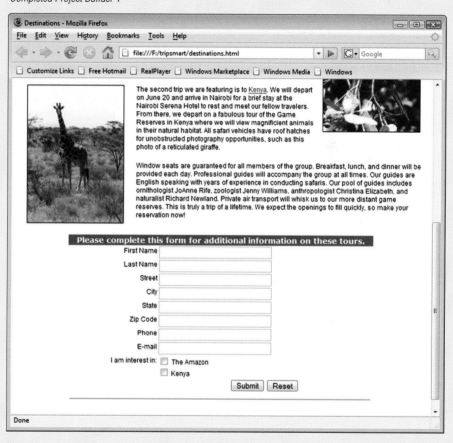

Use Figure 35 as a guide to continue your work on the Carolyne's Catering Web site you created in Project Builder 2 in Chapters 1 through 7. Chef Carolyne asked you to place a simple form on the catering page that will allow customers to fill in and fax lunch orders.

1. Open the Carolyne's Catering Web site.

2. Open the catering page.

3. Add a row to the bottom of the table on the page, then merge the cells in the new row.

4. Insert a form called **orders** in the new row with **POST** as the method.

5. Insert a table in the form that contains **8** rows, **2** columns, and your choice of table width, border thickness, cell padding, and cell spacing. Specify an appropriate table summary.

6. Merge the cells in the top row and type **Lunch Order**.

7. In the first column of cells, type the following labels under the table header: **Please select from the following**:, **Beverage choice**:, **Desired pick-up time**:, **First Name**:, **Last Name**:, **Phone number**:.

8. In the second cell of the second row, insert a radio button group named **boxes** with the following labels and values: **Southwest Club Sandwich, sandwich**; **Chipotle Chicken Wrap, wrap**; **Pecan Chicken Salad, salad**.

9. In the second cell in the third row, insert a radio button group called **beverages** with the following labels and values: **Raspberry tea**, **tea**; **Berry smoothie**, **smoothie**.

10. In the second cell of the fourth row, insert a single line text field named **time** with a character width and maximum characters of **10**.

11. In the second cell of the fifth, sixth, and seventh rows, insert single-line text fields named **first_name**, **last_name**, and **phone** using character widths of **30** and maximum characters of **100**.

12. Merge the cells in the last row and type **Fax order by 9:00 a.m. to 555-963-5938**.

13. Since they are going to fax the form, there is no need for a submit button. You may add a reset button if you like.

14. Format the text in the form with styles of your choice.

15. Save your work, preview the page in a browser, test the form, compare your screen to Figure 35, close your browser, then close the catering page.

FIGURE 35

Completed Project Builder 2

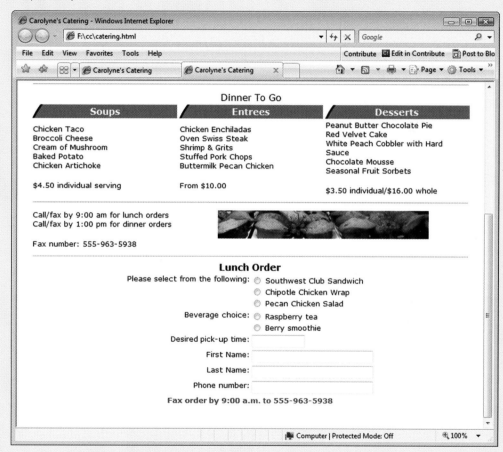

Web sites use many form objects to collect donations from viewers. The form shown in Figure 36 is well organized and requests information that most people are comfortable giving over the Internet, such as name, address, and phone number. The form also contains text fields where viewers can specify a donation amount and pay using a credit card. Because the form is secure, viewers should feel comfortable providing their credit card numbers.

1. Connect to the Internet, then navigate to the Girls and Boys Town Web site, pictured in Figure 36, *www.girlsandboystown.org.*

2. Does this site use forms to collect information? If so, identify each of the form objects used to create the form.

3. Is the form organized logically? Explain why or why not.

4. What CGI script is being used to process the form? And where is that script located? Remember the name of the processing CGI script is included in the Action attribute of your form tag. (*Hint*: To view the code of a page in a browser, click View on the menu bar of your browser, then click Source.)

5. What types of hidden information are being sent to the CGI script?

6. Is this form secure?

7. Could the information in this form be collected with different types of form objects? If so, which form objects would you use?

8. Does the form use tables for page layout?

9. Does the form use fieldsets? If so, identify the fieldset labels used.

10. Does the form use labels for its fields? If so, were the labels created using the <label> element or with text labels in table cells?

FIGURE 36
Design Project

Girls and Boys Town Web site used with permission from Girls and Boys Town: www.girlsandboystown.org

In this project, you will continue to work on the Web site that you have been developing since Chapter 1.

You will continue building your Web site by designing and completing a page that contains a form to collect visitor information as it relates to the topic of your site.

1. Review your storyboard. Choose a page to develop that will use a form to collect information. Choose another page that you already developed on which you will place a jump menu.

2. Plan the content for the new page by making a list of the information that you will collect and the types of form objects you will use to collect that information. Plan to include at least one of every type of form object you learned about in the chapter. Be sure to specify whether you will organize the form into fieldsets and how you will use a table to structure the form.

3. Create the form and its contents.

4. Create the jump menu.

5. Run a report that checks for broken links in the Web site. Correct any broken links that appear in the report.

6. Test the form by previewing it in a browser, entering information into it, and submitting it. Check to make sure the information gets to its specified location, whether that is a database or an e-mail address.

7. Preview all the pages in a browser, then test all menus and links. Evaluate the pages for both content and layout.

8. Review the checklist shown in Figure 37. Make any modifications necessary to improve the form, the jump menu, or the page containing the form.

9. Close all open pages.

FIGURE 37
Portfolio Project checklist

Web Site Checklist
1. Do all navigation links work?
2. Do all images appear?
3. Are all colors Websafe?
4. Do all form objects align correctly with their labels?
5. Do any extra items appear on the form that need to be removed?
6. Does the order of form fields make sense?
7. Does the most important information appear at the top of the form?
8. Did you test the pages in at least two different browsers?
9. Do your pages look good in at least two different screen resolutions?

chapter

9 POSITIONING OBJECTS
WITH CSS

Introduction

If you want to control the position of text and graphic elements with precision on your Web pages, another option you can use is a CSS page layout. With **CSS page layouts**, you use containers formatted with CSS styles to place content on Web pages. These containers can be images, blocks of text, a Flash movie, or any other page element. The appearance and position of the containers is set through the use of HTML tags known as **div tags**. Using div tags, you can position elements next to each other as well as on top of each other in a stack. In this chapter, you will use a CSS predefined page layout with div tags to place text and graphics on a page.

Using Div Tags versus Tables for Page Layout

Like tables, div tags let you control the appearance of your Web page. But unlike tables, div tags allow you to stack your information in a vertical pile, allowing for just one piece of information to be visible at a time. Tables are static, which makes it difficult to change them on the fly. Div tags, on the other hand, are treated as their own documents, so that you can easily change their contents. Dreamweaver includes the JavaScript behavior to do so. **Behaviors** in Dreamweaver are simple action scripts that allow you to perform common tasks quickly, either on a Web page while it is being viewed in a browser, or to a Web page while you are creating it in Dreamweaver.

Building a Web page from scratch with div tags may prove to be a difficult task for beginning designers. Once you are comfortable using tables for placing content, try using one of Dreamweaver's predesigned CSS page layouts as a template. After you master that, try designing a page built with your own div tags.

Tools You'll Use

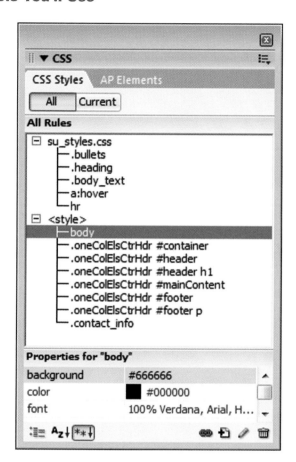

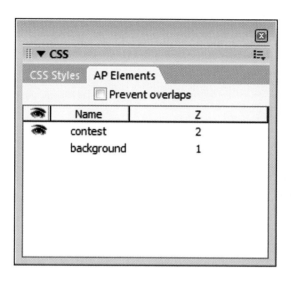

CREATE A PAGE
USING CSS LAYOUTS

What You'll Do

Header

Main Content

Lorem ipsum dolor sit amet, consectetuer adipiscing elit. Praesent aliquam, justo convallis luctus rutrum, erat nulla fermentum diam, at nonummy quam ante ac quam. Maecenas urna purus, fermentum id, molestie in, commodo porttitor, felis. Nam blandit quam ut lacus. Quisque ornare risus quis ligula. Phasellus tristique purus a augue condimentum adipiscing. Aenean sagittis. Etiam leo pede, rhoncus venenatis, tristique in, vulputate at, odio. Donec et ipsum et sapien vehicula nonummy. Suspendisse potenti. Fusce varius urna id quam. Sed neque mi, varius eget, tincidunt nec, suscipit id, libero. In eget purus. Vestibulum ut nisl. Donec eu mi sed turpis feugiat feugiat. Integer turpis arcu, pellentesque eget, cursus et, fermentum ut, sapien. Fusce metus mi, eleifend sollicitudin, molestie id, varius et, nibh. Donec nec libero.

H2 level heading

Lorem ipsum dolor sit amet, consectetuer adipiscing elit. Praesent aliquam, justo convallis luctus rutrum, erat nulla fermentum diam, at nonummy quam ante ac quam. Maecenas urna purus, fermentum id, molestie in, commodo porttitor, felis. Nam blandit quam ut lacus. Quisque ornare risus quis ligula. Phasellus tristique purus a augue condimentum adipiscing. Aenean sagittis. Etiam leo pede, rhoncus venenatis, tristique in, vulputate at, odio.

Footer

In this lesson, you will create a new page based on a predefined CSS layout to become the new home page for the Web site.

Understanding Div Tags

Div tags are HTML tags that define how areas of content are placed and formatted on a Web page. When you center an image on a page or inside a table cell, Dreamweaver automatically inserts a div tag in the HTML code. In addition to being used for aligning page elements, div tags can be used to designate different colors for blocks of content, text that uses a CSS style, and many other properties. One type of div tag is an **AP Div Tag.** AP stands for absolutely positioned, so an **AP Div Tag** is a div tag that has a specified, fixed position on a Web page. The resulting container that an AP div tag creates on a page is called an **AP element.**

Using CSS Page Layouts

Building a Web page using div tags can be a tedious process for beginning designers. Dreamweaver provides 32 predesigned layouts in the New Document dialog box, as shown in Figure 1. These layouts can be used to place the page elements, rather than using tables. Placeholder text is displayed in each div tag until you replace it with your own content. Because div tags use CSS for formatting and positioning, they are the preferred method for building content for Web pages. As you become more comfortable using the predesigned layouts, you will begin to build your own CSS-based pages from scratch. You must be careful, however, to not run into conflicts when your pages are viewed in multiple browsers; some CSS layouts will not render correctly. When you use the Dreamweaver predesigned layouts, you can be sure that your pages will render correctly in all browsers.

QUICK TIP

The Browser Compatibility Check Feature flags code that might present a CSS rendering issue in some browsers by underlining code in green. To access this feature, simply switch to Code view and browse through the code.

Viewing CSS Layout Blocks

Dreamweaver provides information about the blocks of CSS content on Web pages by using outlines in Design view. Any div tag, image, or paragraph that has been aligned, or a tag with the display: block style is outlined by a dotted border. In the Visual Aids list on the View menu, you can select options such as CSS Layout Backgrounds, CSS Layout Box Model, CSS Layout Outlines, and AP Element Outlines. The CSS Layout Box Model displays the padding and margins of a block element.

FIGURE 1

New Document dialog box

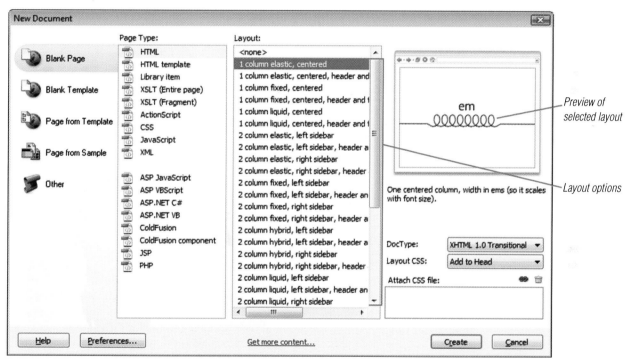

Create a page with a CSS layout

1. Open The Striped Umbrella Web site.

2. Click **File** on the menu bar, click **New**, verify that Blank Page is highlighted in the first category of the New Document dialog box, click **HTML** in the Page Type category, then click **1 column elastic, centered, header and footer** in the Layout category, as shown in Figure 2.

   The term "elastic" means that the page will stretch to fit different size browser windows. A fixed layout will remain the same size regardless of the size of the browser window.

   (continued)

(continued)

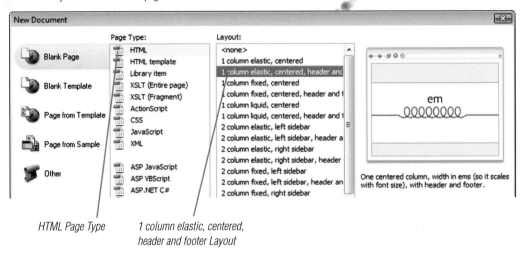

FIGURE 2
Predefined layout selected for new page

HTML Page Type

1 column elastic, centered, header and footer Layout

Using XML and XSL to create and format Web page content

Another option you have with Dreamweaver is to create containers of information with XML, Extensible Markup Language; and XSL, Extensible Stylesheet Language. XML is a language that you use to create the structure of blocks of information, similar to HTML. It uses opening and closing tags and the nested tag structure that is used by HTML documents. However, none of these tags determine how the information is formatted. This is done through XSL. XSL is similar to CSS. The XSL stylesheet information formats the containers created by XML. One more term to learn is XSLT, Extensible Stylesheet Language Transformations. XSLT displays the information on a Web page and transforms it through the use of the style sheet. XSL transformations can be written as client-side or server-side transformations. To create XML documents, use the File, New, XML command.

FIGURE 3

The su_styles.css file is attached to the new page

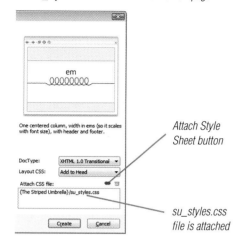

Attach Style
Sheet button

su_styles.css
file is attached

3. Click the **Attach Style Sheet button** 🖿 in the bottom-right corner of the dialog box, then click **Browse** in the Attach External Style Sheet dialog box.

   The Select Style Sheet File dialog box opens.

4. Select the **su_styles.css file** in the Select Style Sheet File dialog box, click **OK**, then click **OK** to close the information box.

   The links will not be relative until the page is saved in the Web site.

5. Verify that the Link option is selected in the Attach External Style Sheet dialog box, then click **OK** to close the Attach External Style Sheet dialog box.

   The su_styles.css file is attached to the new page, as shown in Figure 3.

6. Click **Create** in the New Document dialog box, open the CSS Styles panel, then expand the styles.

   A new page is created based on the CSS predefined layout with placeholder text, as shown in Figure 4, that will be replaced with content for The Striped Umbrella Web site. We will use this new page to create a revised home page for The Striped Umbrella Web site.

You created a new page based on a predefined CSS layout, then attached the style sheet for The Striped Umbrella Web site.

FIGURE 4
New page based on CSS layout

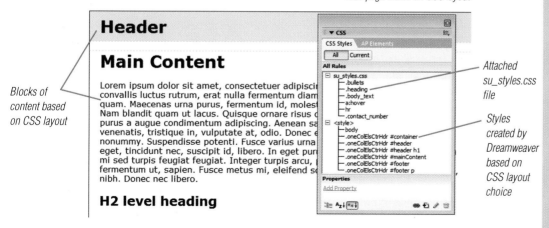

Blocks of
content based
on CSS layout

Attached
su_styles.css
file

Styles
created by
Dreamweaver
based on
CSS layout
choice

ADD CONTENT
TO CSS LAYOUT BLOCKS

What You'll Do

In this lesson, you will copy the text and banner from the index page and paste it into the new page. You will then save over the old index page with this new one.

Understanding Div Tag Content

As you learned in Lesson 1, a div tag is a container that holds blocks of information on a Web page. It contains the same types of elements that a page based on table layout can, such as background colors, images, links, tables, and text.

Also, as with formatting text on a Web page, you should use CSS styles to format your text. You can also add all other properties such as text indent, padding, margins, and background color using CSS styles.

In this lesson, we will copy and paste content from the index page onto the new page, and then save it as a new index page, replacing the old index page with the new page based on CSS.

Using Dreamweaver sample pages

You can use either the Welcome Screen or the New command on the File menu to create several different types of pages. The predesigned CSS page layouts make it very easy to design accessible Web pages based on Cascading Style Sheets without an advanced level of expertise in writing HTML code. Predesigned templates are another time-saving feature that promotes consistency across a Web site. Framesets, CSS Style Sheets, and Starter Pages are a few of the other options. It is worth the time to explore each category to understand what is available to you as a designer. Once you have selected a sample page, you can customize it to fit the needs of your client and the design of your site.

Understanding CSS Code

When you view a page based on a predesigned CSS in Code view, you will notice helpful comments that explain sections of the code, as shown in Figure 5. The comments are in gray to differentiate them from the rest of the code. The CSS rules reside in the Head section. The code that ties the rules to the content is located in the body section.

The code for a CSS container begins with the class, or name of the rule, and is followed by the ID, or the name of the container. A pound sign (#) precedes the ID.

FIGURE 5
Code view for CSS in head content

```
41  }
42  .oneColElsCtrHdr #footer {
43      padding: 0 10px; /* this padding matches the left alignment of the elements in the divs that
    appear above it. */
44      background:#DDDDDD;
45  }
46  .oneColElsCtrHdr #footer p {
47      margin: 0; /* zeroing the margins of the first element in the footer will avoid the possibility
    of margin collapse - a space between divs */
48      padding: 10px 0; /* padding on this element will create space, just as the the margin would have,
    without the margin collapse issue */
49  }
50  -->
51  </style></head>
52
53  <body class="oneColElsCtrHdr">
54
55  <div id="container">
56      <div id="header">
```

Class name preceded by period   *ID preceded by # sign*   *Comments in gray text*

Add text to a CSS container

1. Open the index page and select the paragraph of text that begins "Welcome."

2. Copy the selected text, then switch to the new, unsaved page.

   TIP Press [Ctrl][Tab] (Win) or ⌘ [`] (Mac) to switch between two open pages.

3. Select the content between the Header and Footer in the main section of the page, as shown in Figure 6, click **Edit** on the menu bar, then click **Paste**.

   The paragraph from the index page is pasted into the center container of the new page, replacing the placeholder text.

4. Switch back to the index page, then select and copy the contact information.

5. Switch back to the new, unsaved page, insert a blank line after the pasted paragraph, then paste the contact information.

6. Repeat Step 4 to copy the copyright and last updated information from the index page.

7. Repeat Step 5 to paste the copyright and last updated information in the footer section of the new, unsaved page, replacing the placeholder text, as shown in Figure 7.

You copied text from the index page and pasted it onto the new, unsaved page.

FIGURE 6
Text selected in mainContent block of new, unsaved page

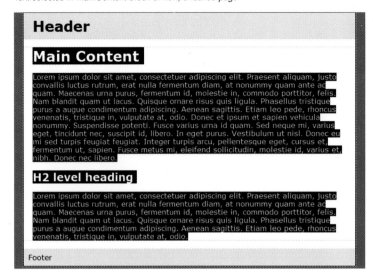

FIGURE 7
Text copied into Footer block of new, unsaved page

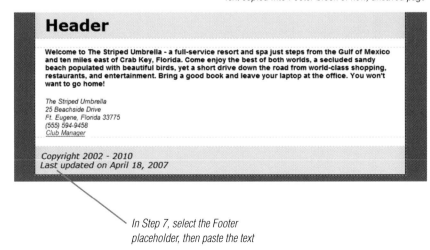

In Step 7, select the Footer placeholder, then paste the text

FIGURE 8
Images appear broken until page is saved

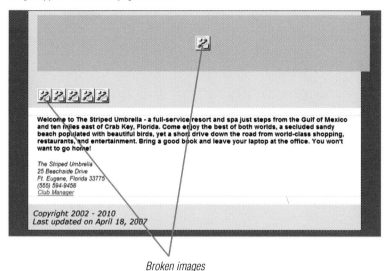

Broken images

FIGURE 9

Images are not broken after page is saved

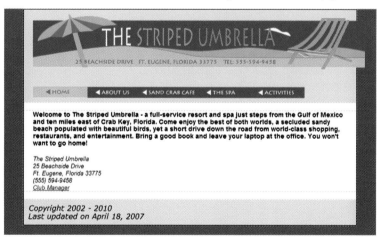

Add images to a CSS container

1. Switch back to the index page and copy both the banner and the navigation bar.

2. Switch back to the new, unsaved page and paste the banner and navigation bar into the header section of the new, unsaved page.

   The banner and navigation bar display as broken links, as shown in Figure 8, but after you save the page in the Web site, the links will not be broken.

3. Close the index page.

4. Save the new, untitled page as **index.html**, overwriting the original index page.

   The banner and navigation bar images are no longer broken, as shown in Figure 9.

You copied the banner and navigation bar from the index page, pasted it onto the new, unsaved page, then saved the new page as the new index page.

EDIT CONTENT
IN CSS LAYOUT BLOCKS

What You'll Do

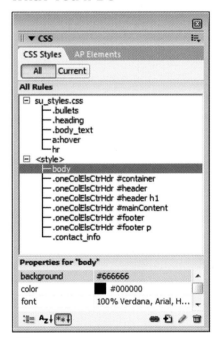

In this lesson, you will center and format the navigation bar. You will then view the Div tag properties.

Edit Content in CSS Layout Blocks

It is unlikely that you will find a preformatted CSS page layout that is exactly what you have in mind for your Web site. However, once you have created a page with a predefined CSS layout, it is easy to modify the properties for individual styles to change the way the content is placed or formatted on the page to better fit your needs. You can easily change it to fit the color scheme of your Web site.

During the process of creating a page, you can attach an external style sheet to the page. If you chose to do this, you will see both the external style sheet and the internal style sheet for the page layout in the CSS Styles panel. Click the plus sign, if necessary, to see the styles listed in each section, and then select the style you want to modify. The properties and values for the selected style appear in the Properties pane, as shown in Figure 10, where you can modify them.

FIGURE 10
Viewing the CSS Styles panel

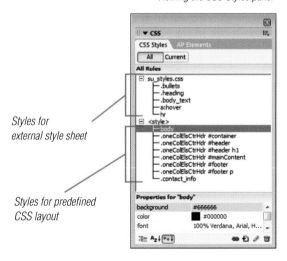

Styles for external style sheet

Styles for predefined CSS layout

Positioning Objects with CSS

FIGURE 11
Centering the navigation bar in the header layout block

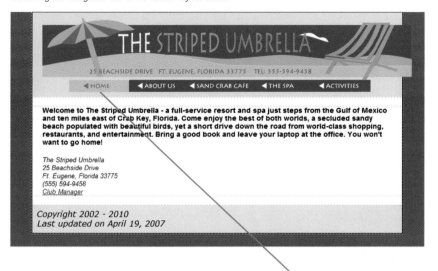

*Navigation bar is centered
in header and extra space
is removed*

Edit content in CSS layout blocks

1. Place the insertion point in front of the navigation bar, press **[Shift]**, then click immediately after the navigation bar to select it.

2. Click the **Align Center button** ≣ in the Property inspector.

   The navigation bar is now centered in the header.

3. Click in front of the navigation bar, then press **[Backspace]** to remove the extra line between the navigation bar and banner (if necessary), then compare your page to Figure 11.

(continued)

Using the Adobe CSS Advisor for cross-browser rendering issues

You can use the Browser Compatibility Check (BCC) feature to check for problems in the HTML code for CSS features that may render differently in multiple browsers. It flags and rates code on three levels: an error that could cause a serious display problem; an error that probably won't cause a serious display problem; or a warning that it has found code that is unsupported, but won't cause a serious display problem. Each bug is linked to the CSS Advisor, a part of the Adobe Web site, that offers solutions for that particular bug and other helpful information for resolving any issues with your pages.

4. Move your mouse over the bottom of the header block, click the **yellow border** to select the block, then move the mouse on the block border until the floating window shown in Figure 12 appears.

The properties of the div tag are displayed in a floating window. The Property inspector displays the Div ID, header, and the Class, OneColElsCtrHdr.

TIP   You can change the border color of div tags in the Preferences dialog box. Select the Highlighting category, then click the Mouse-Over color box to select a different color. You can also disable highlighting by deselecting the Show checkbox for Mouse_Over.

5. Save your work.

You centered the navigation bar and removed an extra line between the banner and the navigation bar. You also viewed the properties of the Div tag.

FIGURE 12
Viewing the div tag properties

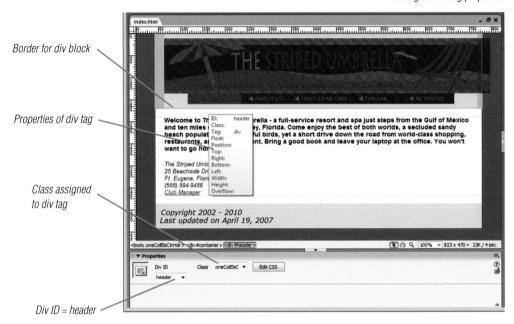

Border for div block

Properties of div tag

Class assigned
to div tag

Div ID = header

Viewing options for CSS layout blocks

There are several options for viewing your layout blocks in Design view. You can choose to show or hide outlines, temporarily assign different background colors to each individual layout block, or view the CSS Layout Box Model (padding and margins) of a selected layout. To change these options, use the View, Visual Aids menu, and then select or deselect the CSS Layout Outlines, CSS Layout Backgrounds, or CSS Layout Box Model menu choice. You can also use the Visual Aids button on the Document toolbar.

FIGURE 13

Clearing prior formatting to allow body_text style to display

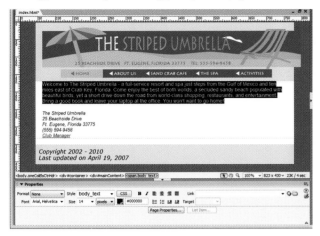

FIGURE 14

Editing the properties of the oneColElsCtrHdr #container style

Select the
oneColElsCtrHdr
#container style

Change the
width of the
block to 48 ems

1. Place the insertion point in front of the word "Welcome" in the text paragraph, press and hold **[Shift]**, then click the space at the end of the paragraph.

2. Click the **Format list arrow** in the Property inspector, then click **None**.

   The Heading 1 tag was picked up from the preformatted text in the main_content block. By removing the Heading 1 tag, the existing body_text style was used to format the paragraph text. See Figure 13.

3. Save your work.

You cleared prior formatting from the predefined CSS layout page to allow the body_text style to format the paragraph of text.

Edit CSS layout block properties

1. Click the **OneColElsCtrHdr #container style** in the CSS Styles panel to select it.

   The properties of the style are displayed in the Properties pane.

2. Click **46em** to select it, type **48**, as shown in Figure 14, then press **[Enter]** (Win) or **[return]** (Mac).

   (continued)

Although the width of the page will adjust to the width of the browser, each container on the page has a set width that will remain fixed. Changing the width of the container enlarges it to make room for the banner. It no longer extends over the edge of the container.

3. Click the **OneColElsCtrHdr #header style** in the CSS Styles panel to select it.

4. Click to select the background color **#DDDDDD**, type **#FFFFFF** as shown in Figure 15, then press **[Enter]** (Win) or **[return]** (Mac).

   The background color of the header is now white, to match the other two layout blocks.

5. Repeat Step 4 to change the footer background color to **#FFFFFF**.

6. Save your work, preview the page in the browser, then compare your screen to Figure 16.

You changed the width of a CSS layout block, then changed the background color of two CSS layout blocks to white.

FIGURE 15

Editing the properties of the oneColElsCtrHdr #header style

Select the oneColElsCtrHdr #header style

Change the background color value to #FFFFFF

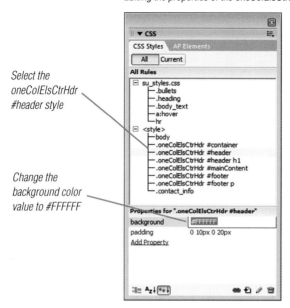

FIGURE 16

The three layout blocks now have a white background

The three sections have the white background color

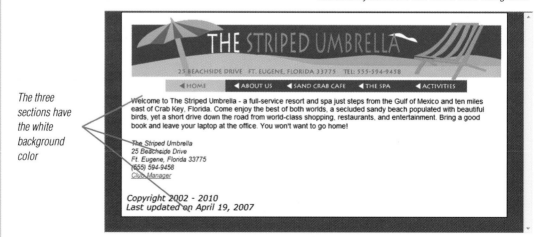

FIGURE 17

Changing the body background value to #FFFFFF

Select the
body style

Change the background
color value to #FFFFFF

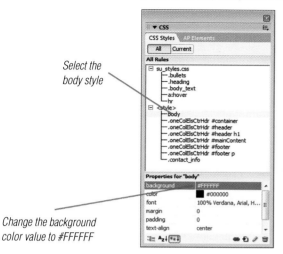

FIGURE 18

Viewing the index page in the browser

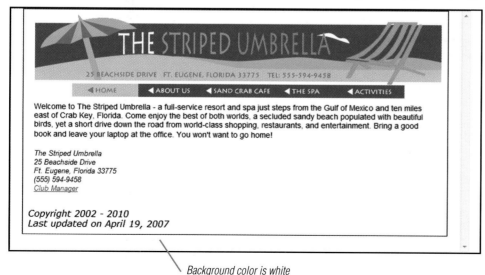

Background color is white

Edit page properties

1. Select the **body tag** in the CSS Styles panel.

2. Click to select the background color **#666666**, type **#FFFFFF**, as shown in Figure 17, then press **[Enter]** (Win) or **[return]** (Mac).

   The body tag for the page is now set to display a white background.

3. Save your work, preview the page in your browser, then compare your screen to Figure 18.

4. Close the browser, select the copyright and last updated statements, then change their style to **contact_info**.

5. Save your work.

You changed the value for the background color to white, then changed the style of the copyright and last updated statements to contact_info.

INSERT
AN AP DIV

What You'll Do

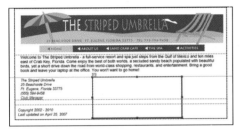

In this lesson, you will draw an AP div on The Striped Umbrella home page and set its properties using the Property inspector.

Understanding AP Elements

AP elements are div tags that are absolutely positioned, or assigned a fixed position on a Web page. Using AP Div Tags, you can stack AP elements on top of each other and specify that only certain elements be visible at certain times or in specified conditions. AP elements can be used to create special effects on a Web page. For instance, you can use AP elements to build a whole image from individual pieces. You can also use them to create a jigsaw puzzle that allows you to slide the pieces into their positions one at a time. You can also use AP elements to create dynamic pages that contain moving parts or objects that become visible or invisible based on a selection made by the Web site viewer.

Using AP elements to lay out a Web page is like working with a stack of transparency sheets that you can stack on top of each other. Figure 19 illustrates how to use AP elements to stack graphical elements on top of each other to create the single image of a flower.

To insert an AP element, you can use the Draw AP Div button in the Layout Category on the Insert bar and drag to draw a rectangular shape anywhere on your page, as shown in Figure 20. You can also insert an AP element using the Insert Layout Objects, AP Div command. Specify the exact dimensions, color, and other attributes of a new AP element by changing the settings in the Preferences dialog box.

Using HTML Tags to Create AP Elements

Dreamweaver uses the <div> tag to create an AP element. Initially, the default value for the first AP Div Tag on a page appears as <div id="apDiv1">. Each additional AP Div Tag will be assigned the next number in sequence. You can use either the Property inspector or the AP Elements panel to rename each AP Div Tag with a name that is relevant to its content. The code for AP Div Tags resides in the head content as part of the CSS code.

Understanding AP Elements Content

An AP element is like a separate document within a Web page. It can contain the same types of elements that a page can, such as background colors, images, links, tables, and text. You can also set the contents of an AP element to work directly with a specified Dreamweaver behavior to make the page interact with a viewer in a certain way.

Using Advanced Formatting

You should be careful not to add too much content to an AP element. If it contains more information than it can readily display, you will need to use advanced formatting controls to format the content. You can control the appearance of a selected AP element by making changes to the Clip, Visibility, and Overflow properties in the Property inspector.

The **Clip property** identifies the portion of an AP element's content that is visible when displayed in a Web browser. By default, the clipping region matches the outside borders of the AP element, but you can change the amount that is visible by clipping one or all sides. For instance, if you set the L (left) Clip property to 10 pixels, then everything from the eleventh pixel to the right will be displayed in the browser. If you clip off 10 pixels from the right side, you will need to subtract 10 from the total width of the AP element and then type this value in the Clip R text box in the Property inspector. The clip setting can be applied only to AP elements that have an Overflow attribute set to a value other than visible.

The **Vis (visible) property** lets you control whether the selected AP element is visible. You can set the Vis property to default, visible, hidden, or **inherit**, which means that the visibility of the AP element is automatically inherited from its parent AP element or page.

The **Overflow property** specifies how to treat excess content that does not fit inside an AP element. You can make the content visible, specify that scroll bars appear, hide the content, or let the current AP element automatically deal with the extra content in the same manner as its parent AP element or page. However, some browsers do not support the overflow property.

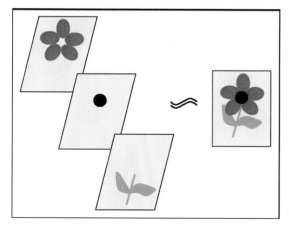

Draw AP Div button

AP Div icon

AP Div border

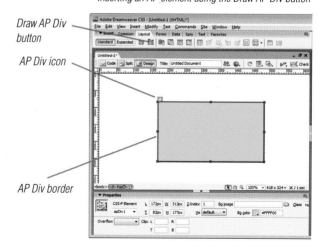

Draw an AP Div

1. Drag a horizontal guide to the **250 pixel mark** on the vertical ruler.

   | TIP   Guides help you place page elements or emulate the fold lines in a browser. Fold lines are similar to the top of a folded newspaper. The most important stories are usually printed at the top of the fold line.

2. Click the **Layout tab** on the Insert bar, then click the **Draw AP Div button** 📰.

3. Using Figure 21 as a guide, drag a **rectangle** in the middle of the home page and under the guide that is approximately 350 pixels wide and 150 pixels tall.

   A new AP element appears on the page, but it is not selected. An AP Div icon ▣ appears above the upper-left corner of the AP element.

   | TIP   You can also insert an AP Div by clicking Insert on the menu bar, pointing to Layout Objects, and then clicking AP Div.

4. Click the **AP Div icon** ▣ above the AP element to select it.

   | TIP   You can also select an AP Div by clicking one of its borders.

You drew an AP Div on the home page, then selected it.

FIGURE 21
New AP element added to the home page

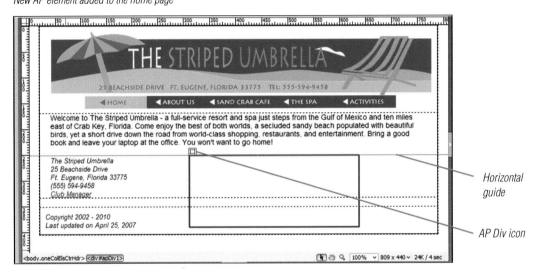

Horizontal guide

AP Div icon

Positioning Objects with CSS

FIGURE 22

Property inspector showing properties of selected AP element

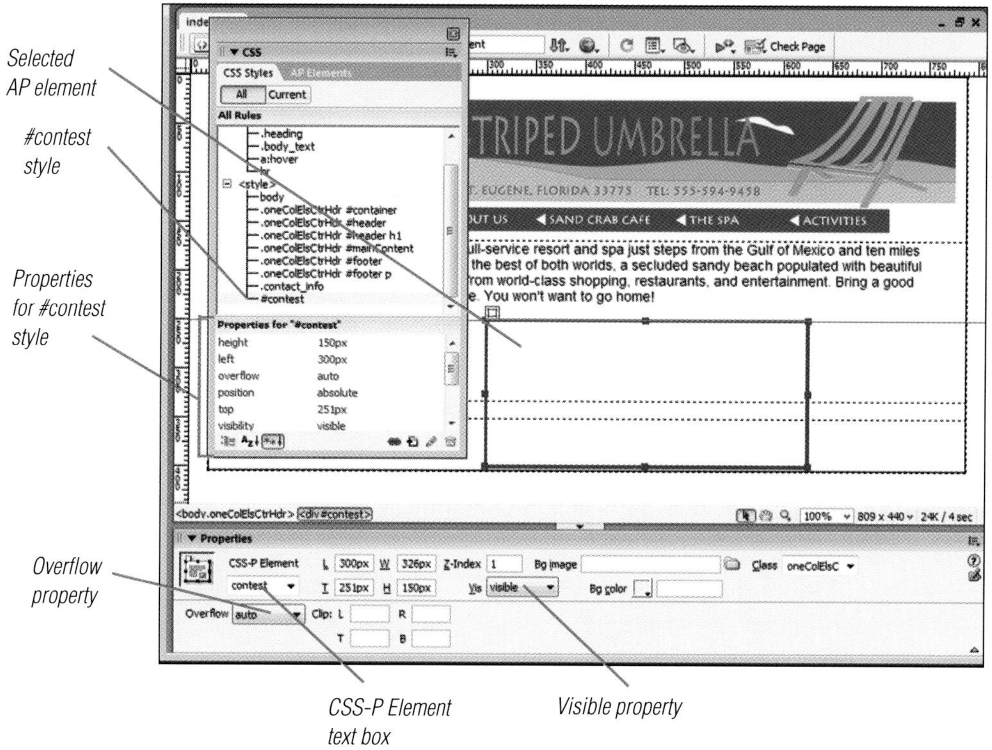

Selected
AP element

#contest
style

Properties
for #contest
style

Overflow
property

CSS-P Element
text box

Visible property

1. With the AP Div selected, select **apDiv1** in the CSS-P Element text box in the Property inspector, type **contest**, then press **[Enter]** (Win) or **[return]** (Mac).

   TIP If the AP element is not selected, click the <div#apDiv1> tag in the Tag selector.

2. Verify that <div#contest> is selected in the Tag selector.

3. Click the **Overflow list arrow** in the Property inspector, then click **auto**.

4. Click the **Vis list arrow**, then click **visible**.

5. Compare your screen to Figure 22.

   The L, T, W, and H settings in the Property inspector specify the position and size of the AP element. Your settings will probably differ from those shown in the figure because you probably drew your layer with slightly different measurements.

   Notice that a new style has been defined in the CSS Styles panel called #contest. The properties for this style are listed in the Properties pane. When you draw an AP Div, Dreamweaver automatically creates a style for it. As you make changes to the element properties, they are displayed in the Properties pane, when the style is selected.

6. Save your work.

You specified a name and other properties for the selected AP element. You viewed the properties in the CSS Styles panel.

SET THE POSITION AND SIZE
OF AN AP ELEMENT

What You'll Do

 In this lesson, you will use the Property inspector to position and size layers on the home page of The Striped Umbrella Web site.

Understanding Absolute Positioning

To use AP elements, you must understand **absolute positioning**. An AP element is positioned absolutely by specifying the distance between the upper-left corner of the AP element and the upper-left corner of the page or parent AP element in which it is contained. Figure 23 illustrates how an AP element keeps its relative position on a page when the page is scrolled. Because Dreamweaver treats AP elements as if they are separate documents contained within a page; they do not interrupt the flow of content on the page or parent AP element in which they are contained. This means that AP elements placed on top of a page can hide the contents on the page.

AP elements have no impact on the location of other AP elements. In other words, if you insert an AP element, the remaining page elements that follow it within the code will continue with the flow of the page, ignoring the presence of the AP element. This means you can create overlapping AP elements. You can create dynamic effects with overlapping AP elements on a Web page. You do so by using JavaScript or CGI programs to change the attributes associated with each AP element in response to actions by the viewer. For instance, an AP element could move or change its size when a viewer clicks or moves the mouse over a link on the page or in the layer.

Setting Positioning Attributes

You can control the placement of AP elements by setting attributes available in the Property inspector. These attributes work together to create an AP element that will hold its position on a page.

The **Left property (L)** in the Property inspector specifies the distance between the left edge of an AP element and the left edge of the page or parent AP element that contains it. The **Top property (T)** in the Property inspector specifies the distance between the top edge of your AP element and the top edge of the page or the AP element that contains it.

The **Width (W)** and **Height (H) properties** specify the dimensions of the AP element most often in pixels, although the AP element can be specified as a percentage of your screen dimension. For instance, you can specify that your AP element be 250 pixels by 250 pixels, or you can set it to 25% by 25%, which will create a layer that is roughly 200 by 150 in a Web browser on an 800×600 resolution monitor.

Use the **Z-Index property** in the Property inspector to specify the vertical stacking order of AP elements on a page. If you think of the page itself as AP element 0, then any number higher than that will appear on top of the page. For instance, if you have three AP elements with the Z-Index values of 1, 2, and 3, then 1 will appear below 2 and 3, while 3 will always appear above 1 and 2. You can create a dynamic Web site by adjusting the Z-Index settings on the fly using Dreamweaver's built-in JavaScript behaviors within the Web page you are creating.

QUICKTIP
You cannot set Z-Index values below 0.

FIGURE 23
Scrolling a page containing an AP element

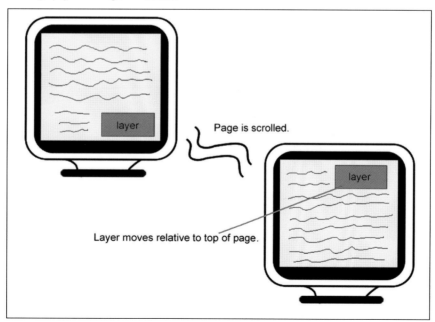

Set the Left and Top position of an AP Div

1. Click the **AP Div border** to select the AP Div element (if necessary).

2. Type **420px** in the L text box in the CSS-P Element section of the Property inspector, then press **[Enter]** (Win) or **[return]** (Mac).

    The AP Div moves automatically to the position you specified.

3. Type **260px** in the T text box, then press **[Enter]** (Win) or **[return]** (Mac).

4. Save your work, then compare your screen to Figure 24.

You adjusted the upper-left corner position of the AP Div.

Set AP Div height and width

1. Click the **AP Div border** to select the AP Div (if necessary).

2. Type **200px** in the W text box, then press **[Tab]**.

    The AP Div automatically adjusts its width to the dimension you specified.

3. Type **175px** in the H text box, then press **[Tab]**.

    The AP Div automatically adjusts to the height you specified. Notice that the upper-left corner stays in the same position.

4. Save your work, then compare your screen to Figure 25.

You adjusted the height and width of the AP Div.

FIGURE 24
AP element moved down and to the right on the page

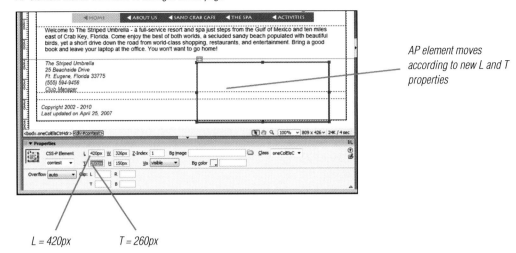

AP element moves according to new L and T properties

L = 420px   T = 260px

FIGURE 25
AP element with width and height adjusted

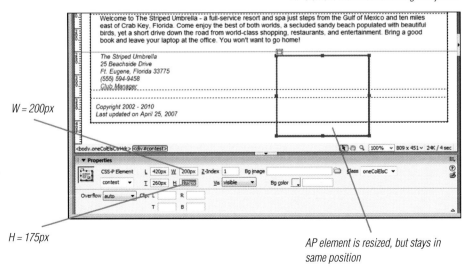

W = 200px

H = 175px

AP element is resized, but stays in same position

FIGURE 26
New background AP element on top of contest AP element

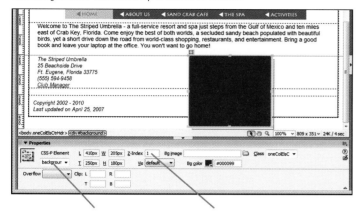

New AP element name = background   *Z-Index = 1*

FIGURE 27
Contest AP element moved on top of background AP element

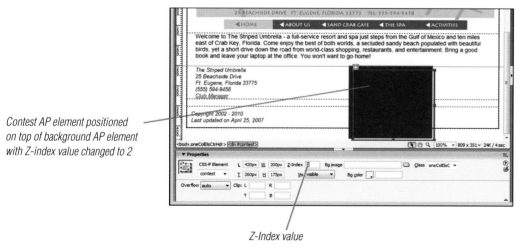

Contest AP element positioned on top of background AP element with Z-index value changed to 2

Z-Index value

Set the Z-Index value for an AP Div

1. Create another AP Div anywhere on the page, select it, then name it **background**.

2. Select the **background AP Div** (if necessary), then adjust its size and position by setting the following properties in the Property inspector: L: **410px**, T: **250px**, W: **205px**, and H: **180px**.

   The new AP Div is now positioned on top of the contest AP Div.

3. Click the **Color picker button** next to the Bg color text box, then change the background color of the background AP Div to dark blue, **#000099**.

   TIP You can also select the color number in the text box and type the new color number to replace it.

4. Change the Z-Index value of the background AP Div to **1** in the Property inspector, as shown in Figure 26.

5. Click the **contest AP Div** to select it.

   TIP Be careful to click the border of the contest AP Div, not the background AP Div.

6. Change the Z-Index value of the contest AP Div to **2** in the Property inspector.

   The background AP Div is now positioned behind the contest AP Div to act as an outline, as shown in Figure 27.

   The contest AP Div does not have content yet, so you can see the background AP Div behind it.

7. Save your work.

You added a new AP Div named background to the home page, and specified its dimensions and position on the page using the Property inspector. You set the background color of the background AP Div, then adjusted the vertical stacking order of the two layers.

ADD CONTENT
TO AN AP ELEMENT

What You'll Do

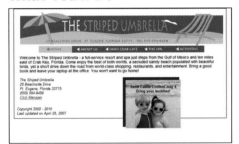

In this lesson, you will copy the text and banner from the index page and paste it into the new page. You will then save over the old index page with this new one.

Understanding Layer Content

As you learned in Lesson 4, an AP element is like a separate document within a Web page. It contains the same types of elements that a page based on table layout can, such as background colors, images, links, tables, and text. If you just want to include an image as part of the content, but not the background, insert the image just as you would insert one on a page using the Property inspector. Figure 28 shows an AP element with a blue background color and an image with a transparent background inserted at the bottom of the cell. If you have an image you would like to be able to type over, insert the image as the background, as shown in Figure 29.

If you add more content than the preset image size, the AP element will enlarge to display the content on your page in Dreamweaver. However, when you preview the page in the browser, the amount displayed will depend on how you set your Overflow settings.

Like a Web page, if you specify both a background color and a background image, the background image will override the background color. As the page is loading, the layer background color may display until the layer background image finishes loading.

Also, as with formatting text on a Web page, you should use CSS styles to format your text on an AP element. You can also add all other layer properties such as text indent, padding, margins, and background color using CSS styles.

FIGURE 28

AP element with a background color and an inserted image

FIGURE 29

AP element with an image inserted as a background image

Set a background color

1. With the contest AP Div selected, click the **Bg color text box** in the Property inspector.

2. Type **#FFFFFF**.

   The AP Div is now filled with white, as shown in Figure 30.

You added a background color to the AP Div.

FIGURE 30
White background color applied to AP element

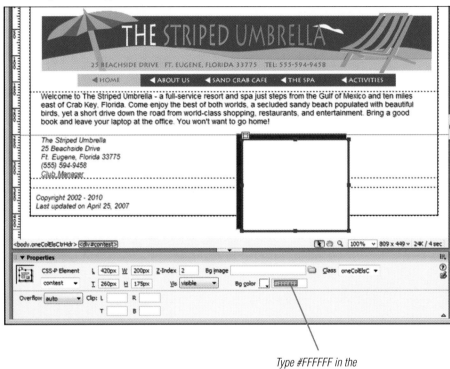

*Type #FFFFFF in the
Bg color text box*

FIGURE 31

Image added to AP element

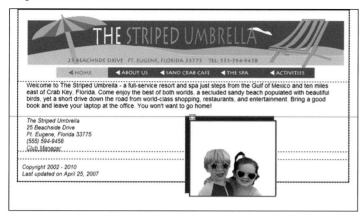

FIGURE 32

AP element displays scroll bars in browser because it has been stretched

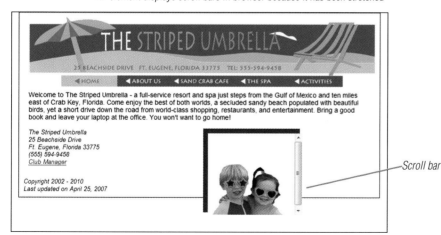

Scroll bar

Add an image to an AP Div

1. Deselect the AP Div, then click inside it to set the insertion point.

2. Click the **Common tab** on the Insert bar, click the **Images list arrow**, then click **Image**.

3. Navigate to where you store your Data Files, then double-click **contestants.gif**.

4. Type **Two young contestants** in the Image Tag Accessibility Attributes dialog box, then click **OK**.

   | TIP   If the Image Tag Accessibility Attributes dialog box does not appear, type appropriate alternate text in the Alt text box in the Property inspector.

5. Click [←] to place the insertion point before the image, insert three line breaks by pressing **[Shift][Enter]** (Win) or **[Shift][return]** (Mac) three times, then compare your screen to Figure 31.

6. Save your work, preview the page in your Web browser, then compare your screen to Figure 32.

   Notice the scroll bar in the AP Div. The AP Div had to stretch to fit in the three page breaks and the image. Because the Overflow is set to Auto, the scroll bar automatically appears when there is more content than can fit in the dimensions.

You added an image to the AP Div, then added alternate text to it.

Set a background image

1. Remove both the background color and the image from the layer.

2. Press **[Backspace]** three times to delete the line breaks.

3. Select the **AP Div**, then click the **Browse for File icon** 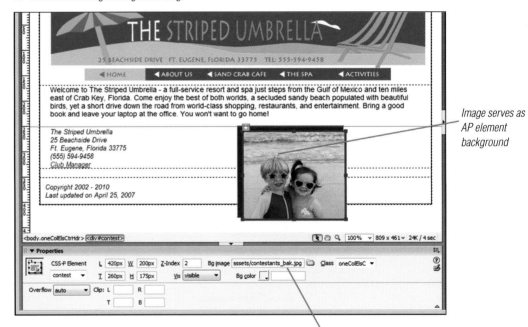 next to the Bg image text box in the Property inspector to open the Select Image Source dialog box.

4. Navigate to where you store your Data Files, then click **contestants_bak.jpg**.

5. Click **OK** (Win) or **Choose** (Mac), then compare your screen to Figure 33.

6. Refresh the Files panel to verify that contestants_bak.jpg was copied to the assets folder of the Web site.

You added a background image to the contest AP Div.

FIGURE 33
AP element containing a background image

Image serves as AP element background

Bg image = contestants_bak.jpg

FIGURE 34

Editing the #contest style

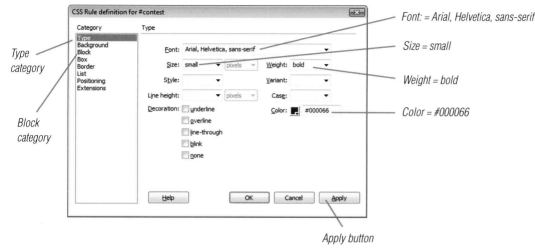

Type category

Block category

Font: = Arial, Helvetica, sans-serif

Size = small

Weight = bold

Color = #000066

Apply button

FIGURE 35

Index page with the formatted AP elements

Add and format text on an AP Div

1. Click inside the AP Div to set the insertion point, then enter a line break.

2. Type **Sand Castle Contest July 4**, press **[Shift][Enter]** (Win) or **[Shift][return]** (Mac), then type **Bring your buddies!**.

3. Select the **contest style** in the CSS Styles panel, then click the **Edit Style button** .

4. Click the **Type category**, as shown in Figure 34, change Font to **Arial, Helvetica, sans-serif**, Size to **small**; Weight to **bold**, Color to **#000066**, then click the **Apply button**.

5. Click the **Block category**, change the Text align setting to **center**, then click **OK**.

   The text changes to reflect the properties you have added to the contest style. It is blue and centered on the AP Div. When you have text on an AP Div, it is strongly recommended that you edit the text using the layer style in the CSS Styles panel, rather than using the Property inspector.

6. Save your work, preview the page in your Web browser, compare your screen with Figure 35, then close your browser.

You added text to the AP Div, and formatted it using the CSS Styles panel.

USE THE
AP ELEMENTS PANEL

What You'll Do

 In this lesson, you will use the AP Elements panel to change the name of an AP element, view and hide an AP element, and work with nested AP elements.

Controlling AP Elements

You can use the **AP Elements panel** to control the visibility, name, and Z-Index order of all the AP elements on a Web page. You can also use the AP Elements panel to see how an AP element is nested within the page structure and to change the nesting status of an AP element. **Nested AP elements** are those whose HTML code is included within another AP element's code. A nested AP element does not affect the way it appears to the page viewer; it establishes a relationship of how it appears in relation to its parent AP element. To change the nesting status of an AP element, drag it to a new location in the AP Elements panel. Figure 36 shows the AP Elements panel with a nested AP element.

You can open the AP Elements panel using the Window menu. The AP Elements panel is very handy when you are trying to select an AP element on the bottom of a stack. Clicking the AP element name selects the AP element on the page. You can access the same information that is available in

the AP Elements panel by selecting the AP element and viewing its settings in the Property inspector.

Using the AP Elements panel is the easiest way to change a series of AP element names, control AP element visibility while testing a site, and control the visible stacking order. The AP Elements panel also keeps track of all the AP elements on a page, making it easy to review the settings for each.

FIGURE 36
AP Elements panel

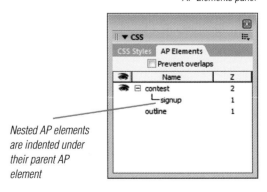

Nested AP elements are indented under their parent AP element

FIGURE 37
Using the AP Elements panel to change an AP element name

AP element names

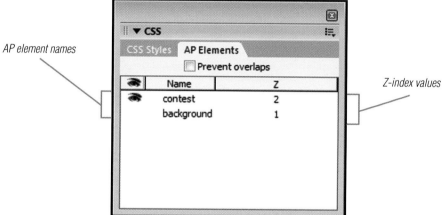

Z-index values

1. Click **Window** on the menu bar, then click **AP Elements,** or click **AP Elements** in the CSS panel group.

   The AP Elements panel appears in the CSS panel group, as shown in Figure 37.

2. Click **background** on the AP Elements panel to select the background AP element.

3. Double-click **background** on the AP Elements panel to edit its name.

4. Type **outline**, then press **[Enter]** (Win) or **[return]** (Mac).

   The AP Element is renamed.

5. With the outline AP element selected, press [→] and [↓] each about seven times to reposition the outline AP element so it is centered behind the contest AP element, serving as an outline for the contest AP element.

You used the AP Elements panel to change the name of one of the AP elements on the home page, then repositioned the AP element.

Controlling AP element visibility

1. Click the **Eye icon column** twice for the contest AP element in the AP Elements panel, then compare your screen with Figure 38.

   The Closed eye icon appears, indicating that the contest AP element no longer appears in the document window.

2. Click the **Closed eye icon** 👁 on the contest AP element.

   Clicking the Closed eye icon makes the AP element visible, as shown in Figure 39. The Eye icon appears in the AP Elements panel.

3. Click the **Eye icon** 👁 on the contest AP element.

   Clicking the Eye icon makes the AP element inherit the visibility status of its parent objects. In this case, the parent object of the contest AP element is the home page. Because the home page is visible, the contest AP element is visible, too.

You used the AP Elements panel to change the visibility status of the contest AP element.

FIGURE 38

Using the AP Elements panel to hide the contest AP element

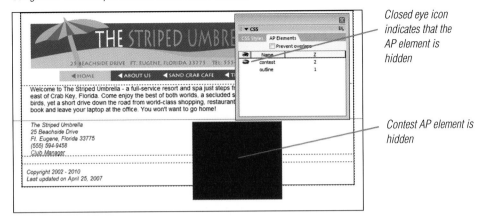

Closed eye icon indicates that the AP element is hidden

Contest AP element is hidden

FIGURE 39

Using the AP Elements panel to make the contest AP element visible

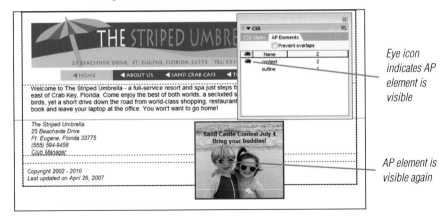

Eye icon indicates AP element is visible

AP element is visible again

FIGURE 40

Nested AP element shown with parent AP element properties

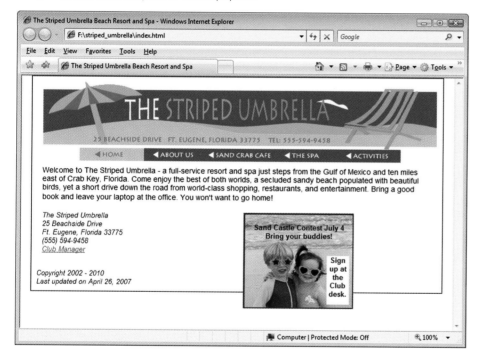

1. Click the **contest AP element** in the AP Elements panel, then click in the contest AP element in the Document window after the word "buddies!" to place the insertion point.

2. Click **Insert** on the menu bar, point to **Layout Objects**, then click **AP Div**.

   A new AP element is inserted as a nested AP element of the contest AP element.

3. Use the AP Elements panel to select this new nested **AP element**, then name it **signup**.

4. Type **152px** in the L text box, then type **77px** in the T text box.

5. Type **42px** in the W text box, then type **92px** in the H text box.

   These dimensions specify the position and size of the nested AP element in relation to the upper-left corner of the contest AP element.

6. Set the background color to **#FFFFFF**.

7. Click in the **sign up AP element** to place the insertion point, then type **Sign up at the Club desk**.

   Notice that the text is automatically formatted using the properties for the contest AP element, the parent AP element for the nested AP element.

8. Enter the page title **The Striped Umbrella Beach Resort and Spa** in the title text box.

9. Save your work, preview the page in your browser, then compare your screen to Figure 40.

You created a nested AP element within the contest AP element.

Create a page using CSS Layouts.

1. Open the blooms & bulbs Web site, then open the home page.

2. Create a new blank HTML page with the 1 column elastic, centered, header and footer style.

3. Link the **blooms_styles.css** file to the page.

4. Add the page title **blooms & bulbs - Your complete garden center** in the Title text box.

Add content to CSS layout blocks.

1. Switch to the index page and copy the block of text and contact information.

2. Paste the text in the center container of the new, unsaved page.

3. Switch back to the index page and copy the copyright and last updated information.

4. Paste the text in the footer container of the new, unsaved page.

5. Switch back to the index page and select both the banner and the navigation bar.

6. Paste the banner and navigation bar in the header section of the new, unsaved page.

7. Close the index page.

8. Save the new, untitled page as **index.html**, overwriting the original index page. (*Hint:* The navigation bar has been placed on two lines because the container is not wide enough. We will fix this in an upcoming set of steps.)

Edit content in CSS layout blocks.

1. Select the **OneColElsCtrHdr #container style** in the CSS Styles panel.

2. Change the width of the container to **48em,** and the float to **Left**.

3. Select the **OneColElsCtrHdr #header style** in the CSS panel and change the background color to **#FFFFFF**.

4. Repeat Step 3 to change the background color of the footer to **white**.

5. Repeat Step 3 to change the body background to **white**.

6. Save your work.

Insert an AP Div

1. Use the Draw AP Div button to draw a long thin rectangle, about 2 inches tall by 1 inch wide on the bottom half of your page.

2. Name this AP Div **organic**.

Set the position and size of an AP Div.

1. Select the organic AP div, then set the Left property to **400 pixels**.

2. Set the Top property to **230 pixels**.

3. Set the Width property to **175 pixels**.

4. Set the Height property to **219 pixels**.

5. Set the Z-Index property to **1** (if necessary).

6. Save your work.

Add content to an AP element.

1. Select the organic AP div, remove the background color (if necessary), then insert the background image **peaches_small.jpg** from where you store your Data Files.

2. Set the Vis property to **default**.

3. Set the Overflow property to **visible**.

4. Place the insertion point in the organic AP div, then type **Organic Gardening**.

5. Insert a line break, then type **Class begins soon!**.

6. Save your work.

Use the AP Elements panel.

1. Open the AP Elements panel (if necessary).

2. Use the Property inspector to change the organic AP div's name to **organic_class**.

3. Set the Vis property to **visible**.

4. Save your work.
5. Preview the page in your browser, compare your screen to Figure 41, close your browser, adjust the AP element position (if necessary), then save and close the home page.

FIGURE 41
Completed Skills Review

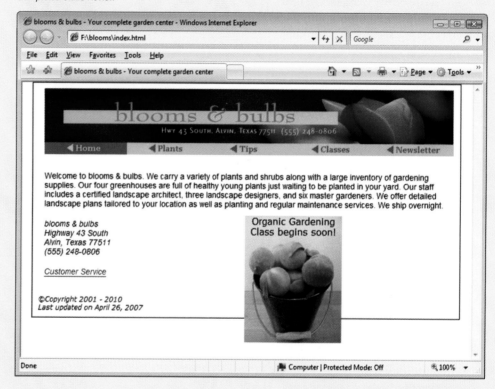

In this exercise, you will continue your work on the TripSmart Web site. The owner, Thomas Howard, wants you to create a section on the index page that advertises a special price on Packing Cubes.

1. Open the TripSmart Web site, then open the index page.

2. Create a new page based on the **one column elastic, centered** CSS page layout.

3. Attach the **tripsmart_styles.css** file.

4. Copy all content from the index page, then paste it in the new, unsaved page.

5. Close the index page.

6. Save the new page as the **index** page, over-writing the original index page.

7. Change the width of the #container to **48em** and the float to **Left**, then edit the container and page properties to have white back-grounds.

8. Draw an AP div that is approximately 1 inch tall and 3 inches wide in the middle of the page, then name it **special**.

9. Set the background color of the AP div to **transparent** by clicking the **Default** button on the color picker toolbar.

10. Insert **packing_cube.jpg** from where you store your Data Files into the AP div, adding appropriate alternate text, then set the Align option to Left.

11. Set the Left property to **300 pixels** and the Top property to **300 pixels**.

12. Set the width to **350 pixels**, the height to **80 pixels**, and the Z-Index property to **1**.

13. Add the following text to the right of the image: **Packing Cubes on sale this week!**, with a line break before the word "this."

14. Format the Packing Cubes on sale this week! text using the **heading** style.

15. Enter a line break, type **Large: $15.00; Medium: $10.00; Small: $5.00**; then format this text with the **item_numbers** style.

FIGURE 42

Sample Project Builder 1

16. Edit the #special style in the CSS Styles panel to add a double border around the AP div with the color **#666666**.

17. Set the Overflow property to **visible**.

18. Set the body tag background color to **#FFFFFF**.

19. Add the page title **TripSmart - serving all your travel needs**.

20. Save your work, preview the page in your browser, compare your screen to Figure 42, close your browser, make any spacing adjust-ments necessary for the AP div size or position, then close the index page.

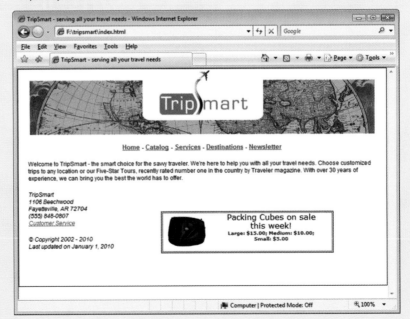

Use Figure 43 as a guide to continue your work on the Carolyne's Creations Web site.

Carolyne's Creations Web site.

1. Open the Carolyne's Creations Web site, then open the index page.

2. Create a new page with a CSS layout of your choice, then attach the cc_styles.css file.

3. Replace the placeholder content with the content from the index page, then save the new page as the index page.

4. Edit the container properties with values of your choice to format the page to blend with the existing pages in the Web site.

5. Create an AP Div on the page, then place the file cc_logo.jpg from your assets folder on the AP div.

6. Adjust the size and position of the AP element with settings of your choice.

7. Add a page title to the page.

8. Save your work, preview the page in your browser, close your browser, then close the index page.

FIGURE 43
Completed Project Builder 2

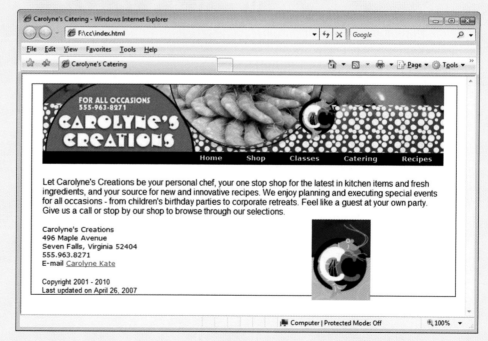

Sharon Woods has recently been asked to redesign a Web site for a small college. She has decided to use CSS for her page layout. Because she has never developed a Web site with these features before, she decides to look at some other college Web sites for ideas and inspiration.

1. Connect to the Internet, then go to *www.hendrix.edu*, as shown in Figure 44.
2. How are CSS used in this site?
3. How are CSS used to prevent an overload of information in one area of the screen?
4. View the source code for the page and locate the HTML tags that control the CSS on the page.
5. Use the Reference panel in Dreamweaver to look up the code used in this site to place the content on the page.

FIGURE 44
Design Project

Hendrix College Web site used with permission from Hendrix College: www.hendrix.edu

For this assignment, you will continue to work on the portfolio project that you have been developing since Chapter 1. There will be no Data Files supplied. You are building this Web site from chapter to chapter, so you must do each Portfolio Project assignment in each chapter to complete your Web site.

You will continue building your Web site by designing and completing a page that uses div tags rather than tables to control the layout of information.

1. Consult your storyboard to decide which page to create and develop for this chapter. Draw a sketch of the page to show how you will use CSS to lay out the content.

2. Create the new page for the site and set the default preferences for div tags and AP elements. Add the appropriate number of div tags and AP elements to the new page and configure them appropriately, making sure to name them and set the properties for each.

3. Add text, background images, and background colors to each container.

4. Create the navigation links that will allow you to add this page to your site.

5. Update the other pages of your site so that each page includes a link to this new page.

6. Add images in the containers (where appropriate), making sure to align them with text so they look good.

7. Check to ensure that all AP elements are properly stacked using the Z-Index property.

8. Review the checklist in Figure 45 and make any necessary modifications.

9. Save your work, preview the page in your browser, make any necessary modifications to make the page look good, close your browser, then close all open pages.

FIGURE 45
Portfolio Project checklist

Web Site Checklist
1. Are all AP Elements properly stacked with Z-Index values assigned correctly?
2. Do all pages have titles?
3. Do all navigation links still work?
4. Are all colors in your layers Websafe?
5. Does the use of CSS containers in your Web site improve the site navigation?
6. Do any extra AP elements appear that need to be removed?
7. Do your pages look acceptable in at least the two major browsers?
8. Do AP elements hide any information on your pages?
9. Do all images in your CSS containers appear correctly?

10

ADDING MEDIA
OBJECTS

1. Add and modify Flash objects

2. Add rollover images

3. Add behaviors

4. Add Flash video

10 ADDING MEDIA
OBJECTS

Introduction

You can use Dreamweaver to add media objects created in other programs to the pages of your Web site. Some of the external media file types include Adobe Fireworks navigation bars, rollover images, and buttons; Flash buttons, video, sound, and animation; Director and Shockwave movies and presentations; Java applets; ActiveX controls; server-side controls; and a variety of plug-ins. This means you can create complex, interactive Web sites with media effects that can be viewed within the pages themselves, rather than loading an external document player such as Windows Media Player or RealPlayer by Real Networks. In this chapter, you will use Dreamweaver to add Flash and Fireworks objects to The Striped Umbrella Web site.

Understanding Media Objects

The term "media objects" has different meanings, depending on who you are talking to, and the industry in which they work. For our purposes, **media objects** are combinations of visual and audio effects and text to create a fully engaging experience with a Web site. Although this might be an open-ended definition, it is the experience you are striving for when you add video and audio elements to a Web page. Think about the experience of watching a movie. You are engaged not just by the actors, but also by the sounds and special effects you experience. You want to create this same type of experience for your Web site viewers by adding media elements to your pages.

You can use Dreamweaver to insert a wide variety of media effects in your Web pages, including Flash buttons, movies, and text; Flash video; and a series of built-in JavaScript behaviors such as sounds, rollover images, pop-up menus, Go to URL, and menus.

Tools You'll Use

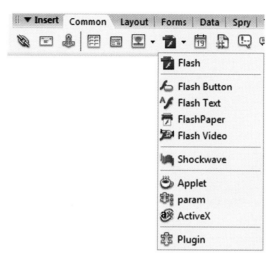

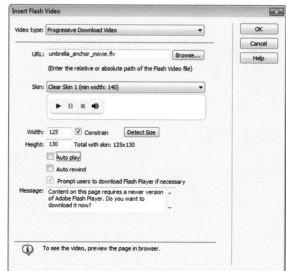

ADD AND MODIFY
FLASH OBJECTS

What You'll Do

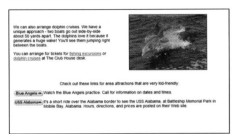

 In this lesson, you will insert and edit two Flash buttons on the activities page of The Striped Umbrella Web site. You will also insert and modify a Flash movie on the cafe page, and then play the movie both in Dreamweaver and in a browser.

Understanding Adobe Flash

Flash is a software program that allows you to create low-bandwidth, high-quality animations and interactive elements that can be placed on your Web pages. These animations use a series of vector-based graphics that load quickly and merge with other graphics and sounds to create short movies. Figure 1 shows a Web page that contains several Flash objects. Figure 2 shows the Flash program used to create Flash objects.

Once these short movies are created, you can place them on your Web pages. To view Flash movies, you need the Flash Player, a software program that is included in the latest versions of both Internet Explorer and Mozilla Firefox. If you are using an older browser that does not support the version of Flash used to create your movie, you can download the latest Flash player from the Adobe Web site, located at *www.adobe.com*. Almost all Internet-enabled desktops worldwide use the Flash player. In addition, other tools, such as cell phones and handheld devices, contain rich Flash content.

Collecting Flash objects

Adobe and their devoted product users provide you with a variety of downloadable Flash buttons that are available on the Adobe Exchange Web site, located at *www.adobe.com/cfusion/exchange*. At this site, you can find collections of different buttons, such as space and planet theme sets, and just about anything else you might want. If you can't find a movie or button that interests you, you can download a demo version of Flash to create your own Flash objects.

Adding Media Objects

Inserting Flash Buttons and Movies

A **Flash button** is a button made from a small, predefined Flash movie that can be inserted on a Web page to provide navigation on your Web site. Like all Flash objects, Flash buttons are saved with the .swf file extension. Using Dreamweaver, you can insert customized Flash buttons on your Web pages without having Flash installed on your computer. To do this, use the Flash Button command in the Media menu on the Insert bar when the Common tab is displayed. The Insert Flash Button dialog box opens, where you can choose from 44 different styles of buttons. You also use this dialog box to specify the button text, formatting, an internal or external page to which to link the button, a background color, and a filename for the button.

Using Flash, you can create Flash movies that include a variety of multimedia elements, such as audio files (both music and voice-overs), animated objects, scripted objects, clickable links, and just about any other animated or clickable object imaginable. Flash movies can be used to add presentations to your existing Web site or to create an entire Web site. To add a Flash movie to a Web page, click Flash from the Media menu on the Common tab on the Insert bar to open the Select File dialog box, and then choose the Flash movie you want to insert.

FIGURE 1
Web site based on Flash

NASA Web site – *www.nasa.gov*

FIGURE 2
Adobe Flash CS3 window

Lesson 1   Add and Modify Flash Objects

Insert Flash buttons

1. Open The Striped Umbrella Web site, then open the activities page.

2. Click before the beginning of the sentence that starts with "Watch the Blue Angels practice" to set the insertion point.

3. Click the **Common tab** on the Insert bar (if necessary), click the **Media button list arrow**, then click **Flash Button** to open the Insert Flash Button dialog box.

4. Select **Chrome Bar** from the Style list.

5. Type **Blue Angels** in the Button text text box.

6. Click the **Font list arrow**, click **Verdana,** then type **14** in the Size text box.

7. Type **http://www.blueangels.navy.mil** in the Link text box.

8. Set the Target to **_blank**.

   The _blank setting ensures that the Blue Angels Web site will open in a new window, keeping The Striped Umbrella Web site open also.

9. Type **angels.swf** in the Save as text box, compare your dialog box to Figure 3, then click **OK**.

   This is a step that is easily overlooked. Be sure to name your new Flash file or it will use the default name "button1.swf," which is not very descriptive.

10. Type **Link to Blue Angels Web site** in the Title text box in the Flash Accessibility Attributes dialog box, then click **OK**.

   (continued)

FIGURE 3

Insert Flash Button dialog box

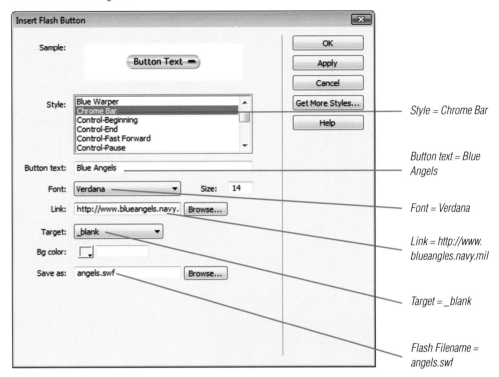

Style = Chrome Bar

Button text = Blue Angels

Font = Verdana

Link = http://www. blueangles.navy.mil

Target = _blank

Flash Filename = angels.swf

Creating FlashPaper Documents

You can also use FlashPaper to incorporate Flash content into your Web site. FlashPaper is a program built into Microsoft Word and PowerPoint. Using the FlashPaper menu command, you can easily convert a Word or PowerPoint file into a Flash .swf file that a browser can open and read. FlashPaper files are accessible by default; all linked text is readable and accessible using keyboard shortcuts. The files FlashPaper generates consistently have readable text and alternate text, and, for multiple column layout, readable content.

FIGURE 4

Flash button added to the activities page

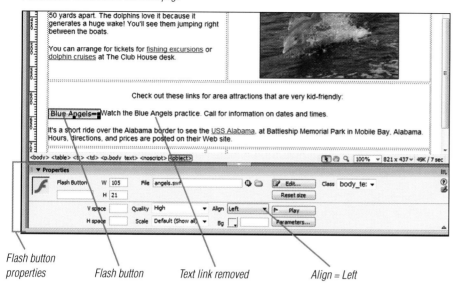

Flash button
properties   Flash button Text link removed   Align = Left

11. With the Flash button selected, click the **Align list arrow** in the Property inspector, then click **Left**.

    The Flash button is aligned to the left of the line of text beside it.

12. Select the **text link** to the Blue Angels Web site, delete the link in the Link text box in the Property inspector, deselect the Blue Angels text, then compare your screen to Figure 4.

    Because you now have a Flash button to serve as the link, you no longer need the text link.

13. Repeat Steps 2 through 12 to create a Flash button that links to the USS Alabama site, using **USS Alabama** as the Button text, **http://www.ussalabama.com** as the link, **alabama.swf** as the Flash file name, and **Link to USS Alabama** as the title in the Flash Accessibility Attributes dialog box.

    TIP If the text on your Flash buttons appears too large, you can choose a smaller font size or a different font.

14. Save your work, preview the page in your browser, test the Flash buttons, compare your screen to Figure 5, then close the browser.

    Notice that both Web sites opened in new windows, leaving The Striped Umbrella Web site window open.

    TIP If warned about Flash Player security issues, click the Settings button and change the security options.

You added two Flash buttons to the activities page of The Striped Umbrella Web site.

FIGURE 5

Viewing the activities page with new Flash buttons added

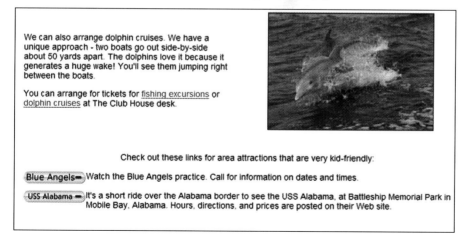

Edit a Flash button

1. Click the **Blue Angels Flash button**, then click **Edit** in the Property inspector.

2. Change the Font to **Arial**, then click **OK**.

3. Repeat Steps 1 and 2 to change the font on the USS Alabama button.

4. Click the **Refresh button** 🅲 on the Files panel to view the two new Flash button files, as shown in Figure 6.

   To work properly, the Flash buttons should be saved in the root folder.

5. Save your work, then close the activities page.

You changed the font of the two Flash buttons to Arial.

FIGURE 6
Viewing the two Flash button files in the Files panel

Two Flash button files

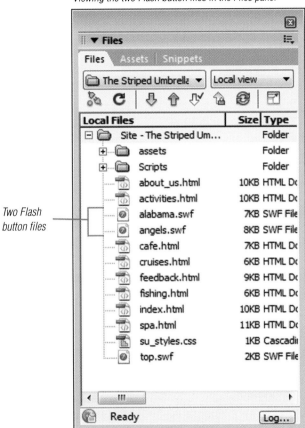

Adding Media Objects

FIGURE 7

Flash movie placeholder on the cafe page

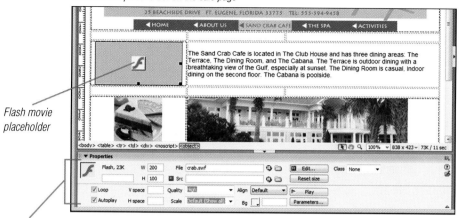

Flash movie placeholder

Properties of selected Flash movie

FIGURE 8

Flash movie playing in Dreamweaver

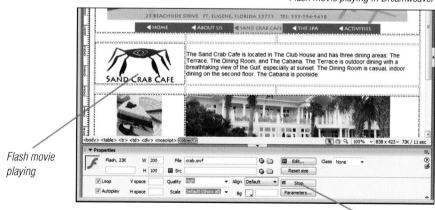

Flash movie playing

Click to stop movie

Insert Flash movies

1. Open the cafe page in The Striped Umbrella Web site.

2. Select the **cafe logo** in the top-left corner of the page, then click **[Delete]** (Win) or **[delete]** (Mac).

3. Click the **Media button list arrow** on the Common tab, then click **Flash**.

4. Navigate to where you store your Data Files, click **crab.swf**, click **OK** (Win) or **Choose** (Mac), save the movie in the root folder of the Web site, type **Crab logo animation** in the Object Tag Accessibility Attributes text box, then click **OK**.

   A Flash movie placeholder appears on the page, as shown in Figure 7.

   TIP   If you already have the Flash file in your root folder, you can drag and drop it from the Assets panel or Files panel instead of using the Insert bar or Insert menu.

You inserted a Flash movie on the cafe page of The Striped Umbrella Web site.

Play a Flash movie in Dreamweaver and in a browser

1. With the placeholder selected, click **Play** in the Property inspector to view the crab.swf movie, as shown in Figure 8, then click **Stop**.

2. Save your work, preview the page in your browser, compare your screen to Figure 9, then close your browser.

(continued)

TIP To play Flash movies in Dreamweaver and in your browser, you must have the Flash Player installed on your computer. If the Flash Player is not installed, you can download it at the Adobe Web site (*www.adobe.com*).

3. If the movie did not play in Internet Explorer, click **Tools** on the menu bar, click **Internet Options**, click the **Advanced tab**, then click the **Allow active content to run in files on my computer check box**.

   TIP If you are using a different browser or a version of Internet Explorer that is earlier than 6.0, look for a similar setting.

You played a Flash movie on the cafe page in The Striped Umbrella Web site in Dreamweaver and in your browser.

Modify a Flash file from Dreamweaver

1. If you have Adobe Flash installed on your computer, go to Step 2. If you do not have it installed, skip to Lesson 2 on page 10-12.

   Remember, if you don't have Flash installed on your computer, you can go to the Adobe Web site at *www.adobe.com* to download a trial version.

2. Use Explorer (Win) or Finder (Mac) to copy the file crab.fla from the Data Files folder to the root folder of The Striped Umbrella Web site.

   To use this source file, you must copy it to your root folder to be able to make changes to it.

3. Close Explorer (Win) or Finder (Mac), then return to Dreamweaver.

4. With the Flash placeholder selected, click **Edit** in the Property inspector.

(continued)

FIGURE 9
Flash movie playing in Internet Explorer

FIGURE 10
Editing the Flash movie and returning to Dreamweaver

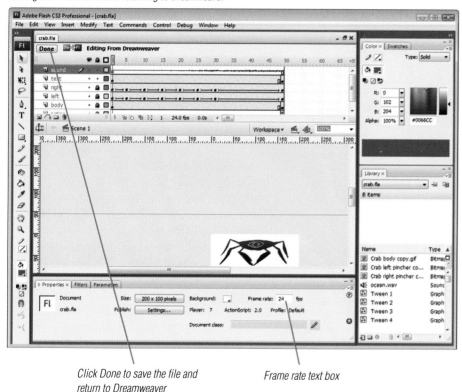

Click Done to save the file and
return to Dreamweaver

Frame rate text box

5. Click **crab.fla** in the striped_umbrella root
folder in the Locate Adobe Flash Document
File dialog box, then click **Open**.

The .swf file is a Flash player file and cannot
be edited. The .fla file is the editable Flash file.
You must have this source file to edit the
movie. After you select the .fla file, the file
opens in Flash.

TIP If you receive a warning that one or
more fonts used for this movie are not
available, click Choose Substitute, then
choose another font.

6. Click in the **Frame rate text box** in the
Property inspector, change the frame rate
from 12 to **24** fps (frames per second), as
shown in Figure 10, then click **Done**.

Flash automatically saves both the crab.fla
file and the crab.swf file, then closes.

7. Save and preview the page in your browser,
then close the browser and close the cafe
page.

Notice that the movie plays a little faster
now. You changed the frames per second to
a larger number, which had the effect of the
movie playing faster. The sound, however,
plays out after the animation stops. A sound
continues playing until it is finished
regardless of how long the Flash movie is.

*You used the Edit button in the Property inspector
to find and modify the Flash movie in Flash, then
returned to Dreamweaver.*

ADD ROLLOVER IMAGES

What You'll Do

 In this lesson, you will add two rollover images to the activities page of The Striped Umbrella Web site.

Understanding Rollover Images

A **rollover image** is an image that changes its appearance when the mouse pointer is placed over it in a browser. A rollover image actually consists of two images. The first image is the one that appears when the mouse pointer is not positioned over it, and the second image is the one that appears when the mouse pointer is positioned over it. Rollover images are often used to help create a feeling of action and excitement on a Web page. For instance, suppose you are creating a Web site that promotes a series of dance classes. You could create a rollover image using two images of a dancer in two different poses. When a viewer places the mouse pointer over the image of the dancer in the first pose, the image would change to show the dancer in a different pose, creating a feeling of movement and action.

QUICKTIP

You can also add a link to a rollover image, so that the image will change only when the image is clicked.

Adding Rollover Images

You add rollover images to a Web page using the Rollover Image command on the Images menu on the Common tab, shown in Figure 11. You specify both the original image and the rollover image in the Insert Rollover Image dialog box. The rollover image is the image that is swapped when the mouse rolls over the original image. To prevent one of the images from being resized during the rollover, both images should share the same height and width dimensions. Another way to create a rollover image, button, or navigation bar is to insert it as a Fireworks HTML file. The code for the rollover is inserted in the file when it is created and exported from

Fireworks. The Fireworks HTML command is also on the Images menu, as shown in Figure 11.

Rollover images can also be used to display an image associated with a text link. For instance, suppose you are creating a Web site for an upcoming election. You could create a Web page that contains a list of candidates for the election and add a rollover image for each candidate's name that would cause a photograph of the candidate to appear when the mouse is placed over his or her name. You can also use this effect to make appropriate images appear when you point to different menu options. For instance, Figure 12 shows the North Arkansas College Web site, which uses rollover images to highlight each menu option on its home page. When a rollover image is inserted onto a page, Dreamweaver automatically adds two behaviors; a Swap Image behavior and a Swap Image Restore behavior. A **Swap Image behavior** is JavaScript code that directs the browser to display a different image when the mouse is rolled over an image on the page. A **Swap Image Restore** behavior restores the swapped image back to the original image.

FIGURE 11

Images menu on the Insert bar

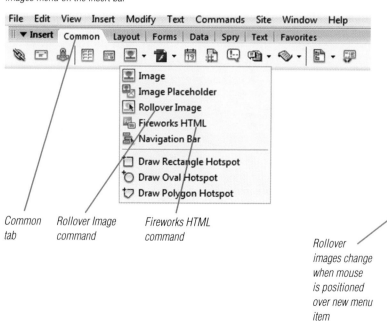

Common tab

Rollover Image command

Fireworks HTML command

FIGURE 12

North Arkansas College Website with rollover image

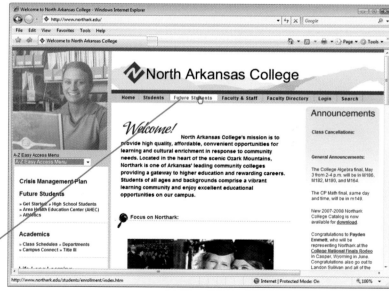

Rollover images change when mouse is positioned over new menu item

North Arkansas College Web site used with permission from North Arkansas College – *www.northark.edu*

Add a rollover image

1. Open the activities page of The Striped Umbrella Web site.

2. Scroll down to find the image of the two dolphins, then delete it.

3. Click the **Images list arrow** on the Common tab, then click **Rollover Image**.

4. Type **dolphins** in the Image name text box.

5. Click **Browse** next to the Original image: text box, browse to where you store your Data Files, then click **one_dolphin.jpg**.

6. Click **Browse** next to the Rollover image text box, then select the **two_dolphins.jpg** file from where you store your Data Files for the Rollover image text box.

7. Type **Dolphins riding the surf** in the Alternate text: text box, compare your screen to Figure 13, then click **OK**.

8. Add a 1-pixel border to the image, save your work, preview the page in your browser, then compare your screen to Figure 14.

   When you point to the image, the one dolphin image is "swapped" with the two-dolphin image.

   (continued)

FIGURE 13
Browsing to find the source files for the rollover image

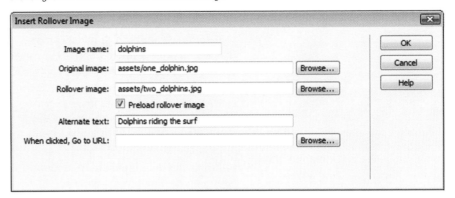

FIGURE 14
Viewing the rollover image in the browser

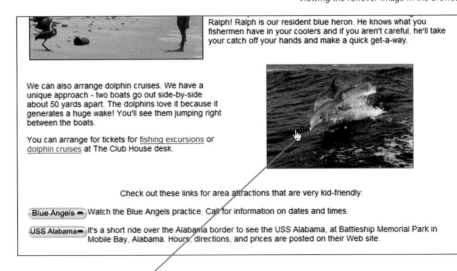

Image is swapped when mouse rolls over it

Adding Media Objects

FIGURE 15

Swap behavior code for rollover image

```
     Beware, though, of Ralph! Ralph is our resident blue heron. He knows what you fishermen have in
     your coolers and if you aren't careful, he'll take your catch off your hands and make a quick
     get-a-way.</span></td>
82     </tr>
83     <tr>
84     <td colspan="2"><p class="body_text">We can also arrange dolphin cruises. We have a unique
     approach - two boats go out side-by-side about 50 yards apart. The dolphins love it because it
     generates a huge wake! You'll see them jumping right between the boats. </p>
85     <p class="body_text">You can arrange for tickets for <a href="fishing.html">fishing excursions
     </a> or <a href="cruises.html">dolphin cruises</a> at The Club House desk.</p></td>
86     <td align="center"><a href="#" onmouseout="MM_swapImgRestore()" onmouseover=
     "MM_swapImage('dolphins','','assets/two_dolphins.jpg',1)"><img src="assets/one_dolphin.jpg" alt=
     "Dolphins riding the surf" name="dolphins" width="252" height="180" border="1" id="dolphins" /></a>
          </div></td>
87     </tr>
```

Code for
rollover
image

9. Close the browser.

10. Switch to Code view, then locate the code for the swap image behavior, as shown in Figure 15.

The code directs the browser to display the image with one dolphin "onmouseout"— when the mouse is not over the image. It directs the browser to display the image with two dolphins "onmouseover"—when the mouse is over the image.

> TIP If your code is selected in Code view, that means the image is selected in Design view.

11. Return to Design view.

You replaced an image with a rollover image on the activities page of The Striped Umbrella Web site.

ADD
BEHAVIORS

What You'll Do

 In this lesson, you will add an action that plays a sound effect to the activities page of The Striped Umbrella Web site. You will then change the event for that action.

Adding Interactive Elements

You can make your Web pages come alive by adding interactive elements such as sounds to them. For instance, if you are creating a Web page about your favorite animals, you could attach the sound of a dog barking to a photograph of a dog so that the barking sound would play when the viewer clicks the photograph. You can add sound and other multimedia actions to elements by attaching behaviors to them. **Behaviors** are sets of instructions that you can attach to page elements that tell the page element to respond in a specific way when an event occurs, such as when the mouse pointer is positioned over the element. When you attach a behavior to an element, JavaScript code for the behavior is automatically generated and inserted into the code for your page.

Using the Behaviors Panel

You can use the Behaviors panel located in the Tag panel group to insert a variety of JavaScript-based behaviors on a page. For instance, using the Behaviors panel, you can automate tasks, respond to visitor selections and mouse movements with pop-up menus, add sounds, create games, go to a different URL, or add automatic dynamic effects to a Web page. To insert a behavior, click the Add behavior button on the Behaviors panel to open the Actions menu, as shown in Figure 16, then click a behavior from the menu.

Inserting Sound Effects

Sound effects can add a new dimension to any Web site. You can use sounds to enhance the effect of positioning the mouse on a rollover image, clicking a link, or even loading or closing a page. By adding sounds, you can make your pages cheep, chirp, click, or squawk.

To apply a sound effect, select the link or object to which you want the sound effect added, and then select the Play

Sound behavior located in the Actions menu of the Behaviors panel. Sound effects should be used very sparingly, and only if they add to the overall good design for the page. Sound effects that loop, or repeat continuously, may be annoying to viewers.

Understanding Actions and Events

Actions are triggered by events. For instance, if you want your viewer to hear a sound when an image is clicked, you would attach the Play Sound action using the onClick event to trigger the action. Other examples of events are onMouseOver and onLoad. The onMouseOver event will trigger an action when the mouse is placed over an object. The onLoad event will trigger an action when the page is first loaded in the browser window.

Using the Spry Framework

Some of the behaviors that can be added to Web pages use a JavaScript library called the **Spry framework for AJAX**.

Asynchronous JavaScript and XML (AJAX) is a method for developing interactive Web pages that respond quickly to user input, such as a map. In the library, you will find **spry widgets**, which are prebuilt components for adding interaction to pages; and **spry effects**, which are screen effects such as fading and enlarging page elements. When a spry effect is added to a page element, a SpryAssets folder is automatically added to the root folder with the supporting files inside the folder.

FIGURE 16

Behaviors panel with the Actions menu displayed

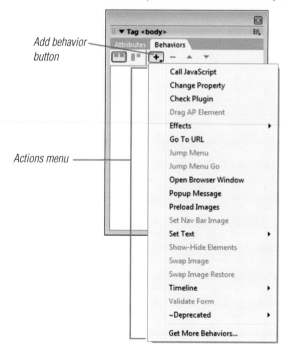

Add behavior button

Actions menu

Add a behavior

1. Open the file **dw10_1.html**, then save it in the root folder as **wildlife_message.html**. Do not update links.

2. Select the **fishing image** on the activities page, click **Window** on the menu bar, then click **Behaviors** to open the Behaviors panel.

3. Click the **Add behavior button** [+] on the Behaviors panel toolbar to open the Actions menu, as shown in Figure 17, then click **Open Browser Window** to open the Open Browser Window dialog box.

4. Click **Browse** next to the URL to display: text box, navigate to the root folder, then double-click **wildlife_message.html**.

5. Type **300** in the Window width: text box, type **300** in the Window height: text box, type **message** in the Window name: text box, compare your screen to Figure 18, then click **OK**.

6. Save your work, preview the page in your browser, test the Open Browser Window effect by clicking the fishing image, as shown in Figure 19, then close both browser windows.

You added an Open Browser Window effect to an image on the activities page of The Striped Umbrella Web site.

FIGURE 17

Adding the Open Browser Window behavior to the fishing image

Click Open Browser Window

In Step 2, select this image

FIGURE 18

Setting Open Browser Window options

FIGURE 19

Viewing the wildlife message in the browser

FIGURE 20

Viewing the edited window size for the behavior

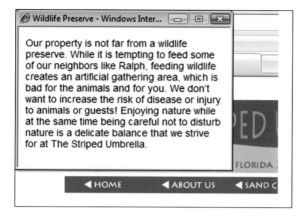

FIGURE 21

Changing the event

onMouseOver action

Edit a behavior

1. Right-click (Win) or [control]-click (Mac) the **right column** of the Open Browser Window action in the Behaviors panel, then click **Edit Behavior.**

    The Open Browser Window dialog box opens.

2. Change the window height to **200**, save your changes, preview the page in your browser, then click the **fishing image**.

    The browser window with the wildlife message is shorter in height, as shown in Figure 20.

3. Close the browser windows.

4. Click the **left column** of the Open Browser Window action in the Behaviors panel to display the events list arrow, click the **arrow**, then click **onMouseOver**, as shown in Figure 21.

    This will change the event that triggers the action from clicking the image to simply placing the mouse over the image.

5. Save your work, open the page in the browser, then move the mouse over the fishing image.

    Now, simply placing the mouse over the image triggers the Open Browser Window event.

6. Close the browser windows, close the Behaviors panel, then close the wildlife_ message page. Leave the activities page open.

You edited the behavior in the Behaviors panel.

ADD FLASH
VIDEO

What You'll Do

In this lesson, you will insert a Flash video on the activities page.

Insert Flash Video

Another option you have to present rich media content on your Web pages is to insert video files. Although you can use several different formats for video, one of the most popular formats is the Flash video file. **Flash video files** are files that include both video and audio and have an .flv file extension. Like the Flash .swf file, the Flash video file is played through the Flash Player. Since most viewers have the Flash Player installed on their computers, it is a nice format to use without fear of losing viewers. You have two choices for delivering your Flash movie on your Web site: using a progressive video download or a streaming video download. A **progres-sive video download** will download the video to the viewer's computer, then allow the video to play before it has completely downloaded. It will finish the download as the video plays, but the viewer will not notice that this is taking place. A **streaming video download** is very similar to a progressive download, except streaming video downloads use buffers to gather the content as it is downloading to ensure a smoother playback. Flash video is not the only video format that can be viewed on a Web page. You can also link or embed **AVI (Audio Visual Interleave)**, the Microsoft standard for digital video, or **MPEG (Motion Picture Experts Group)** files.

Figure 22 is a page on the GAP Web site that features a funny promotional video. It also includes a link to instructions for viewers to create their own holiday video clip and download it to the GAP Web site for their friends and family to enjoy. This is an effective way of engaging viewers to keep them interested in returning to the Web site. Video used sparingly can be very effective and add much interest to a site.

FIGURE 22
Viewing video content

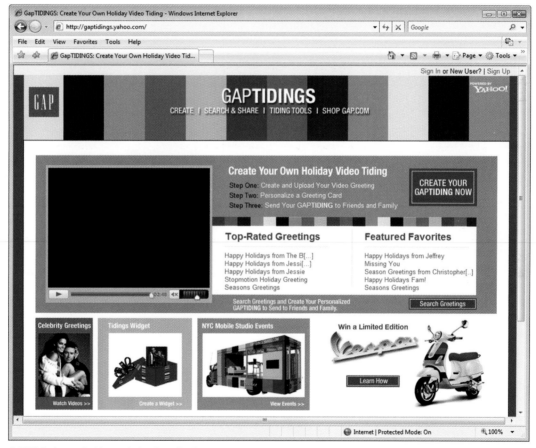

GAP Web site used with permission from Gap Inc. - www.gap.com

Add Flash video

1. Using Windows Explorer (Win) or Finder (Mac), copy the file **umbrella_anchor_ movie.flv** from where you store your Data Files, then paste it into your Striped Umbrella root folder.

2. Click to place the insertion point in the cell under the two Flash buttons.

3. Click the **Media list arrow**, then click **Flash Video**.

4. Verify that the Video type: list menu shows Progressive Download Video as the type for the video.

5. Click the **Browse button** next to the URL: text box, browse to your root folder, then select **umbrella_anchor_movie.flv**.

6. Choose the **Halo Skin 1 (min width: 180) option** in the Skin: menu if (necessary).

7. Type **180** in the W: text box, **180** in the H: text box, verify that the Constrain check box is checked, compare your screen to Figure 23, then click **OK**.

   A placeholder for the movie is displayed in the cell. You will only be able to view the video in the browser.

8. Type **Stop by The Club House to pick up your complimentary Umbrella Anchor before you head to the beach!** in the cell next to the cell with the Flash video, then apply the body_text style.

(continued)

FIGURE 23
The Insert Flash Video settings for the umbrella anchor movie

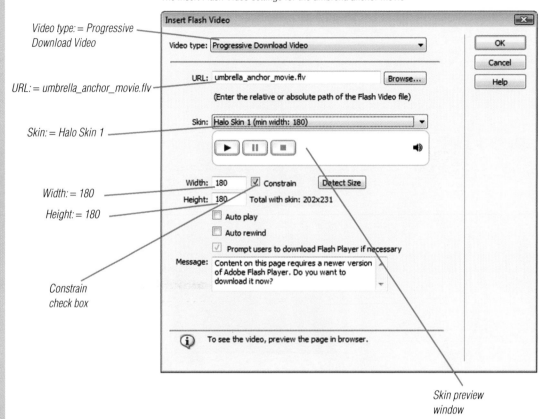

Video type: = Progressive Download Video

URL: = umbrella_anchor_movie.flv

Skin: = Halo Skin 1

Width: = 180

Height: = 180

Constrain check box

Skin preview window

FIGURE 24

Viewing the video in the browser

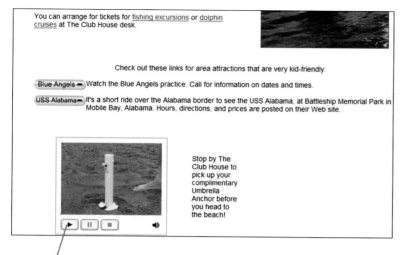

Play button on skin

9. Center the video placeholder in the cell, save your work, preview the page in the browser, then compare your screen to Figure 24.

The skin is the bar at the bottom of the video with the control buttons. You click the Play button ▶ to play the movie and the Stop button ■ to stop the movie.

10. Play the movie, then close the browser window.

11. Notice the two additional files that have been added to the Files panel: Halo_Skin_1.swf and FLVPlayer_Progressive.swf, as shown in Figure 25.

These two files provide the instructions for the skin to display and function and for the movie to start playing in the browser before it is completely downloaded

12. Close all open pages.

You inserted a Flash video on the page, then viewed the additional files added to the Web site as supporting files by Dreamweaver.

FIGURE 25

Supporting video files added to the Web site

FLVPlayer_Progressive.swf

Halo_Skin_1.swf

umbrella_anchor_movie.flv

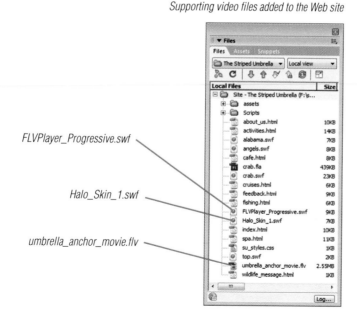

Add and modify Flash objects.

1. Open the blooms & bulbs Web site, then open the classes page.
2. Click after the paragraph about Master Gardeners, then insert a Flash button with the following settings: Style: **Glass-Purple**; Button Text: **Master Gardeners**; Font: **Comic Sans MS**; Size: **11** pixels; Link: **http://aggie-horticulture.tamu.edu/ mastergd/becomingMG.html**; Target: **_blank**; Save as: **m_gardeners.swf**, then click OK.
3. Type **Link to Texas Master Gardeners** in the Flash Accessibility Attributes dialog box.
4. Set the alignment to **Top** and add H space of **10**.
5. Insert the **garden_quote.swf** Flash movie located where you store your Data Files directly below the paragraph about registration, then type **Garden quote** in the Object Tag Accessibility Attributes dialog box.
6. Play the garden_quote.swf movie in Dreamweaver, save your work, preview the page in your browser, compare your screen to Figure 26, then close your browser.
7. Close the classes page.

Add rollover images.

1. Open the tips page, then delete the Garden Tips graphic text at the top of the page.

2. Verify that your insertion point is still where you just deleted the garden tips graphic.
3. Insert a rollover image from where you store your Data Files by clicking Insert on the menu bar, pointing to **Image Objects**, then clicking **Rollover Image**. Type **rollover** as the name, insert **garden_tips2.jpg** as the original image, **garden_tips2.jpg** from where you store your Data files, as the rollover image, type **Garden tips with flower** as the alternate text, then click OK.

4. Save your work, preview the page in the browser to test the rollover, then close the tips page.

Add behaviors.

1. Open the water_plants page.
2. Select the water plants image, then use the Behaviors panel to add the **Appear/Fade effect** that will fade from **100% to 50%**, then select the Toggle check box.

FIGURE 26
Completed Skills Review 1

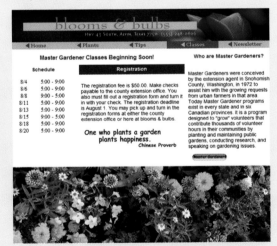

Adding Media Objects

3. Edit the behavior to use the **onMouseOver** action. (*Hint*: Dreamweaver will add a new SpryAssets folder in the Web site with the SpryEffects.js supporting file.)

4. Save your work, then preview the page in the browser. (*Hint*: Place the mouse over the image to test the behavior.)

5. Close the browser, then close the water_plants page.

Add Flash video.

1. Open the plants page, then add a new row to the bottom of the page.

2. Insert the hanging_baskets.flv file into the new row using the following settings: Video Type: **Progressive Download**, URL: **hanging_baskets.flv,** Skin: **Clear Skin 1**, Width: **150**, Height: **150**. (*Hint:* Remember to copy the file to your root folder first.)

3. Insert a line break after the video place-holder, type **Join us this Saturday for a class on hanging baskets.**, then apply the subheading style to the sentence and set the cell alignment to **center**.

4. Save your work, preview the page and play the movie in the browser, then compare your screen to Figure 27.

5. Close the browser, then close all open pages.

FIGURE 27
Completed Skills Review

Moonlight White Petunia (Mini-Spreading)

Pretty petunias blanket your beds with lush green leaves and bright blooms in assorted colors. Shown is the Moonlight White Petunia (Mini-Spreading). This variety is fast-growing and produces spectacular blooms. Cut them back in July for blooms that will last into the fall. Full sun to partial shade. Great for border plants or hanging baskets.

Verbena is one of our all-time favorites. The variety shown is Blue Silver. Verbena grows rapidly and is a good choice for butterfly gardens. The plants can spread up to two feet wide, so it makes excellent ground cover. Plant in full sun. Heat resistant. Beautiful also in rock gardens. We have several other varieties equally as beautiful.

Silver Blue Verbena

Golden Dream Lantana

Dramatic masses of Lantana display summer color for your beds or containers. The variety shown is Golden Dream. Blooms late spring through early fall. This variety produces outstanding color. Plant in full sun with well-drained soil. We carry tall, dwarf, and trailing varieties. You can also overwinter with cuttings.

Stop by to see us soon. We will be happy to help you with your selections. We have many annuals, perennials, and water plants that have just arrived.

Join us this Saturday for a class on hanging baskets.

In this exercise, you will continue your work on the TripSmart Web site. The owner of TripSmart would like you to work on the amazon page. He gives you a Flash file that shows the route of the ship that will take visitors down the Amazon river.

1. Open the TripSmart Web site, then open the amazon page.
2. Place the insertion point at the end of the second paragraph, then split that cell into two rows.
3. Insert the **amazon_map.swf** file in the new row, then add the text **Amazon map animation** in the Object Tag Accessibly Attributes dialog box.
4. Center the Flash object in the cell, then save the file.
5. Preview the amazon page in the browser.
6. Close the browser, then close the amazon page.
7. Open the file dw10_2.html from where you store your Data Files, then save it in the TripSmart root folder as amazon_trip.html.

8. Attach the **tripsmart_styles.css** file to the page, then apply the **bullets style** to the text.
9. Save and close the page.
10. Open the amazon page, then attach a behavior to the water lily image that will open a new browser window when the mouse rolls over it that displays the amazon_trip.html file. Use **300** for the window width and **100** for the window height. Name the window **soldout**.
11. Save your work, then preview the page in the browser to test the behavior, as shown in Figure 28.
12. Close the browser, then close all open pages.

FIGURE 28
Sample Project Builder 1

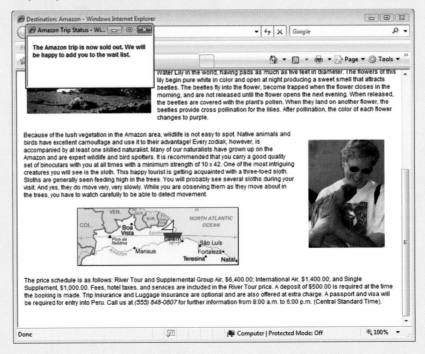

Adding Media Objects

Use Figures 29 and 30 as a guide to continue your work on Carolyne's Creations. You have decided to add a video demonstrating how to sugar flowers for decoration.

1. Open the Carolyne's Creations Web site.
2. Open the index page.
3. Select the logo in the bottom-right corner of the page, then attach a behavior and an action of your choice to it.
4. Save and close the index page, then open the adults page.
5. Insert a new row at the bottom of the page, then insert a table in the new row with **one** row and **three** columns.
6. Set each column width to **fixed widths**, then insert the Flash video **sugared_flowers.flv** in the center cell, using settings of your choice for the video.
7. Refer to the text in Figure 30 to add short descriptive text on each side of the video, then format the text with the **sub_head style**.
8. Make any other adjustments you wish, save your page, then preview the page in the browser.
9. Close the browser, then close all open pages.

FIGURE 29 AND 30

Completed Project Builder 2

Henry Fisher is an astronomer. He would like to design a Web site about planets, like the example shown in Figure 31. He would like his Web site to incorporate Flash elements, rollovers, and video and would like to use Dreamweaver to build his site.

1. Connect to the Internet and go to *www.nasa.gov.*
2. Which elements in the site are Flash objects?
3. Which objects in the site are made with rollover images?
4. How has adding the Flash effects improved the appearance of this site?
5. Go through the site and locate some Flash video.
6. Create a sketch of Henry's site that contains at least five pages. Indicate in your sketch what media elements you plan to insert in the site, including where you would add Flash objects, rollover images, and video.

FIGURE 31
Design Project

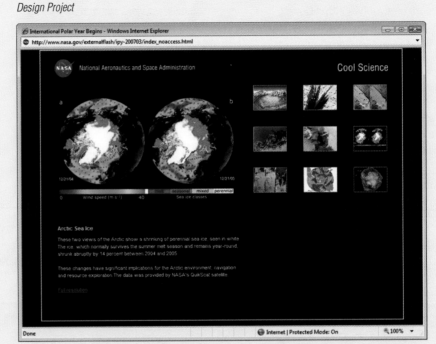

NASA Web site — *www.nasa.gov*

In this assignment, you will continue to work on the group Web site that you started in Chapter 1. There will be no Data Files supplied. You are building this Web site from chapter to chapter, so you must do each Portfolio Project assignment in each chapter to complete your Web site.

You will continue building your Web site by designing and completing a page that contains rich media content or by adding media content to existing pages. After completing your Web site, be sure to run appropriate reports to test the site.

1. Evaluate your storyboard, then choose a page, or series of pages, to develop in which you will include Flash objects as well as other media content, such as rollover images, video, and behaviors.
2. Plan the content for your new page so that the layout works well with both the new and old pages in your site. Sketch a plan for the media content you wish to add, showing which media elements you will use and where you will place them.

3. Create the Flash buttons and Flash text you identified in your sketch, choosing appropriate formatting.
4. Add the rollover images to the page.
5. Add a video, if possible, to the page.
6. Run a report on your new page(s) to ensure that all links work correctly.

7. Preview the new page (or pages) in your browser and test all links. Evaluate your pages for content and layout. Use the checklist in Figure 32 to make sure your Web site is complete.
8. Make any modifications that are necessary to improve the page.

FIGURE 32
Portfolio Project checklist

Web Site Checklist
1. Do all Flash buttons load correctly?
2. Do all Flash movies play properly in your browser?
3. Do all links work?
4. Do all sounds play correctly?
5. Are there any missing images or links on the pages?
6. Do all pages have a title?
7. Do all rollover images display properly?

chapter

11

CREATING AND
USING TEMPLATES

1. Create templates with editable regions

2. Use templates to create pages

3. Use templates to update a site

4. Use advanced template options

11

CREATING AND
USING TEMPLATES

Introduction

When you create a Web site, it's important to make sure that each page has a unified look so that viewers know they are in your site no matter what page they are viewing. For instance, you should make sure that common elements such as the navigation bar and company banner appear in the same place on every page and that every page has the same background color. One way to make sure that every page in your site has a consistent appearance is through the use of templates. A **template** is a special kind of page that contains both **locked regions**, which are areas on the page that cannot be modified by users of the template, as well as other types of regions that users can change or edit. For instance, an **optional region** is an area in the template that users can choose to show or hide, and an **editable region** is an area where users can add or change content.

Using templates not only ensures a consistent appearance throughout a Web site, but also saves considerable development time. Templates are especially helpful if different people will be creating pages in your site. In this chapter, you will create a template from an existing page in The Striped Umbrella Web site and define editable regions in it.

Understanding How to Use Templates

The ideal process for using templates is for one person (the template author) to create a template that has locked regions containing the design elements common to every page in the site, as well as regions where content can be added or changed. Once the template is fully developed, other team members can use it to create each page of the site, adding appropriate content to the editable regions of each page. If the template author makes changes to the template, all pages to which the template is attached can be automatically updated to reflect those changes.

Tools You'll Use

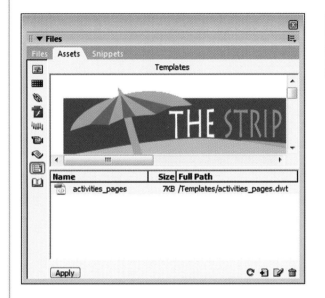

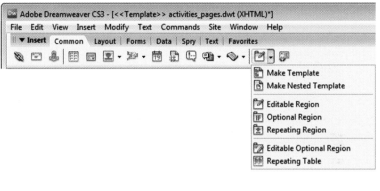

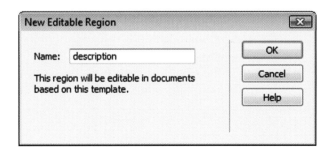

CREATE TEMPLATES WITH
EDITABLE REGIONS

What You'll Do

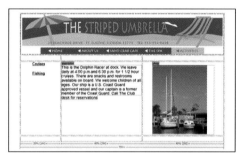

In this lesson, you will create a template based on the cruises page of The Striped Umbrella Web site. You will then define editable regions in the template, rearrange some of the cell content, change the cell alignment of several cells, and add two Flash buttons to link to the cruises and fishing pages. Finally, you will delete the template page title.

Creating a Template from an Existing Page

If you have already created and designed a page that you think looks great, and you want to use the layout and design for other pages in your site, you can save the page as a template using the Save as Template command. Templates are saved with a .dwt extension and are stored in the Templates folder in the root folder of your Web site. If your site does not have a Templates folder, one will automatically be created for you the first time you save a template. To view a list of templates in your site, open the Templates folder in the Files panel. To preview a template before opening it, open the Assets panel, click the Templates button on the Assets panel toolbar, and then click a template in the list. The template appears in the preview window above the templates list, as shown in Figure 1.

Defining Editable Regions

By default, when you save a template, all content on the page will be locked, which

means that no one else will be able to add content or modify any part of the template to create new pages. If your template is going to be used effectively, you need to have at least one editable region in it so that other users can add content. You can specify a name for the region using the New Editable Region dialog box. Editable regions are outlined in blue on the template page, and the names of the editable regions appear in blue shaded boxes, as shown in Figure 2.

Defining Optional Regions

In addition to editable regions, you can also add optional regions to a template. An optional region is an area in a template that users can choose to either show or hide. For instance, you could place a graphic in an optional region, so that users of the template can decide whether or not to show it on the page they are creating. An optional region's visibility is controlled by the conditional statement **if**. You can specify a page element as an optional region using the New Optional Region dialog box. You can name the region and specify whether to show or hide it by default. The Editable and Optional Region dialog boxes are both accessed by clicking the Templates list arrow on the Common tab of the Insert bar.

Defining Editable Optional Regions

If you want to give users the ability to show or hide a page element, as well as make modifications to it, then you can define the element as an **editable optional region**. For instance, you might want to make an advertisement an editable optional region so that users of the template could change its text and specify whether to show or hide it. Using the New Optional Region dialog box, you can name the region and specify whether to show or hide it by default.

FIGURE 1
Template in the assets panel

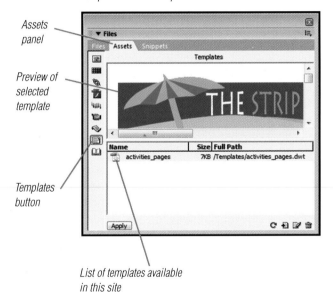

Assets panel

Preview of selected template

Templates button

List of templates available in this site

FIGURE 2
Template with locked and editable regions

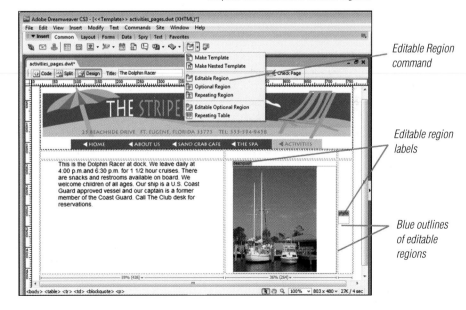

Editable Region command

Editable region labels

Blue outlines of editable regions

Create a template from an existing page

1. Open the cruises page.

2. Click **File** on the menu bar, then click **Save as Template** to open the Save As Template dialog box.

3. Type **activities_pages** in the Save as text box, compare your screen to Figure 3, click **Save**, update the links, then click the **Refresh button** 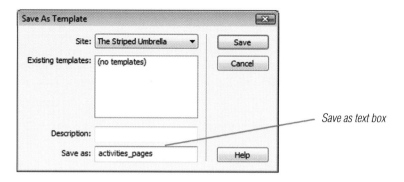 on the Files panel toolbar.

   Notice that the Templates folder, which contains the activities_pages template, appears in the Files panel.

4. Display the Assets panel, click the **Templates button** to view the list of templates in the site, click the **activities_pages template** in the list (if necessary), then compare your Assets panel to Figure 4.

   TIP To create a template from scratch, click File on the menu bar, click New to open the New Document dialog box, click Blank Template, click the type of template you want to create in the Template Type list, then click Create.

You created a template from the cruises page of The Striped Umbrella Web site.

FIGURE 3
Save As Template dialog box

Save as text box

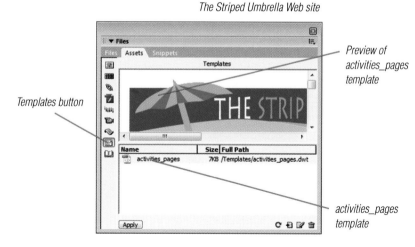

Preview of activities_pages template

Templates button

activities_pages template

FIGURE 5
New Editable Region dialog box

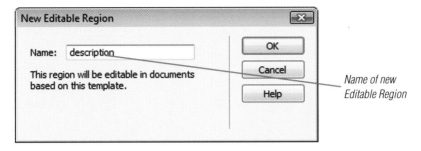

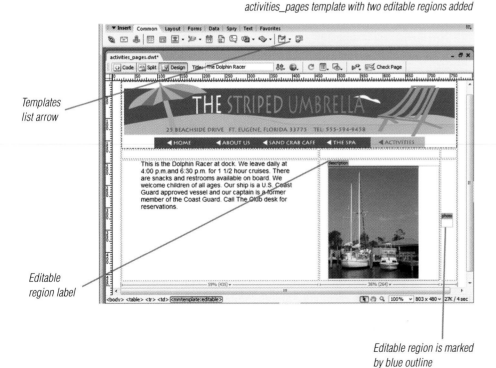

*Name of new
Editable Region*

FIGURE 6
activities_pages template with two editable regions added

*Templates
list arrow*

*Editable
region label*

*Editable region is marked
by blue outline*

Create an editable region

1. Click to place the insertion point in the cell with the boat graphic, then click the **<td> tag** in the tag selector to select all of the content in that cell.

2. Click the **Common tab** on the Insert bar.

3. Click the **Templates list arrow** on the Common tab, then click **Editable Region** to open the New Editable Region dialog box.

   TIP You can also press [Ctrl][Alt][V] (Win) or ⌘[option][V] (Mac) to open the New Editable Region dialog box.

4. Type **description** in the Name text box, as shown in Figure 5, click **OK**, then press [→] to deselect the graphic.

   A blue shaded box containing "description" appears above the picture of the boat.

5. Press **[Tab]**, then repeat Steps 3 and 4 to create an editable region in the next empty cell to the right of the boat, name it **photo**, press **[Delete]** (Win) or **[delete]** (Mac) to remove the word "Photo" below the photo label, then compare your screen to Figure 6.

   TIP To remove an editable region from a template, select the editable region in the document window, click Modify on the menu bar, point to Templates, then click Remove Template Markup.

You created two editable regions in the activities_pages template.

Modify a template

1. Select the **boats image**, then drag it into the photo editable area.

   You must drop the image inside the blue rectangle for it to be included in the editable area.

2. Select the paragraph of **text**, then drag it into the description editable area.

3. Place the insertion point in the empty cell to the left of the cell with the description and set the column width to **20%**.

4. Repeat Step 3 to set the widths of the two cells containing content to **40%** each, then compare your screen to Figure 7.

   > TIP You may have to select the cell tag to be able to enter the width setting. Make sure no other cells have a width setting. If you find any, delete them.

5. Select the cell with the boats image, then change the horizontal alignment (Horz) to **Center** and the vertical alignment (Vert) for the cell to **Top**.

6. Select the cell with the description editable region, then change the horizontal alignment (Horz) to **Left**.

(continued)

FIGURE 7
Editing the activities_pages template

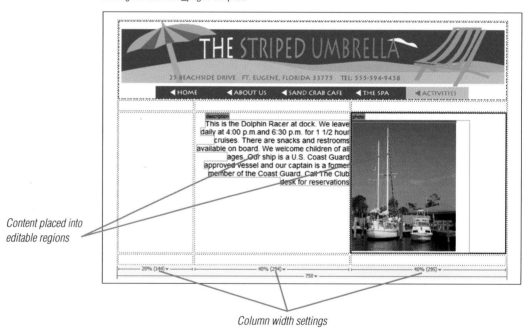

Content placed into editable regions

Column width settings

Creating and Using Templates

FIGURE 8

Links added to the activities_pages template

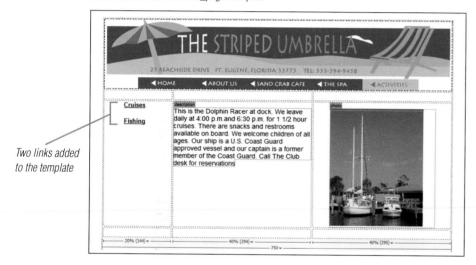

Two links added
to the template

7. Place the insertion point in the cell to the left of the cell with the description editable region, then type **Cruises**.

8. Press **[Enter]** (Win) or **[return]** (Mac), type **Fishing**, then apply the **bullets style** to the two words.

9. Link the **Cruises text** to cruises.html, then link the **Fishing text** to fishing.html.

   Don't be concerned with the leading periods before the link in the Src text box. They are simply indicating that the template file is in a different folder from the CSS file.

10. Delete the page title from the Title text box on the Document window toolbar, click **File** on the menu bar, click **Save as Template**, click **Save**, click **Yes** to overwrite the existing template, then compare your screen to Figure 8.

11. Close the activities_pages template.

You rearranged some of the content on the activities_pages template, changed the alignment of some cells, then added links to the cruises and fishing pages. Last, you deleted the page title from the template.

USE TEMPLATES
TO CREATE PAGES

What You'll Do

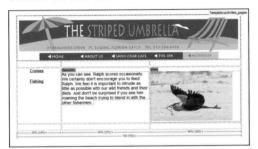

In this lesson, you will use the activities_pages template to create a new page in The Striped Umbrella Web site. You will add content to the editable regions, then apply the template to two existing pages in the Web site. You will also create a new page based on the template.

Creating Pages with Templates

There are many advantages to using a template to create a page. First, it saves a lot of time, because part of the content and format of your page is already set. Second, it ensures that the page you create matches the look and format of other pages in the site. You can create a page based on a template using many different methods. One way is to click File on the menu bar, click New to open the New Document dialog box, click Page from Template, select the template you want to use, and then click Create. Templates can be used only in the Web site that contains them.

QUICKTIP

You can also create a new page based on a template by right-clicking (Win) or [control]-clicking (Mac) a template in the Assets panel, and then clicking New from Template.

Modifying Editable Regions

When you create a new page that is based on a template, certain areas of the new page will be locked. You can tell which areas are locked by the appearance of the mouse pointer. When positioned over a locked region, the mouse pointer will appear in the shape of a circle with a line cutting through it, as shown in Figure 9. Editable regions are outlined in blue and marked with a blue, shaded label.

Editing, deleting, or adding content in editable regions of a template-based page works just like it does on any other page. Simply select the element you want to modify and make your changes, or click in the editable region and insert the new content.

Creating Links in Template-Based Pages

When you add a link to a page that is based on a template, it is important to use document-relative links; otherwise, they will not work. The path to a link actually goes from the template file (not from the template-based page) to the linked page. To ensure that all of your links are document-relative, select the page element to which you want to add a link, and then drag the Point to File icon from the Property inspector to the page you want to link to in the Files panel, as shown in Figure 10.

FIGURE 9

Working with a template-based page

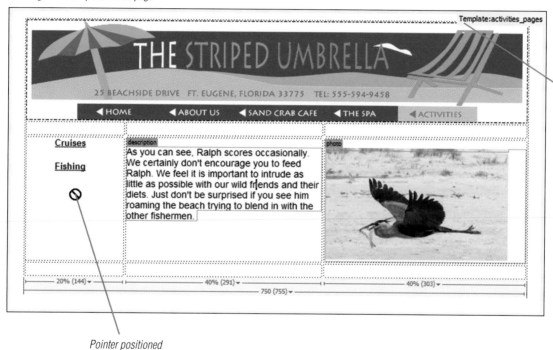

Template:activities_pages

Notation that this page is based on the activities_pages template

Pointer positioned over a locked region

Attaching a Template to an Existing Page

Sometimes you might need to apply a template to a page that you have already created. For example, suppose you create a page for your department in your company's Web site, and then your manager tells you that it must be based on the template created by the marketing department. Before you attach a template to an existing page, you should delete any elements from your page that also appear in the template. For instance, if both your page and the template have a company logo, you should delete the logo on your page. If you don't delete it, the logo will appear twice. Once you delete all the duplicate content on your page, attach the template by opening your page, selecting the template in the Assets panel, and clicking Apply in the Assets panel. When you do this, the Inconsistent Region Names dialog box opens, allowing you to specify in which regions of the template to place the document head and body content from your page.

QUICKTIP

You can also attach a template to an open page by dragging the template from the Assets panel to the Document window.

FIGURE 10
Using the Point to File icon to specify a document-relative link

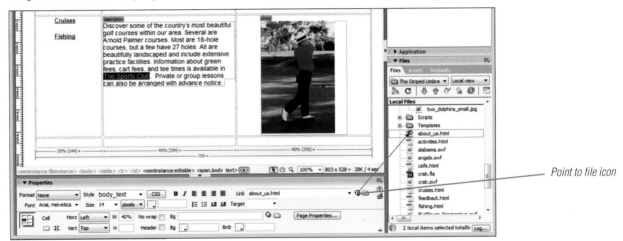

Point to file icon

FIGURE 11

New Document dialog box

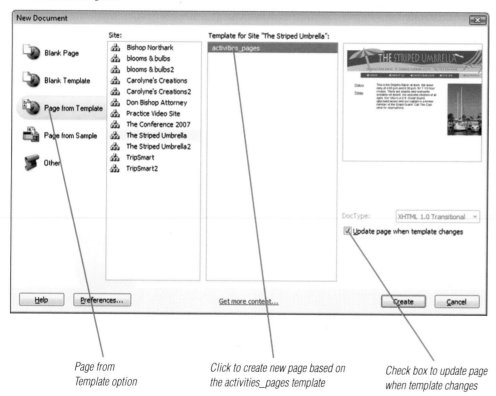

Page from
Template option

Click to create new page based on
the activities_pages template

Check box to update page
when template changes

1. Click **File** on the menu bar, click **New** to open the New Document dialog box, then click **Page from Template**.

2. Click **"The Striped Umbrella"** in the Site list box (if necessary), click **activities_pages** in the Template for Site "The Striped Umbrella" list box (if necessary), verify that the **Update page when template changes check box** is selected, compare your screen to Figure 11, then click **Create**.

   A new untitled page opens with the activities_pages template applied to it.

3. Click **File** on the menu bar, click **Save As** to open the Save As dialog box, type **golf.html** in the File name text box, then click **Save**.

   TIP Another way to create a new page based on a template is to open a new untitled page, click the Templates list arrow on the Insert bar, click Make Template to open the Save As Template dialog box, select a template in the Existing templates text box, then click Save.

You created a new page in The Striped Umbrella Web site that has the activities_pages template applied to it. You then saved this page as golf.html.

Modify editable regions in a template

1. Type **Area Golf Courses** in the Title text box.

2. Select the **boats image**, delete it, then insert **golfer.jpg** from where you store your Data Files in the photo editable region, adding **Golfer swinging a club** as the alternate text.

3. Place the insertion point in the description editable region, select and delete the existing text, then use the Import Word Document command to import **golf.doc** (Win).

   TIP If you are using a Macintosh, you'll need to copy and paste the text into Dreamweaver.

4. Select all of the new text, then apply the **body_text style** to it.

5. Compare your screen to Figure 12.

You deleted content from the editable region of a new golf page based on the activities_pages template. You then replaced the image in the photo editable region and imported text to replace the text in the description editable region.

Add links to template-based pages

1. Select the text "The Sports Club" in the paragraph, then link the file **about_us.html** to the selected text, as shown in Figure 13.

2. Save and close the golf.html page.

You used the Point to File icon to link a file to the selected text.

FIGURE 12
Golf page with revised content in editable regions

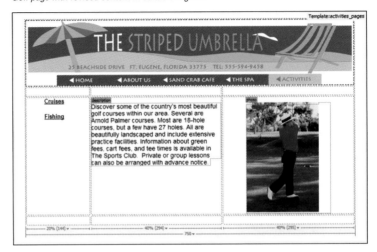

FIGURE 13
Linking to the about_us.html page

Select text
for link

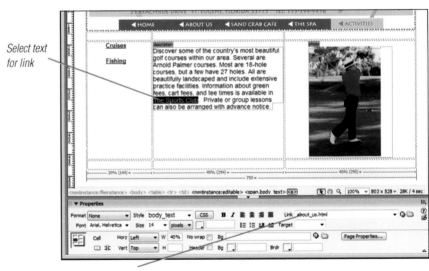

Link to about_us.html page

Creating and Using Templates

1. Open the fishing page.

2. Copy the paragraph of text on the right side of the page, then close the fishing page.

3. Create a new HTML page based on the activities_pages template, then save the page as **fishing.html**, overwriting the original fishing.html page.

4. Replace the paragraph in the template with the paragraph you copied from the fishing page, as shown in Figure 14.

5. Delete the boat image and replace it with the **heron_small.jpg** image by dragging it from the assets folder into the photo editable region, adding **Ralph and his "catch"** for the alternate text.

6. Title the page **Fishing at The Striped Umbrella**, save the file, compare your screen with Figure 14, then close the page.

7. Repeat Step 3 to create a new cruises page based on the activities_pages template. You will not have to replace any of the content because this is the page that was used for the template.

8. Enter **The Dolphin Racer** as the page title, then save and close the file.

You created a new HTML page based on a template and replaced text and images in the page. You then made an existing page into a template-based page.

FIGURE 14
New fishing page based on a template

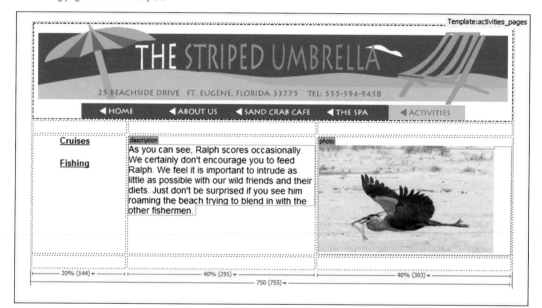

Template:activities_pages

THE STRIPED UMBRELLA

25 BEACHSIDE DRIVE FT. EUGENE, FLORIDA 33775   TEL: 555-594-9458

◀ HOME   ◀ ABOUT US   ◀ SAND CRAB CAFE   ◀ THE SPA   ◀ ACTIVITIES

Cruises

Fishing

description
As you can see, Ralph scores occasionally. We certainly don't encourage you to feed Ralph. We feel it is important to intrude as little as possible with our wild friends and their diets. Just don't be surprised if you see him roaming the beach trying to blend in with the other fishermen.

photo

20% (144) ▾   40% (291) ▾   40% (303) ▾
750 (755) ▾

USE TEMPLATES TO
UPDATE A SITE

What You'll Do

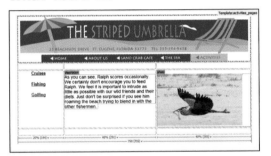

In this lesson, you will make a change to the activities_pages template, then update the site so that all pages based on the template reflect the change.

Making Changes to a Template

If you create a successful site that draws large numbers of faithful viewers, your site will probably enjoy a long life. However, like everything else, Web sites need to change with the times. Your company might decide to make new products or offer new services. After a relatively short time, a Web site can look dated, even with no changes in the company. When changes occur in your company, on a large or small scale, you will need to make changes to your Web site's appearance and functionality. If your Web site pages are based on a template or group of templates, you will have a much easier time making those changes.

You use the same skills to make changes to a template as you would when creating a template. Start by opening the template from the Files panel or Assets panel, then add, delete, or edit content as you would

Using Adobe templates

If you are a licensed Dreamweaver user, you can take advantage of the large collection of beautiful templates that Adobe creates for the exclusive use of its customers. The wide-ranging templates are a great starting point for many different types of Web sites—from weddings, to clubs, to professions, and even to special events. To preview and download the templates, go to *www.adobe.com* and type Dreamweaver templates in the Search text box. You can also find other Web sites that offer templates for downloading. Go to your favorite search engine and type templates in the Search text box. Some of these sites will have a fee for downloading a template.

on any non-template-based page. You can turn locked regions into editable regions using the New Editable Region command. To change an editable region back into a locked region, select the region, click Modify on the menu bar, point to Templates, and then click Remove Template Markup.

Updating All Pages Based on a Template

One of the greatest benefits of working with templates is that any change you make to a template can be made automatically to all nested templates and pages that are based on the template. When you save a template to which you have made modifications, the Update Template Files dialog box opens, asking if you want to update all the files in your site that are based on that template, as shown in Figure 15. When you click Update, the Update Pages dialog box opens and provides a summary of all the files that were updated.

FIGURE 15
Update Template Files dialog box

Files based on activities_pages template

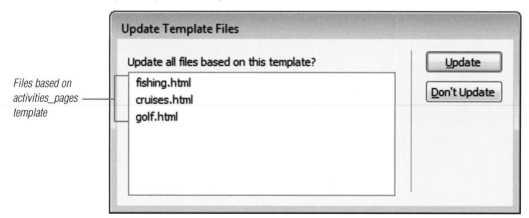

Make changes to a template

1. Open the activities_pages template.

2. Click the insertion point after the second link, then press **[Enter]** (Win) or **[return]** (Mac).

3. Create a third link using the word **Golfing**, link it to the golf page, apply the **bullets style**, then compare your screen to Figure 16.

4. Open the fishing page.

   The new link does not appear because you have not yet saved the template and updated the site.

5. Close the fishing page.

You opened the activities_pages template and added a new link.

FIGURE 16
activities_pages template with new link added

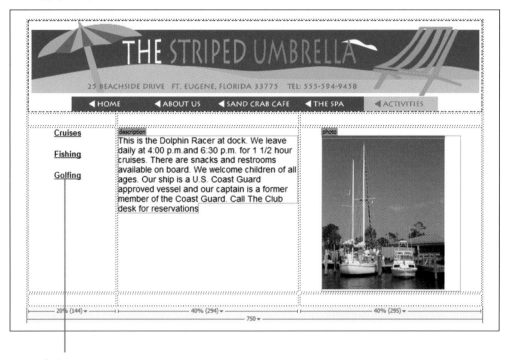

Golfing link

FIGURE 17
Update Template Files dialog box

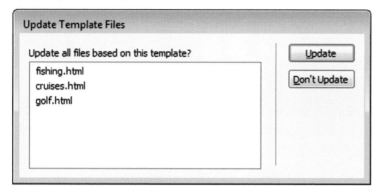

Update all template-based pages in a site

1. Return to the activities_pages template (if necessary), click **File** on the menu bar, then click **Save All**.

   The Update Template Files dialog box opens, as shown in Figure 17.

2. Click **Update** to open the Update Pages dialog box, then click **Close** after it has finishing updating the pages.

3. Open the fishing page, then compare your screen to Figure 18.

   The fishing page, the cruises page, and the golf page in the Web site now show the new link.

4. Close the fishing page and the activities_pages template.

5. Open the activities page, then type **We can also arrange tee times for you at area golf courses.** at the end of the paragraph with the links to the cruises and fishing pages.

6. Link the text **tee times** to golf.html, then save and close the activities page.

You saved the activities_pages template and used the Update Template Files dialog box and the Update Pages dialog box to specify that all pages in the site based on the template be updated to reflect the template modifications.

FIGURE 18
Fishing page with template changes incorporated

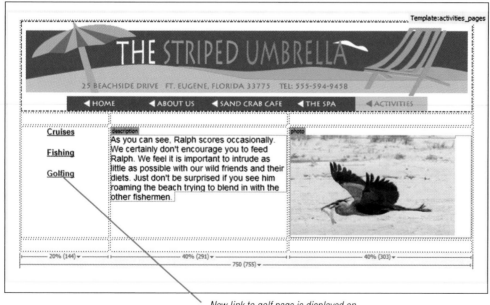

New link to golf page is displayed on fishing page

USE ADVANCED TEMPLATE
OPTIONS

What You'll Do

 In this lesson, you will learn about advanced template settings that can be used for more complex templates.

Setting Parameters for Optional Regions

If your template will be used by many people, it might be a good idea to include several optional regions in it so that users of the template can pick and choose from a wide range of content elements. You might also want to set parameters for optional regions, specifying that they are displayed or hidden based on specific conditions. For instance, let's say you have two optional regions named red and blue, respectively. You could set the blue optional region parameter to red so that the blue optional region would appear only when the red optional region is showing, and would be hidden only when the red optional region is hidden. Use the Advanced settings in the New Optional Region dialog box to set the parameters of an optional region. You can also write

a conditional expression based on JavaScript. For instance, you could write the expression *red == false* to specify that the blue optional region appear only when the red optional region is hidden.

Nesting Templates

If you are working on a complex Web site that has many different pages used by different people or departments, you might need to create **nested templates**, which are templates that are based on another template. Nested templates are helpful when you want to define a page or parts of a page in greater detail. An advantage of using nested templates is that any changes made to the original template can be automatically updated in the nested template.

To create a nested template, create a new page based on the original template, then use the Save as Template command to save the page as a nested template. You can then make changes to the nested template by adding or deleting content and defining new editable regions. Note that editable regions in the original template are passed on as editable regions to the nested template. However, if you add a new editable or optional region to an editable region that was passed on from the original template, the original editable region changes to a locked region in the nested template.

Creating Editable Attributes

There might be times when you want users of your template to be able to change certain attributes of an element in a locked region. For instance, perhaps you want to give users the ability to change the cell background color of the top row in a repeating table, or change the source file for an image in a locked area of the template. You can use the Editable Tag Attributes dialog box, shown in Figure 19, to specify that certain attributes of locked regions be editable. To do this, choose an attribute of a selected element, specify to make it editable, assign it a label, and specify its type and its default setting. For instance, in Figure 19, the table was first selected in the template. Then, the Editable Tag Attributes dialog box was opened by clicking Modify on the menu, clicking Templates, and then clicking Make Attribute Editable. From that dialog box, you can choose the attribute and settings that you want to make editable. When you define editable attributes of elements in locked regions, template users can make changes to the element's attributes using the Template Properties dialog box.

FIGURE 19

Editable Tag Attributes dialog box

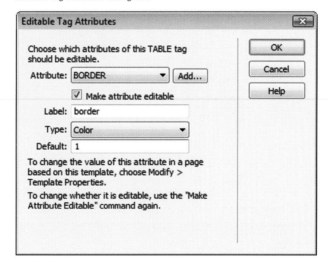

Create templates with editable and optional regions.

1. Open the blooms & bulbs Web site, then open the plants page.
2. Save the plants page as a template called **plant_categories** and update the links.
3. Delete the four rows in the table beneath the photo and description of "Moonlight White Petunia," then delete the content from the two remaining rows beneath the nav bar. You should have only the banner, navigation bar, and two empty rows left.
4. Type **Annuals - Perennials - Water Plants** in the top row (make sure there is a space before and after each dash).
5. Link the **Annuals text** to the annuals.html page, the **Perennials text** to the perennials.html page, and the Water Plants text to the water_plants.html page.
6. Insert an editable region named **image** in the first cell in the bottom row and an editable region named **description** in the second cell in the bottom row.
7. Set the horizontal alignment of the first cell in the bottom row to **Center** (if necessary), then set the vertical alignment to **Top**.
8. Set the horizontal alignment of the second cell in the bottom row to **Left** (if necessary), then set the vertical alignment to **Top**.
9. Save and close the plant_categories template.

Use templates to create pages.

1. Create a new page from the plant_categories template, then save it as **annuals.html**, overwriting the existing file.
2. Replace the placeholder text in the image editable area with the **fuchsia.jpg** file from the Web site assets folder and type **Fuchsia** as the alternate text.
3. Use a word processing program to open the file annuals.doc from where you store your Data Files, then copy and paste the text from the file into the description editable area.
4. Apply the **seasons style** to the Annuals heading and the **bodytext style** to the paragraph text, then save and close the page.
5. Repeat Steps 1 through 4 to create a new perennials page based on the plant_categories template, using the **iris.jpg** file and the **perennials.doc** text.
6. Repeat Steps 1 through 4 to create a new water_plants page based on the plant_categories template, using the **water_hyacinth.jpg** file and the **water_plants.doc** text.

Use templates to update a site.

1. Open the plant_categories template, then insert a horizontal rule that is **100%** wide and **left-aligned** in the right cell in the last row under the plant description.
2. Create a style that defines the hr tag in the blooms_styles.css file as color **#000066**.
3. Change the width of the first cell in the last row to **45%** and the width of the second cell in the last row to **55%.**
4. Apply the **subheading style** to the three links.
5. Save the template and the style sheet file, then update all files in the site that are based on the template.
6. Preview all pages in your browser, compare your annuals page to Figure 20, close the browser, then close all open pages.

FIGURE 20
Completed Skills Review

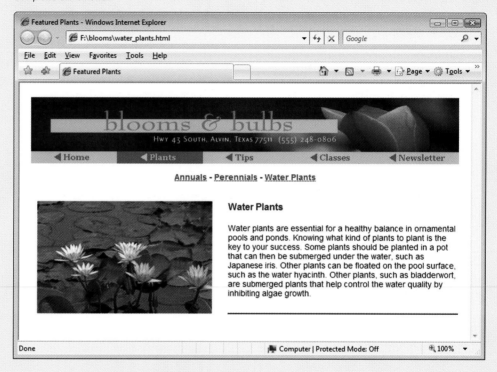

In this Project Builder, you will use a template to enhance the TripSmart Web site. Use Figure 21 as a guide as you work with the template.

1. Open the TripSmart Web site.
2. Open the catalog page, save it as a template named **catalog_pages**, update the links, then delete the catalog.html page.
3. Open the services page, select the text link "on-line catalog," remove the link to the catalog page because it has been deleted, then save and close the page.
4. Switch back to the template, then select the text "Protection from harmful UV rays" and use it to create an editable region named **description1**.
5. Select the text "Cool, lightweight, versatile" and use it to create an editable region named **description2**.
6. Select the text "Pockets for everything" and use it to create an editable region named **description3**.
7. Select the hat and use it to create an editable region named **image1**.

8. Repeat Step 7 to make editable regions called **image2** from the pants image and **image3** from the vest image.
9. Create editable regions called **name1**, **name2**, and **name3** using the text Safari Hat, Kenya Convertible Pants, and Photographer's Vest.
10. Select each item number and create editable regions called **item_number1**, **item_number2**, and **item_number3**.
11. Select each price and make editable regions named **price1**, **price2**, and **price3**.
12. Save and close the template.
13. Create a new page based on the catalog_pages template and save it as **clothing.html**. Because all the information is intact from the template, you do not need to alter it.
14. Close the clothing.html page.
15. Create a new page based on the catalog_pages template and save it as **accessories.html**.
16. Use Figure 21 as a guide to replace the images in the editable regions with the images **packing_cube_large.jpg**, **head-**

phones.jpg, and **passport_holder.jpg** from where you store your Data Files, then add appropriate alternate text.
17. Refer to Figure 21 and the following text to replace the text in the rest of the editable regions:

description1	**Makes packing a snap**
description2	**Block out annoying noises**
description3	**Organize your documents**
name1	**Packing Cube**
name2	**Headphones**
name3	**Passport Holder**
item_number1	**74983**
item_number2	**29857**
item_number3	**87432**
price1	**$20, $15, $10**
price2	**$40.00**
price3	**$22.50**

18. Save and close the accessories page.
19. Open the catalog_pages template and replace the catalog navigation bar link with two links: **Clothing** and **Accessories**.

20. Link the **Clothing text** to the clothing.html file and link the **Accessories text** to the accessories.html file.
21. Save the template and update the pages based on the template.
22. Open each page in the Web site and replace the catalog link with the two new links. (*Hint*: You can copy the new links and paste them in place on each page as long as you do not copy them from the template page. Because the template is in the Templates folder, the links are slightly different.)
23. Save all pages and preview them in the browser, testing each link.

FIGURE 21

Sample Project Builder 1

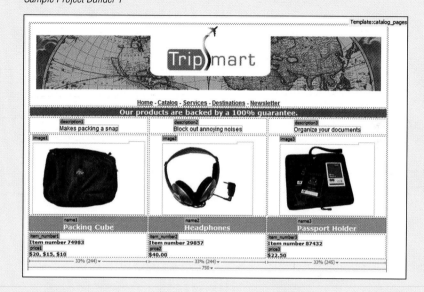

In this Project Builder, you will continue your work on the Carolyne's Creations Web site. Carolyne would like to make sure that the pages of the Web site have a consistent appearance. She has asked you to create a template based on the recipes page to use for adding new recipes on the Web site.

1. Open the Carolyne's Creations Web site, then create a new template from the recipes page named **recipes** and update the links. Click OK to close the warning message.
2. Select the paragraph beginning "This is one" and create an editable region from it named **description**.
3. Select the text including the recipe name and description and create an editable region named **name_ingredients**.
4. Select the directions text and create an editable region named **directions**.
5. Select the last sentence on the page and create an editable region named **notes**.
6. Select the photo and create an editable region named **photo**.
7. Add a row right below the navigation bar and type **Featured Recipes: Cranberry Ice - Rolls**, then insert an horizontal rule below the text.
8. Compare your screen to Figure 22, then save and close the template.
9. Create a new file based on the recipes template and name it **recipes.html**, overwriting the original recipes.html file.
10. Close the new recipes page.
11. Create another new page based on the recipes template, and name it **rolls.html**.
12. Using the rolls.doc Data File, replace the editable regions text in the rolls.html file with the rolls text from the Word file.
13. Replace the cranberry_ice.jpg image with the rolls.jpg image.
14. Apply styles to all text, compare your screen to Figure 23, then save your work.
15. Open the recipes template and link the text under the navigation bar as follows: Cranberry Ice to recipes.html, and Rolls to rolls.html.
16. Save and close the template, updating the pages based on the template.
17. Save all files, preview the pages in the browser, testing all links, then close the browser and make any spacing adjustments as needed.
18. Close and save all open files.

FIGURE 22
Completed Project Builder 2

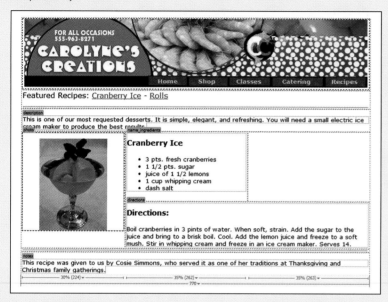

FIGURE 23
Completed Project Builder 2

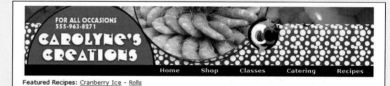

Adobe offers registered users of Dreamweaver the benefit of downloading and using professionally designed templates from their Web site. There are a wide range of templates that are appropriate for different kinds of organizations and events. Figure 24 shows the Adobe Web site with several templates available as free downloads for licensed Dreamweaver customers.

1. Connect to the Internet, then go to *www.adobe.com/products/dreamweaver/download/templates/*.

2. Spend some time exploring the templates on this site by previewing each one and opening each page. You might also check out *www.dreamweaver-templates.org* for additional ideas.

3. Think of an idea for a new site that you would like to create. The site can be for a club, organization, event, or any topic or person that interests you. Draw an outline and a sketch of the site, including the content that will be on each page.

4. After you have completed your sketch, look through the Dreamweaver templates available, then choose an appropriate template for your site. (*Note*: Skip to Step 9 if your educational institution does not allow you to download files.)

5. Download the template and copy the folder that contains the template files to a folder on your computer or external drive.

6. Use Dreamweaver to define a new site with an appropriate name that uses the site folder you downloaded as the root directory. Specify the Images folder as the default folder for images.

7. Open the site, then modify the pages of the sample site to match your site sketch. Replace any placeholder graphics, text, and other elements with content that is appropriate for your site's subject.

8. Save all pages in your site, preview them in a browser, print each page, then close your browser and close all open pages.

9. If you are unable to download files, choose an appropriate template from the site and print each page. Mark up each printed page, indicating how you would modify the template elements or replace particular elements with content appropriate for your site.

FIGURE 24
Design Project

Adobe Web site used with permission from Adobe Systems Inc.
- www.adobe.com/products/dreamweaver/download/templates/

In this assignment, you will continue to work on the Web site that you created in earlier chapters.

You will continue to enhance your Web site by using templates. You will first create a template from one of your existing pages and define editable regions in it. You will then apply the template to a page and add content to the editable regions.

1. Consult your storyboard and decide which page you would like to save as a template. You will use the template to create at least one other page in your site.
2. Create a sketch of the template page you will create. Mark the page elements that will be in locked regions. Identify and mark at least one area that will be an editable region.
3. Create a new template, then define the editable regions in the template.

4. Make any necessary formatting adjustments to make sure it looks attractive, and then save the template. Create a new page based on the template, using the same name as the page on which the template is based, so that the earlier version of the page is overwritten.
5. Apply the template to another existing page in the site, making sure to delete all repeating elements contained in the template.

6. Review the template(s) and the template-based pages, and decide if you need to make improvements. Use the checklist in Figure 25 to make sure you completed everything according to the assignment.
7. Make any necessary changes.
8. Save your work, then close all open pages.

FIGURE 25
Portfolio Project checklist

Web Site Checklist
1. Does your template include at least one editable region?
2. Are all links on templates-based pages document-relative?
3. Do all editable regions have appropriate names?
4. Do all links work correctly?
5. Do all pages view well using at least two different browsers?

12

WORKING WITH LIBRARY
ITEMS AND SNIPPETS

1. Create and modify library items

2. Add library items to pages

3. Add and modify snippets

12 WORKING WITH LIBRARY
ITEMS AND SNIPPETS

Introduction

When creating a Web site, chances are good that you will want certain graphics or text blocks to appear in more than one place in the site. For instance, you might want the company tag line in several different places, or a footer containing links to the main pages of the site at the bottom of every page. Library items and snippets can help you work with these repeating elements more efficiently.

Understanding Library Items

If you want an element to appear repeatedly, then it's a good idea to save it as a library item. A **library item** is content that can contain text or graphics and is saved in a separate file in the Library folder of your Web site. The advantage of using library items is that when you make a change to the library item and then update the site, all instances of that item will be updated to reflect the change.

Understanding Snippets

Another way to use the same content repeatedly throughout a site is to insert code snippets. **Code snippets** are reusable pieces of code that can be inserted on a page. Dreamweaver provides a wide variety of ready-made code snippets you can use to create footers, drop-down menus, headers, and other page elements.

In this chapter, you will work with library items and code snippets to enhance The Striped Umbrella Web site.

Tools You'll Use

Library button

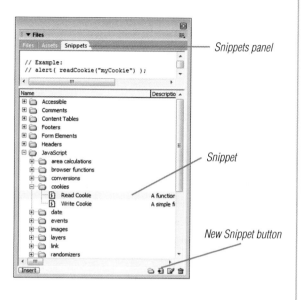

Snippets panel

Snippet

New Snippet button

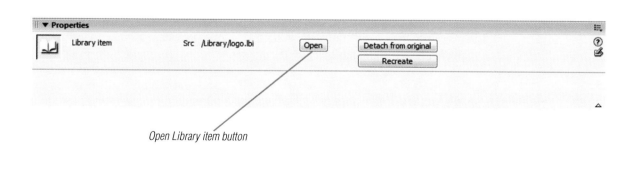

Open Library item button

CREATE AND MODIFY
LIBRARY ITEMS

What You'll Do

In this lesson, you will create a text-based library item. You will also create a library item that contains an image in the activities_pages template. You will then edit both library items and update the site to reflect those edits.

Understanding the Benefits of Library Items

Using library items for repetitive elements—especially those that need to be updated frequently—can save you considerable time. For instance, suppose you want to feature an employee of the month photograph on every page in your site. You could create a library item named employee_photo and add it to every page. Then, when you need to update the site to show a new employee photo, you could simply replace the photo contained in the library item, and the photo would be updated throughout the site. Library items can contain a wide range of content, including text, images, tables, Flash files, and sounds.

Viewing and Creating Library Items

To view library items, show the Assets panel, then click the Library button. The library items appear in a list, and a preview of the selected library item appears above the list,

as shown in Figure 1. To save text or an image as a library item, select the item in the Document window, and then drag it to the Assets panel. You can also click Modify on the menu bar, point to Library, and then click Add Object to Library. The item that you dragged will appear in the preview window in the Assets panel and in the library item list with the temporary name Untitled assigned to it. Type a new name, and then press [Enter] (Win) or [return] (Mac) to give the library item a permanent name. Library items on a Web page appear in shaded yellow in the Document window, but not in a browser. When you click a library item in the Document window, the entire item is selected and the Property inspector changes to display three buttons that you can use to work with the library item, as shown in Figure 2.

QUICKTIP
You can also view a list of available library items by expanding the Library folder in the Files panel.

Modifying Library Items

You cannot edit library items on the Web pages in which they appear. To make changes to a library item, you have to open it. To open a library item, select the item in the Document window, and then click Open in the Property inspector. The library item will appear in the Document window, where you can make edits or add content to it. When you are satisfied with your edits, save the library item using the Save command on the File menu. When you do this, the Update Library Items dialog box will appear, asking if you want to update all instances of the library item throughout the site.

FIGURE 2
Web page containing library item

FIGURE 1
Library items in Assets panel

Preview of selected library item

Library button

Library items

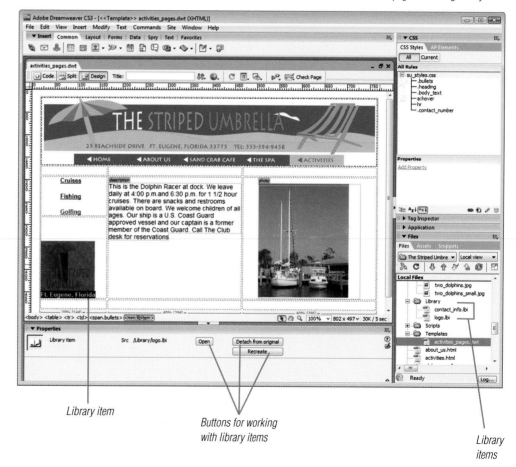

Library item

Buttons for working with library items

Library items

Create a text-based library item

1. Open The Striped Umbrella Web site, then open the index page.

2. Create a new rule in the su_styles.css file called **contact_number** with the following settings: Font = **Arial**, **Helvetica**, **sans-serif**, Size = **small**, Color = **#000099**, Weight = **bold**, Text align = **center**.

3. Insert two paragraph returns at the bottom of the index page, then type **The Striped Umbrella 1-555-594-9458**.

4. Apply the **contact_number style** to the text you typed in Step 3.

5. Click to place the insertion point before the telephone number, click **Insert**, point to **HTML**, point to **Special Characters**, click **Other**, click the **Em dash symbol** in the Insert Other Character dialog box, then add a space after the Em dash, as shown in Figure 3.

   TIP You can also insert an Em dash by clicking Insert on the menu bar, pointing to HTML, pointing to Special Characters, and clicking Em-Dash.

   (continued)

FIGURE 3

Inserting an Em dash using the Insert Other Character dialog box

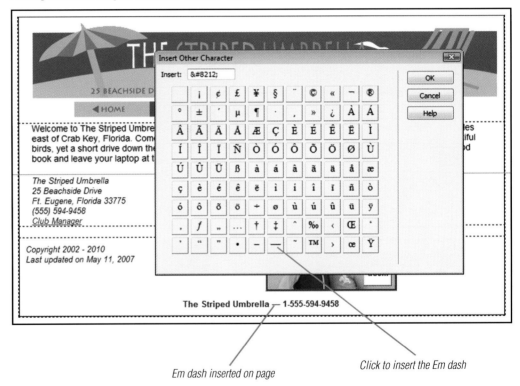

Em dash inserted on page

Click to insert the Em dash

FIGURE 4

Assets panel showing new contact_info library item

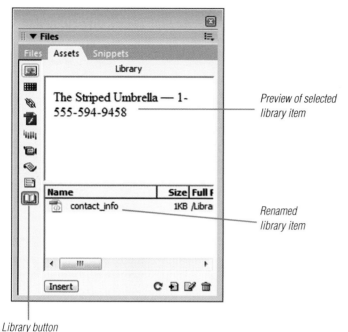

Preview of selected
library item

Renamed
library item

Library button

FIGURE 5

Viewing the new contact_info library item in Code view

```
165  rt. Eugene, florida 55775<br />
166  (555) 594-9458 <br />
167  <a href="mailto:manager@stripedumbrella.com">Club Manager</a></span></p>
168    <!-- end #mainContent --></div>
169    <div id="footer">
170      <p class="contact_info"><em>Copyright 2002 - 2010<br />
171  Last updated on
172      <!-- #BeginDate format:Am1 -->May 11, 2007<!-- #EndDate -->
173      </em></p>
174      <p class="contact_info"> </p>
175      <p class="contact_number"><!-- #BeginLibraryItem "/Library/contact_info.lbi" -->The Striped
     Umbrella &#8212; 1-555-594-9458<!-- #EndLibraryItem --></p>
176    <!-- end #footer --></div>
177  <!-- end #container --></div>
178  </body>
179  </html>
```

Code for library item

6. Display the Assets panel, then click the **Library button** 📖.

7. Select the line of text with the telephone number, then drag it to the Assets panel.

8. Click **OK** to close the dialog box warning you that the library item is not displayed with the style information (if necessary).

   The text that you dragged is now an unnamed library item in the Assets panel.

9. Type **contact_info** in the Name text box to replace "Untitled," press **[Enter]** (Win) or **[return]** (Mac) to name the library item, deselect the library item on the page, then compare your screen to Figure 4.

   If you look closely, you will see that the contact information now has a very lightly shaded yellow background on the page indicating it is a library item.

10. Switch to Code view to view the library item, as shown in Figure 5, then switch back to Design view.

    The library item file has the file extension .lbi.

11. Save and close all open files.

You created a text-based library item from text on the index page.

Create an image-based library item

1. Click the **Templates button** 🗔 on the Assets panel, then double-click the **activities_pages template** to open it.

2. Click the **Library button** 📖 on the Assets panel to display the library item in the Assets panel.

3. Split the cell with the three text links into two rows, then insert the **su_logo.jpg** from where you store your Data Files in the bottom cell of the newly split cells.

4. Type **The Striped Umbrella logo** as the alternate text.

5. Click to the right of the logo, press **[Shift] [Enter]** (Win) or **[Shift][return]** (Mac) to insert a line break, type **Ft. Eugene**, **Florida**, apply the **bullets style** to the text, then deselect the text, as shown in Figure 6.

6. Click the **Vert list arrow** on the Property inspector, then click **Bottom** to set the cell's vertical alignment.

(continued)

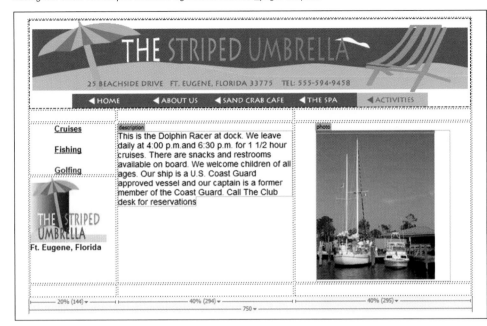

FIGURE 7
logo library item added to Assets panel

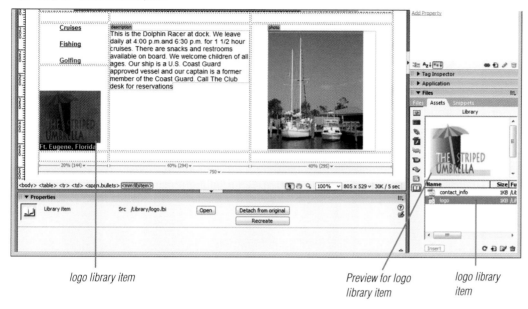

logo library item Preview for logo logo library
library item item

FIGURE 8
Update Pages dialog box with Library items and Templates checkboxes checked

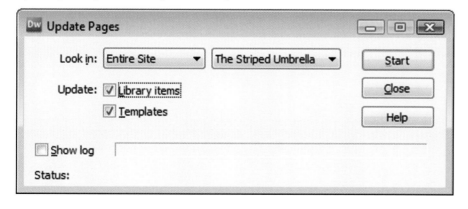

7. Select the logo and address, drag the selection to the Library in the Assets panel, then click **OK** to close the dialog box warning you that the style was not copied (if necessary).

   The image and text are stored as one library item and appear in the preview window at the top of the Assets panel. A new untitled library item appears selected in the library item list.

8. Type **logo** to replace "Untitled," press **[Enter]** (Win) or **[return]** (Mac) to name the library item in the Assets panel, then compare your screen to Figure 7.

9. Save your changes, then click **Update** in the Update Template Files dialog box to open the Update Pages dialog box.

10. Click the **Look in list arrow**, click **Entire Site**, check the **Library items** and **Templates** checkboxes, as shown in Figure 8, then click **Start**.

    Dreamweaver updates your files based on the changes made to the library item.

11. Click **Close**, open the golf page to view the library item on the page, then close the golf page.

You created a library item named logo that contains an image and text in the activities_pages template. You then saved the template and updated all pages in the site.

Edit an image-based library item

1. Click the **su_logo.jpg** image at the bottom of the activities_pages template.

2. Click **Open** in the Property inspector to open the logo library item.

   The image and text appear in the Document window. The title bar displays the filename logo.lbi. The file extension .lbi denotes a library file.

   | TIP You can also open a library item by double-clicking it in the Assets panel.

3. Click the **image** in the Document window, then click the **Crop button** ⊠ in the Property inspector.

4. Click **OK** to the message warning "The action you are about to perform will permanently alter the selected image."

   An outline surrounds the image, as shown in Figure 9. The outline is used to crop the image.

   (continued)

FIGURE 9
Preparing to crop the logo

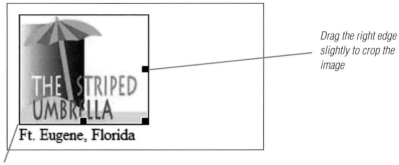

Drag the right edge slightly to crop the image

The border and handles indicate you can crop the image

FIGURE 10

Viewing the cropped logo

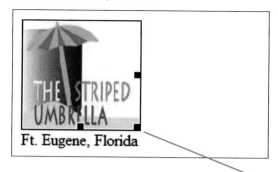

Edge of image is
more in line with text

5. Drag the right edge toward the center of the image to crop the right edge of the graphic, lining it up with the line of text underneath it.

6. When you are satisfied with the crop, double-click on top of the logo to execute the crop, then compare your screen to Figure 10.

> TIP You can also press [Enter](Win) or [return](Mac) to execute a crop.

You opened the logo library item, then cropped the image.

Update library items

1. Click **File** on the menu bar, then click **Save** to open the Update Library Items dialog box.

   The dialog box asks if you want to update the library item on the pages shown.

2. Click **Update** to open the Update Pages dialog box.

3. Click the **Look in list arrow**, click **Entire Site**, check the **Library items** and **Templates** check boxes, then click **Start**.

   Dreamweaver updates your files based on the changes made to the library item.

4. Click **Close**, close the logo.lbi file, then switch to the activities_pages template.

   Notice that the page reflects the change you made to the logo library item.

5. Compare your screen to Figure 11.

6. Save and close the activities_pages template, updating the pages in the site again.

You saved the logo library item and updated all pages in the site to incorporate the changes you made.

FIGURE 11
activities_pages template showing the updated logo library item

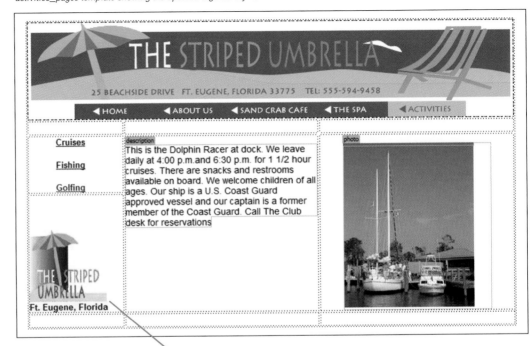

Logo is slightly cropped

FIGURE 12

contact_info library item after editing

The Striped Umbrella — (555) 594-9458 or (800) 594-9458 toll free

*Phone number edited and
toll free number added*

FIGURE 13

Page reflects edits made to contact_info library item

Edit a text-based library item

1. Open the index page (if necessary), then click the **telephone text** to select the contact_info library item.

2. Click **Open** in the Property inspector to open the contact_info library item.

3. Edit the telephone number to read **(555) 594-9458 or (888) 594-9458 toll free**, then compare your screen to Figure 12.

4. Save your changes, update the site, then close the contact_info library item.

5. Switch to the index page, then compare your screen to Figure 13.

   The text reflects the edits you made to the contact_info library item.

6. Save and close the index page.

You edited the text in the contact_info library item, then saved the changes and updated the site.

ADD LIBRARY ITEMS
TO PAGES

What You'll Do

 In this lesson, you will add a text-based library item you created to the about us, activities, cafe, feedback, and spa pages. You will detach the library item on the index page and edit it. You will then delete one of the library items and restore the deleted item using the Recreate command.

Adding Library Items to a Page

Once you create a library item, it's easy to add it to any page in a Web site. All you do is drag the library item from the Assets panel to the desired location on the page. When you insert a library item, the actual content and a reference to the library item are copied into the code. The inserted library item is shaded in yellow in the Document window and will be automatically updated to reflect any changes you make to the library item.

> **QUICK**TIP
>
> You can also insert a library item on a page by selecting the item in the Assets panel, then clicking Insert.

There may be times when you don't want content to be updated when you update the library item. For instance, suppose you want one of your pages to include photos of all past employees of the month. You would insert content from the current library item, but you do not want the photo to change when the

library item is updated to reflect next month's employee photo. To achieve this, you would insert the content of a library item on a page without inserting the reference to the library item. To do this, press and hold [Alt] (Win) or [option] (Mac) as you drag the library item from the Assets panel to the Document window. The content from the library item will be inserted on the page, but it will not be linked to the library item.

Making Library Items Editable on a Page

There may be times when you would like to make changes to a particular instance of a library item on one page, without making those changes to other instances of the library item in the site. You can make a library item editable on a page by breaking its link to the library item. To do this, select the library item, and then click Detach from original in the Property inspector. Once you have detached the library item, you can edit the content like you would any other element on the page.

Keep in mind, though, that this edited content will not be updated when you make changes to the library item.

Deleting and Recreating Library Items

If you know that you will never need to update a library item again, you might want to delete it. To delete a library item, select it in the Assets panel, and then click the Delete button. Deleting a library item removes it from only the Library folder; it does not change the contents of the pages that contain that library item. All instances of the deleted library item will still appear in shaded yellow in the site unless you detach them from the original. Be aware that you cannot use the Undo command to restore a library item. However, you can undelete a library item by selecting any instance of the item in the site and clicking Recreate in the Property inspector. You can also recreate a library item after you have exited and started Dreamweaver again, provided a deleted library item still has an instance remaining on a page. After you recreate a library item, it reappears in the Assets panel and you can make changes to it and update all pages in the site again. Figure 14 shows the Property inspector with Library item settings.

FIGURE 14
Property inspector with Library item settings

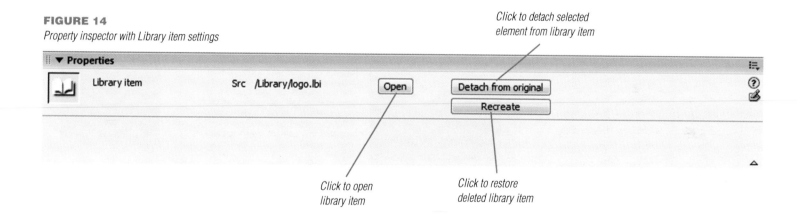

Click to detach selected element from library item

Click to open library item

Click to restore deleted library item

Add a library item to a page

1. Open the about_us page.

2. Insert a new row at the bottom of the table.

3. Open the Assets panel (if necessary), then drag the **contact_info library item** from the Assets panel to the new row.

   The contact_info heading now appears where you dragged it. Notice that it is shaded in yellow, indicating it is a library item.

4. Click to the right of the library item on the page, then use the Property inspector to apply the **bullets style**.

5. Center the cell contents, deselect the text, then compare your screen to Figure 15.

   (continued)

FIGURE 15

about_us page with library item added

The main swimming pool is directly behind The Club House. A lifeguard is on duty from 8:00 a.m. until 9:00 p.m. The pool area includes a wading pool, a lap pool, and a large pool with a diving board. Showers are located in several areas for your use before and after swimming. We also provide poolside service from the cafe for snacks and lunch.

Enjoy our lush landscaping as you explore the grounds. The beautiful sago palms flourish in our Florida weather! We have many native plants that we hope you will enjoy, both within our manicured grounds and along the beach. Remember, the wild vegetation are all protected species.

native vegetation. The sea oats and other flora are tender. Please do not step on them or pick them.

If you would like to play tennis, we have a very nice sports club. Call to reserve court times. Our clay courts are generally busy, so it's not a bad idea to schedule your games as soon as you arrive. We also have a very extensive pro shop where you can find anything you need to play. We can even restring your racket if the need arises.

Please give us your feedback so that we may make your next stay the best vacation ever.
The Striped Umbrella — (555) 594-9458 or (888) 594-9458 toll free

Library item

FIGURE 16

activities page with library item added

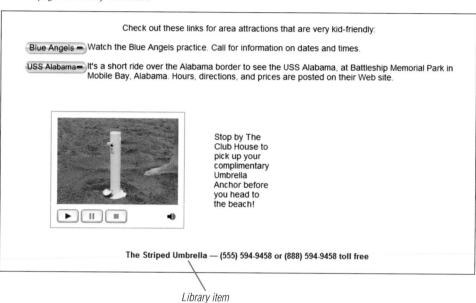

Library item

6. Save and close the about_us page.

7. Repeat Steps 2 through 5 to add the **contact_info** library item to the activities page, as shown in Figure 16, then continue with the cafe, feedback, and spa pages.

   If the page already has an empty row, there is no need to add a new row. If the row contains multiple cells, merge the cells before you insert the library item.

8. Preview all of the edited pages in the browser, then close the browser.

9. Save and close all open pages.

You added the contact_info library item to the about_us, activities, cafe, feedback, and spa pages.

Creating library items

Although you can create library items with images, text, or a combination of the two, you can use only items that contain body elements. For instance, when editing a library item, the CSS Styles panel will be unavailable because style sheet code is embedded in the head section, rather than just the body section. Likewise, the Page Properties dialog box will be unavailable because library items cannot include a body tag attribute such as text color. You can apply a style after you have placed the library item on the page.

Make a library item editable on a page

1. Open the index page, then click the **contact_info library footer** on the index page.

   The Property inspector displays three buttons relating to library items.

2. Click **Detach from original** in the Property inspector.

   A dialog box opens, warning you that the item will no longer be automatically updated when the original library item changes.

3. Click **OK**.

   Notice that the contact information no longer appears in shaded yellow, indicating it is no longer a library item.

4. Type **in Florida** after the first telephone number, then compare your screen to Figure 17.

   The contact information is edited on the page.

5. Save and close the index page.

You detached the contact information from the contact_info library item to make the text editable on the index page. You then added two words to the contact information.

FIGURE 17
Editing a library item on a page

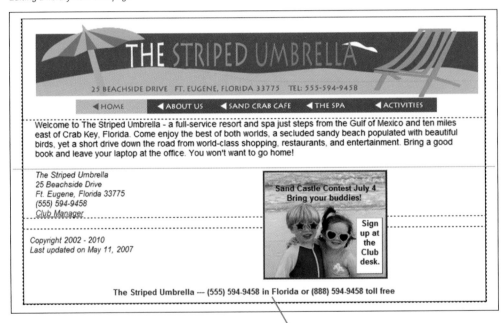

"in Florida" added to text

FIGURE 18

Assets panel after deleting the logo library item

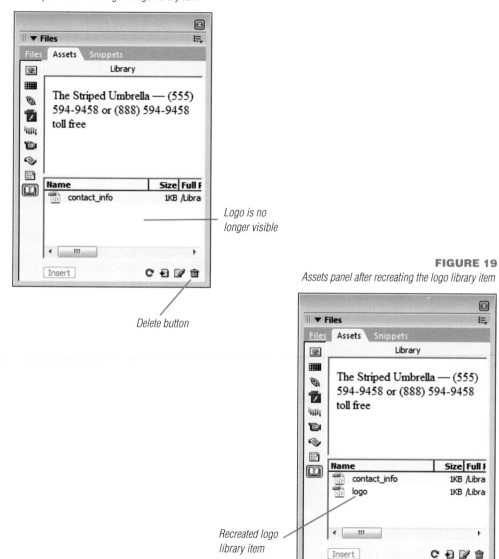

Logo is no longer visible

Delete button

FIGURE 19

Assets panel after recreating the logo library item

Recreated logo library item

Delete a library item

1. Select the **logo library item** in the Assets panel.

2. Click the **Delete button** 🗑 in the Assets panel.

    A dialog box opens, asking if you are sure you want to delete the library item.

3. Click **Yes**, then compare your screen to Figure 18.

    The logo library item no longer appears in the Assets panel. Mac users may need to select the contact_info library item to see the change.

You deleted the logo library item in the Assets panel.

Recreate a library item

1. Open the activities_pages template.

    The logo still appears in shaded yellow, indicating it is still a library item, even though you deleted the library item to which it is attached.

2. Click the **logo** to select it.

3. Click **Recreate** in the Property inspector, then compare your screen to Figure 19.

    The logo library item is added to the Assets panel.

    If you do not see the logo library item, recreate the site cache, then refresh the Assets panel.

4. Save and close the activities_pages template.

You recreated the logo library item that you deleted in the previous set of steps.

ADD AND MODIFY
SNIPPETS

What You'll Do

 In this lesson, you will add a predefined snippet from the Snippets panel to create a new footer for the index page. You will then replace the placeholder text and links in the snippet with appropriate text and links. Finally, you will save the modified snippet as a new snippet and add it to other pages.

Using the Snippets Panel

Creating a Web site is a huge task, so it's nice to know that you can save time by using ready-made code snippets to create various elements in your site. The Snippets panel, located in the Files panel group, contains a large collection of reusable code snippets organized in folders and named by element type. The Snippets panel contains two panes, as shown in Figure 20. The lower pane contains folders that can be expanded to view the snippets. The upper pane displays a preview of the selected snippet. Use the buttons at the bottom of the Snippets panel to insert a snippet, create a new folder in the Snippets panel, create a new snippet, edit a snippet, or remove a snippet.

Inserting and Modifying Snippets

Adding a snippet to a page is an easy task; simply drag the snippet from the Snippets panel to the desired location on the page. Once you position a snippet, you will need to replace the placeholder text, links, and images with appropriate content.

> **QUICK**TIP
>
> You can also add a snippet to a page by selecting the snippet in the Snippets panel, then clicking the Insert button on the Snippets panel.

Creating New Snippets

Once you've modified a snippet so that it contains text and graphics appropriate for your site, you might want to save it with a new name. Doing this will save time when using this snippet on other pages. To save a modified snippet as a new snippet, select the snippet content in the Document window, and then click the New Snippet button in the Snippets panel to open the Snippet dialog box. Use this dialog box to name the snippet and give it a description. Because the Snippet dialog box displays the snippet code, you can make edits to the code here if you wish. Any new snippets you create will appear in the Snippets panel.

FIGURE 20
Snippets panel

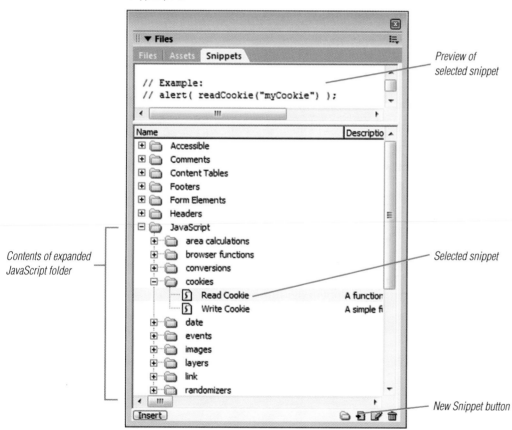

Preview of selected snippet

Contents of expanded JavaScript folder

Selected snippet

New Snippet button

Add a predefined snippet to a page

1. Open the index page.

2. Scroll to the bottom of the page, click to the right of the contact telephone numbers at the bottom of the page, then press **[Shift][Enter]** (Win) or **[Shift][return]** (Mac) to add a line break.

3. Click the **Snippets tab** to open the Snippets panel.

4. Click the **plus sign (+)** (Win) or the **triangle** (Mac) next to the Navigation folder in the Snippets panel to display the contents of the Navigation folder, then click the **plus sign (+)** (Win) or **triangle** (Mac) next to the Horizontal folder to display the contents of the Horizontal folder.

5. Drag the **Bullet as Separator** in the Horizontal folder to the bottom of the index page, under the contact telephone numbers at the bottom of the page, as shown in Figure 21.

   This text will serve as placeholder text until you replace it with the appropriate links for The Striped Umbrella Web site.

   TIP Having a navigation bar with plain text links on each main page of a Web site ensures maximum accessibility for users.

6. Save your changes.

You added a predefined navigation bar from the Snippets panel.

FIGURE 21
index page after inserting snippet

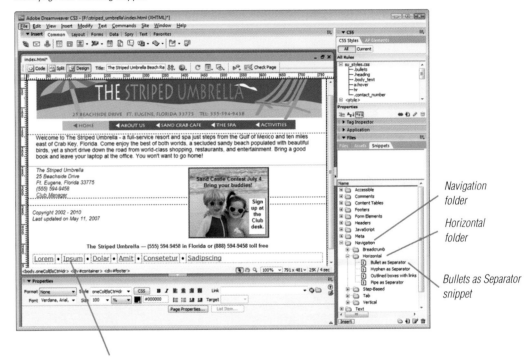

Navigation folder

Horizontal folder

Bullets as Separator snippet

Bullets as Separator snippet dragged from the Snippets panel

FIGURE 22
index page after editing snippet placeholder text

Bullet separator and last link are deleted

1. Click in the last cell of the navigation snippet with the text placeholder **Sadipscing**, click the **<td> tag** in the tag selector, then press **[Delete]** (Win) or **[delete]**(Mac).

   The last link and the cell it was in are deleted.

2. Repeat Step 1 to delete the next cell to the left with the bullet.

   The bullet and cell are deleted.

3. Save your changes, then compare your screen to Figure 22.

You edited the placeholder text contained in the navigation snippet on the index page.

Modify snippet links

1. Select the **Lorem placeholder link** in the bottom row of the table, then type **Home**.

2. Replace the Ipsum placeholder link with **About Us**, replace the Dolar placeholder link with **Sand Crab Cafe**, replace the Amit placeholder link with **The Spa**, then replace the Consetetur placeholder link with **Activities.**

3. Select all of the text in the snippet and apply the **contact_number** style.

4. Select the **table tag** in the tag selector, center the table, then change the width for the table with the navigation snippet to **60%**.

   The links are now spaced closer together.

5. Display the Files panel, select the **Home link text** at the bottom of the home page, then use the Point to File icon ⊕ in the Property inspector to set the Link property to the index page, as shown in Figure 23.

6. Use the Point to File icon ⊕ to set the Link property for the About Us, Sand Crab Cafe, The Spa, and Activities links.

7. Save your changes.

8. Preview the index page in your browser, test all the new navigation links, then close your browser.

You changed the names of the placeholder links and used the Point to File icon to create links to the five main pages in The Striped Umbrella Web site.

FIGURE 23

Using the Point to File icon to create document-relative links in the new links

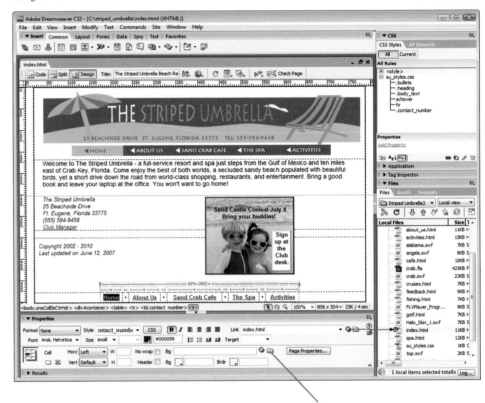

Point to File icon

Create a new snippet

1. Select the **navigation footer** on the index page by clicking to place the insertion point in the footer, then selecting the table tag for the footer.

2. Click the **New Snippet button** 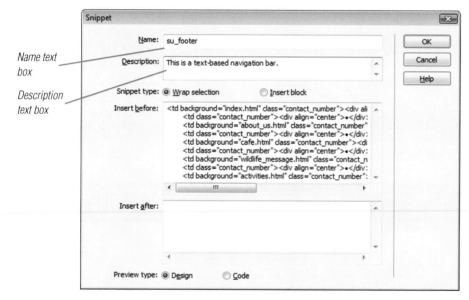 in the Snippets panel to open the Snippet dialog box.

3. Type **su_footer** in the Name text box.

4. Type **This is a text-based navigation bar.** in the Description text box, compare your screen to Figure 24, then click **OK**.

5. Open the about us page, place the insertion point to the right of the telephone contact information, press **[Shift][Enter]** (Win) or **[Shift][return]** (Mac), then drag the **su_footer** from the Snippets panel to the page.

   You can also double-click a snippet to insert it on a page.

6. Repeat Step 6 to insert the **su_footer snippet** on the cafe, spa, and activities pages.

7. Save and preview all open pages in the browser, close each page, then close the browser.

8. Run reports for Untitled Documents, Missing Alt Text, Broken Links, Orphaned Files, and non-Websafe Colors; then correct any errors.

9. Publish your completed site, then exit Dreamweaver.

You copied the text-based navigation bar from the index page and saved it as a snippet called su_footer. You then copied it to the rest of the main pages in the Web site.

FIGURE 24

Snippet dialog box

Name text box

Description text box

Snippet	
Name: su_footer	OK
Description: This is a text-based navigation bar.	Cancel
	Help

Snippet type: ⦿ Wrap selection ◯ Insert block

Insert before:
```
<td background="index.html" class="contact_number"><div ali
  <td class="contact_number"><div align="center">•</div>
  <td background="about_us.html" class="contact_number"
  <td class="contact_number"><div align="center">•</div>
  <td background="cafe.html" class="contact_number"><di
  <td class="contact_number"><div align="center">•</div>
  <td background="wildlife_message.html" class="contact_n
  <td class="contact_number"><div align="center">•</div>
  <td background="activities.html" class="contact_number":
```

Insert after:

Preview type: ⦿ Design ◯ Code

Create and modify library items.

1. Open the blooms & bulbs Web site, then open the index page.
2. Create a new style in the blooms_styles.css file called **telephone** with the following settings: Font: **Verdana**, **Arial**, **Helvetica**, **sans-serif**; Size: **14** pixels; Weight: **bold**; Style: **normal**; Color: **#000033.**
3. Insert a new paragraph at the bottom of the index page, type **blooms & bulbs 555-248-0806**, then apply the telephone style to the text. (*Hint*: You may need to enter two paragraph breaks to be able to see the text below the AP element.)
4. Select the text you typed in Step 3, drag it to the Assets panel with the Library category displayed to create a new library item, then name it **telephone**.
5. Center the line with the telephone number, then save the page.
6. Edit the library item to read **(555) 248-0806**, then save the library item and update all pages with the library item.
7. Open the newsletter page, insert **blooms_logo.jpg** from where you store your Data Files right after the e-mail link near the bottom of the page, then type **blooms & bulbs logo** as the alternate text.
8. Right-align the logo, then drag it to the Assets panel to create a new library item, then name it **logo**.
9. Save and close the newsletter page.

Add library items to pages.

1. Open the classes page, then add a new row to the bottom of the table.
2. Insert the telephone library item in the new row, apply the telephone style to the cell contents, then center the telephone number.
3. Repeat Steps 1 and 2 to add the telephone number to the newsletter, plants, and tips pages, then save all pages.
4. Delete the telephone library item from the Assets panel.
5. Switch to the index page, select the telephone library item on the page, then re-create it.
6. Insert a horizontal rule that is **90% wide** and **centered** immediately before the telephone library item on the index, classes, plants, and newsletter pages. (*Hint*: The tips page already has a horizontal rule at the bottom of the page.)
7. Save your work and preview all pages in the browser, then adjust the spacing on the index page to prevent overlap.

Add and modify snippets.

1. Scroll to the bottom of the index page and insert a line break.
2. Insert the **Bullet as Separator Horizontal Navigation snippet** in the new line.

3. Delete the last link and separator, then delete the last two empty cells.
4. Replace the placeholder links in the footer with text to link to the home, plants, tips, classes, and newsletter pages.
5. Create a link for each link in the navigation bar to the appropriate page.
6. Set the width of the table with the snippet to **50%** and **center** the table in the row.
7. Create a new snippet from the footer you just inserted. Name the snippet **blooms_footer**, then give it an appropriate description.
8. Insert the new footer at the bottom of the classes, newsletter, plants, and tips pages.
9. Delete the a:link and a:hover styles from the CSS Styles panel so your navigation footer will be displayed as plain text links.
10. Save all pages, then preview each page in the browser to test the links in the footer to make sure they work, as shown in Figure 25.
11. Close the browser, then close all open pages.
12. Run reports for Untitled Documents, Missing Alt Text, Broken Links, Orphaned Files, and non-Websafe Colors; then correct any errors that you find.
13. Publish your completed site, then exit Dreamweaver.

FIGURE 25
Completed Skills Review

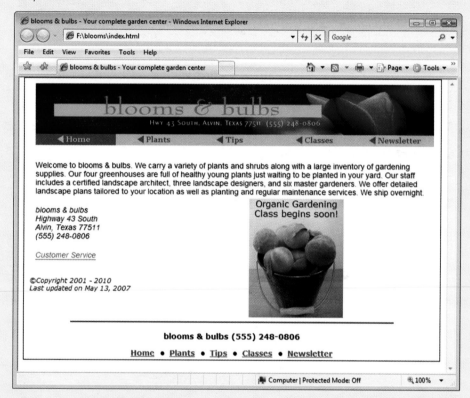

In this Project Builder, you will continue your work on the TripSmart Web site. You have been given the TripSmart logo to use in the Web site and decide to create a library item from the logo combined with the copyright statement.

1. Open the TripSmart Web site, then open the index page.
2. Place the insertion point after the last updated statement, then enter a line break.
3. Insert the file **tripsmart_logo.jpg** from where you store your Data Files onto the page, adding **TripSmart logo** for the alternate text.
4. Drag the copyright statement to the right of the logo.
5. Select both the logo and copyright statement, then use them to create a new library item named **logo**.
6. Save the file, preview the page in the browser, then compare your screen to Figure 26.
7. Close the browser, then make any spacing adjustments necessary to improve the page appearance.
8. Open the services page, then insert a line break after the last line on the page.
9. Drag the **logo library item** onto the page.
10. Repeat Steps 8 and 9 to add the logo library item to the rest of the pages in the Web site. (*Hint*: To add the logo library item to the accessories and clothing pages, add it to the catalog_pages.dwt file.)

11. Save the file, then preview the page in the browser.
12. Close the browser, then make any necessary adjustments to improve the page appearance.
13. Close all files, run reports for Untitled Documents, Missing Alt Text, Broken Links, Orphaned Files, and non-Websafe Colors, then correct any errors that you find.
14. Publish your completed site, then exit Dreamweaver.

FIGURE 26
Sample Project Builder 1

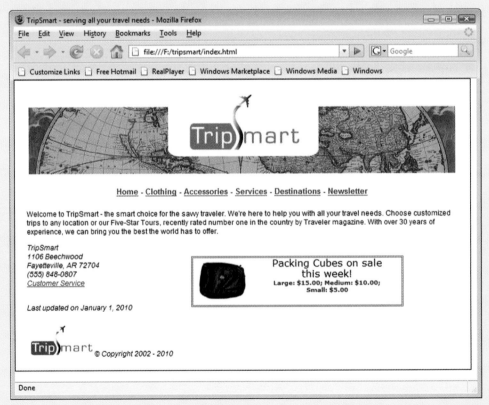

Working with Library Items and Snippets

In this Project Builder, you will continue your work on the Carolyne's Creations Web site. Chef Carolyne has asked you to add some plain text links at the bottom of each page to provide viewers with more accessible links that do not depend on the image map at the top of each page.

1. Open the Carolyne's Creations Web site.
2. Open the index page.
3. Insert a line break after the last updated statement.
4. Insert the **Pipe as Separator snippet**. (*Hint*: This snippet is located in the Snippets panel. Open the Accessible folder, then the Navigation folder, and finally the Horizontal folder.)
5. Delete the two cells with the last text placeholder and pipe, then replace each placeholder with links to the main pages, using Figure 27 as a guide.
6. Apply the **body_text style** to the navigation bar, set the table width to **65%**, then **center** it.
7. Insert a horizontal rule that is **80%** wide and **centered** above the navigation bar.
8. Save your work, then preview the page in the browser.
9. Close the browser, then insert the horizontal line and navigation bar snippet at the bottom of the adults, children, classes, catering, recipes, and shop pages.

10. Make any adjustments to the pages to improve the appearance, save your work , then preview each page in the browser.
11. Close the browser, then close all open pages.

12. Run reports for Untitled Documents, Missing Alt Text, Broken Links, Orphaned Files, and non-Websafe Colors; then correct any errors.
13. Publish your completed site, then exit Dreamweaver.

FIGURE 27
Completed Project Builder 2

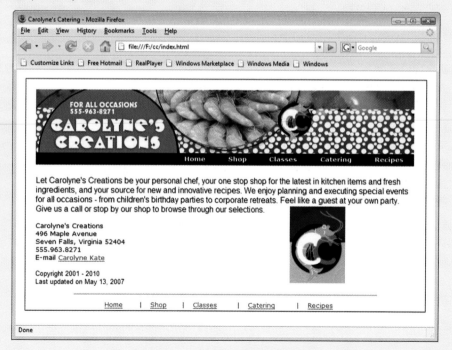

Library items and snippets are commonly used in Web sites to ensure that repetitive information is updated quickly and accurately.

1. Connect to the Internet, then go to *www.bostonchefs.com*, as shown in Figure 28.

2. Spend some time exploring the pages of this site to become familiar with its elements. Do you see many repeating elements?

3. If you were developing this site, which images or text would you convert into library items? Print two pages from this Web site and write a list of all the text and visual elements from these pages that you would make into library items.

4. Link to at least two of the restaurants listed on the Web site, then print two pages from each of these sites.

5. Write a list of all the elements shown on the printed pages that you think should be made into library items.

FIGURE 28
Design Project

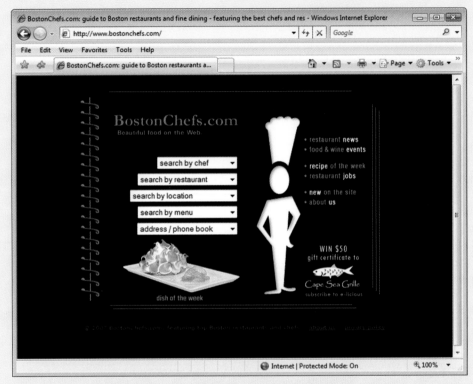

Boston Chefs.com Web site used with permission from Boston Chefs.com: www.bostonchefs.com

In this project, you will continue to work on the Web site that you created in Chapter 1.

You will continue to enhance your Web site by using library items and snippets.

1. Consult your storyboard and decide which text and graphic elements in the site should be converted into library items. Write a list of these items.

2. Discuss what content to include in a footer that you will add to each page of the site using a snippet.

3. Convert all the text elements you identified in your list into library items.

4. Insert the library items that you created in Step 3 in appropriate places in the Web site.

5. Convert all the graphic elements you identified in Step 1 into library items.

6. Insert the graphic library items that you created in Step 5 in appropriate places in the Web site.

7. Edit two of the library items that you created, then save and update all instances of the library item in the site.

8. Add a footer to the Web site using one of the snippets in the Footers folder of the Snippets panel. Replace all placeholder links with appropriate links to each major page in the site and replace placeholder text with text that is suitable for your site.

9. Create a new snippet from the footer that was created in Step 8. Insert this snippet on the other pages of the site.

10. Save your work, preview all pages in a browser, then test all the links. Use the checklist in Figure 29 to make sure your Web site is complete.

11. Make any necessary changes, then save and close all open pages.

12. Run reports for Untitled Documents, Missing Alt Text, Broken Links, Orphaned Files, and non-Websafe Colors; then correct any errors that you find.

13. Publish your completed site, then exit Dreamweaver.

FIGURE 29
Portfolio Project checklist

Web Site Checklist

1. Have you converted all repeating text elements into library items?
2. Have you converted all repeating graphic elements, such as logos, into library items?
3. Did you save and update the library items after making edits to them?
4. Do all links work?
5. Did you add the footer to all pages in the Web site?

Topic Area	Objectives	Chapter
1.0 Understanding Web technologies	1.1 Given an HTML tag, explain the purpose of that tag. (Tags include: <div> <span><table> <a>.)	2 3 4 5
	1.2 Describe the difference between CSS classes and IDs.	7 9
	1.3 Explain how JavaScript is used on the client in Web pages.	4 8
	1.4 List and describe the features and functionality of ftp and how it is used in Dreamweaver.	1 6
2.0 Planning sites	2.1 Define a local site by using the Manage Sites dialog box.	1 6
	2.2 Manage site definitions for local, remote, and testing server information.	1 6 8
	2.3 Describe considerations related to case-sensitive links.	2 4
	2.4 Given a scenario, define the structure of a site.	1
	2.5 Given a scenario, select and set the appropriate resolution for a site.	2 6
	2.6 List and describe considerations related to designing a site for multiple platforms and browsers.	3 6 9
	2.7 List and describe the features Dreamweaver provides for Accessibility Standards/Section 508 compliance.	2 3 4 5
	2.8 Explain how templates are used to architect for reuse and consistency.	2 11
	2.9 Create pages by using CSS starter pages.	9
	2.10 Explain how to extend Dreamweaver by using Extensions.	8
	2.11 Given a scenario, set development Preferences.	2
	2.12 Given a scenario, choose the proper method to lay out a page. (Methods include: tables, layers, CSS Box model.)	5 9

CERTIFICATION GRID

DREAMWEAVER 1

Topic Area	Objectives	Chapter
	2.13 Incorporate graphics and rich media into a Web site.	2
		3
		10
3.0 Designing pages		
	3.1 List and describe how to navigate the Dreamweaver UI.	1
	3.2 Use Find and Replace, including support for regular expressions.	6
	3.3 Create and use page templates.	11
	3.4 Create and maintain Cascading Style Sheets (CSS).	3
		7
		9
	3.5 Create and use reusable page objects by using library items.	12
	3.6 Explain the purpose of and how to use Server-side includes.	8
	3.7 Create and use code Snippets.	12
	3.8 Given a method, lay out a page. (Methods include: Table Layout, Layers, Expanded Tables mode.)	5
		9
	3.9 List and describe the options for creating and saving new pages.	9
	3.10 Set document properties by using the Document Properties dialog box.	2
	3.11 Lay out a page by using guides.	5
		9
	3.12 List and describe the options available for formatting the structure of a Document.	2
	(Options include: paragraph breaks, line breaks, non-breaking	3
	spaces, tables.)	5
	3.13 List and describe, and then resolve issues related to browser	3
	compatibility.	6
		9
	3.14 Use JavaScript behaviors to implement page functionality. (Behaviors include: Pop-Up Menus, Open Browser Window, Swap Image, Go To URL.)	10
	3.15 Add Flash elements to a Web page. (Options include: text, buttons, video, paper.)	4
		10
	3.16 List and describe the functionality provided by Dreamweaver for XML.	1
		7
		9

Topic Area	Objectives	Chapter
	3.17 Given a coding tool or feature, describe the purpose of or how to use that tool or feature. (Tools or features include: Code and Design View, Code Collapse, Code Navigation, Code Hinting, Coding Context Menu option.)	1 2 7
	3.18 Discuss considerations related to naming conventions and case sensitivity (e.g., variations between UNIX and Windows).	2 4
	3.19 Annotate files by using Design Notes and Comments.	2 6
4.0 Managing and maintaining sites		
	4.1 Manage collaboration with multiple developers by using Check In-Check Out.	6
	4.2 List and describe the different methods for accessing a remote site. (Methods include: FTP, LAN, VSS, WebDAV.)	6
	4.3 Given an access method, configure site definitions.	6
	4.4 Transfer and synchronize files to and from a remote server. (Options include: Cloaking, background file transfer, Get, Put.)	6
	4.5 Manage assets, links, and files for a site.	3 4 6
	4.6 Configure preferences, and explain the process required to compare files.	6
	4.7 Validate a site prior to deployment. (Options include: link checking, Accessibility checking, validating markup.)	6 9

CERTIFICATION GRID

DREAMWEAVER 3

Read the following information carefully.

Find out from your instructor the location where you will store your files.

- To complete many of the chapters in this book, you need to use the Data Files provided on the CD at the back of this book.

- Your instructor will tell you whether you will be working from the CD or copying the files to a drive on your computer or on a server. Your instructor will also tell you where you will store the files you create and modify.

- All the Data Files are organized in folders named after the chapter in which they are used. For instance, all Chapter 1 Data Files are stored in the chapter_1 folder. You should leave all the Data Files in these folders; do not move any Data File out of the folder in which it is originally stored.

Copy and organize your Data Files.

- Copy the folders that contain the Data Files to a USB storage device, network folder, hard drive, or other storage device if you will not be working from the CD.

- As you build each Web site, the exercises in this book will guide you to copy the Data Files you need from the appropriate Data Files folder to the folder where you are storing the Web site. Your Data Files should always remain intact because you are copying (and not moving) them to the Web site.

- Because you will be building a Web site from one chapter to the next, sometimes you will need to use a Data File that is already contained in the Web site you are working on.

Find and keep track of your Data Files and completed files.

- Use the **Data File Supplied** column to make sure you have the files you need before starting the chapter or exercise indicated in the **Chapter** column.

- Sometimes the file listed in the **Data File Supplied** column is one that you created or used in a previous chapter, and that is already part of the Web site you are working on. For instance, if the file tripsmart/amazon_trip.html is listed in the **Data File Supplied** column, this means that you need to use the amazon_trip.html file in the tripsmart site that you already created.

- Use the **Student Creates File** column to find out the filename you use when saving your new file for the exercise.

Files used in this book

Adobe Dreamweaver CS3

Chapter	Data File Supplied	Student Creates File	Used In
1	dw1_1.html about_us.swf accommodations.swf activities.swf cafe.swf index.swf shop.swf spa.swf assets/pool.jpg assets/su_background.jpg assets/su_banner.gif		Lesson 2
	dw1_2.html assets/su_banner.gif	about_us.html activities.html cafe.html cruises.html fishing.html spa.html	Lesson 4
	dw1_3.html dw1_4.html assets/blooms_banner.jpg assets/blooms_logo.jpg	annuals.html classes.html newsletter.html perennials.html plants.html tips.html water_plants.html	Skills Review
	dw1_5.html assets/tripsmart_banner.jpg	amazon.html catalog.html destinations.html kenya.html newsletter.html services.html	Project Builder 1
	dw1_6.html assets/cc_banner.jpg	adults.html catering.html children.html classes.html recipes.html shop.html	Project Builder 2

Chapter	Data File Supplied	Student Creates File	Used In
	none		Design Project
	none		Group Project
2	dw2_1.html spa.doc assets/su_banner.gif assets/the_spa.jpg		Lesson 2
	dw2_2.html gardening_tips.doc assets/blooms_banner.jpg assets/garden_tips.jpg		Skills Review
	none		Project Builder 1
	none		Project Builder 2
	none		Design Project
	none		Group Project
3	questions.doc		Lesson 1
		su_styles.css	Lesson 2
	dw3_1.html assets/boardwalk.jpg assets/club_house.jpg assets/pool.jpg assets/sago_palm.jpg assets/sports_club.jpg assets/su_banner.gif		Lesson 4
	assets/stripes_back.gif assets/umbrella_back.gif		Lesson 6
	dw3_2.html assets/blooms_banner.jpg assets/daisies.jpg assets/lantana.jpg assets/petunias.jpg assets/verbena.jpg	blooms_styles.css	Skills Review
	dw3_3.html dw3_4.html assets/tripsmart_banner.jpg assets/lion.jpg assets/zebra_mothers.jpg	tripsmart_styles.css	Project Builder 1

Chapter	Data File Supplied	Student Creates File	Used In
	dw3_5.html dw3_6.html assets/cc_banner.jpg assets/cranberry_ice.jpg assets/pot_knives.jpg	cc_styles.css	Project Builder 2
	none		Design Project
	none		Group Project
4	dw4_1.html assets/heron_waiting_small.jpg assets/su_banner.gif assets/two_dolphins_small.jpg		Lesson 1
		top.swf	Lesson 3
	assets/about_us_down.gif assets/about_us_up.gif assets/activities_down.gif assets/activities_up.gif assets/cafe_down.gif assets/cafe_up.gif assets/home_down.gif assets/home_up.gif assets/spa_down.gif assets/spa_up.gif		Lesson 4
	dw4_2.html dw4_3.html assets/boats.jpg assets/heron_small.jpg		Lesson 6
	dw4_4.html dw4_5.html dw4_6.html dw4_7.html assets/b_classes_down.jpg assets/b_classes_up.jpg assets/b_home_down.jpg assets/b_home_up.jpg assets/b_newsletter_down.jpg assets/b_newsletter_up.jpg assets/b_plants_down.jpg assets/b_plants_up.jpg	top.swf	Skills Review

Chapter	Data File Supplied	Student Creates File	Used In
	assets/b_tips_down.jpg assets/b_tips_up.jpg assets/blooms_banner.jpg assets/fuchsia.jpg assets/iris.jpg assets/water_hyacinth.jpg		
	dw4_8.html dw4_9.html dw4_10.html assets/giraffe.jpg assets/parrot.jpg assets/sloth.jpg assets/tripsmart_banner.jpg assets/water_lily.jpg		Project Builder 1
	dw4_11.html dw4_12.html dw4_13.html assets/cc_banner.jpg assets/cc_banner_with_text.jpg assets/children_cooking.jpg assets/cookies_oven.jpg assets/dumplings1.jpg assets/dumplings2.jpg assets/dumplings3.jpg assets/fish.jpg		Project Builder 2
	none		Design Project
	none		Group Project
5	assets/cafe_logo.gif assets/cafe_photo.jpg assets/cheesecake.jpg		Lesson 3
	cafe.doc		Lesson 4
	gardeners.doc registration.doc assets/flower_bed.jpg		Skills Review

Chapter	Data File Supplied	Student Creates File	Used In
	assets/hat.jpg assets/pants.jpg assets/vest.jpg		Project Builder 1
	menu items.doc assets/cell_back.jpg assets/muffins.jpg		Project Builder 2
	none		Design Project
	none		Group Project
6		The Striped Umbrella.ste	Lesson 4
		blooms & bulbs.ste	Skills Review
		TripSmart.ste	Project Builder 1
		Carolyne's Creations.ste	Project Builder 2
	none		Design Project
	none		Group Project
7	The Striped Umbrella.ste striped_umbrella folder containing these files: about_us.html activities.html cafe.html cruises.html feedback.html fishing.html index.html spa.html su_styles.css top.swf assets/about_us_down.gif assets/about_us_up.gif assets/activities_down.gif assets/activities_up.gif assets/boardwalk.jpg assets/boats.jpg assets/cafe_down.gif assets/cafe_logo.gif assets/cafe_photo.jpg assets/cafe_up.gif assets/cheesecake.jpg assets/club_house.jpg assets/heron_small.jpg		Lesson 1

Chapter	Data File Supplied	Student Creates File	Used In
	assets/heron_waiting_small.jpg		
	assets/home_down.gif		
	assets/home_up.gif		
	assets/pool.jpg		
	assets/sago_palm.jpg		
	assets/spa_down.gif		
	assets/spa_up.gif		
	assets/sports_club.jpg		
	assets/striped_umbrella_banner.gif		
	assets/the_spa.jpg		
	assets/two_dolphins_small.jpg		
	Scripts/AC_RunActiveContent.js		
	blooms & bulbs.ste		Skills Review
	blooms folder		
	containing these files:		
	annuals.html		
	blooms_styles.css		
	classes.html		
	index.html		
	newsletter.html		
	perennials.html		
	plants.html		
	tips.html		
	top.swf		
	water_plants.html		
	assets/b_classes_down.jpg		
	assets/b_classes_up.jpg		
	assets/b_home_down.jpg		
	assets/b_home_up.jpg		
	assets/b_newsletter_down.jpg		
	assets/b_newsletter_up.jpg		
	assets/b_plants_down.jpg		
	assets/b_plants_up.jpg		
	assets/b_tips_down.jpg		
	assets/b_tips_up.jpg		
	assets/blooms_banner.jpg		
	assets/flower_bed.jpg		
	assets/fuchsia.jpg		
	assets/garden_tips.jpg		

Chapter	Data File Supplied	Student Creates File	Used In
	assets/iris.jpg assets/lantana.jpg assets/petunias.jpg assets/verbena.jpg assets/water_hyacinth.jpg Scripts/AC_RunActiveContent.js		
	tripsmart folder containing these files: amazon.html catalog.html destinations.html index.html kenya.html newsletter.html services.html tripsmart_styles.css assets/giraffe.jpg assets/hat.jpg assets/lion.jpg assets/pants.jpg assets/parrot.jpg assets/sloth.jpg assets/tripsmart_banner.jpg assets/vest.jpg assets/water_lily.jpg assets/zebra_mothers.jpg		Project Builder 1
	cc folder containing these files: adults.html catering.html cc_styles.css children.html classes.html index.html recipes.html shop.html _notes/dwsync.xml assets/cc_banner_with_text.jpg assets/cc_logo.jpg assets/cell_back.jpg assets/children_cooking.jpg assets/cookies_oven.jpg		Project Builder 2

Chapter	Data File Supplied	Student Creates File	Used In
	assets/cranberry_ice.jpg assets/dumplings1.jpg assets/dumplinsg2.jpg assets/dumplings3.jpg assets/fish.jpg assets/muffins.jpg assets/pot_knives.jpg		
	none		Design Project
	none		Group Project
8	No files provided		
9	contestants.gif contestants_bak.jpg		Lesson 6
	peaches_small.jpg		Skills Review
	packing_cube.jpg		Project Builder 1
	assets/cc_logo.jpg		Project Builder 2
10	crab.fla crab.swf	angels.swf alabama.swf	Lesson 1
	assets/one_dolphin.jpg assets/two_dolphins.jpg		Lesson 2
	dw10_1.html		Lesson 3
	umbrella_anchor_movie.flv		Lesson 4
	garden_quote.swf assets/garden_tips.jpg assets/garden_tips2.jpg hanging_baskets.flv	m_gardeners.swf	Skills Review
	dw10_2.html amazon_map.swf		Project Builder 1
	sugared_flowers.flv		Project Builder 2
11		Templates/activities_pages.dwt	Lesson 1
	golf.doc assets/golfer.jpg	golf.html	Lesson 2
	annuals.doc perennials.doc water_plants.doc	annuals.html water_plants.html Templates/plant_categories.dwt	Skills Review
	assets/headphones.jpg assets/packing_cube_large.jpg assets/passport_holder.jpg	accessories.html clothing.html Templates/catalog_pages.dwt	Project Builder 1

Chapter	Data File Supplied	Student Creates File	Used In
	rolls.doc assets/rolls.jpg	Templates/recipes.dwt	Project Builder 2
	none		Design Project
	none		Group Project
12	assets/su_logo.jpg		Lesson 1
	assets/blooms_logo.jpg		Skills Review
	assets/tripsmart_logo.jpg		Project Builder 1
	none		Project Builder 2
	none		Design Project
	none		Group Project

Absolute path

A path containing an external link that references a link on a Web page outside the current Web site, and includes the protocol "http" and the URL, or address, of the Web page.

Absolute positioning

The positioning of an AP element according to the distance between the AP element's upper-left corner and the upper-left corner of the page or AP element in which it is contained.

Action

A response to an event trigger that causes a change, such as text changing color.

Action property

Property that specifies the application or script that will process form data.

Adobe Flash Player

A program that must be installed on a computer to view Flash movies.

Advanced style

A style used to format combinations of page elements.

Aligning an image

Positioning an image on a Web page in relation to other elements on the page.

Alternate text

Descriptive text that can be set to appear in place of an image while the image is downloading or when a user places the mouse pointer over the image.

AP div tag

A div tag that is assigned a fixed position on a page (absolute position).

AP elements panel

Panel in the CSS panel group that is used to control the visibility, name, and Z-Index stacking order of AP elements on a Web page.

ASP

The acronym for Active Server Pages. ASP is a server-side application tool.

Assets folder

A subfolder in a Web site in which you store most of the files that are not Web pages, such as images, audio files, and video clips.

Assets panel

A panel that contains nine categories of assets, such as images, used in a Web site. Clicking a category button will display a list of those assets.

Background color

A color that fills an entire Web page, frame, table, cell, or document.

Background image

A graphic file used in place of a background color.

Banner

Graphic that generally appears across the top of a Web page that can incorporate the company's logo, contact information, and navigation buttons.

Behavior

A preset piece of JavaScript code that can be attached to page elements. A behavior tells the page element to respond in a specific way when an event occurs, such as when the mouse pointer is positioned over the element.

BMP

Bitmapped file. A file format used for images that is based on pixels.

Body

The part of a Web page that is seen when the page is viewed in a browser window.

Border

An outline that surrounds a cell, table, or frame.

Broken links

Links that cannot find the intended destination file for the link.

Browser

Software used to display Web pages, such as Microsoft Internet Explorer or Mozilla Firefox.

Bullet

A small raised dot or similar icon.

Bulleted list

The name that is sometimes given to unordered lists using bullets.

Cascading Style Sheet (CSS)
A file used to assign sets of common formatting characteristics to page elements such as text, objects, and tables.

CAST
Acronym for the Center for Applied Special Technology.

Cell padding
The distance between the cell content and cell walls in a table.

Cell spacing
The distance between cells in a table.

Cell walls
The edges surrounding a cell.

Cells
Small boxes within a table that are used to hold text or graphics. Cells are arranged horizontally in rows and vertically in columns.

Checkbox
Form object that can be used on a Web page to let viewers choose from a range of possible options.

Checked out files
Files that are being used by other team members.

Child page
A page at a lower level in a Web hierarchy that links to a parent page.

Class style
See **custom style**.

Client-side scripting
A method used to process information a form collects by using the user's computer.

Clip property
Property that determines the portion of a layer's content that will be visible when displayed in a Web browser.

Cloaked file
File that is marked to be excluded from certain processes, such as being transferred to the remote site.

Code and Design view
A view that is a combination of Code view and Design view.

Code Inspector
A window that works just like Code view except that it is a floating window.

Code snippet
See **snippets**.

Code view
A view that shows the underlying HTML code for the page. Use this view to read or edit the code.

Coding toolbar
A toolbar that contains buttons that are used when working directly in the code.

ColdFusion
Development tool that can be used to build data-driven Web applications.

Columns
Table cells arranged vertically.

Comments
Comments are notes of explanation that are inserted into the code and are not visible in the browser window.

Common Gateway Interface (CGI)
Server-side application used for processing data in a form.

Copyright
A legal protection for the particular and tangible expression of an idea.

CSS page layout
A method of positioning objects on Web pages through the use of containers formatted with CSS styles.

Custom style
A style that can contain a combination of formatting attributes that can be applied to a block of text or other page elements. Custom style names begin with a period (.). Also known as a class style.

Debug
To find and correct coding errors.

Declaration
The property and value of a style in a Cascading Style Sheet.

Default base font
The font that is applied by default to any text that is entered on a page created in Dreamweaver.

Default font color
The color the browser uses to display text if no other color is assigned.

Default link color
The color the browser uses to display links if no other color is assigned. The default link color is blue.

Definition lists
Lists composed of terms with indented descriptions or definitions.

Delimited files
Database or spreadsheet files that have been saved as text files with delimiters.

Delimiter
A comma, tab, colon, semicolon, or similar character that separates tabular data.

Dependent file
File that another file needs to be complete, such as an image or navigation bar element.

Derivative work
An adaptation of another work, such as a movie version of a book.

Description
A short summary of Web site content that resides in the head section.

Design view
The view that shows the page as it would appear in a browser and is primarily used when designing and creating a Web page.

Diagonal symmetry
A design principle in which page elements are balanced along the invisible diagonal line of the page.

Div tag
An HTML tag that is used to format and position Web page elements.

Document
For this book, an HTML document created in Dreamweaver.

Document toolbar
A toolbar that contains buttons and drop-down menus you can use to change the current work mode, preview Web pages, debug Web pages, choose visual aids, and view file-management options.

Document-relative path
A path referenced in relation to the Web page that is currently displayed.

Document window
The large white area in the Dreamweaver workspace where you create and edit Web pages.

Domain name
An IP address expressed in letters instead of numbers, usually reflecting the name of the business represented by the Web site.

Down image state
The state of a page element when the element has been clicked.

Download
Transfer a file or files from a remote server to a computer.

Download time
The time it takes to transfer a file to another computer.

DSL
Digital Subscriber Line. A type of high-speed Internet connection.

Dynamic content
Content on a Web page that allows the user to interact with the page by clicking or typing, and then responds to the input in some way.

Editable optional region
An area in a template where users can add or change content, and that users can also choose to show or hide.

Editable region
An area in a template where users of the template can add or change content.

Element
A graphic link that is part of a navigation bar and can have one of four possible appearances.

Embedded CSS style sheet
Styles that are part of an HTML page and that reside in the head content.

Enable cache
A setting to direct the computer system to use space on the hard drive as temporary memory or cache while you are working in Dreamweaver.

Event trigger
An event, such as a mouse click on an object, that causes a behavior to start.

Expanded Tables mode
A Dreamweaver viewing mode that includes expanded table borders and temporary cell padding and cell spacing.

Export data
To save data by using a special file format so that you can open it in another application.

External CSS style sheet
Collection of rules stored in a separate file that control the formatting of content in a Web page. External CSS style sheets have a .css file extension.

External links
Links that connect to Web pages in other Web sites or to e-mail addresses.

Fair use
A concept that allows consumers to copy all or part of a copyrighted work in support of their First Amendment rights.

Favorites
Assets that are used repeatedly in a Web site and are included in their own category in the Assets panel.

Field
See **form object**.

Fieldset
HTML tag used to group related form elements together.

File field
Form object that allows viewers to upload files to a Web server.

Files panel
The panel you use to manage your Web site files.

Flash button object
Button made from a small, predefined Flash movie that can be inserted on a Web page to provide navigation in a Web site.

Flash Paper
A program built into Microsoft Word and PowerPoint that allows you to easily convert a Word or PowerPoint file into a Flash .swf file that a browser can open and read.

Flash player
A free program included with many browsers that allows you to view content created with Adobe Flash.

Flash text
A vector-based graphic file that contains text.

Flash video files
Flash files that include both video and audio and have an .flv file extension.

Focus group
A marketing tool where a group of people are asked for feedback about a product.

Font combination
A set of three fonts that specifies which fonts a browser should use to display the text on a Web page.

Form control
See **form object**.

Form element
See **form object**.

Form object
An object on a Web page, such as a text box, radio button, or checkbox, that collects information from viewers. Also referred to as **form element**, **form control**, or **field**.

FormName property
Property that specifies a unique name for a form.

Frame

Fixed region in a browser that can display a Web page and act independently from other pages displayed in other frames within the browser window.

Frameset

A document that contains the instructions that tell a browser how to lay out a set of frames showing individual documents on a page, including the size and position of the frames.

Frames panel

Panel in the Advanced Layout panel group that shows a visual representation of the frameset and is used for selecting frames.

FTP

File Transfer Protocol. The process of uploading and downloading files to and from a remote site.

Get

Transferring files from a remote location.

GET method

Method property that specifies that ASCII data collected in a form will be sent to the server appended to the URL or file included in the Action property.

GIF

Graphics interchange format. Type of file format used for images placed on Web pages that can support both transparency and animation.

Graphics

Pictures or design elements that add visual interest to a page.

Grids

Horizontal and vertical lines that fill the page and are used to place page elements

Guides

Horizontal or vertical lines that you can drag onto the page from the rulers to use to align page elements.

Head content

The part of a Web page that is not viewed in the browser window. It includes meta tags, which are HTML codes that include information about the page, such as keywords and descriptions.

Headings

Six different styles that can be applied to text: Heading 1 (the largest size) through Heading 6 (the smallest size).

Height property

Property that specifies the height of an AP layer either in pixels or as a percentage of the screen's height.

Hexadecimal value

A value that represents the amount of red, green, and blue in a color and is based on the Base 16 number system.

Hidden field

Form object that makes it possible to provide information to the Web server and form-processing script without the viewer knowing that the information is being sent.

History panel

A panel that lists the steps that have been performed in Dreamweaver while editing and formatting a document.

Home page

Usually the first Web page that appears when viewers visit a Web site.

Horizontal symmetry

A design principle in which page elements are balanced across the page.

Hotspot

An area on a graphic, that, when clicked, links to a different location on the page or to another Web page.

HTML

Hypertext Markup Language. A language Web developers use to create Web pages.

HTML style

A style used to redefine an HTML tag.

Hyperlink

Graphic or text element on a Web page that users click to display another location on the page, another Web page on the same Web site, or a Web page on a different Web site. Hyperlinks are also known as links.

Image field
Form object used to insert an image in a form.

Image map
A graphic that has been divided into sections, each of which contains a link.

Import data
To bring data created in another software program into an application.

Inherit
An AP element value of the Vis (visible) property that sets the visibility of the AP element to be the same as its parent AP element or page.

Inline CSS rule
A CSS rule whose code is contained within the body section of the HTML code on a Web page.

Insert bar
Groups of buttons for creating and inserting objects displayed as tabs.

Intangible assets
Assets that are referred to as intellectual property.

Intellectual property
A product resulting from human creativity such as a movie or a song.

Interactivity
Allows visitors to your Web site to affect its content.

Internal links
Links to Web pages within the same Web site.

IP address
An assigned series of numbers, separated by periods, that designates an address on the Internet.

ISP
Internet Service Provider. A service to which you subscribe to be able to connect your computer to the Internet.

JavaScript
A Web-scripting language that interacts with HTML code to create interactive content.

JPEG file
Joint photographic experts group. Type of file format used for images that appear on Web pages, typically used for photographs.

Jump menu
Navigational menu that lets viewers go quickly to different pages in a site or to different sites on the Internet.

Keywords
Words that relate to the content of a Web site and reside in the head content.

Layout mode
A Dreamweaver mode that is used for drawing tables.

Left property
Property that specifies the distance between the left edge of an AP element and the left edge of the page or AP element that contains it.

Library item
Content that can contain text or graphics and is saved in a separate file in the Library folder of a Web site.

Licensing agreement
The permission given by a copyright holder that conveys the right to use the copyright holder's work.

Link
See hyperlink.

List
Element on a Web page from which viewers can make a choice from several options. Lists are often used in order forms.

List form object
A form object that lets users choose one or more options from a list of choices.

Local site
The location of your local root folder where your Web site files are stored while being developed.

Locked region
An area on a template that cannot be changed by users of the template.

M

mailto: link

A common point of contact that viewers with questions or problems can use to contact someone at a company's headquarters.

Media objects

Combinations of visual and audio effects and text to create a fully engaging experience with a Web site.

Menu

Element on a Web page from which Web viewers can make choices. Menus are often used for navigation in a Web site.

Menu bar

A bar located above the document window that includes names of menus, each of which contain Dreamweaver commands.

Menu form object

A form object, commonly used for navigation on a Web site, that lets viewers select a single option from a list of choices.

Menu list

Lists that are very similar to unordered lists.

Merge cells

To combine multiple cells in a table into one cell.

Meta data

Information about a file, such as keywords, descriptions, and copyright information.

Meta tags

HTML codes that include information about the page, such as keywords and descriptions, and reside in the head content.

Method property

Property that specifies the HyperText Transfer Protocol (HTTP) method used to send form data to a Web server.

Multiple Document Interface

A Dreamweaver interface choice in which all document windows and panels are positioned within one large application window.

N

Named anchor

A specific location on a Web page that has a specific name.

Navigation bar

Bar that contains multiple links, usually organized in rows or columns, that link to the major pages in a Web site.

Navigation structure

The way viewers navigate from page to page in a Web site.

Nested AP element

AP element whose HTML code is included within another AP element's code.

Nested table

A table within a table.

Nested template

A template that is based on another template.

Non-Websafe colors

Colors that might not be displayed uniformly across computer platforms.

Numbered lists

Lists of items that are presented in a specific order and are preceded by numbers or letters in sequence. Also called ordered lists.

O

Objects

The individual elements in a document, such as text or images.

Optional region

Region in a template that template users can choose either to show or hide.

Ordered list

List of items that need to be placed in a specific order, where each item is preceded by a number or letter. Also called numbered lists.

Orphaned files

Files that are not linked to any pages in a Web site.

Overflow property

Property that specifies how to handle excess content that does not fit inside a layer.

Over image state
The state of a page element when the mouse pointer is positioned over it.

Over While Down image state
The state of a page element when the mouse pointer is clicked and held over it.

Panel
A window that contains related commands or displays information on a particular topic.

Panel groups
Sets of related panels that are grouped together.

Paragraph style
HTML style that is applied to an entire paragraph.

Parent page
A page at a higher level in a Web hierarchy that links to other pages on a lower level.

Path
The location of a file in relation to other folders in the Web site.

PICS
The acronym for Platform for Internet Content Selection. This is a rating system for Web pages.

PNG
Portable network graphics. A type of file format for graphics.

Point of contact
A place on a Web page that provides viewers a means of contacting a company.

Pop-up menu
A menu that appears when you move the pointer over a trigger image in a browser.

Pop-up message
Message that opens in a browser to either clarify or provide information, or alert viewers of an action that is being taken.

Position property
Property used to define an AP element's position on a page.

POST method
Method property that specifies that form data be sent to the processing script as a binary or encrypted file, so that data will be sent securely.

Progressive video download
A download type that will download a video to the viewer's computer, and then allow the video to play before it has completely downloaded.

Property inspector
A panel located at the bottom of the Dreamweaver window that lets you view and change the properties of a selected object.

Public domain
Work that is no longer protected by copyright. Anyone can use it for any purpose.

Publish a Web site
To make a Web site available for viewing on the Internet or on an intranet.

Put
Transfer files to a remote location.

Radial symmetry
A design principle in which page elements are balanced from the center of the page outward, like the petals of a flower.

Radio button
Form object that can be used to provide a list of options from which only one selection can be made.

Radio group
A group of radio buttons from which viewers can make only one selection.

Ransom note effect
A phrase that implies that fonts have been randomly used in a document without regard to style.

RDS
Remote Development Services, used with Web servers using ColdFusion for transferring files.

Reference panel
A panel used to find answers to coding questions, covering topics such as HTML, JavaScript, and Accessibility.

Refresh Local File List Automatically option
A setting that directs Dreamweaver to automatically reflect changes made in your file listings.

Regular expressions
Combinations of characters, such as a phrase that begins or ends with a particular word or tag.

Relative path
A path containing a link to a page within a Web site.

Remote server
A Web server that hosts Web sites and is not directly connected to the computer housing the local site.

Remote site
A Web site that has been published to a remote server.

Repeating region
An area in a template whose format is repeated over and over again. Used for presenting information that repeats, such as product listings in a catalog.

Repeating table
A table in a template that has a predefined structure, making it very easy for template users to add content to it.

Required field
A field on a form that must be completed before the form can be processed.

Reset button
A button that, when clicked, will clear data from a form and reset it to its default values.

Resolution
The number of pixels per inch in an image; also refers to an image's clarity and fineness of detail.

Rollover
A special effect that changes the appearance of an object when the mouse rolls over it.

Rollover color
The color in which text will appear when the rollover is taking place.

Rollover image
An image on a Web page that changes its appearance when the mouse pointer is positioned over it.

Root folder (local root folder)
A folder used to store all Web pages or HTML files for the site. The root folder is given a name to describe the site, such as the company name.

Root relative path
A path referenced from a Web site's root folder.

Rows
Table cells arranged horizontally.

Rule of Thirds
The rule of thirds is a design principle that entails dividing a page into nine squares and then placing the page elements of most interest on the intersections of the grid lines.

Rules
Sets of formatting attributes in a Cascading Style Sheet.

Sans-serif fonts
Block-style characters used frequently for headings and subheadings.

Screen reader
A device used by the visually impaired to convert written text on a computer monitor to spoken words.

Selector
The name or the tag to which the style declarations have been assigned.

Serif fonts
Ornate fonts with small extra strokes at the beginning and end of characters. Used frequently for paragraph text in printed materials.

Server-side application
An application that resides on a Web server and interacts with the information collected in a form.

Server-side scripting
A method used to process information a form collects that uses applications that reside on the Web server and interact with the information collected in the form.

Site definition
Information about the site, including the URL, preferences, and password information.

Site map
A graphical representation of the Web pages in a Web site. A site map is used to view and edit the navigation structure of your Web site.

Site usability test
A process of using and evaluating a Web site for ease of use.

Snippet
A reusable piece of code that can be inserted on a page to create footers, headers, drop-down menus, and other items.

Split cells
To divide cells into multiple cells.

Spry effects
Screen effects such as fading and enlarging page elements.

Spry framework for AJAX
Asynchronous JavaScript and XML (AJAX). A method for developing interactive Web pages that respond quickly to user input, such as a map.

Spry widgets
Prebuilt components for adding interaction to pages.

Standard toolbar
A toolbar that contains buttons you can use to execute frequently used commands that are also available on the File and Edit menus.

Standard mode
A mode that is used to insert a table using the Insert Table button or command.

States
The four appearances a button can assume in response to a mouse action. These include: Up, Over, Down, and Over While Down.

Static content
Content on a Web site that does not change or allow user interaction.

Status bar
A bar located below the document window that displays HTML tags being used at the insertion point location as well as other information, such as estimated download time for the current page and window size.

Step
Each task performed in the History panel.

Storyboard
A small sketch that represents every page in a Web site.

Streaming video download
Similar to a progressive download, except streaming video downloads use buffers to gather the content as it is downloading to ensure a smoother playback.

Styles
Preset attributes, such as size, color, and texture, that you can apply to objects and text. Styles are also called rules.

Style Rendering toolbar
A toolbar with options for rendering a Web page in different media types, such as a handheld device.

Submit button
A button which when clicked, will send the data from a form on a Web page to a Web server to be processed.

Swap image
A behavior similar to a rollover effect.

Swap Image Restore
A behavior that restores a swapped image back to the original image.

Synchronize files
To synchronize files is to compare the dates of the files in a remote and local site and then transfer only the files that have changed.

Table
Grid of rows and columns that can either be used to hold tabular data on a Web page or can be used as a basic design tool for page layout.

Table header
Text placed at the top or sides of a table on a Web page that is read by screen readers.

Tabular data
Data that is arranged in columns and rows and separated by a delimiter.

Tag selector
A location on the status bar that displays HTML tags for the various page elements, including tables and cells.

Tags
HTML codes that define the formatting of page elements. They are usually, but not always, written in pairs with beginning and ending tags that surround the affected content in the code.

Target
The location on a Web page that the browser will display in full view when an internal link is clicked, or the frame that will open when a link is clicked.

Target property
Property that specifies the window in which you want form data to be processed.

Template
A template contains the basic layout for pages in Web sites and contains both locked regions, which are areas on the template page that cannot be modified by users of the template, as well as other types of regions that users can change or edit.

Terms of use
The rules that a copyright owner uses to establish use of his work.

Testing server
A server used to test a Web site to evaluate the way that features such as a form work.

Text area field
A text field in a form that can store several lines of text.

Text field
Form object used for collecting a string of characters such as a name, address, or password.

TIFF
Tagged image file format.

Tiled image
A small graphic that repeats across and down a Web page, appearing as individual squares or rectangles.

Top property
Property that specifies the distance between the top edge of an AP element and the top edge of the page or AP element that contains it.

Trademark
Protects an image, word, slogan, symbol, or design used to identify goods or services.

Tree structure
A diagram that visually represents the way the pages in a Web site are linked to each other.

Unordered lists
Lists of items that do not need to be placed in a specific order and are usually preceded by bullets.

Unvisited links
Links that have not been clicked by the viewer.

Up image state
The state of a page element when the mouse pointer is not on the element.

Upload
Transfer files to a remote server.

URL
Uniform resource locator. An address that determines a route on the Internet or to a Web page.

Vector based graphics
Graphics that are based on mathematical formulas.

Vertical symmetry
A design principle in which page elements are balanced down a page.

Visible property
Property that lets you control whether the selected layer is visible or hidden.

Visited links
Links that have been previously clicked or visited. The default color for visited links is purple.

VSS
Microsoft Visual SafeSource, used with the Windows operating system for transferring files.

Web design software
Software for creating interactive Web pages containing text, images, hyperlinks, animation, sounds, and video.

Websafe colors
Colors that are common to both Macintosh, UNIX, and Windows platforms.

Web server
A computer dedicated to hosting Web sites that is connected to the Internet and configured with software to handle requests from browsers.

Web site
A group of related Web pages that are linked together and share a common interface and design.

WebDav
Web-based Distributed Authoring and Versioning, used with the WebDav protocol for transferring files.

White space
An area on a Web page that is not filled with text or graphics.

Width property
Property that specifies the width of an AP element either in pixels or as a percentage of the screen's width.

Workspace
The area in the Dreamweaver program window where you work with documents, movies, tools, and panels.

WYSIWYG
An acronym for What You See is What You Get, meaning that your Web page should look the same in the browser as it does in the Web editor.

XHTML
The acronym for eXtensible HyperText Markup Language, the most current standard for developing Web pages.

XML site map
A listing of a Web site's links that can be made available to search engines.

Z-Index property
Property that specifies the vertical stacking order of AP elements on a page. A Z-Index value of 1 indicates that an AP element's position is at the bottom of the stack. A Z-Index position of 3 indicates that the AP element is positioned on top of two other AP elements.

INDEX

Dreamweaver Chapter Opener Art Credits

Dreamweaver Chapter #	Credit
Dreamweaver 1	© Chris Gomersall/Alamy
Dreamweaver 2	© Art Wolfe/Getty Images
Dreamweaver 3	© Martin Siepmann/RF/Alamy
Dreamweaver 4	© Jose B. Ruiz/Nature Picture Library/Alamy
Dreamweaver 5	© Keren Su/China Span/Alamy
Dreamweaver 6	© Mervyn Rees/Alamy
Dreamweaver 7	© David Davis Productions/RF/Alamy
Dreamweaver 8	© Veer
Dreamweaver 9	© Michale & Patricia Fogden/Corbis
Dreamweaver 10	© Don Hammond/Design/Corbis
Dreamweaver 11	© Ralph A. Clevenger/Corbis
Dreamweaver 12	© Dave Marsden/RF/Alamy
End Matter opener	© Hal Beral/Corbis